Praise for *Effective DevOps*

"Excellent reading for anyone interested in understanding devops and how to foster a devops culture."

—*James Turnbull, CTO at Kickstarter*

"Devops is not another "tech movement" that can be deferred and discarded; it has tentacles throughout the organization from concept to cash. Anyone who has watched their cost of building new features increase, or has lived through the frustrations of unplanned downtime, will understand the intrinsic values espoused by the devops movement.

"*Effective DevOps* is the most comprehensive book I've seen on the topic; and one that is completely digestible and applicable for those within technology *and* the lines of business. I particularly enjoyed the sections debunking common myths and memes regarding devops; such as it being cost prohibitive, only applicable to startups, or that it's a position to be filled. Such resounding rebuttals help preserve the spirit of devops and keeps commoditization of the movement at bay. This book will become recommended reading for any organization that conceives, develops, and deploys software."

—*Nivia S. Henry, Sr. Agile Coach at Summa*

"High performance organizations see technology as a strategic capability. However, they understand that technology is often not the most challenging dimension. Culture matters. How well your organization collaborates, experiments and seeks to learn and share knowledge dictates the level it not only accepts but will achieve. In this book, Jennifer and Ryn have outlined the necessary conditions to create a system of work for your business to develop its own path towards continuous improvement, growth and transformation. Read it, reflect on it, then deploy it."

—*Barry O'Reilly, Founder and CEO, ExecCamp and coauthor of*
Lean Enterprise: How High Performance Organizations Innovate At Scale *(O'Reilly)*

Effective DevOps
Building a Culture of Collaboration,
Affinity, and Tooling at Scale

Jennifer Davis and Ryn Daniels

Beijing · Boston · Farnham · Sebastopol · Tokyo

Effective DevOps

by Jennifer Davis and Ryn Daniels

Published by O'Reilly Media, Inc., 1005 Gravenstein Highway North, Sebastopol, CA 95472.

O'Reilly books may be purchased for educational, business, or sales promotional use. Online editions are also available for most titles (*http://oreilly.com/safari*). For more information, contact our corporate/institutional sales department: 800-998-9938 or *corporate@oreilly.com*.

Editor: Brian Anderson	**Indexer:** WordCo Indexing Services
Production Editor: Colleen Lobner	**Interior Designer:** David Futato
Copyeditor: Rachel Monaghan	**Cover Designer:** Randy Comer
Proofreader: Jasmine Kwityn	**Illustrator:** Rebecca Demarest

June 2016:   First Edition

Revision History for the First Edition

2016-05-23:   First Release
2018-01-19:   Second Release
2018-04-06:   Third Release

See *http://oreilly.com/catalog/errata.csp?isbn=9781491926307* for release details.

978-1-491-92630-7

[LSI]

Table of Contents

Part II.   Collaboration

Part III.   Affinity

Part IV.   Tools

Part VI.   Bridging Devops Cultures

Foreword by John Allspaw

There is a sea change happening in software development and operations, and it is not simply the introduction of a new word into our lexicon—it's much more than that. It is a fundamental shift of perspective in the design, construction, and operation of software in a world where almost every successful organization recognizes that software is not something you simply build and launch—it is something you operate.

What makes this shift unique is that it's more encompassing, more holistic, and more reflective of the reality that engineering teams face on a daily basis. Long gone are the days that manufacturing and assembly-line metaphors could be used in software development and operations. Long gone are the days that products are things that are designed, planned, and then finally launched. There is no "finally" anymore. There is only an endless cycle of adaptation, change, and learning.

What Ryn and Jennifer have laid out in this volume is a myriad of threads to pull on as engineers in teams and organizations cope with the complexity that comes with trying to make their work "simple."

Ryn and Jennifer do not paint a picture of one-size-fits-all or deterministic solutionism. Instead, they describe a landscape of topic areas, practices, and observations of teams and organizations that understand the idea that at the heart of good products, good user experiences, and good software is the elegantly messy world of human cooperation, thoughtful critique, effective collaboration, and judgment.

In 2009, my friend Paul Hammond and I gave a presentation at O'Reilly's Velocity Conference entitled "10+ Deploys a Day: Dev and Ops Cooperation at Flickr." While some of the material was about perspectives on continuous deployment, many chose to focus on the "10+ Deploys" part rather than the "Cooperation" part. I believe it is a mistake to think that the technology or "hard parts" can be seen as somehow distinct or separate from the social and cultural "soft parts"—they cannot. They are inextricably linked and equally critical to success. In other words, people and process influence tools and software in more ways than most are willing to admit or even know.

My strong advice to readers: do not make the mistake of thinking that technology is not about people and process, first and foremost. Your competition will eat you alive the second you start thinking this.

These topics of concern are not found in typical computer science curriculums, nor are they found in typical professional leadership and development courses. These topics are born out of the pragmatic maturity that only hard-won work in the field can produce.

Ryn and Jennifer have given you an in-depth set of signposts in this book. My genuine request to you, dear reader, is to use these signposts to think with, in your own context and environment.

—John Allspaw
Chief Technology Officer, Etsy
Brooklyn, NY

Foreword by Nicole Forsgren

In 2003, Nicholas Carr declared to the world that IT didn't matter—and because he said it in *Harvard Business Review*, organizations (and the executives that run them) believed him. Well, times have changed, and so has IT. Since 2009, the most innovative teams and organizations have shown that technology can play a key role in delivering real value and competitive advantage. This technology revolution is known as DevOps, and this book can show you how to join those innovative companies to deliver value with technology as well.

Here, Jennifer and Ryn draw on their experiences at innovative companies as well as their backgrounds as prominent experts in the community to highlight what it really takes to do DevOps—or as they call it, devops—effectively. This vantage point brings unique insights that can be applicable and useful to any reader, because they combine knowledge from several companies and across industries. This gives readers something to take away regardless of where you are in your journey, no matter how big (or small) your organization is.

The tales and advice found in *Effective DevOps* parallel those I've seen in my own work for the past decade. As a leading researcher in the field and the lead investigator on the *State of DevOps Reports*, I know that a strong organizational culture that prioritizes information flow and trust is a key component of any DevOps transformation, and the factor that sets the DevOps movement apart from traditional IT. Data I've collected from over 20,000 DevOps professionals also shows that this culture drives IT and organizational performance, helping the best IT organizations see double productivity, profitability, and market share when compared to their peers. It's no mistake that Jennifer and Ryn start the book with a discussion on aspects of culture, communication, and trust, and devote a good portion of their time addressing the importance of these factors to any transformative work. As technologists, we love to start with the tools and maybe even the processes, but time and again, the data shows that culture is essential for tooling and technology success in addition to the aforementioned IT and organizational performance. Parts II–III on collaboration and affinity, respectively, are must-reads here, whether you are just starting your DevOps transformation and want to know what to implement and watch for, or you are taking your existing DevOps practice to the next level and looking for ways to optimize and troubleshoot.

As a consultant to some of the most innovative companies, I've found that the most challenging part of implementing DevOps and planning a technology transformation roadmap is helping teams and organizations understand that there isn't just one right answer—it always depends on what is right for your team and your organization. I love that Ryn and Jennifer embrace the ambiguity so well in this book, knowing that there is no way to "plug and play" a single solution, and lay out the tools and pieces you need to construct your own DevOps solution and journey successfully. In addition to Parts II–III, be sure to check out Part IV on tools, which are essential to any DevOps transformation. I especially love how they're framed as not only technology, but also key components of the culture in which they perform.

My favorite aspect of this book is how accessible it is to so many different audiences. Part V on scalability is particularly relevant for individual contributors and team leaders, and I'll be using it as a reference both personally and for my clients. Chapter 4 on terminology and Chapter 11 on ecosystem overview come in handy both for technologists (to make sure we're all on the same page, as different tribes often use different words) and for executives who could use a current reference. The whole book is a welcome and much-needed introduction to the field for university students who just don't get this training in their studies, and I wish I'd had it when I was a professor.

We live and work in exciting times, and the integration of technology into our core businesses has made every firm a software firm. Technology now provides opportunities to deliver features to customers in new ways and at speeds not possible before. Organizations often find themselves struggling to keep up. Old IT and waterfall methods just don't allow organizations to deliver value fast enough—I've seen it in the data, and I've seen it among the customers and companies I work with to create solutions for their own DevOps journeys. Jennifer and Ryn have also seen the challenges to technology transformation in the old way, and the exciting opportunities that are possible with DevOps, and they've responded by writing this book to guide us all through our own journeys. So read through, and choose your own adventure! Iterate, learn, grow, and choose your own adventure again!

—Nicole Forsgren, PhD
Director, Chef Software
Seattle, WA

Preface

Imagine this scenario: a small web company is starting to run into problems—its website is straining and experiencing regular failures under unprecedented growth. Employees are increasingly unhappy with the number of hours required to maintain services while also trying to implement and deploy new features. Language and time zone barriers are contributing to friction between globally distributed teams. A culture of blame has grown around the tense reactions during site outages, resulting in increased suspicion and decreased transparency between teams.

Given these problems, the organization decides that devops sounds like a good solution. Management hires several new people to join their new devops team. The devops team has on-call responsibilities, where the existing operations team can call them to escalate issues that they don't know how to address. The devops team members have more industry experience than the people on the ops team, so they are generally better equipped to handle production issues. Without the time or opportunity to learn new skills, however, the operations staff keeps escalating the same issues over and over again.

The devops team gets tired of acting as go-between for both the development and operations teams. Rather than defusing the culture of blame, management's "solution" has produced twice as much miscommunication, because none of the teams are privy to the planning processes, emails, chat messages, or even bug trackers of the other teams.

Thus, management declares "this devops thing" is a failure and is unwilling to invest any more time, effort, or money into either the ops or devops teams, viewing them as incompetent people who keep "taking down the site" and "getting in the way" of the "real" development work being done. The members of these two teams who are able to find better jobs leave for organizations where yelling and blame aren't acceptable workplace practices, making the remaining team even less effective.

Introducing Effective Devops

Where did things go wrong here? Devops sounded like a good idea, but creating a devops team led to less desirable outcomes. What could this organization have done differently to see meaningful improvements to their situations and actual solutions to their problems? Throughout this book, we will show you what it looks like to make effective changes with a devops mindset.

This book is not a prescription for the One True Way of doing devops. We don't offer you devops in a box, devops-as-a-service, or tell you that you are Doing Devops Wrong. This book offers a collection of ideas and approaches for improving individual collaboration, team and organizational affinity, and tool usage throughout a company or organization, and explains how these concepts allow organizations to change and adapt as necessary. Every organization is unique, and so while there is no one-size-fits-all way of doing devops, these common themes can be applied in different ways to every organization that wants to improve both the quality of their software and the efficiency and well-being of their employees.

> Efficiency is doing the thing right. Effectiveness is doing the right thing.
>
> —Peter F. Drucker

Effectiveness is defined as doing the right things and achieving the desired results. To do the right things, we must understand our goals and how specific short-term objectives serve those goals.

We hope to help you identify what the right things are in your environment based on your current culture, including the processes and tools in use. The principles and insights we share throughout the book are applicable across your organization, not only to development and operations teams. We even found ourselves applying them throughout our process of writing this book.

While our overall goal in writing *Effective DevOps* was to share common stories, tips, and practices that every organization can adopt and apply to their own work methodologies, we each have our own stories and experiences. From private to public sector, small startups to large corporate environments, and roles ranging from development to operations, quality assurance, consulting, and more, our collective experiences gave us a wealth of insights that complemented our writing process.

"Devops," "devops," or "DevOps"?

We have had many discussions over the capitalization (or lack thereof) of the term "devops." A simple online poll showed overwhelming support for "DevOps." We also found a focus on the "Dev" and "Ops" within organizations. This has lead to the creation of "DevSecOps" and "DevQAOps," as "DevOps" implies an exclusivity of just "Dev" and "Ops."

Ultimately, this is why we've chosen "devops"—it reflects the original hashtag on Twitter used to connect people who want to help change conversations from *us versus them* to *enabling the business* with sustainable work practices that focus on people.

Successful projects require input, effort, insight, and collaboration from people across the organization; the problems inherent in your organization may not be limited to just developers and operations teams. We have deliberately chosen to use lowercase "devops" throughout the text of this book to reflect our view that this is an inclusive movement, not an exclusive one.

Who This Book Is For

This book is aimed primarily at managers and individual contributors in leadership roles who see friction within their organizations and are looking for concrete, actionable steps they can take toward implementing or improving a devops culture in their work environment. Individual contributors of all levels looking for practical suggestions for easing some of the pain points will find actionable takeaways.

Our readers have a mix of professional roles, as devops is a professional and cultural movement that stresses the iterative efforts to break down information silos, monitor relationships, and repair misunderstandings that arise between teams within an organization.

The book covers a wide range of devops skills and theory, including an introduction to the foundational ideas and concepts. We assume you will have heard of the term "devops" and perhaps have a basic understanding of the tools and processes commonly used in the field.

We encourage you to put aside any hard-and-fast definitions and to keep an open mind to the principles of devops that we have seen to be most effective.

After reading this book, you will have a solid understanding of what having a devops culture means practically for your organization, how to encourage effective collaboration such that individual contributors from different backgrounds and teams with different goals and working styles can work together productively, how to help teams collaborate to maximize their value while increasing employee satisfaction and balancing conflicting organizational goals, and how to choose tools and workflows that complement your organization.

How This Book Is Organized

We put a great deal of thought into the ordering and organization of the chapters. Just as there is no One True Way of doing devops, there is no one true ordering of "how to do devops." Everyone reading this book will be at a slightly different stage in their devops journey, and each journey is a different story that is being told, taking a different path, with different problems and conflicts that need to be addressed.

This book is broken down into multiple parts (in Part I, we share the big picture and then zoom in closer to devops ideas, definitions, and principles; Parts II–V cover the central four pillars of effective devops; and Part VI concludes with a discussion of how we can use stories to build connections between individuals, teams, and organizations):

- Part I, *What Is Devops?*
- Part II, *Collaboration*
- Part III, *Affinity*
- Part IV, *Tools*
- Part V, *Scaling*
- Part VI, *Bridging Devops Cultures*

Parts II–V each end with a chapter that discusses various misconceptions about that particular pillar of effective devops, as well as some common troubleshooting scenarios related to that topic. Readers who are struggling a bit with implementing one or more of these areas within their own organization will find even more practical advice to help guide them in these "Misconceptions and Troubleshooting" chapters.

It might be tempting for readers who feel more comfortable working with computers than with people to skip over the interpersonal and cultural material in this book, but these aspects give us an understanding of how we work together, including how culture and technology interact, and that combination is part of what gives effective devops its strength.

Choose to read the chapters in the order that is most relevant to you for where you are in your own story; feel free to treat this as a "Choose Your Own Adventure"–style book. The pillars are all intertwined and interrelated, and it is our hope that people will be able to come back, reread the parts that speak to them at the time, and continue to learn from these principles as they continue along their devops journeys.

Methodology of Case Studies

Throughout the book, we share the stories of individuals at a number of companies from the industry. Information was gathered through interviews with people at different levels within organizations, published blog posts, presentations, and company filings. While the theme for each chapter informs the direction of the case study, the nature of devops means that each case study will touch many, if not all, of the four pillars.

In addition, we share a combination of more formal case studies, informal stories, and our own personal experiences to demonstrate the breadth of ways that devops can impact decisions and narratives.

Read the stories we have shared in the upcoming chapters. Recognize the stories within your organization now; what influences and informs your teams? Share your stories at internal community events or external industry events, and always keep an ear open to how you can learn from other people's devops stories in addition to sharing your own.

Conventions Used in This Book

The following typographical conventions are used in this book:

Italic
> Indicates new terms, URLs, email addresses, filenames, and file extensions.

`Constant width`
> Used for program listings, as well as within paragraphs to refer to program elements such as variable or function names, databases, data types, environment variables, statements, and keywords.

`Constant width bold`
> Shows commands or other text that should be typed literally by the user.

`Constant width italic`
> Shows text that should be replaced with user-supplied values or by values determined by context.

 This element signifies a general note, tip, or suggestion.

 This element indicates a warning or caution.

 This element signifies an actionable suggestion based on the four pillars of effective devops.

Using Code Examples

We have a web page for this book, where we list errata, share more stories, and post additional material. This material is available at *http://effectivedevops.net*.

This book is here to help you get your job done. In general, if example code is offered with this book, you may use it in your programs and documentation. You do not need to contact us for permission unless you're reproducing a significant portion of the code. For example, writing a program that uses several chunks of code from this book does not require permission. Selling or distributing a CD-ROM of examples from O'Reilly books does require permission. Answering a question by citing this book and quoting example code does not require permission. Incorporating a significant amount of example code from this book into your product's documentation does require permission.

We appreciate, but do not require, attribution. An attribution usually includes the title, author, publisher, and ISBN. For example: "*Effective DevOps* by Jennifer Davis and Ryn Daniels (O'Reilly). Copyright 2016 Jennifer Davis and Ryn Daniels, 978-1-491-92630-7."

If you feel your use of code examples falls outside fair use or the permission given above, feel free to contact us at *permissions@oreilly.com*.

Safari® Books Online

Safari Books Online is an on-demand digital library that delivers expert content in both book and video form from the world's leading authors in technology and business.

Technology professionals, software developers, web designers, and business and creative professionals use Safari Books Online as their primary resource for research, problem solving, learning, and certification training.

Safari Books Online offers a range of plans and pricing for enterprise, government, education, and individuals.

Members have access to thousands of books, training videos, and prepublication manuscripts in one fully searchable database from publishers like O'Reilly Media, Prentice Hall Professional, Addison-Wesley Professional, Microsoft Press, Sams, Que, Peachpit Press, Focal Press, Cisco Press, John Wiley & Sons, Syngress, Morgan Kaufmann, IBM Redbooks, Packt, Adobe Press, FT Press, Apress, Manning, New Riders, McGraw-Hill, Jones & Bartlett, Course Technology, and hundreds more. For more information about Safari Books Online, please visit us online.

How to Contact Us

Please address comments and questions concerning this book to the publisher:

O'Reilly Media, Inc.
1005 Gravenstein Highway
North Sebastopol, CA 95472
(800) 998-9938 (in the United States or Canada)
(707) 829-0515 (international or local)
(707) 829-0104 (fax)

We have a web page for this book, where we list errata, examples, and any additional information. You can access this page at *http://bit.ly/orm-effective-devops*.

To comment or ask technical questions about this book, send email to *bookquestions@oreilly.com*.

Acknowledgments

Effective DevOps would not have been possible without the help and guidance of many friends, colleagues, and family members. We'd like to thank the entire team at O'Reilly, with special thanks to Courtney Nash for encouraging us to write this; our editor, Brian Anderson, for all of his support; the secret cabal of animal choosers, who blessed us with the unshaven yak as our official animal; and everyone else involved in making this book a reality. We'd also like to thank John Allspaw, Lara Hogan, and Jon Cowie at Etsy; Nicole Forsgren, and Yvonne Lam at Chef; Bridget Kromhout at Pivotal; and Tom Limoncelli at Stack Exchange for all of their help, support, and encouragement along the way.

Thank you to our public case study participants: Alex Nobert, Bridget Kromhout, Tim Gross, Tina Donbeck, and Phaedra Marshall.

Thank you to all of the individuals who shared their stories, including Davida Marion, Linda Laubenheimer, Hollie Kay, Nicole Johnson, and Alice Goldfuss.

Thank you to our technical reviewers who helped hone our narrative: Alice Goldfuss, Dustin Collins, Ernest Mueller, Matthew Skelton, Olivier Jacques, Bridget Kromhout, Yvonne Lam, and Peter Nealon.

Thank you to Andy Paroff for *Ed*, our sparkly devops yak on our website and stickers.

From Ryn

Thank you to Etsy for providing me the opportunity to work on this book, to speak at so many conferences, and for being an all-around excellent place to work. Extra thanks to the web operations team for their support and patience during this project—working with all of you has helped me remember why I love this work in the first place. Special shoutouts to Mike Rembetsy for not taking "no" for an answer all those times I said I wasn't good enough to even interview here, to John Allspaw for encouraging and believing in me, and to Laurie Denness and Jon Cowie for all their support and knowledge, and for helping me grow so much as an operations engineer.

Thank you to Lara Hogan, Bridget Kromhout, Cate Huston, and Melissa Santos for being excellent friends, role models, and generally bad-ass women. Getting to know and talk with you has helped me keep going even when things get tough, and your feedback and support has helped me immensely.

Thank you to James Turnbull for reaching out to me on Twitter all those years ago, and by doing so introducing me to the operations community. I've appreciated getting to know you; your support, wisdom, and encouragement on the writing process; and having another member of the operations face-metal cabal.

Thank you to Jason Dixon for giving me my first invitation to speak at a conference and believing that I had something worthwhile to say, even before I believed that myself.

Thank you to the operations and devops communities as a whole, and especially to the NYC ops folks for providing support, new opportunities, and friends to enjoy a good Sysdrink beer with.

Thank you to Jennifer Davis, for being a great friend, conference buddy, and coauthor. Brainstorming, writing, ranting, training, and editing with you has been an amazing adventure, and I'm immensely thankful for getting to work with you and for all the cupcakes we celebrated with, both remotely and together.

Finally, thank you to my mother for supporting, encouraging, and believing in me—I told you I could get a real job even with weird-colored hair! Also, this book would not have been possible without the continual love, support, lap-warming, and armchair-editing of my cats throughout the entire project.

From Jennifer

Thank you to Chef for creating the work opportunities to learn from so many different organizations and for supporting sharing that learning through speaking and training.

Thank you to all the women in the industry, who change the way we work through introducing new perspectives and acceptable behaviors and norms: your voice matters. Keep sharing your experiences and finding your support.

Thank you to the devops community at large, who has helped reignite my desire to be a part of community. This community has provided a support system and encouraged sustainable workplace practices. Thank you to all the individuals who shared their individual stories and experiences.

Thank you to Yvonne Lam, Bridget Kromhout, Dominica DeGrandis, Mary Grace Thengvall, Amye Scavarda, Nicole Forsgren, and Sheri Elgin for the invaluable friendship. Your thoughts and feedback have helped me understand and grow my perspective. Your support has strengthened and invigorated me.

Thank you to Ryn Daniels, my friend and coauthor, for the thoughtful, collaborative, and inspiring thinking, writing, and editing as we journeyed through this project together, exemplifying our thoughts on devops in practice. Through the laughter and tears, the rants and raves, it has been an honor and inspiration to devops with you.

Thank you to my grandmother, elementary school teacher Frances Wadsworth Hayes, for inspiring me to share my stories, and pursue lifelong teaching and learning. My contributions wouldn't have been possible without the love and support of my family, Brian Brennan and George.

PART I

What Is Devops?

CHAPTER 1

The Big Picture

Devops is a way of thinking and a way of working. It is a framework for sharing stories and developing empathy, enabling people and teams to practice their crafts in effective and lasting ways. It is part of the cultural weave that shapes how we work and why. Many people think about devops as specific tools like Chef or Docker, but tools alone are not devops. What makes tools "devops" is the manner of their use, not fundamental characteristics of the tools themselves.

In addition to the tools we use to practice our crafts, an equally important part of our culture is our values, norms, and knowledge. Examining how people work, the technologies we use, how technology influences the way we work, and how people influence technology can help us make intentional decisions about the landscape of our organizations, and of our industry.

Devops is not just another software development methodology. Although it is related to and even influenced by software development methodologies like Agile or XP, and its practices can include software development methods, or features like infrastructure automation and continuous delivery, it is much more than just the sum of these parts. While these concepts are related and may be frequently seen in devops environments, focusing solely on them misses the bigger picture—the cultural and interpersonal aspects that give devops its power.

A Snapshot of Devops Culture

What does a successful devops culture look like? To demonstrate this, we will examine the intersection of people, process, and tools at Etsy, an online global marketplace for handmade and vintage goods. We chose Etsy as an example not only because they are well-known in the industry for their technical and cultural practices, but also because Ryn's experiences working there allow us a more detailed look at what this culture looks like from the inside.

A new engineer at Etsy starts her first day with a laptop and a development virtual machine (VM) already set up with the appropriate accounts for access and authorization, the most common GitHub repositories cloned, aliases and shortcuts to relevant tools precreated, and a guide with new hire information and links to other company resources on her desktop. Standardization of tools and practices between teams makes it easier for new people to get up to speed regardless of what team they are joining, but every team also has the flexibility to customize as they see fit.

A current employee will pair with the new employee to walk through what testing and development processes she will use in her day-to-day work. She starts by writing code on her local development VM, which is set up with configuration management to be nearly identical to the live production environment. This development VM is set up to be able to run and test code locally, so she can quickly work and make changes without affecting anyone else's development work during these early stages.

Etsy engineers can achieve a good degree of confidence that a change is working locally by running a suite of local unit and functional tests. From there, they test changes against the try server (*http://bit.ly/etsy-try*), a Jenkins cluster nearly identical to the organization's production continuous integration (CI) cluster but with the added bonus of not requiring any code to be committed to the master branch yet. When try passes, engineers have an even higher degree of confidence that their changes will not break any tests.

Depending on the size and complexity of the change, this new engineer might choose to open a pull request or more informally ask for a code review from one of her colleagues. This is not mandated for every change, and is often left up to individual discretion—in Etsy's high-trust, blameless environment, people are given the trust and authority to decide whether a code review is necessary. Newer or more junior employees are given the guidance to help them figure out what changes merit a code review and who should be involved. As a new employee, she has a teammate glance over her changes before she starts deploying them.

When local and try tests have passed, the developer then joins what Etsy calls a *push queue* to deploy her changes to production. This queue system uses Internet Relay Chat (IRC) and an IRC bot to coordinate deploys when multiple developers are pushing changes at once. When it is her turn, she pushes her commits to the master branch of the repository she is working in and uses Deployinator (*https://github.com/etsy/deployinator*) to deploy these changes to QA. This automatically starts builds on the QA server as well as running the full CI test suite.

After the builds and tests have completed successfully, she does a quick manual check of the QA version of the site and its logs to look for any problems that weren't caught by the automated tests. From there, she uses the same Deployinator process to deploy her code to production and make sure that the tests and logs look good there as well. If something does break that the tests don't catch, there are plenty of dashboards of graphs to watch, and Nagios monitoring checks to alert people to problems. In addition, many teams have their own Nagios checks that go to their own on-call rotations, encouraging everyone to share the responsibilities of keeping everything running smoothly. And if something doesn't run so smoothly, people work together to help fix any issues, and blameless postmortems mean that people learn from their mistakes without being chastised for making them.

This process is so streamlined that it takes only around 10 minutes on average from start to finish, and Etsy engineering as a whole deploys around 60 times a day. Documentation is available for anyone interested to peruse, and every engineer pushes code to production on their first day, guided by a current team member to help familiarize them with the process. Even nonengineers are encouraged to participate by way of the *First Push Program*, pairing with engineers to deploy a small change such as adding their photo to the staff page on the website. In addition to being used for regular software development, the try and Deployinator process works so well that it is used for nearly everything that can be deployed, from the tools that developers use to build virtual machines to Kibana dashboards for searching logs, from Nagios monitoring checks to the Deployinator tool itself.

The Evolution of Culture

This story of Etsy today is in stark contrast to how things were several years ago with a less transparent and more error-prone deployment process that took close to four hours. Developers had their own blade servers to work on, rather than virtual machines, but the blade servers weren't powerful enough to run the automated test suites to completion. Tests that were run in the staging environment took a couple of hours to complete, and even then they were flaky enough to make their results less than useful.

Teams within the engineering organization were siloed. There were a lot of developers throwing code over the metaphorical wall to ops, who were solely responsible for deployments and monitoring and thus tended to be incredibly change-averse. Developers wrote code, executing handcrafted shell scripts to create a new SVN branch which would be deployed using svn merge—not known for being the easiest merging tool to work with—to merge in all the developers' changes to this deploy branch. Developers would tell the one operations engineer who had permissions to deploy which branch to use. This would begin the painstaking, multihour deployment process (see Figure 1-1). Because the process was so painful, it happened only once every two or three weeks.

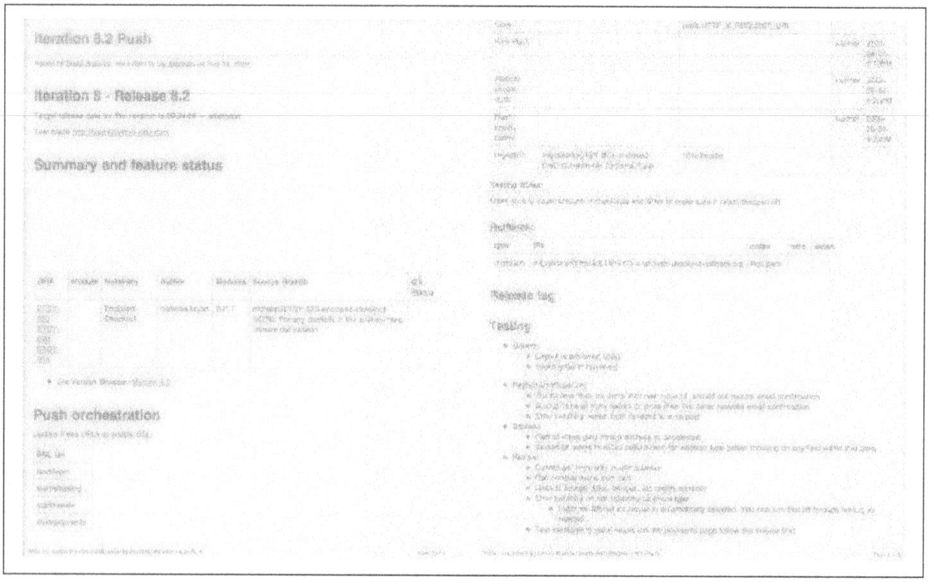

Figure 1-1. Before Deployinator, a complex and error-prone deploy process

People became fed up with this process. They realized something had to change. It would be hard for the deployment situation to get any worse. The organization was made up of smart and talented people with the motivation and now frustration to solve this problem. They had buy-in from the CEO and CTO down, which was key to having resources available to make change.

The keys to the deployment kingdom were shared from the one operations engineer to two developers, who were given the time and go-ahead to hack on this process as much as they needed. They say when you have a hammer, everything looks like a nail, and when you have a web application developer, everything looks like it needs a web app—and so the first Deployinator was born (Figure 1-2). At first, it was a web wrapper around the existing shell scripts, but over time, more people began to work and improve it. While the underlying mechanisms doing the heavy lifting changed, the overall interface stayed largely the same.

It became evident to everyone that empowering these employees to create tools to improve their jobs made it a lot easier for people to do said jobs. Deploys went from being in people's way to helping them accomplish the goal of getting features in front of users. Tests went from being flaky wastes of time to helping catch bugs. Logs, graphs, and alerts made it possible for everyone, not just a select few individuals, to see the impact of their work.

The key takeaway from the stories of all these tools isn't so much the specifics of the tools themselves, but the fact that someone realized that they needed to be built, and was also given the time and resources to build them.

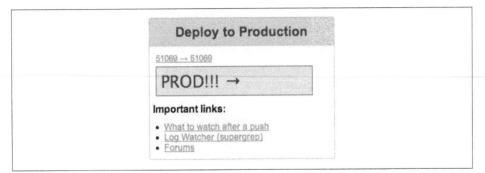

Figure 1-2. After Deployinator, a simple web interface that anyone can use

 Buy-in from management, freedom to experiment and work on non-customer-facing code, and trust across various teams all allowed these tools to be developed and along with them, a culture of tooling, sharing, and collaboration.

These factors made Etsy the so-called devops unicorn (they prefer to call themselves just a sparkly horse) they are known as today, and maintaining that culture is prioritized at all levels of the company. This example embodies our definition of effective devops—an organization that embraces cultural change to affect how individuals think about work, value all the different roles that individuals have, accelerate business value, and measure the effects of the change. It was these principles of devops that helped take Etsy from a state of frustration and silos to industry-renowned collaboration and tool builders. While the details may differ, we have seen these guiding principles in success stories throughout the industry, and in sharing them we provide a guide for organizations looking to make a similar transformation.

The Value of the Story

> Each of us thinks our own thoughts. Our concepts we share.
>
> —Stephen Toulmin, *Human Understanding*

Effective DevOps contains case studies and stories from both teams and individuals. When looking at the devops books that already existed, we found that there were fewer direct real-world experiences for people to draw from; so many stories focus on a specific tool or an abstract cultural practice. It is one thing to talk about how something should work in theory, but there is often a great deal of difference between how something should work in theory and how things turn out in practice. We want to share the actual stories of these practices, what did and didn't end up working, and the thought processes behind the decisions that were made, so that people have as much information as possible as they undertake their own devops journey.

Ryn's Story

My devops story begins around the same time as the devops movement itself. I made an accidental career change into operations shortly after the idea of devops was first formalized and the first devopsdays conference events had been held. As luck would have it, I found myself working as a one-person operations team at a small startup in the ecommerce space, and discovered I loved operations work. Even though I was a one-person team for so long, the idea of devops immediately made sense to me—it seemed to be a common sense, no-bullshit approach to working more effectively with other parts of an organization outside of your own team. At the time, I was the grumpy system administrator who spent their days hiding in the data center. I was the only person on-call, and was so busy fighting the fires that I had inherited that I had little to no idea what the developers (or anyone else, for that matter) were working on. So the ideas of sharing responsibilities and information and breaking down barriers between teams really spoke to me.

Some organizations are much more open to change and new ideas than others, and in addition to being rather change-resistant, this startup wasn't keen on listening to anything a very junior system administrator had to say. "You're not even a real sysadmin," they said as a way of dismissing my ideas. There also wasn't enough budget to even buy me a couple of books (I bought Tom Limoncelli's *The Practice of System and Network Administration* and *Time Management for System Administrators* on my own dime, and they were worth every penny), let alone send me to LISA or Velocity, and devopsdays New York wouldn't be started for another couple of years.

Luckily, I started to find the devops community online, and being able to talk to and learn from people who shared my passions for operations and learning and working together revitalized me. James Turnbull, now CTO of Kickstarter but who was at the time working at Puppet, found me on Twitter, struck up a conversation with me, and sent me a copy of his excellent *Pro Puppet* book at a time when I was struggling with having inherited 200 snowflake servers with not even a bash script to manage them. That small action introduced me to a growing and thriving community of people, and gave me hope that I could one day be a part of that community.

As Jennifer will note in her story as well, it's hard to effect change when you're burnt out, and after a year or so of trying to help change and improve my current company and being shut down for my lack of experience (which was growing by the day) every time, I also made the choice to move on. I kept learning and growing my skills, but still didn't feel totally aligned with the places I ended up working. I still seemed to be fighting against my coworkers and organizations, rather than working with them.

In January 2013, I went to the first devopsdays New York, soaking up all the talks and listening to as much of the hallway track as I could, even if I didn't feel like I was experienced enough to add anything to the conversations. I lived vicariously through following #VelocityConf on Twitter. In October of that year, I gave a lightning talk at the second devopsdays New York, and through that met Mike Rembetsy, one of the co-organizers of that conference. He told me I should come work for Etsy, but after years of feeling like an impostor in my own field, I thought he was joking. I'd followed Code as Craft and the Etsy operations team online since I first discovered the operations and devops communities, but I didn't think I was good enough to join them.

I've never been more happy to be proven so wrong. My career in operations has taken me on a journey through several different organizational structures and ways that development, operations, and sometimes even "devops" teams worked together. Having worked at companies as small as a 25-person startup and as large as a decades-old enterprise organization with hundreds of thousands of employees, I've seen many ways of developing and delivering software and systems—some more effective than others.

Having spent time being the one person on-call 24/7 for the better part of a year and in other less-than-ideal workplace scenarios, I want to share the techniques and methods that have worked best for both me and my teams over the years to help reduce the number of people who might also find themselves being the single point of failure for part of their organization. A large part of my motivation for writing this book was being able to tell these stories—both ones that I've lived personally and ones told to me by others—so that we can share, learn, and grow as a community. Community helped me get to where I am today, and this book is just one way I have of giving back.

Jennifer's Story

In 2007, I was contacted by Yahoo management about a position that was "a little dev" and "a little ops"—a Senior Service Engineer position building out a multitenanted, hosted, distributed, and geographically replicated key/value data store called Sherpa.

As a service engineer at Yahoo, I honed my skills in programming, operations, and project management. I worked alongside the development and quality assurance teams building Sherpa, coordinating efforts with the data center, network, security, and storage teams. In 2009, as the murmurings of devops trickled into Yahoo, I discounted its value, as I already was a devops!

Fast-forward to the summer of 2011, and Jeff Park took over the leadership of my team. He helped grow the team so that we had multiple people in Service Engineering in the United States as well as in India. It wasn't enough. Jeff had concerns about me as an employee working nonstop and almost single-handedly keeping the service up. He was also concerned about the business and wanted to build resiliency into the support model through redundant staff support. In December, he told me to take a real vacation—to not read my email or take phone calls but to disconnect.

I told him that I felt like something wasn't quite right, something wasn't working as expected. He told me that he'd fire me if I didn't take the time off. He reassured me that everything would be fine. I set up a simple visualization of the concerning metrics with JavaScript and a Perl script running on a cron job the evening before my vacation, confident that it would be enough to provide warning.

I came back from vacation to a degraded service. So many small issues that I had found over the years impacted the overall event, making it more difficult to debug. I felt like a complete failure, even though my last-minute visualization had been critical to identifying and monitoring the issue.

Jeff took me aside and said that he knew there was a high risk that things would break while I was out and additional risk of issues resulting from the team's historical complete reliance on me. My *heroics* were disguising the failures inherent in the system.

He felt that sometimes short-term setbacks are an OK thing, if you later use them as a lesson to right things over the long term. If things broke, it would help prioritize the criticality of further sharing, documenting, and distributing my knowledge and expertise to the business. Ultimately, that would lead to more stability and a better overall outcome for the organization and individuals on the team.

That event united the Sherpa team as we tried to repair the service and understand what happened. We divided into cross-functional teams to address the different components of the problem: failure handlers, communication group, tools, monitoring, and cleanup crew. Key individuals from management were available at all times and prepared to make hard decisions. These hard decisions helped us limit the overall length of the outage.

> Failure sucks but instructs.
>
> —Bob Sutton, *Stanford Management Instructor*

A key takeaway from this event for me was the value of failure. We couldn't be afraid to fail, and we needed to learn from the failure. We had ongoing meetings to resolve the operational issues that had been highlighted in the event. We continued to remediate outages as a cross-discipline team rather than limiting those activities to the Service Engineering team. We promoted discussions between our consumers and providers to better understand the weak points in the system.

Having spent over 10 years building work practices based on operations' tribal cultures of long hours, isolation, and avoiding system failures, how was I going to evoke the change I needed?

I was ready for devops. For me, the value of devops wasn't the mantra of "devs do X and ops do Y, or dev versus ops", but the shared stories, solving problems in a collaborative manner across the industry, and strengthening community. From the open spaces to the collaborative hacking, a new support system was emerging that strengthened the foundations of sustainable workplace practices and cultivated relationships between people.

Collaborating with Ryn on this book has strengthened my understanding of devops. Being able to share the working strategies and techniques from around the world to help improve and create sustainable work practices has been an incredible journey. It doesn't end with the final words in this book.

We are all gaining so much experience each and every day based on our different, diverse perspectives. Whether you are at the beginning of your career, knee-deep in cultural transformation, or about to change roles and responsibilities, your experiences can inform and educate others. I look forward to hearing and amplifying your stories so that together we grow as a community and collectively learn from our failures and successes.

Illustrating Devops with Stories

We have selected a variety of case studies to help illustrate the different ways in which a culture of effective devops can manifest. The goal of these stories is not to provide templates that can be followed exactly; blindly copying another organization or individual discounts all of the circumstances and reasoning that went into the choices they made.

These stories are illustrations or guides. Our hope is that you read these stories and see reflections of your experiences, perhaps as they are today, but maybe as how they could be in the future. We included stories from a variety of sources, both formal case studies and informal personal stories. While some stories are from organizations that are more well known, we deliberately chose to include stories from lesser-known sources as well, to showcase the variety of devops narratives that exist.

When you read these studies, consider not only the choices that were made and their outcomes, but also their circumstances and situations. What similarities can you see between their circumstances and your own, and what are the key differences? If you made the same choice in your own organization, what factors that are unique to your workplace would change the outcome? By reading and understanding these stories, we hope that you will be able to see their underlying themes, and start applying them to your own devops narrative.

Learning shouldn't stop at these shared stories. Experiment with new processes, tools, techniques, and ideas. Measure your progress, and most importantly, understand your reasons why. Once you start realizing what does and doesn't work with the things you try, you can begin to do more sophisticated experiments.

CHAPTER 2

What Is Devops?

Devops is a cultural movement that changes how individuals think about their work, values the diversity of work done, supports intentional processes that accelerate the rate by which businesses realize value, and measures the effect of social and technical change. It is a way of thinking and a way of working that enables individuals and organizations to develop and maintain sustainable work practices. It is a cultural framework for sharing stories and developing empathy, enabling people and teams to practice their crafts in effective and lasting ways.

A Prescription for Culture

Devops is a prescription for culture. No cultural movement exists in a vacuum; social structure and culture are inherently intertwined. The hierarchies within organizations, industry connections, and globalization influence culture, as well as the values, norms, beliefs, and artifacts that reflect these areas. Software we create does not exist separately from the people who use it and the people who create it. Devops is about finding ways to adapt and innovate social structure, culture, and technology together in order to work more effectively.

The Devops Equation

> The danger for a movement that regards itself as new is that it may try to embrace everything that is not old.
>
> —Lee Roy Beach et al., *Naturalistic Decision Making and Related Research Lines*

This book is not a prescription for the One True Way of doing devops. While we will describe commonly seen misconceptions and anti-patterns, we are more interested in describing what a successful devops culture looks and acts like and how these principles can be applied across a variety of organizations and environments.

While the term *devops* itself is a portmanteau of "development" and "operations," the core concepts of devops can and should be applied throughout the entire organization. A sustainable, successful business is more than the development and operations teams. Limiting our thinking to just those teams who write software or deploy it into production does the entire business a disservice.

Devops as Folk Model

In many ways, devops has become a *folk model*, a term used with different intent that leads to miscommunication and misunderstanding. In the field of cognitive science, a folk model is used as an abstraction for more concrete ideas and often substituted, being easier to understand than the concept ultimately being discussed. An example of this is the term *situational awareness*, which is often used as a stand-in for more specific ideas like perception and short-term memory. Folk models are not necessarily bad. They become problematic when different groups use the same term with different intent.

People will often spend more time arguing over what "devops" means—what folk model they are using for it—than they spend focusing on the ideas that they really want to discuss.[1] Sometimes, in order to get around the issue of defining devops and get people talking about concepts and principles, individuals will exaggerate "bad" behaviors as a way of focusing on the "good" behaviors that are seen as being "devops." To talk about effective interteam collaboration, someone might use a cartoonish example of a company that creates a devops team that serves only to act as go-betweens for the development and operations teams, as we did in the Preface. It is an extreme example, but it gets people talking about something more meaningful and practical than a definition.

The Old View and the New View

In an environment where humans are blamed and punished for errors, a culture of fear can build up walls that prevent clear communication and transparency. Contrast this with a blameless environment, where issues are addressed cooperatively and viewed as learning opportunities for individuals and the organization. Professor Sidney Dekker described these two environments as the "old view" and the "new view" of human error in his book, *The Field Guide to Understanding Human Error*.[2]

The first environment views "human error as the cause of trouble." This "old view" is described as a mindset in which the focus is on elimination of human error. Mistakes

---

1 Sidney Dekker and Erik Hollnagel, "Human Factors and Folk Models." *Cognition, Technology & Work* 6, no. 2 (2004): 79–86.

2 Sidney Dekker, *The Field Guide to Understanding Human Error* (Farnham, UK: Ashgate Publishing Ltd, 2014).

---

are made by "bad apples" who need to be thrown out. This view is found in blameful cultures, as it assumes that errors are often caused by malice or incompetence. Individuals responsible for failure must be blamed and shamed (or simply fired).

The second environment views "human error as a symptom of trouble deeper in the system." This "new view" is a mindset that sees human errors as structural rather than personal. People make choices and take the actions based on their context and what makes most sense to them, not intentional malice or incompetence. Organizations should consider systems holistically when looking to minimize or respond to issues.

Understanding and embracing the "new view" is key to understanding the devops movement. This view encourages us to share stories, as everything is a learning opportunity.

Shared stories:

- lead to increased transparency and trust within a team;
- instruct our coworkers in how to avoid a costly mistake without having to directly experience it; and
- increase the time spent on solving new problems, allowing for more innovation.

When these stories are shared throughout the industry, we impact the industry as a whole, creating new opportunities, knowledge, and shared understanding.

The Devops Compact

The heart of devops starts with people working not only as groups but as teams with a desire for mutual understanding. This can be described as a compact that teams will work together, communicate their intentions and the issues that they run into, and dynamically adjust in order to work toward their shared organizational goals.

Example of a compact

We can visualize this critical compact by examining the communication, clarification, and mutual trust of two rock climbers. Rock climbing is an activity that involves participants climbing up, down, or across natural rock formations or synthetic walls. The shared goal is to reach the top or end point of a specific route, usually without falling. It is a combination of the physical endurance required to navigate the problem as well as the mental acuity to understand and prepare for the next steps.

In some forms of rock climbing, one individual, the *climber*, will use a rope and a harness as protection against falls. The second individual, the *belayer*, monitors the tension in the rope, giving the climber enough tension to prevent a long fall while also providing enough slack to give her room to maneuver as she climbs.

Belaying properly and safely requires both a shared understanding of the tools and process as well as ongoing communication. The climber will securely knot into her harness. The belayer will make sure his belay device is properly attached to his climbing harness. Each will trust but verify the status of the other's work before starting the climb.

The climb itself has a set of verbal cues to indicate readiness prior to approaching the climb, with the climber asking "on belay?" and the belayer communicating "belay on." The climber responds with "climbing" to indicate her readiness. Finally, the belayer acknowledges with "climb on."

The principles of this compact that make it work include:

- Shared, clearly defined goals
- Ongoing communication
- Dynamic adjustment and repairs of understanding

As we will illustrate next, these principles bring just as much to devops in the workplace as they do to climbers on the wall.

Example of the devops compact

Two employees work on separate teams at Sparkle Corp. The General is a senior developer with a number of different experiences in her background and has worked at Sparkle Corp for two years. George is an operations engineer with some experience and is relatively new to Sparkle Corp.

Their two teams support the global community of people that depend on the Sparkle Corp website for their creative endeavors. Their shared goal is to implement a new feature that will increase the value to end users, hopefully without impacting the site.

As the one with more experience at the company, the General will be really clear with George about the expectations, values, and processes in place at Sparkle Corp. In turn, George will be really clear with the General about when he needs help or doesn't understand part of the process. Both the General and George will check in with each other's work before proceeding to next steps—an example of the *trust-but-verify* model, as described with the climbing process.

The General and George have a shared understanding of their goals:

- Implementing a new feature that increases the value to Sparkle Corp customers
- Maintaining safety and trust in their communication with each other

In a siloed, nondevops environment, the lack of a shared understanding would be like the General trying to start coding without making sure George understands the requirements—it might end up working, but without communication of intentions, the odds are stacked against it.

An organization will certainly run into unexpected issues or roadblocks along the way, but with the shared understanding that everyone is still a part of the compact, actions turn into repairs. We repair our misunderstandings about who would be working on a particular feature or when something would get done. We repair bugs that affect our understanding of how the software is supposed to behave. We repair processes and their documentation when things don't go the way we expect in production.

Throughout the book, we're going to take this idea of a devops compact and show how both the technological and cultural aspects of devops are ways of developing and maintaining this shared mutual understanding.

CHAPTER 3

A History of Devops

Examining the history of the industry and the recurring patterns and ideas within it helps us to understand what shaped the devops movement. With that understanding we can make sense of where we are today and understand how, through effective devops, we can break the cycle of increasing specialization that creates silos and devaluation of specific roles.

Developer as Operator

In the beginning, the developer was the operator. When World War II broke out, the United States government put out a call for math majors to become "computers," a job in which they were responsible for calculating ballistics firing tables for the war effort. Jean Bartik was one of the many women that responded. Her college advisor encouraged her to ignore the call, worrying that the repetitive tasks were not as admirable as continuing her family's tradition of education.

While her advisor was right about the repetitious nature of calculating numbers, the job put Bartik in the right place at the right time to become one of the first programmers of the Electronic Numeric Integrator and Computer, or ENIAC (*http://eniacprog rammers.org*), the first all-electronic, programmable computer system.

With no documentation and no plans, Bartik and the other five women working on the ENIAC figured out how to program it by reviewing the device's hardware and logic diagrams. Programming the machine and its 18,000 vacuum tubes meant setting dials and changing out cable connections across 40 control panels.

At the time, the industry focused on hardware engineering and not on the programming required to make the system work. When problems arose, hardware engineers would come in and proclaim, "It's not the machine; it's the operators." The programmers felt the pain of managing and operating these systems as they had to replace fuses and cables and remove literal bugs in the system.

The Advent of Software Engineering

In 1961, President John F. Kennedy set the challenge that within the decade the United States would land a person on the moon, and return them safely to Earth. Faced with this deadline but lacking employees with the necessary skills, the National Aeronautics and Space Administration (NASA) needed to find someone to write the onboard flight software required to accomplish this task. NASA enlisted Margaret Hamilton, a mathematician at the Massachusetts Institute of Technology (MIT) to lead the effort.[1]

Hamilton recalls:

> Coming up with new ideas was an adventure. Dedication and commitment were a given. Mutual respect was across the board. Because software was a mystery, a black box, upper management gave us total freedom and trust. We had to find a way and we did. Looking back, we were the luckiest people in the world; there was no choice but to be pioneers; no time to be beginners.[2]

In her pursuit of writing this complex software, Hamilton is credited with coining the term *software engineering*. She also created the concept of *priority displays*, software that alerts astronauts to information that requires their attention in real time. She instituted a set of requirement gathering that added quality assurance to the list of software engineering concerns, which included:

- debugging all individual components;
- testing individual components prior to assembly; and
- integration testing.

In 1969, during the Apollo 11 mission, the lunar module guidance computer software was tasked with too many calculations for its limited capacity. Hamilton's team had programmed the software such that it could be manually overridden, allowing Neil Armstrong to step in and pilot the lunar module using manual controls.

The freedom and trust that the management team afforded the team of engineers working on the onboard flight software, as well as the mutual respect between team members, led to software that facilitated one of humankind's great leaps in technol-

---

1 Robert McMillan, "Her Code Got Humans on the Moon—And Invented Software Itself," *WIRED*, October 13, 2015.

2 A. S. J. Rayl, "NASA Engineers and Scientists—Transforming Dreams Into Reality," 2008, *http://www.nasa.gov/50th/50th_magazine/scientists.html*.

ogy as Neil Armstrong stepped on the moon. Without this high-trust environment, this manual override ability (something that turned out to be of critical importance) might not have been present, and the moon landing story might have had a very different outcome.

The Problems of Software

Space flight was not the only area in which software was becoming critical in the 1960s. As hardware became more readily available, people became more concerned about the impending complexity of software that did not follow standards across other engineering disciplines. The growth rate of systems and the emerging dependence upon them were alarming.

In 1967, the NATO Science Committee, comprising scientists across countries and industries, held discussions to assess the state of software engineering. A Study Group on Computer Science was formed in the fall of 1967, whose goal was to focus attention on the problems of software. They invited 50 experts from all areas of industry, with three working groups focusing on the design of software, production of software, and service of software, in an effort to define, describe, and begin solving the problems of software engineering.

At the NATO Software Engineering Conference of 1968, key problems with software engineering were identified, including:

- defining and measuring success;
- building complex systems requiring large investment and unknown feasibility;
- producing systems on schedule and to specification, and;
- putting economic pressures on manufacturers to build specific products.

The identification of these problems would help to define and shape areas of focus for the industry in years to come, and still impacts us to this day.

The Advent of Proprietary Software and Standardization

Until 1964, the practice was to build computers that were specific and targeted to customer requirements. Software and hardware were not standardized or interchangeable. In 1964, International Business Machines (IBM) announced a family of computers known as the System/360—computers designed to support a wide range of utility from small to large and for commercial and scientific purposes.

The goal was to reduce the cost of product development, manufacturing, service, and support while also facilitating the ability for customers to upgrade as needed. The System/360 became the dominant mainframe computer, providing customers the flexibility to start small and grow computing resources as needed. It also enabled job flexibility, as individuals could learn the software and hardware, which at the time were still tightly coupled, and then have the requisite skills needed for a similar job in another location.

Up until the late 1960s, computers were leased rather than bought outright. The cost of the hardware was high and incorporated the cost of software and services. Source code for the software was generally provided. In 1969, faced with a US antitrust lawsuit, IBM again impacted the industry by decoupling the software and hardware of their product, charging separately for the software associated with their mainframe hardware. This changed how software was viewed; software had suddenly acquired significant monetary value in and of itself and was not provided openly.

The Age of the Network

In 1979, a worldwide distributed discussion platform called Usenet was started by Tom Truscott and Jim Ellis, then students at Duke University. Usenet started out as a simple shell script that would automatically call different computers, search for changes in files on those computers, and copy changes from one computer to another using UUCP (Unix-to-Unix copy, a suite of programs allowing for file transfer and remote command execution between computers). Ellis gave a talk on the "Invitation to a General Access UNIX Network"[3] at a Unix users group known as USENIX. This was one of the first ways to communicate and share knowledge across organizations with computers, and its use grew rapidly.

While this tool started to facilitate the sharing of knowledge across universities and corporations, this was also a time when the details of how companies were run were considered part of their "secret sauce." Talking about solving problems outside of the company was not done, because such knowledge was viewed as a competitive advantage. There was an intentional cultural drive for competitors to work inefficiently. This stymied a great deal of collaboration and limited the effectiveness of the communication channels that were available. This cultural siloization led to companies growing in complexity.

Increasingly complex systems in turn led to the need for specialization of skills and role proliferation. Such roles included system administrators, specializing in systems management and minimizing system costs, and software engineers, specializing in creating of new products and features to address the new needs. Other more specialized groups were siloed off as well, with the NOC (network operations center), QA, security, databases, and storage all becoming separate areas of concern.

---

3 Ronda Hauben and Michael Hauben, *Netizens: On the History and Impact of Usenet and the internet* (Los Alamitos, CA: IEEE, 1997).

This situation created the institutional Tower of Babel, with the different silos all speaking different languages due to differing concerns. Along with this siloization, the specific pains of software and the hardware on which it ran were also separated. No longer were developers exposed to the late-night pages of down systems, or the anger expressed by unsatisfied users. Additionally, programming's trend toward higher-level languages meant that development became more abstracted, moving further and further away from the hardware and the systems engineers of the past.

In an effort to be proactive and prevent service outages, system administrators would document the set of steps required to do regular operations manually. System administrators borrowed the idea of "root cause analysis" from total quality management (TQM). This led in part to additional attention and effort toward minimizing risk. The lack of transparency and change management created growing amounts of entropy that engineers had to deal with more and more.

The Beginnings of a Global Community

As interconnected networks allowed programmers and IT practitioners to share their ideas online, people began looking for ways to share their ideas in person as well. User groups, where practitioners and users of various technologies could meet to discuss their fields, began to grow in number and popularity. One of the biggest worldwide user groups was DECUS, the Digital Equipment Computer Users' Society, which was founded in 1961 with members consisting mostly of programmers who wrote code for or maintained DEC computer equipment.

The US chapter of DECUS ran a variety of technical conferences and local user groups (LUGs) throughout the United States, while chapters in other countries were doing the same globally. These conferences and events began to publish their papers and ideas in the form of DECUS proceedings, which were made available to members as a way of sharing information and growing both the total knowledge of the community and the interconnectedness of its members.

A similar community specifically for system administrators was found with USENIX and its special interest group, the System Administrators Group. Known later as SAGE, today the group is known as the special interest group LISA (Large Installation System Administration), and it runs an annual conference with the same name.[4] Separately, NSFNET "Regional-Tech" meetings evolved into the North American Network Operators' Group (NANOG), a community specifically for network administrators to increase collaboration to make the internet better.

---

4 USENIX has announced that LISA will be retired at the end of 2016. For details, see *https://www.usenix.org/blog/refocusing-lisa-community*.

Contrary to the focus on knowledge sharing that was a primary feature of these local and global user groups, at the same time there was a great deal of secrecy within technology companies regarding their practices. Companies, in their quests for their own financial and material successes, kept their processes as closely guarded secrets, because if their competitors had inefficient practices, that improved the likelihood of their own relative success. Employees were strongly discouraged or even explicitly forbidden from sharing knowledge at industry conferences to try to maintain this sort of competitive advantage. This is in stark contrast to more recent developments, where communities and conferences are growing around knowledge sharing and cross-collaboration between companies.

Trade Secrets and Proprietary Information

Information that is not generally known to the public that is sufficiently secret to confer economic or business advantage is considered a trade secret. Information a company possesses, owns, or holds exclusive rights to is considered proprietary. Software, processes, methods, salary structure, organizational structure and customer lists are examples of items that can be considered a company's proprietary information. For example, proprietary software is software for which the source code is generally not available to end users. All trade secrets are proprietary; not all proprietary information is secret.

In addition to the changes in culture in the industry, commoditization and the costs of knowledge and technology impact what companies keep secret within their organizations.

The Age of Applications and the Web

An early example of successful cooperation across organizational boundaries, the very popular Apache HTTP Server (*https://httpd.apache.org/ABOUT_APACHE.html*) was released in 1995. Based on the public domain NCSA HTTP daemon developed by Robert McCool, an undergraduate at the University of Illinois at Urbana-Champaign, the modular Apache software enabled anyone to quickly deploy a web server with minimal configuration. This marked the beginning of a trend toward this and other open source solutions. Open source software, with licenses that allow users to read, modify, and distribute its source code, began to compete with proprietary, closed source solutions.

Combined with the availability of various distributions of the Linux operating system and the growth in popularity of scripting languages such as PHP and Perl, the open source movement led to the proliferation of the LAMP stack (most commonly Linux, Apache, MySQL, and PHP) as a solution for building web applications. MySQL, a relational database first released in 1995, combined with the server-side scripting capabilities of PHP, allowed developers to create dynamic websites and applications, with more rapidly updated or dynamically generated content than before. Given the ease with which these new web applications could be created, people and organizations in the late 1990s had to begin working with more speed and flexibility in order to stay competitive.

It was a time of angst and frustration for both system administrators and computer programmers. Endemic in system administration, there was a long-standing culture of saying "no" and "it's critical to preserve stability." In 1992, Simon Travaglia started posting a series on Usenet called The Bastard Operator From Hell (BOFH) (*http://bit.ly/wiki-bofh*) that described a rogue sysadmin who would take out his frustration and anger on the users of the system. Toxic operations environments led some individuals in this field to view that rogue sysadmin as a hero and emulate his behaviors, often to the detriment of others around them.

In development, there was a culture of "it's critical to get these changes out" and "I don't want to know how to do that because I'll get stuck doing it." In some environments, this prompted developers to risk system stability by finding unofficial ways to work around the established processes in order to meet their own goals. This in turn led to additional massive cleanups, further solidifying the idea that change is extremely risky. The singletons in either group who tried to make changes to the overall processes often found themselves stuck in the mire of becoming the subject matter expert, locked into the positions of support that became critical to maintain.

The Growth of Software Development Methodologies

In 2001, an invitation to discuss software development went out to people interested and active in the Extreme Programming (XP) community and others within the field. XP was a form of Agile development that was designed to be more responsive to changing requirements than previous development software methodologies, known for short release cycles, extensive testing, and pair programming. In response to this invitation, 17 software engineers got together in Snowbird, Utah. They summarized their shared common values to capture the adaptiveness and response to change that they wanted to see in development with an explicit emphasis on human factors. This Agile Manifesto was the rallying cry that started the Agile movement.

In 2004, Alistair Cockburn, a software developer who was one of the coauthors of the Agile Manifesto, described Crystal Clear,[5] a software development methodology for small teams based on his 10 years of research with successful teams. It described three common properties:

---

5 Alistair Cockburn, *Crystal Clear: A Human-Powered Methodology for Small Teams: A Human-Powered Methodology for Small Teams* (Boston: Addison Wesley, 2004).

- frequent delivery of usable code, moving toward smaller, more frequent deployments rather than large, infrequent ones;

- reflective improvement, or using reflections on what worked well and what worked poorly in previous work to help guide future work; and

- osmotic communication between developers—the idea that if developers are in the same room, information will drift through the background to be picked up informally, as by osmosis.

This movement continued in software development for several years, and later expanded its influence. Around that time, a system administrator named Marcel Wegermann wrote an essay on how to take the principles of Crystal Clear, Scrum, and Agile and apply them to the field of system administration. In addition to giving a lightning talk on the subject where he suggested ideas such as version control for the Linux operating system's /etc directory, pair system administration, and operational retrospectives, he also started the Agile System Administration mailing list in 2008.

Open Source Software, Proprietary Services

As open source software proliferated and software in general became more modular and interoperable, engineers found themselves with more and more choices as they worked. Instead of being restricted to one hardware vendor and whatever operating system and proprietary software would run on that hardware, developers were now able to pick and choose which tools and technologies they wanted to use. As software, especially web software, became more commoditized, it became at once both more and less valuable, being less exclusive and more commonplace, but with software developers being highly paid and widely sought after.

In 2006, Amazon.com, Inc., an ecommerce company that until then had mostly been known as a website selling books and other goods to consumers, launched two services, Amazon Elastic Compute Cloud (EC2) and Amazon Simple Storage Service (S3), a first foray into providing virtualized compute instances and storage through a proprietary service. This allowed individuals to spin up compute resources quickly without a large upfront expenditure of hardware, and request more as needed. As with the introduction of the System/360, the service was quickly adopted, becoming the de facto standard due to its ease of use, low entry cost, and flexibility.

As web technology continued to grow and evolve, the ways that people communicated and collaborated online did too. Twitter, an online social networking service, was introduced to the world in 2006. At first it seemed very much like a tool for people wanting to share information in an abbreviated format, for short attention spans or for celebrities to reach out to fans. In 2007, however, its usage skyrocketed thanks to the South by Southwest Interactive (SXSW) conference streaming live tweets about the conference on screens in the hallways.

Twitter quickly became a way for ad hoc communities to form across the globe. For conferences, it was a way to get additional value out of the multitrack systems and connect with like-minded individuals. The hallway track, a phrase often used to describe the interactions and conversations that take place in the hallways of conferences, had expanded from the physical world to the web, where anyone could discover and participate in these ad hoc interactions.

Agile Infrastructure

At the Agile 2008 conference in Toronto, system administrator and IT consultant Patrick Debois spoke about incorporating Scrum into operations with his talk, "Agile Operations and Infrastructure: How Infra-gile are You?" Patrick worked with development and operations teams on a project to test data center migration. In his work he might be doing development one day and fighting fires with the operations team the next; this context switching began to take a toll on him. Indeed, switching between even two tasks instead of focusing on just one can cause a nearly 20 percent drop in productivity due to the overhead of context switching.[6]

At that same conference, Andrew Clay Shafer, a former software developer who was starting to take a great interest in IT concerns, proposed an Agile Infrastructure session. He thought, however, that nobody would be interested in this topic, and ended up not attending the session that he himself proposed. When Patrick saw this, he realized that he wasn't the only one interested in Agile system administration and contacted Andrew out of band to discuss the concept further.

Around the same time, individual companies were beginning not only to make great strides toward processes that allowed them to keep up with the increasingly rapid changes of the internet, but also to share some of their stories publicly through communities that were building up around popular conferences like the O'Reilly Velocity Conference (*http://velocityconf.com/*).

One such company was Flickr, a popular community site for photographers. After being purchased by Yahoo in 2005, Flickr needed to migrate all of its services and data from Canada to the United States. John Allspaw, a web operations enthusiast who had worked in systems operations for years, had joined the company as the Flickr operations engineering manager to help with scaling this new migration project. Paul Hammond joined the Flickr development team in 2007, and became the

---

6 Gerald Weinberg, *Quality Software Management: Systems Thinking* (New York: Dorset House Publishing Company, 1997).

Flickr engineering manager in 2008, heading the development organization in collaboration with Allspaw.

At Velocity Santa Clara 2009, Hammond and Allspaw co-presented "10+ Deploys per Day: Dev and Ops Cooperation at Flickr," highlighting the revolutionary change that allowed the team to move rapidly. They didn't do this by setting out to break down silos or start a big professional and cultural movement. They were able to collaborate a great deal in their work at Flickr, which was in contrast to Allspaw's previous experiences at Friendster, where emotions and pressures ran high and there was little in the way of interteam collaboration.

 You can't declare that you're "doing devops successfully" simply because you are "doing 10 deploys a day." Pay attention to the specific problems that you are trying to solve in your organization, not the metrics you hear from other organizations. Keep in mind why you are making specific changes rather than simply looking at the number of deploys or any other arbitrary metrics.

The opportunities to work together that presented themselves were something that both managers took advantage of. Neither of them woke up one day and decided that the company needed a big change; rather, they recognized the little pieces of working together that made things work well. They took note of these little things, which ended up becoming much bigger cultural changes, and that cooperation had a much larger impact than just the number of deploys.

The Beginning of devopsdays

> Don't just say 'no', you aren't respecting other people's problems... #velocityconf #devops #workingtogether
>
> —Andrew Clay Shafer (@littleidea)

This tweet, from Andrew Clay Shafer on June 23, 2009, prompted Patrick Debois to lament on Twitter that even though he was watching remotely, he was unable to attend that year's Velocity conference in person. Pris Nasrat, at the time a lead systems integrator at the *Guardian*, tweeted in reply, "Why not organize your own Velocity event in Belgium?" Inspired, Patrick did almost exactly that, creating a local conference that would allow for developers, system administrators, toolsmiths, and other people working in those fields to come together. In October of that year, the first devopsdays conference took place in Ghent. Two weeks later, Debois wrote (*http://bit.ly/debois-devopsdays*):

> I'll be honest, for the past few years, when I went to some of the Agile conferences, it felt like preaching in the desert. I was kinda giving up, maybe the idea was too crazy: developers and ops working together. But now, oh boy, the fire is really spreading.

That first devopsdays event ignited the powder keg of unmet needs; people separated in silos and frustrated with the status quo identified with devops and a way of describing the work they felt they were already doing. The conference grew and spread as individuals started up new local devopsdays events across the world. With the real-time communication made available by Twitter, the hallway track never ended and #devops took on a life of its own.

The Current State of Devops

It is inspiring to see how far the devops movement has come in the six years since Patrick Debois held the first devopsdays in Belgium. The 2015 State of Devops Report (*http://bit.ly/2015-state-of-devops*), published by Puppet, found that companies that are doing devops are outperforming those that aren't, finally showing numerically what many people have already suspected—that an emphasis on having teams and individuals work together effectively is better for business than silos full of engineers who don't exactly play well with others. High-performing devops organizations deploy code more frequently, have fewer failures, recover from those failures faster, and have happier employees.

The number of devopsdays conferences has increased from 1 in 2009 to 22 all over the world in 2015. Each year brings devopsdays events in new locations worldwide; this is not a phenomenon limited to technology hubs like Silicon Valley or New York. There are dozens of local Meetup groups with thousands of members in even more locations around the globe, not to mention the conversations about the topic happening daily on Twitter.

Summary

Reflecting on our history, we see the trend of focusing on outcomes rather than people and processes. Many took away from John Allspaw and Paul Hammond's "10+ Deploys a Day" presentation that what was important was the quantity of deployments—10+ deploys in a day. The subtitle "Dev & Ops Cooperation at Flickr" was missed behind the hook.

Fixation on a specific outcome increases stress for those who are already stressed out by limitations within the organization. Unlike mechanical processes, outcomes in software rely heavily on human factors. Software can be outdated before completion, neglect to meet customer expectations, and fail in unexpected ways with drastic impact.

Focusing on the culture and processes encourages iteration and improvement in how and why we do things. When we shift our focus from *what* to *why*, we are given the freedom and trust to establish meaningfulness and purpose for our work, which is a key element of job satisfaction. Engagement with work impacts outcomes without concentrating on achieving a specific outcome, allowing for happy and productive humans building the next leap for humankind.

The introduction of devops has changed our industry by focusing on people and processes across roles to encourage collaboration and cooperation, rather than competing with specialization.

CHAPTER 4

Foundational Terminology and Concepts

Building a strong foundation for effective devops requires discussing some key terms and concepts. Some of these concepts may be familiar to readers; many have been mentioned in the preceding history of software engineering or will be well known to readers who have experience with various software development methodologies.

Throughout the history of computer engineering, a number of methodologies have been described to improve and ease the process of software development and operations. Each methodology splits work into phases, each with a distinct set of activities. One issue with many methodologies is a focus on the development process as something separate from operations work, leading to conflicting goals between teams. Additionally, forcing other teams to follow particular methodologies can cause resentment and frustration if the work doesn't fit their processes and goals. Understanding how these different methodologies work and what benefits each might bring can help increase understanding and reduce this friction.

Devops is not so rigidly defined as to prohibit any particular methodology. While devops arose from practitioners who were advocating for Agile system administration and cooperation between development and operations teams, the details of its practice are unique per environment. Throughout this book, we will reiterate that a key part of devops is being able to assess and evaluate different tools and processes to find the most effective ones for your environment.

Software Development Methodologies

The process of splitting up development work, usually into distinct phases, is known as a *software development methodology.*

These different phases of work may include:

- Specification of deliverables or artifacts
- Development and verification of the code with respect to the specification
- Deployment of the code to its final customers or production environment

Covering all methodologies is far beyond the scope of this chapter, but we will touch on a few that have in one way or another impacted the ideas behind devops.

Waterfall

The waterfall methodology or model is a project management process with an emphasis on a sequential progression from one stage of the process to the next. Originating in the manufacturing and construction industries and adopted later by hardware engineering, the waterfall model was adapted to software in the early 1980s.[1]

The original stages were requirements specification, design, implementation, integration, testing, installation, and maintenance, and progress was visualized as flowing from one stage to another (hence the name), as shown in Figure 4-1.

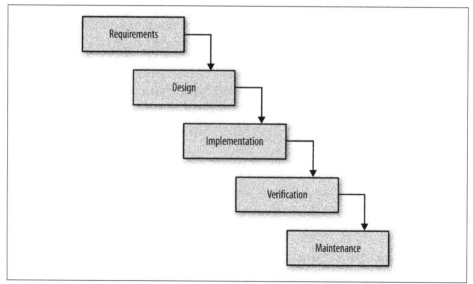

Figure 4-1. The waterfall model

---

1 Herbert D. Benington, *Production of Large Computer Programs*. IEEE Annals of the History of Computing, October 1, 1983, *http://bit.ly/benington-production*.

Software development under the waterfall model tended to be very highly structured, based on a large amount of time being spent in the requirements and design phases, with the idea that if both of those were completed correctly to begin with it would cut down on the number of mistakes found later.

In waterfall's heyday, there was a high cost to delivering software on CD-ROMs or floppy disks, not including the cost to customers for manual installation. Fixing a bug required manufacturing and distributing new floppies or CD-ROMs. Because of these costs, it made sense to spend more time and effort specifying requirements up front rather than trying to fix mistakes later.

Agile

Agile is the name given to a group of software development methodologies that are designed to be more lightweight and flexible than previous methods such as waterfall. The Agile Manifesto, written in 2001 and described in the previous chapter, outlines its main principles as follows:

> We are uncovering better ways of developing software by doing it and helping others do it. Through this work we have come to value:
>
> > *individuals and interactions* over *processes and tools*
> > *working software* over *comprehensive documentation*
> > *customer collaboration* over *contract negotiation*
> > *responding to change* over *following a plan*
>
> That is, while there is value in the items on the right, we value the items on the left more.

Agile methodologies include processes such as Scrum, which we will define next, and other methods that place a heavy emphasis on collaboration, flexibility, and the end result of working software.

Is Devops Just Agile?

Devops shares many characteristics with the Agile movement, especially with the focus on individuals, interactions, and collaboration. You might wonder if devops is just "rebranded" Agile. While devops has certainly grown around Agile methodology, it is a separate cultural movement steeped in the history of the computing industry with a broad reach that includes more than just developers. Devops adopts and extends Agile principles and applies them to the entire organization, not only the development process. As we will see in detail in later chapters, devops has cultural implications beyond Agile and a focus that is broader than speed of delivery.

Scrum

In the mid-1990s, Ken Schwaber and Dr. Jeff Sutherland, two of the original creators of the Agile Manifesto, merged individual efforts to present a new software development process called Scrum. Scrum is a software development methodology that focuses on maximizing a development team's ability to quickly respond to changes in both project and customer requirements. It uses predefined development cycles called *sprints*, usually between one week and one month long, beginning with a sprint planning meeting to define goals and ending with a sprint review and sprint retrospective to discuss progress and any issues that arose during that sprint.

One key feature of Scrum is the *daily Scrum* or *daily standup*, a daily meeting where team members (rather rapidly) each answer three questions:

- What did I do yesterday that helped the team meet its sprint goals?
- What am I planning to do today to help the team meet those goals?
- What, if anything, do I see that is blocking either me or the team from reaching their goals?

These meetings, which take place in the morning in order to help people align with what they are planning to do that day and help each other with any blocking issues, are often facilitated by the *Scrum master*. The Scrum master is an important role that also includes responsibilities such as helping the team self-organize and coordinate work efforts, helping remove blockers so the team will continue making progress, and involving project owners and stakeholders so there is a shared understanding of what "done" means and what progress is being made. The principles of Scrum are often seen applied less formally in many software development practices today.

Operations Methodologies

Similar to how software development methodologies split up software development work into different phases or otherwise try to bring more order to those processes, IT or operations work can be split up or organized as well. As with the software methodologies, covering all methodologies is far beyond the scope of this chapter.

ITIL

ITIL, formerly known as Information Technology Infrastructure Library, is a set of practices defined for managing IT services. It is published as a series of five volumes that describe its processes, procedures, tasks, and checklists, and is used to demonstrate compliance as well as measure improvement toward that end. ITIL grew out of a trend that saw the growing number of IT organizations in the 1980s using an increasingly diverse set of practices.

The British Central Computer and Telecommunications Agency developed the set of recommendations as a way to try to standardize these practices. First published in 1989, the books and practices have grown over the years, with the five core sections in the most recent (2011) version being service strategy, service design, service transition, service operation, and continual service improvement.

IT analyst and consultant Stephen Mann notes that while there are many benefits that come with ITIL's standardization and there are over 1.5 million ITIL-certified people worldwide, it has some areas where practitioners might want to put additional focus. Mann has said that ITIL is often more on the side of being reactive rather than proactive, so we suggest that organizations that have been using ITIL take note of ways that they can try to add more proactive planning and customer focus to their practices.

COBIT

Control Objectives for Information and Related Technology (COBIT) is an ISACA framework for governance and management of information and technology first released in 1996. A core principle of COBIT is to align business goals with IT goals.

COBIT is based on 5 principles:

- meeting stakeholder needs;
- covering the enterprise from end to end;
- applying a single integrated framework;
- enabling a holistic approach; and
- separating governance from management.

Systems Methodologies

Some methodologies focus on thinking about systems as a whole, rather than limiting focus to more specific areas such as software development or IT operations. Systems thinking skills are crucial for anyone working with complex systems like many of the software products that are created today; readers interested in learning more about systems thinking in general would do well to read *Thinking in Systems* by Donella Meadows and *How Complex Systems Fail* by Dr. Richard Cook.

Lean

After a five-year study on the future of automobile production and the Toyota Production System (TPS), James P. Womack, Daniel T. Jones, and Daniel Roos coined the term *Lean Production*.[2] Womack and Jones defined the five principles of Lean Thinking as follows:[3]

- Value
- Value stream
- Flow
- Pull
- Perfection

These ideas, especially the pursuit of perfection through systemic identification and elimination of waste, drove the definition of *Lean* as the maximization of customer value and minimization of waste.

Lean systems focus on the parts of the system that add value by eliminating waste everywhere else, whether that be overproduction of some parts, defective products that have to be rebuilt, or time spent waiting on some other part of the system. Stemming from this are the concepts of Lean IT and Lean software development, which apply these same concepts to software engineering and IT operations.

Waste to be eliminated in these areas can include:

- Unnecessary software features
- Communication delays
- Slow application response times
- Overbearing bureaucratic processes

Waste in the context of Lean is the opposite of value. Mary Poppendieck and Thomas Poppendieck have mapped Lean manufacturing waste to software development waste as follows:[4]

- Partially done work
- Extra features
- Relearning
- Unnecessary handoffs

---

2 James P. Womack, Daniel T. Jones, and Daniel Roos, *The Machine That Changed the World* (New York: Rawson Associates, 1990).

3 James P. Womack and Daniel T. Jones, *Lean Thinking* (New York: Simon & Schuster, 1996).

4 Mary Poppendieck and Thomas David Poppendieck. *Implementing Lean Software Development* (Upper Saddle River, NJ: Addison-Wesley, 2007).

- Task switching
- Delays
- Defects

As with devops, there is no one way to do Lean software development. There are two main approaches to Lean: a focus on waste elimination through a set of tools, and a focus on improving the flow of work, also known as *The Toyota Way*.[5] Both approaches have the same goal, but due to the differing approaches may result in different outcomes.

Development, Release, and Deployment Concepts

There are several terms related to the development, release, and deployment of software that have not previously been covered in the definitions of the methodologies discussed so far in this chapter. These are concepts that describe the *hows* of developing and deploying software, and understanding what they are and how they relate will give readers a more mature understanding of how tools can be used to facilitate these practices down the line.

Version Control

A version control system records changes to files or sets of files stored within the system. This can be source code, assets, and other documents that may be part of a software development project. Developers make changes in groups called *commits* or *revisions*. Each revision, along with metadata such as who made the change and when, is stored within the system in one way or another.

Having the ability to commit, compare, merge, and restore past revisions to objects to the repository allows for richer cooperation and collaboration within and between teams. It minimizes risks by establishing a way to revert objects in production to previous versions.

Test-Driven Development

In test-driven development, the code developer starts by writing a failing test for the new code functionality, then writes the code itself, and finally ensures that the test passes when the code is complete. The test is a way of defining the new functionality clearly, making more explicit what the code should be doing.

---

5 Jeffrey K. Liker, *The Toyota Way: 14 Management Principles from the World's Greatest Manufacturer* (New York: McGraw-Hill, 2004).

Having developers write these tests themselves not only greatly shortens feedback loops but also encourages developers to take more responsibility for the quality of the code they are writing. This sharing of responsibility and shorter development cycle time are themes that continue to be important parts of a devops culture.

Application Deployment

Application deployment is the process of planning, maintaining, and executing on the delivery of a software release. In the general sense, the craft of application deployment needs to consider the changes that are taking place underneath the system. Having infrastructure automation build the dependencies required to run a specific application—whether they be compute, operating system, or other dependencies—minimizes the impact of inconsistencies on the released software.

Depending on the application type, different engineering concerns may be important. For example, databases may have strict guarantees in terms of consistency. If a transaction occurs, it must be reflected in the data. Application deployment is a critical aspect to engineering quality software.

Continuous Integration

Continuous integration (CI) is the process of integrating new code written by developers with a mainline or "master" branch frequently throughout the day. This is in contrast to having developers working on independent feature branches for weeks or months at a time, merging their code back to the master branch only when it is completely finished. Long periods of time in between merges means that much more has been changed, increasing the likelihood of some of those changes being breaking ones. With bigger changesets, it is much more difficult to isolate and identify what caused something to break. With small, frequently merged changesets, finding the specific change that caused a regression is much easier. The goal is to avoid the kinds of integration problems that come from large, infrequent merges.

In order to make sure that the integrations were successful, CI systems will usually run a series of tests automatically upon merging in new changes. When these changes are committed and merged, the tests automatically start running to avoid the overhead of people having to remember to run them—the more overhead an activity requires, the less likely it is that it will get done, especially when people are in a hurry. The outcome of these tests is often visualized, where "green" means the tests passed and the newly integrated build is considered clean, and failing or "red" tests means the build is broken and needs to be fixed. With this kind of workflow, problems can be identified and fixed much more quickly.

Continuous Delivery

Continuous delivery (CD) is a set of general software engineering principles that allow for frequent releases of new software through the use of automated testing and continuous integration. It is closely related to CI, and is often thought of as taking CI one step further, that beyond simply making sure that new changes can be integrated without causing regressions to automated tests, continuous delivery means that these changes can *be deployed*.

Continuous Deployment

Continuous deployment (also referred to as CD) is the process of deploying changes to production by defining tests and validations to minimize risk. While continuous delivery makes sure that new changes can be deployed, continuous deployment means that they *get deployed* into production.

The more quickly software changes make it into production, the sooner individuals see their work in effect. Visibility of work impact increases job satisfaction, and overall happiness with work, leading to higher performance. It also provides opportunities to learn more quickly. If something is fundamentally wrong with a design or feature, the context of work is more recent and easier to reason about and change.

Continuous deployment also gets the product out to the customer faster, which can mean increased customer satisfaction (though it should be noted that this is not a panacea—customers won't appreciate getting an updated product if that update doesn't solve any of their problems, so you have to make sure through other methods that you are building the right thing). This can mean validating its success or failure faster as well, allowing teams and organizations to iterate and change more rapidly as needed.

 The difference between Continuous Delivery and Continuous Deployment is one that has been discussed a great deal since these topics became more widely used. Jez Humble, author of *Continuous Delivery* defines continuous delivery as being a general set of principles that can be applied to any software development project, including the *internet of things* (IoT) and embedded software, while continuous deployment is specific to web software. For more information on the differences between these two concepts, see the Further Resources for this chapter.

Minimum Viable Product

One theme that has become apparent especially in recent years is the idea of reducing both development costs and waste associated with creating products. If an organization were to spend years bringing a new product to market only to realize after the fact that this new product didn't meet the needs of either new or existing customers, that would have been an incredible waste of time, energy, and money.

The idea of the minimum viable product (MVP) is to create a prototype of a proposed product with the minimum amount of effort required to determine if the idea is a good one. Rather than developing something to 100 percent completion before getting it into users' hands, the MVP aims to drastically reduce that amount, so that if significant changes are needed, less time and effort has already been spent. This might mean cutting down on features or advanced settings in order to evaluate the core concept, or focusing on features rather than design or performance. As with ideas such as Lean and continuous delivery, MVPs allow organizations to iterate and improve more quickly while reducing cost and waste.

Infrastructure Concepts

All computer software runs on infrastructure of some sort, whether that be hardware that an organization owns and manages itself, leased equipment that is managed and maintained by someone else, or on-demand compute resources that can easily scale up or down as needed. These concepts, once solely the realm of operations engineers, are important for anyone involved with a software product to understand in environments where the lines between development and operations are starting to blur.

Configuration Management

Started in the 1950s by the United States Department of Defense as a technical management discipline, configuration management (CM) has been adopted in many industries. Configuration management is the process of establishing and maintaining the consistency of something's functional and physical attributes as well as performance throughout its lifecycle. This includes the policies, processes, documentation, and tools required to implement this system of consistent performance, functionality, and attributes.

Specifically within the software engineering industry, various organizations and standards bodies such as ITIL, IEEE (the Institute of Electrical and Electronics Engineers), ISO (the International Organization for Standardization), and SEI (the Software Engineering Institute) have all proposed a standard for configuration management. As with other folk models, this has led to some confusion in the industry about a common definition for the term.

Often this term is conflated with various forms of infrastructure automation, version control, or provisioning, which creates a divide with other disciplines' usage of the term. To ensure a common understanding for this book's audience, we define configuration management as the process of identifying, managing, monitoring, and auditing a product through its entire lifecycle, including the processes, documentation, people, tools, software, and systems involved.

Cloud Computing

Cloud computing, often referred to as just "the cloud," refers to a type of shared, internet-based computing where customers can purchase and use shared computing resources offered by various cloud providers as needed. Cloud computing and storage solutions can spare organizations the overhead of having to purchase, install, and maintain their own hardware.

The combination of high performance, cost savings, and the flexibility and convenience that many cloud solutions offer has made the cloud an ideal choice for organizations that are looking to both minimize costs and increase the speed at which they can iterate. Iteration and decreased development cycle time are key factors in creating a devops culture.

 While some see the cloud as being synonymous with devops, this is not universally the case. A key part of devops is being able to assess and evaluate different tools and processes to find the most effective one for your environment, and it is absolutely possible to do that without moving to cloud-based infrastructure.

Infrastructure Automation

Infrastructure automation is a way of creating systems that reduces the burden on people to manage the systems and their associated services, as well as increasing the quality, accuracy, and precision of a service to its consumers. Indeed, automation in general is a way to cut down on repetitious work in order to minimize mistakes and save time and energy for human operators.

For example, instead of running the same shell commands by hand on every server in an organization's infrastructure, a system administrator might put those commands into a shell script that can be executed by itself in one step rather than many smaller ones.

Artifact Management

An artifact is the output of any step in the software development process. Depending on the language, artifacts can be a number of things, including JARs (Java archive files), WARs (web application archive files), libraries, assets, and applications. Artifact management can be as simple as a web server with access controls that allow file management internal to your environment, or it can be a more complex managed service with a variety of extended features. Much like early version control for source code, artifact management can be handled in a variety of ways based on your budgetary concerns.

Generally, an artifact repository can serve as:

- a central point for management of binaries and dependencies;
- a configurable proxy between organization and public repositories; and
- an integrated depot for build promotions of internally developed software.

Containers

One of the bigger pain points that has traditionally existed between development and operations teams is how to make changes rapidly enough to support effective development but without risking the stability of the production environment and infrastructure. A relatively new technology that helps alleviate some of this friction is the idea of *software containers*—isolated structures that can be developed and deployed relatively independently from the underlying operating system or hardware.

Similar to virtual machines, containers provide a way of sandboxing the code that runs in them, but unlike virtual machines, they generally have less overhead and less dependence on the operating system and hardware that support them. This makes it easier for developers to develop an application in a container in their local environment and deploy that same container into production, minimizing risk and development overhead while also cutting down on the amount of deployment effort required of operations engineers.

Cultural Concepts

The final concepts we define in this chapter are cultural ones. While some software development methodologies, such as Agile, define ways in which people will interact while developing software, there are more interactions and related cultural concepts that are important to cover here, as these ideas will come up later in this book.

Retrospective

A retrospective is a discussion of a project that takes place after it has been completed, where topics such as what went well and what could be improved in future projects are considered. Retrospectives usually take place on a regular (if not necessarily frequent) basis, either after fixed periods of time have elapsed (every quarter, for example) or at the end of projects. A big goal is local learning—that is, how the successes and failures of this project can be applied to similar projects in the future. Retrospective styles may vary, but usually include topics of discussion such as:

What happened?
   What the scope of the project was and what ended up being completed.

What went well?
   Ways in which the project succeeded, features that the team is especially proud of, and what should be used in future projects.

What went poorly?
   Things that went wrong, bugs that were encountered, deadlines that were missed, and things to be avoided in future projects.

Postmortem

Unlike the planned, regular nature of a retrospective, a postmortem occurs after an unplanned incident or outage, for cases where an event's outcome was surprising to those involved and at least one failure of the system or organization was revealed. Whereas retrospectives occur at the end of projects and are planned in advance, postmortems are unexpected before the event they are discussing. Here the goal is organizational learning, and there are benefits to taking a systemic and consistent approach to the postmortem by including topics such as:

What happened?
   A timeline of the incident from start to finish, often including communication or system error logs.

Debrief
   Every person involved in the incident gives their perspective on the incident, including their thinking during the events.

Remediation items
   Things that should be changed to increase system safety and avoid repeating this type of incident.

In the devops community, there is a big emphasis placed on postmortems and retrospectives being *blameless*. While it is certainly possible to have a blameful postmortem that looks for the person or people "responsible" for an incident in order to call them out, that runs counter to the focus on learning that is central to the devops movement.

Blamelessness

Blamelessness is a concept that arose in contrast to the idea of blame culture. Though it had been discussed for years previously by Sidney Dekker and others, this idea really came to prominence with John Allspaw's post on blameless postmortems (*http://bit.ly/blameless-postmortems*), with the idea that incident retrospectives would be more effective if they focused on learning rather than punishment.

A culture of blamelessness exists not as a way of letting people off the hook, but to ensure that people feel comfortable coming forward with details of an incident, even if their actions directly contributed to a negative outcome. Only with all the details of how something happened can learning begin to occur.

Organizational Learning

> A learning organization is one that learns continuously and transforms itself…Learning is a continuous, strategically used process—integrated with and running parallel to work.
>
> —Karen E. Watkins and Victoria J. Marsick, *Partners for Learning*

Organizational learning is the process of collecting, growing, and sharing an organization's body of knowledge. A learning organization is one that has made their learning more deliberate, setting it as a specific goal and taking actionable steps to increase their collective learning over time.

Organizational learning as a goal is part of what separates blameful cultures from blameless ones, as blameful cultures are often much more focused on punishment than on learning, whereas a blameless or learning organization takes value from experiences and looks for lessons learned and knowledge gained, even from negative experiences. Learning can happen at many different levels, including individual and group as well as organization, but organizational learning has higher impact to companies as a whole, and companies that practice organizational learning are often more successful than those that don't.

Summary

We have discussed a variety of methodologies relating to the development, deployment, and operation of both software and the infrastructure that underlies it, as well as cultural concepts addressing how individuals and organizations deal with and learn from incidents and failures.

This is far from an exhaustive list, and new methodologies and technologies will be developed in the future. The underlying themes of development, deployment, operations, and learning will continue to be core to the industry for years to come.

CHAPTER 5

Devops Misconceptions and Anti-Patterns

When talking about concepts such as devops, it can also be helpful to discuss what the concept is *not*. This process will help clear up some common misconceptions or misconstrued ideas about devops. In this chapter, we will provide additional context around devops as well as define some common anti-patterns.

Common Devops Misconceptions

Throughout the industry, there are common misconceptions about devops. Within your organization, your teams may struggle to clarify and articulate beliefs and values. In this section, we'll examine some of the issues people run into when trying to establish this common language in their organization.

Devops Only Involves Developers and System Administrators

While the name is a portmanteau of *development* (or *developers*) and *operations*, this is more of a signal of the origin of the movement than a strict definition of it. While the devopsdays conference tagline is "the conference that brings development and operations together," the concepts and ideas of devops include all roles within an organization. There is no one definitive list of which teams or individuals should be involved or how, just as there is no one-size-fits-all way to "do devops."

Ideas that help development and operations teams communicate better and work more efficiently together can be applied throughout a company. Any team within the organization should be considered—including security, QA, support, and legal—in order to be most effective. For example, effective devops processes between legal and sales allow for automated contract creation based on a consistent sales catalog.

Any two or more teams can benefit from devops principles, and it is important not to limit the potential reach of these ideas, nor to replace one group of silos with another. In Part III, we will discuss considerations for effectively engaging teams.

Devops Is a Team

In general, the creation of a designated "devops team" is a less-than-ideal circumstance. Creating a team called devops, or renaming an existing team to devops, is neither necessary nor sufficient for creating a devops culture. If your organization is in a state where the development and operations teams cannot communicate with each other, an additional team is likely to cause more communication issues, not fewer. Underlying issues need to be addressed for any substantial and lasting change to stick.

Creating a separate team as an environment in which to kickstart new processes and communication strategies can be effective if it is seen as a greenfield project. In large companies this is generally a useful short-term strategy to kick off meaningful change and usually results in blending the team members back into designated-role teams as time progresses.

In a startup environment, having a single team that encompasses both functions can work if it allows for the team to embrace the responsibility and mission of the service as a collaborative unit rather than burning out a single individual on-call. Management will still need to facilitate clear roles and responsibilities to ensure that as the company grows the team can scale out as required.

This book will cover different team organizational options and interteam communication and coordination strategies, but ultimately it is important to remember that there is no one right or wrong way of doing devops, and if having a team with devops in its name genuinely works for you, there's no reason to change it. Keep in mind that devops is a culture and a process, and name and structure your teams accordingly.

Devops Is a Job Title

The "devops engineer" job title has started a controversial debate. The job title has been described in various ways, including:

- a system administrator who also knows how to write code;
- a developer who knows the basics of system administration; or
- a mythical 10x engineer (said to be 10 times as productive as other engineers, though this is difficult to measure and often used figuratively) who can be a full-

time system administrator and full-time developer for only the cost of one salary without any loss in the quality of their work.

In addition to being totally unrealistic, this concept of a devops engineer doesn't scale well. It might be necessary to have the developers deploying the code and maintaining the infrastructure in the early days of an organization, but as a company matures and grows, it makes sense to have people become more specialized in their job roles.

It doesn't usually make much sense to have a director of devops or some other position that puts one person in charge of devops. Devops is at its core a cultural movement, and its ideas and principles need to be used throughout entire organizations in order to be effective.

Still, "devops engineer" is a job title that keeps appearing in the wild. Engineers with "devops" in their title earn higher salaries than regular system administrators, according to the 2015 DevOps Salary Report from Puppet (*http://bit.ly/2015-devops-salary*). With the lack of parity between roles at different organizations based on different interpretations of what a devops engineer role looks like, this is a very slippery slope. Who wouldn't want to be called a devops engineer if it immediately gave them a $10K bump in salary?

A concerning trend as reported by the 2015 DevOps Salary Report is that "more devops engineers reported working in excess of 50 hours, systems engineers reported working 41–50 hours per week, and system administrators reported working 40 or fewer hours per week." When choosing your job, make sure that the higher salary doesn't come at the cost of less personal time and higher rates of burnout.

Devops Is Relevant Only to Web Startups

A primary product of web-based companies is the web application that the user sees when browsing the company website. These websites can often be implemented without relying on information stored between interactions with the website (i.e., stateless sessions). Upgrading the site can be done in stages or through the migration of live traffic to a new version of the site, making the process of continuous deployment easy.

It is easy to see why devops makes sense for web-based companies like this: the movement helps break down barriers that can impede development and deployment. If a web company's processes are so slow that it takes a matter of weeks to fix a typo, chances are they aren't going to do very well compared to newer, more Agile companies in the space.

Web startups are not alone in benefiting from improved collaboration, affinity, and tools. It is easier to iterate on team structures and processes at a small startup; enterprises have been trained to resist rapid change and governmental agencies even more so with laws that may actively restrict and impede change. Change is possible even in these sorts of organizations, however. Later in this book we will share examples of how these cultural ideas can be applied even to enterprise and government organizations.

You Need a Devops Certification

A significant part of devops is about culture: how do you certify culture? There is no 60-minute exam that can certify how effectively you communicate with other people, how well teams in your company work together, or how your organization learns. Certifications make sense when applied to specific technologies that require a high level of expertise to use, such as specific software or hardware. This allows companies that require that specific technology or expertise to gain some understanding of a particular individual's knowledge in that area.

Devops doesn't have required technology or one-size-fits-all solutions. Certification exams are testing knowledge where there are clear right or wrong answers, which devops generally does not have. What works best for one company won't necessarily be optimal for another; there's no easy way to write questions that would be universally correct for devops. A devops certification is likely to be a money-making opportunity or specific to a vendor's solution and mislabeled devops certification.

Devops Means Doing All the Work with Half the People

There are some people under the impression that devops is a way to get both a software developer and a system administrator in one person—and with one person's salary. Not only is this perception incorrect, but it is often harmful. At a time when too many startups are offering perks such as three meals a day in the office and on-site laundry as a way of encouraging workers to spend even more time at work, and when too many engineers find themselves working 60–80 hours a week, misconceptions that drive people further away from work–life balance and more toward overwork are not what our industry needs.

During very early stages, it is true that a startup can benefit from having developers who understand enough about operations to handle deployments as well, especially with cloud providers and other "as a services" to handle a lot of operational heavy lifting. Once an organization gets past the point where every single employee must wear multiple hats out of sheer necessity, expecting one person to fill two full-time roles is asking for burnout.

Devops doesn't save money by halving the number of engineers your company needs. Rather, it allows organizations to increase the quality and efficiency of their work, reducing the number and duration of outages, shortening development times, and improving both individual and team effectiveness.

There Is One "Right Way" (or "Wrong Way") to Do Devops

Early adopters of devops practices and principles, especially those well-known for this in the industry such as Netflix and Etsy, are often regarded as "unicorns"[1] who have cornered the market on the "right" way to do devops. Other companies, eager to get the benefits of a devops culture, will sometimes try to emulate their practices.

Just because a company presents their successful devops strategy does not mean that these same processes will be the right way of doing devops within every environment. Cargo culting[2] processes and tools into an environment can lead to the creation of additional silos and resistance to change.

Devops encourages critical thinking about processes, tools, and practices; being a learning organization requires questioning and iterating on processes, not accepting things as the "one true way" or the way that things have always been done.

One should also beware of people saying that anyone who isn't following their example is doing devops "the wrong way." It bears repeating that while there are valid criticisms of devops teams or devops engineers, there are also documented cases of companies and people who make those terms work for them. Devops intentionally is not rigidly defined like Scrum or ITIL. The companies that are doing devops most successfully are comfortable learning and iterating to find what tools and processes are most effective for them.

It Will Take X Weeks/Months to Implement Devops

If some sort of management buy-in is required for an organizational transformation such as those involved in devops, one of the questions often asked about the transformation is how long it will take. The problem with this question is that it assumes that devops is an easily definable or measurable state, and once that state is reached then the work is done.

---

1 Within devops, a *unicorn* is an internet company that is a practitioner, innovator, and early adopter of devops. This is not to be confused with the financial definition of *unicorn* as a startup valued at over $1 billion.

2 *Cargo culting* describes the practice of emulating observed behaviors or implementing tools into an environment without fully understanding the reasoning or circumstances that led to success using those strategies.

In reality, devops is an ongoing process; it is the journey, not the destination. Some parts of it will have a fixed end point (such as setting up a configuration management system and making sure that all the company's servers are being managed by it), but the ongoing maintenance, development, and use of configuration management will continue.

Because so much of devops is cultural, it is harder to predict how long some of those changes will take: how long will it take people to break old siloed habits and replace them with new collaborative ones? This cannot be easily predicted, but don't let that stop you from working toward these kinds of significant cultural transformations.

Devops Is All About the Tools

While tools are valuable, devops does not mandate or require any particular ones. This misconception is a contributing factor to the idea that devops is only for start-ups, as enterprise companies are often less able to adopt new technologies.

Devops is a cultural movement. Within your environment the tools you use currently are part of your culture. Before deciding on a change, it behooves you to recognize the tools in the environment that have been part of the existing culture, understand individuals' experiences with those tools, and observe what is similar and different between others' experiences. This examination and assessment helps clarify what changes need to be made.

Technology impacts velocity and organizational structures within your organization. Making drastic changes to tools, while they may have value to an individual or team, may have a cost that decelerates the organization as a whole.

The principles discussed in this book don't require a specific set of tools and are applicable to any technology stack. There is a fair amount of overlap between companies that practice devops and those who use containers or cloud providers, but that doesn't mean that those particular technologies are required—there are certainly companies successfully implementing devops while running on bare metal. Part IV will discuss how to assess, choose, and implement tools effectively.

Devops Is About Automation

Many innovations in devops-adjacent tools help to codify understanding, bridging the gaps between teams and increasing velocity through automation. Practitioners have focused on tools that eliminate tasks that are boring and repetitive, such as with infrastructure automation and continuous integration. In both of these cases, automation is a result of improved technology.

If there are repetitive tasks that could be automated to free up a human from having to do them, that automation helps that person work more efficiently. Some cases like this have fairly obvious gains: automating server builds saves hours per server that a system administrator can then spend on more interesting or challenging work. But if more time is spent trying to automate something than would be saved by having it be automated, that is no longer time well spent (see Figure 5-1).

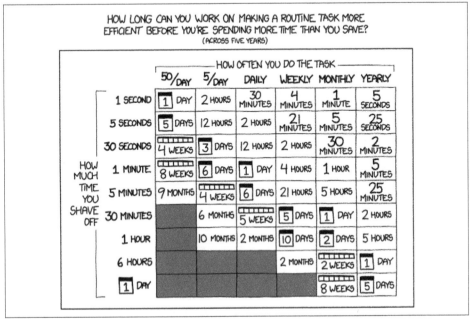

Figure 5-1. A comic from XKCD on time spent versus time saved (https://xkcd.com/ 1205); originally published with the alt text: "Don't forget the time you spend finding the chart to look up what you save. And the time spent reading this reminder about the time spent. And the time trying to figure out if either of those make sense. Remember, every second counts toward your life total, including these right now."

There has been a great deal of discussion about the role of automation in any environment and the way that human factors affect what and how we choose to automate. Paying attention to these stories is an example of cross-discipline affinity; other industries may have much to teach us about our own if we pay attention to them.

Automation is critical to us as systems become more complex and organizations become interdependent due to shared services. Without shared mutual context or concern for human needs, however, automation creates unknown additional risk. Automation may make work faster, but in order to be most effective it must also increase transparency, collaboration, and understanding.

Early Automation in the Aviation Industry

While reviewing the aviation industry in 1977, the House Committee on Science and Technology identified cockpit automation as a leading safety concern. Studies of the aviation field discovered that while pilots could still fly planes, the automation in use was causing their critical thinking skills to atrophy. Pilots were losing the ability to track position without the use of a map display, decide what should be done next, or recognize instrument system failures. This is a warning for us as we implement automation within our environments. Tools change our behavior and the way that we think.

In July 2013, Asiana Airlines flight 214 struck a seawall at San Francisco International Airport, with three people being fatally injured. During the investigation, the National Transportation Safety Board (NTSB) identified a number of issues, among them that there was insufficient monitoring of airspeed due to an overreliance on automated systems that the pilots didn't fully understand.

> In their efforts to compensate for the unreliability of human performance, the designers of automated control systems have unwittingly created opportunities for new error types that can be even more serious than those they were seeking to avoid.

—James Reason, *Managing the Risks of Organizational Accidents*

Devops Is a Fad

As devops is not specific to a technology, tool, or process, it is less likely to become obsolete or replaced with something new. A movement about improving organizational effectiveness and individual employee happiness may be absorbed into common use, but it will not age out.

One of the primary differences between devops and methodologies like ITIL and Agile is that the latter have strict definitions, with context being added over time. Devops, on the other hand, is a movement defined by stories and ideas of individuals, teams, and organizations. It is the continuing conversations and evolution of processes and ideas that lead growth and change.

There has been some discussion in the devops community as to whether or not devops has lost its direction. Critics of the movement say that it is too defined by negative spaces, by people saying what devops isn't rather than what it is (or not providing a concise definition for it at all). They also claim that devops isn't unique, that it is merely a rebranding of ideas that have come before it, and that it will be abandoned as soon as the next name or trend comes along.

Many of the driving ideas behind the devops movement have indeed been around for some time under different names, but the zeitgeist of devops as something more than the sum of its parts is new and different. People have certainly argued against functional silos before, suggested learning organizations, advocated for humane systems, or advocated for automation and measurement.

The devops movement is the first to combine all of these ideas, and to do so with measurable success. (*http://bit.ly/2015-state-of-devops*) Harnessing and leveraging effective devops will lead to growth and evolution in tools, technology, and processes in your organization.

Devops Anti-Patterns

In this section, we will define some more terms that it will help you to be familiar with. Unlike the terms defined in the previous chapter, however, these concepts are generally seen as being anti-patterns, with ideas that run counter to those that give devops its strength and effectiveness.

Blame Culture

A *blame* (or *blameful*) *culture* is one that tends toward blaming and punishing people when mistakes are made, either at an individual or an organizational level. In this kind of culture, a root cause analysis as part of a postmortem or retrospective is generally misapplied, with a search for one thing that ultimately caused a failure or incident. If this analysis happens to point toward a person's actions as being the "root cause," that person will be blamed, reprimanded, or even fired for their role in the incident. This sort of culture often arises from one that must answer to external auditors, or where there is some top-down mandate to improve performance according to a given set of metrics.

Heavily segregated or segmented environments that lack an appreciation for transparency are fertile ground for blame culture. If management is set on finding one person or group of people to blame for each incident that occurs, in order to get rid of that "bad apple," individual contributors will be motivated to try to shift blame away from themselves and their own teams onto somebody else. While this sort of self-preservation is understandable in such an environment, it doesn't lend itself well to a culture of openness and collaboration. More than likely, people will begin withholding information about incidents, especially with regards to their own actions, in an effort to keep themselves from being blamed.

Outside of incident response, a culture of blame that calls people out as a way of trying to improve performance (e.g., which developers introduced the most bugs into the codebase, or which IT technician closed the fewest tickets) will contribute to an atmosphere of hostility between coworkers as everyone tries to avoid blame. When people are too focused on simply avoiding having a finger pointed at them, they are less focused on learning and collaboration.

Silos

A departmental or organizational silo describes the mentality of teams that do not share their knowledge with other teams in the same company. Instead of having common goals or responsibilities, siloed teams have very distinct and segregated roles. Combined with a blameful culture, this can lead to information hoarding as a form of job security ("If I'm the only one who knows how to do X, they won't be able to get rid of me"), difficulty or slowness completing work that involves multiple teams, and decreases in morale as teams or silos start to see each other as adversaries.

Often in a siloed environment you will find different teams using completely different tools or processes to complete similar tasks, people having to go several levels up the managerial chain of command in order to get resources or information from people on another team, and a fair amount of "passing the buck"—that is, moving blame, responsibility, or work to another team.

The issues and practices that can come from organizational silos take time, effort, and cultural change to break down and fix. Having silos for software developers and system administrators or operations engineers, and trying to fix the issues in the software development process that came from that environment, was a big part of the root of the devops movement, but it is important to note that those are not the only silos that can exist in an organization. Cross-functional teams are often touted as being the anti-silos, but these are not the only two options, and just because a team serves only one function it's not necessarily a silo. Silos come from a lack of communication and collaboration between teams, not simply from a separation of duties.

Root Cause Analysis

Root cause analysis (RCA) is a method to identify contributing and "root" causes of events or near-misses/close calls and the appropriate actions to prevent recurrence. It is an iterative process that is continued until all organizational factors have been identified or until data is exhausted. Organizational factors are any entity that exerts control over the system at any stage in its lifecycle, including but not limited to design, development, testing, maintenance, operation, and retirement.

One method of identifying root causes is known as the *5 Whys*. This method entails asking "why" until the root causes are identified. It requires that the individuals answering "why" have sufficient data to answer the question appropriately. A second and more systematic approach is to create an *Ishikawa diagram*. Developed by Kaoru Ishikawa in 1968, this causal diagram helps teams visualize and group causes into major categories to identify sources of variation, discover relationships among sources, and provide insight into process behaviors.

Often RCA is associated with determining a single root cause. Tools that provide event management often allow only a single assignment of responsibility. This limits

RCA's usefulness, as it focuses attention on the direct causes rather than the additional elements that may be contributing factors. There is an implicit assumption with root cause analysis that systems fail (or succeed) in a linear way, which is not the case for any sufficiently complex system.

Human Error

Human error, the idea that a human being made a mistake that directly caused a failure, is often cited as the root cause in a root cause analysis. With this often comes the implication that a different person would not have made such a mistake, which is common in a blame culture when somebody has to be reprimanded for their role in an incident. Again, this is an overly simplistic view, and is used prematurely as the stopping point for an investigation. It tends to assume that human mistakes are made due to simple negligence, fatigue, or incompetence, and neglects to investigate the myriad factors that contributed to the person making the decision or taking the action they did.

In a blameful culture, discussion stops with the finding that a specific person made a mistake, with the focus often being on who made the mistake and its end result. In a blameless culture or a learning organization, a human error is seen as a starting point rather than an ending one, sparking a discussion on the context surrounding the decision and why it made sense at the time.

Summary

Familiarity with these terms provides a more in-depth understanding of the rest of the material in this book. Combined with the foundational terminology and concepts in the previous chapter and the patterns and themes gleaned from history in the chapter prior to that, you now have a much clearer picture of the landscape that makes up devops in our industry today. With this foundation of understanding in place, we can now define and discuss our four pillars of effective devops.

CHAPTER 6

The Four Pillars of Effective Devops

Patrick Debois has said that devops is a human problem (*http://bit.ly/debois-devops-culture*), implying that every organization will have a devops culture that is unique to the humans within it. While there is no one "true" way of doing devops that will be identical for every organization, we have identified four common themes that any team or organization looking to implement devops will need to spend time and resources on.

Here are the four pillars of effective devops:

- Collaboration
- Affinity
- Tools
- Scaling

The combination of these four pillars will enable you to address both the cultural and technical aspects of your organization. It makes sense for your organization to focus on one or two pillars at a time while trying to make changes, but ultimately it is the combination of all four working together that will enable lasting, effective change.

It is important not to gloss over the first two pillars, which cover the norms and values of our cultures and interpersonal interactions, in favor of skipping straight to reading about tools. Effective tool usage is necessary for a successful devops transformation, but not sufficient—if that were the case, we could just provide a list of best practices for Chef or Docker and be done. However, resolving the interpersonal and interteam conflicts that arise within organizations is critical to fostering the lasting relationships that ultimately make a devops environment.

Collaboration

Collaboration is the process of building toward a specific outcome through supporting interactions and the input of multiple people. A guiding principle that shaped the devops movement was the cooperation of software development and operations teams (*http://bit.ly/allspaw-flickr*). Before one team can successfully work with another team with a different focus, the individuals on a team need to be able to work with each other. Teams that don't work well on an individual or intrateam level have little hope of working well at the interteam level.

Affinity

In addition to the growth and maintenance of collaborative relationships between individuals, teams and departments within an organization and across the industry at large need to have strong relationships. Affinity is the process of building these interteam relationships, navigating differing goals or metrics while keeping in mind shared organizational goals, and fostering empathy and learning between different groups of people. Affinity can be applied between organizations as well, enabling companies to share stories and learn from each other as we build a collective body of cultural and technical knowledge within our industry.

Tools

Tools are an accelerator, driving change based on the current culture and direction. Tool choices can be perceived as easy wins. Understanding why they are wins, and their impact on existing structures, is important to prevent obscuring issues in teams and organizations. Failure to examine the problems in values, norms, and organizational structure leads to invisible failure conditions as cultural debt builds up. If tools, or lack thereof, get in the way of individuals or teams working well together, your initiatives will not succeed. If the cost of collaboration is high, not investing in tools (or worse, investing in poor tools) raises this cost.

Scaling

Scaling is a focus on the processes and pivots that organizations must adopt throughout their lifecycles. Beyond simply considering what it means to address devops in large enterprise organizations, scaling takes into account how the other pillars of effective devops can be applied throughout organizations as they grow, mature, and even shrink. There are different considerations, both technical and cultural, for organizations operating at different scales, and we will examine those considerations for organizations that do not fall into the category of "typical" smaller devops cultures.

Summary

Taken together, the four pillars of effective devops will allow you to solve both cultural and technical problems that can impact software development. In each of the next four parts of this book, we cover these pillars in depth. Examples have been pulled from the industry, covering a diverse set of companies from web startups to large enterprises. While it isn't strictly necessary to read the chapters in order, it is recommended that you eventually read all chapters, as it is the combination and harmony of these four pillars that truly make devops effective.

PART II

Collaboration

CHAPTER 7

Collaboration: Individuals Working Together

With individuals spending many hours a week at work together, building durable and long-lasting relationships with others is crucial. Collaboration is the process of building toward a specific outcome through the interactions, input, and support of multiple people. Pair programming, a technique first introduced with Agile software development where two people work on the same piece of code at the same time, is one example of collaboration, but far from the only one.

Sparkle Corp Weekly Planning Meeting

"I really think that we have a great opportunity to use MongoDB in our new reviews service. I saw this great tutorial that showed how fast and easy it is to get it up and running without all the administrative costs of other solutions," said Geordie, a front-end developer for Sparkle Corp.

Listening to Geordie's enthusiasm, the General jotted down the potential benefits of bringing MongoDB into the stack at Sparkle Corp. "Does anyone else have thoughts or concerns about using MongoDB?" she asked of the development team.

"Based on our current stack, we already support MySQL and all of its dependencies. We've already invested a fair amount of work in MySQL integrations. Adding MongoDB adds extra costs to support and maintenance. Is there something that MongoDB offers us that improves on what we already use to offset this cost?" asked Alice, a senior developer at Sparkle Corp.

This kind of disagreement happens all the time within a team. How the individuals respond to one another next will either help or harm their ongoing relationship. Let's dig into the devops compact and examine how collaboration can strengthen or weaken it within our organizations.

Defining Collaboration

As a pillar of devops, collaboration refers to the intentional processes and common purpose of individuals. Examples of collaboration in action include:

- Asynchronous code review
- Documentation
- Updating issues and bug reports
- Demonstrating weekly progress
- Regular status updates
- Pairing

It's important to recognize the value and purpose of different forms of collaboration. Some collaborative work is done in coordination with others, with a single individual responsible for some piece of the collective work and focused on accomplishing her part toward the mutual goal. Other collaborative work is done continuously, with two or more individuals working together to accomplish an objective. These collaborative approaches are the right choice depending on the work and surrounding context.

Rewarding one type of collaborative work over another is somewhat like telling everyone that running is the only successful form of exercise.

In January 2015, Anita Woolley and colleagues published findings from their analysis of teams in an article for the *New York Times* called "Why Some Teams Are Smarter Than Others" (*http://bit.ly/nyt-smarter*). Woolley's smarter teams outperformed other teams based on the following characteristics:

- Communication
- Equal participation
- Theory of Mind

In other words, effective collaboration includes communication, equal participation, and Theory of Mind (ToM). ToM is the ability to recognize one's own perspective, and that others have a distinct and different perspective born from their own context. Examining how individuals are different, and exploring how these differences impact potential perspective, helps expand our own ToM, builds mutual understanding, and helps to resolve conflict crucial to the devops compact, in effect leveling up our capacity as smarter teammates.

Individual Differences and Backgrounds

Each of us has a different cultural background with unique experiences that inform our choices of how and why we work. Respecting our individual differences can help build mutual understanding and resolve conflict in a way that is crucial to the devops compact. There are great benefits to be gained from diverse teams in terms of creativity, problem solving, and productivity, but this differentiation can lead to short-term interpersonal conflicts, either personally or professionally.

Professional Backgrounds

Professional backgrounds, or the types of previous work-related experience that people bring with them to their current positions, vary. As much as we'd like to believe that we judge people only on their current work, there are multiple ways in which people's backgrounds do impact our thinking, our interactions, and our collaborative efforts.

Enterprise versus startup experience

One difference in professional backgrounds is the size of companies that people have worked for previously. In the startup world, there is a strong preference for hiring and working with people with previous startup experience. This makes sense to some extent—especially in early-stage startups, success may be more likely when key individuals have had successful startup experiences before—but beware of being overly biased against people who have worked mostly (or exclusively) at larger organizations. Enterprise experience does not disqualify someone from being able to work well at a much smaller company—not everyone in the enterprise is a "dinosaur," and that kind of bias or ageism should be avoided.

The challenge is balancing the specialization of tasks that can occur with large teams with the context switching that occurs with small teams with too much assigned work, rather than dismissing the suitability of the enterprise-experienced individual out of hand.

Technical fluency

A technical versus nontechnical background can cause friction between people. This can take place in a company-wide context, where engineers are seen as being more valuable to the company. Support, sales, and marketing teams are often treated like second-class citizens. If these feelings are mirrored at all by management, such as at an early-stage startup with engineering cofounders, this can cause a serious loss of morale among non-engineering employees. People need to feel that their work is appreciated.

Role hierarchies

This is not limited to nontechnical roles, of course. In many traditional software development shops, IT and related roles (system and network administrators, operations engineers, QA engineers, and database administrators, among others) are often treated similarly. Operations is often primarily classified as a cost center within accounting. Any costs that are incurred to support the organization as a whole are viewed as liabilities caused by operations rather than through the lens of what value that team or department brings to the organization.

Further, the value that operations provides for the organization is invisible, and its impacts are observed only when something goes wrong and there is some sort of outage or degraded service. Often the operations teams are viewed by other teams as barriers, blockers, or gatekeepers—and these sorts of challenges are part of what spurred the devops movement in the first place.

Different paths to engineering

Even among engineers, there can be differences in people's backgrounds as well. It used to be that software engineers almost exclusively had technical backgrounds, whether that be one or more degrees in a field like computer science or computer engineering or a lifelong history of working with computers. It's easy to look at someone who started tinkering with their parents' computers as a young child and taught themselves to program soon after that as a "natural" engineer.

The barriers to entry into development have changed drastically in the last few years as mechanisms to teach necessary job skills have evolved. Coding bootcamps, short (three- to six-month) skill programs, and educational meetups have changed how people get into the field. These are ways of making tech jobs available to people who are changing careers but don't have the money or time to spend on a traditional four-year degree program.

Bootcamps designed specifically to provide safe learning spaces for underrepresented groups in tech, such as women or people of color, can be a great resource for companies looking to improve the diversity of their engineering staff as well. However, there is still bias in some places toward candidates with "traditional" engineering backgrounds. These biases can impact the value that employers place on nonengineering skills, leading to teams lacking key *soft skills*, abilities that impact how people can relate to, get along with, and work with others.

Years of experience

Friction between team members also comes from job level or experience. When looking to hire, teams may express a preference for more experienced candidates or "senior" engineers because they believe that a more senior person will be quicker to get up to speed and start contributing to the team.

 There are a limited number of senior engineers—far fewer than the number of companies looking to hire them. In addition to simply getting more years of technical experience, junior employees need guidance and coaching to help grow into senior ones. When looking at the people on your team, it's important to consider how effective they are at teaching or mentoring, in addition to just their technical skills, to ensure that your growth isn't blocked by access to the experienced talent pool.

Personal Backgrounds

Increasing the diversity of a team means ensuring a wider range of personal backgrounds. Including aspects such as gender, sexuality, race, class, primary language, ability, and education level, diverse personal backgrounds can increase the strength of an engineering, product-focused, or customer-support-driven organization by bringing a greater number of experiences and points of view to the table.

A diverse workforce benefits teams, organizations, and the industry as a whole. Diversity also leads to increased friction, however. If a team comprising one predominant group—for example, white heterosexual men—hires a woman, LGBTQ individual, or person of color, they will need to make adjustments to their expectations, processes, and potentially behaviors in order to alleviate this friction.

An example of these adjustments may be as simple as modifying how the team members address each other—for instance, from "Hey guys"; "What's up, dudes"; or "Gentlemen," to more neutral greetings like "Hey, folks." Similarly, risqué jokes may create unwelcome tension rather than releasing it. Another example is addressing working hours and expectations of work–life balance. Imagine a team of young, single individuals who are accustomed to working a long day and then drinking together after work. If they hire a single father who is unavailable from 4 pm until 8 pm, he will find himself excluded from the majority of his team's socializing and bonding activities.

An HR department that understands diversity-related concerns is a critical part of the organization in helping prevent friction between individuals due to these kind of personal differences. Individual contributors and managers should be able and encouraged to take unconscious bias training to help explore the assumptions that are impacting and influencing their work interactions.

The value of these initiatives is to foster an environment of safety, respect, and inclusion. Without personal safety, there is unlikely to be trust between employees. Personal backgrounds tend to contribute to power differentials that can affect or even prevent negotiation.

It's also important to keep in mind that, especially with increases in globalization and remote work, it is more likely that teams will have members from different cultures and nationalities. An example might be bowing versus shaking hands as a form of professional greeting. There are many ways in which cultural or regional differences can manifest themselves.

Goals

While team members work toward the same goals and share responsibility for success, individuals on a team may have different personal and professional goals that can add to conflict when these differences are construed negatively. Being aware of these different motivations can help establish better understanding and empathy between team members.

- Some people value their current position as a stepping stone in their career progression, while others may think of it as "just a job," something to do while they consider a career change, pursue side projects, or support their families. Assigning work to reflect individual priorities can help avoid situations such as critical projects being blocked by people whose attention or focus is elsewhere.

- Many people want to learn and grow their skills, but the specifics of this can vary from person to person. Align working assignments with the individual's learning goals and clarify the impact and value to the team's overall goals.

- Some people focus more on individual work, while others place value on growing their networks or participating in more community-focused activities such as mentoring or speaking at industry conferences. The latter group might perceive heads-down, coding-only sorts of engineers as aloof or not interested enough in the bigger picture, while people who are more focused on how many lines of code they write or how many tickets they close might see more community-driven issues as not contributing enough to "real" work. Clarifying team and company expectations around different types of contributions can go a long way toward minimizing resentment.

Cognitive Styles

Friction between individuals can also arise from the different ways people process information, or their *cognitive style*. These include:

- how they think about things;
- how they learn and absorb more information; and
- how they mentally engage with their work, their environments, and the people around them.

Some of the different cognitive styles can be described as a group of different axes or spectra. While this is not an exhaustive list, it covers some of the key styles that might come into play in a workplace environment:

Introvert, ambivert, and extrovert
> This dimensonality of an individual measures how people draw energy, the "recharging of internal battery." Introverts recover energy by being alone or in small well-known groups, while extroverts recharge by being around and interacting with lots of people. Ambiverts are somewhere in the middle, capable of recharging alone or with others depending on circumstances. Extroverts may enjoy group projects or organizational roles where they get to interact with many people and open space work environments, while introverts may prefer focusing on completing work tasks alone and find open space work environments draining.

Asker versus guesser
> Ask versus guess culture came from an internet forum post (*http://bit.ly/ask-vs-guess*) written in 2007 about the different ways that people ask for things from others. Askers feel that it's all right to ask for most things, with the understanding that they may well get "no" for an answer, while guessers tend to read more into situations and avoid asking for things unless they're fairly certain that the answer will be "yes."

 Clarifying and documenting how your team members are expected to communicate can help them come to a mutual understanding and avoid resentment.

Starter versus finisher
> Starters are people who love coming up with new ideas and getting them off the ground; they are energized by the process of beginning a new project. Finishers like tying up loose ends, fixing any remaining issues in a project. Starters will

likely get bored if asked to do a great deal of finisher work, while finishers might feel overwhelmed and not know where to begin if they find themselves asked to be starters.

Analytical, critical and lateral thinkers

Analytical thinking focuses on facts and evidence, dissects complex issues into simpler pieces, and eliminates extraneous information or invalid alternatives. Lateral thinking gathers information more indirectly, finds missing elements, examines issues from multiple perspectives, and eliminates stereotypical patterns of thought. Critical thinking involves evaluating and analyzing information and reflecting upon it in order to form judgments. This might involve evaluating arguments for logical soundness or biases, weighing different opinions or pieces of evidence in order to make a decision, or examining whether or not a conclusion logically follows from the arguments being made or if there are holes or gaps in someone's reasoning.

Purist versus pragmatist

Purists look to use the absolute best technology to solve a problem, and if that perfect technology doesn't exist, they will want to create their own. Purists are much less comfortable with projects that require workarounds or compromise around their engineering principles. Pragmatists instead are much more focused on practicality, weighing the cost of trying to create an ideal solution versus working within the realities of their current environments and constraints. Pragmatists will think about how to operationalize something and get it working in their actual production environment, rather than the purist approach of focusing on a technology in and of itself.

It's important to create and maintain a work environment that supports people across the style spectra. Watch out for office policies that unnecessarily favor certain styles—for example, requiring employees to be in at 8:00 am sharp in the mornings and not allowing them to attend meetings remotely, or a loud, open-office floor plan without any areas where people can work when they need quiet, distraction-free focus.

 When thinking about hiring, you'll want to keep these axes in mind. Take a look at where your current team members fall on the spectra, and keep an eye out for any imbalances on the team. While it probably doesn't matter so much if you have more night owls than early birds, if your team doesn't have a good balance between starters and finishers, and purists and pragmatists, that can lead to issues with overall team productivity and quality. If you find that you need to hire one or the other to address this imbalance, keep that in mind throughout your hiring processes.

Opportunities for Competitive Advantage

Companies have the opportunity to spend money and resources on instilling quality processes that imbue the individual with value that is critical to the organization.

Mentorship

Paying attention to teaching and mentoring is important, as truly mature or senior engineers cannot be expected to come from an environment that does not help guide and support them. Organizations that are willing to invest in the growth and development of junior engineers will have a competitive advantage, not only because it grows the organization's talent pool, but because skilled engineers are much more likely to stay in a place where they feel supported regardless of their current level of experience. Setting up a formal mentoring program can go a long way here.

Sponsorship

In addition to mentors, individuals can also benefit from sponsors, or champions within the organization that advocate and provide guidance for their protégé. Sponsors are also invested in the relationship, as it is a mutually beneficial alliance. Sponsors advocate for that desired promotion, call in potential favors, expand the protégé's perception of self, and provide valuable senior leadership connections. Protégés are trusted individuals that promote and build upon the sponsor's legacy. Economist Sylvia Ann Hewlett studied 12,000 men and women across Britain and the United States and found that sponsorship was more important than mentorship for measurable career progression (*http://bit.ly/nyt-sponsorship*). It's important for organizations to create a comprehensive program that educates employees on what is required to be a sponsor, how to assess a potential protégé, and how to find and assess a sponsor.

Education

Some organizations worry that providing too much training will encourage people to take their new skills and use them to get a better job elsewhere. A bigger risk when considering training and growth is that employees who are truly motivated to learn will leave for places where those goals are supported, with untrained or less motivated employees being the ones that stay. In addition to giving your organization a reputation as a less-than-ideal place to work, it will not help the overall talent of your workforce.

> Train people well enough so they can leave, treat them well enough so they don't want to.
>
> —Richard Branson

Mentorship

A successful formal mentorship program educates mentors and mentees to their respective purposes, roles, and obligations. A healthy mentorship flows both ways, allowing for each participant in the relationship to grow and learn. Understanding this relationship can help you become a mentor even if you've never had one yourself.

Senior-to-Junior Mentoring

The most traditional type of mentoring is senior-to-junior, where a senior engineer mentors a junior one, usually in a more organized capacity as part of some formal mentoring program. This is good for leveraging the expertise of more senior team members to help grow the skills of the junior ones. This works best when the senior employees have enough communication skills, teaching abilities, and patience to help other people truly learn (an impatient person will just grab the keyboard and do the work themselves). In the best case, the questions from the junior employee can help the senior one think through things they took for granted before, to question whether a solution is the best one rather than just "the way we've always done it."

Senior-to-Senior Mentoring

Senior-to-senior mentoring is less common, where two senior-level employees mentor each other. There can be a lot of deep knowledge sharing in these types of cases, but if both people have been senior for a while at the same company, they might lose the questioning and new perspectives that can come from having a fresh set of eyes looking at things.

Junior-to-Senior Mentoring

Junior-to-senior mentoring is the process of a junior employee mentoring a senior one. When done well, it can reinforce an ethic of the importance of trying to learn from everyone. We all have different levels of aptitude in particular skills. What we choose to focus on at a particular time will be where we are strongest. This means that quite often an individual who is junior may be more skilled on a topic than someone more senior.

Junior-to-Junior Mentoring

Finally, junior-to-junior mentoring happens when two junior-level employees work to help each other learn. This might happen on rapidly growing teams, where either there was no senior engineer involved in the process or any senior staff were too busy. Learning alongside someone else can enable both people to learn more quickly than they might on their own, but without any experienced people to steer them toward good practices or help when they get stuck, can also result in some less-than-ideal outcomes.

Introducing Mindsets

Mindsets are our personal beliefs about ourselves, and how we approach our possibilities. After years of research in the field of motivation, Carol S. Dweck, PhD, described fixed and growth mindsets.[1] With a *fixed mindset*, people believe talents and abilities are innate, fixed traits—either they are naturally good at something or they aren't, and that state is immutable. In a *growth mindset*, talents and abilities are learned and improved with effort and practice. Mindsets can greatly impact how people work, approach challenges, and deal with failure.

Cultivating the Right Mindset

Jason Moser, an assistant professor of psychology at Michigan State University, examined the neural mechanisms of different mindsets, publishing his results (*http://bit.ly/moser-mindsets*) in 2011. He noted that during the trial of completing tasks and making mistakes, those with a fixed mindset displayed less brain activity than those with a growth mindset, which is consistent with the findings that growth mindsets are associated with adaptive responses to mistakes. Changing how we think literally changes how the brain functions and respond to mistakes.

Research has shown that people's mindset about their own abilities and, more specifically, where those abilities come from, can have a significant impact on how they learn and grow. A growth mindset can allow people and organizations to learn and adapt more quickly in their environments. In practice, this means individuals and teams are able to react more quickly to production-impacting events or respond and change direction faster during the course of a project's lifecycle, which has benefits for the entire business.

Fixed Mindset

A fixed mindset—believing that skills and traits are innate and static—makes people feel that they have to constantly prove themselves to others. If someone believes that characteristics are innate and people are either smart or not smart, they will obviously want to prove to themselves and those around them that they fall into the smart category.

Someone with a fixed mindset views failures of any kind as proof that the individual is inherently not smart, not talented, or not enough of whatever quality is valued. In

---

1 Carol Dweck, *Mindset: The New Psychology of Success* (New York: Ballantine Books, 2006).

order to avoid failures and those feelings of inadequacy, people operating with a fixed mindset may stay away from situations in which they might fail. They are less likely to work on projects where they would have to learn new skills.

People avoid uncertainty as a way of avoiding failure and disapproval. This means that people with fixed mindsets are less likely to pick up new skills on the job. They also tend to focus a great deal on comparing themselves with their peers—a very competitive mindset—to confirm their beliefs about their traits.

Growth Mindset

Growth mindsets, on the other hand, lend themselves much more to individual learning and learning environments. Someone with a growth mindset believes that their skills and knowledge change over time; if they are currently not knowledgeable about a particular area, they believe that with enough time, effort, teaching, and practice, they can become knowledgeable about it. This isn't to say that everyone has the potential to be the next Albert Einstein or Marie Curie, but rather that nearly every skill can at least be improved, if not mastered or perfected.

In this case, challenges are viewed as learning opportunities, ways to gain new skills and knowledge or practice and level up existing ones. Without the fear of failure that often characterizes a fixed mindset, those with a growth mindset can take more risks and grow more. Failure is viewed not as a sign of an inherent personal flaw, but simply as a natural part of the learning process.

Focus on Individual Growth

How can someone foster a growth mindset? The combination of the following six strategies will help individuals prepare for future challenges and develop more flexibility in changing times.

Learn the fundamentals

When joining a team, learn the fundamental skills necessary for the position and team. Even if you have years of experience in the industry, do you understand the required skills to be successful on your specific team?

Often we approach a position with the idea that we should know everything in order to be given the opportunity to work. We're so busy proving that our new coworkers and manager made the right decision that we often don't take the time to understand what the fundamentals of our job are, including all of the cultural differences associated with each unique environment.

Likewise, when we've been working at a position for a long time, we don't always consider how it's changed over the course of that time. A key aspect to preparing for additional support is to understand the fundamentals well.

Who does what, how, and why? You don't want to be learning for the first time who has various responsibilities and how they work during an outage. Rather, you should take the time to learn these things and make sure you have the fundamentals solidly in hand before the metaphorical firefighting begins.

One fundamental of every position is the ability to observe and be observed. Watch others handling the complex situations in their environments, whether this is within your organization on the same team, other teams, or outside of your organization. Coworking and exchange programs provide direct access to individuals tackling similar problems without the "hindsight effect" of shared stories; that is, they help you better identify and address the issue in the moment rather than after the fact.

Observing is a case where notebooks are more helpful than laptops to track what is going on. Write down who is doing what and why. For example, in an incident, is the manager the incident manager or does that role get passed along to other individuals? Write down the actionable results to learn what you can do better going forward.

Research[2] has shown that taking notes by hand leads to better memory retention and absorption of new materials.

Develop your niche

Within your environment, there is something that you can excel at categorically. You know your current skills, so look for something you can do that you don't already know. If you keep doing the same thing over time, you are essentially repeating the same year of learning. This is a recipe for losing the ability to learn, and you will have to relearn that process.

This new skill doesn't have to be directly related to what you do now; it could be a gap that exists in the team or organization. For example, if you are on the operations team, and your supported application is storage, you might study up on different storage algorithms like LevelDB, a fast key/value storage library written at Google.

In this example, you should spend time exploring how LevelDB is installed, and how its performance characteristics could provide background knowledge and perspective when you are examining your own supported application characteristics. This type of learning will strengthen your overall skills such that you can better operate and manage your application.

---

2 P. A. Mueller and D. M. Oppenheimer, "The Pen Is Mightier Than the Keyboard: Advantages of Longhand Over Laptop Note Taking," *Psychological Science* 25, no. 6 (2014): 1159–1168.

Depending on your team size and the number of projects assigned to your team, there may be more or less slack available for learning. Choose the skill you are strengthening based on need and availability, as well as the size of your team and how this skill will fit in with the other work and learning being done within it.

Once you have learned one new chosen topic, your journey doesn't end there. Share your learning and educate others through writing or speaking, and then choose a new topic to learn. The industry is rapidly changing—new tools and practices are released every day. You can't be an expert at everything, but you can strengthen your ability to learn so that when you do pivot your career, you are ready to take on new challenges. You can also share your expertise to help level up the people around you.

Recognize your strengths and progress

How do you know when you have done something well? How can you be sure that you have learned something well enough that you can choose something new or take your current learning to the next level?

While we can appreciate external sources of feedback, whether that comes in the form of appreciation, coaching, or formal evaluations, for the most part we can't rely on outside systems to identify and rate our progress. The systems in place in most environments do not encourage us to be the best that we can be or understand what elements of development matter most to us as individuals.

It is important to be able to accurately gauge your own performance and efficiency on the job. There are many different mechanisms in place for providing individual feedback, some more useful than others, but you should be able to give yourself feedback in the absence of or regardless of outside systems. Being able to assess ourselves honestly, and be satisfied with our mechanisms for measurement, allows us to steer our careers in the direction that we want to go.

> Yo soy yo y mi circunstancia. (I am I and my circumstance.)
>
> —José Ortega y Gasset

In the late 1960s, while studying individual programming productivity, Sackman, Erikson, and Grant found that some engineers are more productive than others. Over time, the idea of the more productive engineer has turned into some companies' mantra, "We only hire 10x engineers."

If someone consistently works at levels 10 times the productivity of others within the group, it could be a sign that the individual is no longer challenged in their current position. Becoming an expert in a single topic is admirable, but not at the sacrifice of continued learning, resilience, and flexibility.

Many signals tell us to strive to be the best at an activity. The Ortega hypothesis is the idea that the average or mediocre scientists contribute substantially to the advancement of science. We propose a corollary that the average technologist contributes substantially to advancement of technology. As we celebrate the well-known thought leaders, so too should we celebrate the unnamed masses who—through stories, one-off tools, processes, and documentation—have impacted the state of our industry. They've shown that more than just productivity, the evolution of standards is what has produced a common core of tools, platforms, and interfaces, thereby decreasing the overall cost to others to design, build, test, and use software.

Ensure deliberate, quality practice

Use the skill you are learning. Learning literally rewires our brain as we create new myelin, the white matter in the brain that speeds up and strengthens our nerve impulses.[3] It's key to ensure, then, that we put not only the effort to have sufficient quantity of practice, but quality as well; that is, we must make sure not to practice the wrong way of doing things and thus strengthen imperfect mechanisms. One of the benefits of coaching or mentoring, regardless of skill level, is to be able to get outside monitoring or feedback to help guide our practice and activities.

Every day, much of our work can be perceived as practice toward the moments when our performance really changes outcomes. Practice that essentially repeats the same thing over and over again is the *broken record* method. In order to really grow in skills, we need to do different things and progress over time.

A second method of nondeliberate practice is *autopilot*. For many people, after years of driving we act on autopilot—even as we age and our capabilities potentially change, making it a much more difficult activity. The challenge is recognizing that the environment is changing, and not allowing ourselves to become stuck in rote practices, coasting through our careers.

As the industry is changing and technology's impact is advancing at a leapfrog pace, it is critical to recognize these coasting habits—that is, when we are stagnating or becoming too comfortable with an activity because it seems like it could never change. We must continually challenge and improve ourselves, working to learn new skills and strengthen existing ones, to make sure we maintain a high quality of work and the ability to react to nonroutine events.

Develop your working style

We will always have more work to do. We will always leave an environment knowing there was more work that could have been done. We will join environments seeing all the possible things that can be done, but not necessarily seeing the circumstances that

---

3 Alison Pearce Stevens, "Learning Rewires the Brain." *Society for Science*, September 3, 2014, *http://bit.ly/ learning-rewires*.

explain why things happened the way they did. Rather than start a new job or continue in a current role critiquing what exists, which limits one's perspective, examine what is working successfully and identify the strengths of the environment as well as opportunities to improve it.

There's a variety of individual working styles. It's important to figure out which styles work for you and which ones don't in order to get the most out of your work as well as to provide the most value to your team. In the process of this learning, you will also start to develop your own style when it comes to the tools and techniques you use.

Look around for inspiration. In the process of observing others, don't be afraid to try out the tools and methods that they use. With the advent of transparency and open source, individuals have gotten into the habit of sharing dotfiles (*https://dotfiles.github.io/*), configuration files on Unix systems that begin with a period, and using other shortcuts to get work done.

If you have been in the industry for a while, you may already have a style. Assess and identify aspects of your style to understand why you do things the way you do. It's important to understand that the way you complete aspects of your job may be habits you've picked up over time that are not necessarily the best way to do them, but simply what you're familiar with. By understanding what you like and where it comes from, you gain the freedom and flexibility to grow by adopting nonfamiliar styles to try out.

Enhance the team style

Once you understand your own style, you can learn to differentiate between your preferences and those of the team you are currently working on. One of the aspects of turning a group into a team is figuring out how everyone will align and work together.

An organization's behaviors and attitudes toward failure will impact how individuals cling to their own methodologies. If individual team members feel they will be held accountable for failure, they may be more resistant to change processes that work for them.

Mindsets and Learning Organizations

This view of failure applies at the organizational level as well as the individual one. A blameful culture, when dealing with a failure, looks for the individual(s) who supposedly "caused" it so they can be removed, either from the project or the organization. This is often because these cultures view failure in a fixed way. They believe that if someone made a mistake, it was because they were not good enough or smart enough, and because the culture sees this as immutable, they don't give the person chances to improve. The organization as a whole tends to stagnate in this way. Focus is placed not on dealing with failure well and learning from it, but rather on avoiding it altogether.

A blameless view of failure works so well in part because it adopts a growth mindset, acknowledging that mistakes happen but operating under the assumption that both people and organizations are capable of learning, growing, and improving. The team might not currently be good at something, but it *can get better* if people are looking for ways to get better, ways to learn, and ways to improve. This focus on learning, education, and self-improvement produces smarter and more robust individuals and teams.

 In this way, growth mindsets and learning organizations do a good job of upholding the devops compact as well, by enabling more frequent feedback and communication about what state things are in, what the goals are, and how these two aspects are currently aligning.

The Role of Feedback

Dweck's years of research found that the nature of the feedback people received was a key factor in whether they developed a fixed or a growth mindset. If someone does well at something and the praise they receive is, "Good job, you're so smart," the emphasis on smartness pushes them toward a fixed mindset, making them less likely to take on challenging tasks or anything that might call that smartness into question. If, on the other hand, someone is given the praise, "Good job, you worked so hard on that," they will associate their successes with the effort they put in, not an innate quality, making them more likely to take on challenges and try again after setbacks in the future.

The original studies in the area of feedback and mindsets were conducted with school-age children, but the idea that the type of feedback people receive can shape their mindset certainly applies to adults as well. A mindset might originally form during the childhood years, but even a fixed mindset is not static—someone who learned a fixed mindset as a child has the potential to develop a more learning-focused growth mindset as an adult.

This is very important when considering employee growth and performance. People with fixed mindsets tend to pay attention only to feedback that relates directly to their present abilities, tuning out feedback that speaks to how they can improve in the future. Growth mindset individuals, on the other hand, are very attentive to any feedback that could help them do better, being focused on learning and improving themselves rather than on their current state.

Keep both of these things in mind during employee reviews and feedback periods. When someone is giving feedback, either as a manager or as an individual contributor, they should be emphasizing the employee's efforts, actions, and the work and thought they put into things, focusing on what the employee *can do* rather than what they *are* and thus guiding them toward a growth mindset.

This is the case for both positive and more negative feedback. For instance, compare these two approaches:

A fixed mindset approach
Alice is clearly very intelligent—she intuitively understands the way that distributed systems behave and interact. She isn't very good with people, though, and isn't the kind of person that others go to when they need help.

A growth mindset approach
Alice has clearly put a great deal of work into understanding the distributed systems that she works with, and that effort shows in her deep knowledge of how these systems behave and interact. I'd love for her to find ways to share her knowledge more effectively in both formal presentations and less formal one-on-one interactions.

How is Alice likely to respond to this feedback? Though the "good at distributed systems, needs improvement on people skills" messages are consistent, the framing of the feedback is completely different. The fixed mindset phrases—"an intelligent person," "intuitively understands," "isn't the kind of person"—imply innate traits and unchangeable facts about Alice. The growth mindset phrases—"a great deal of work," "that effort shows," "find ways to share her knowledge"—focus on Alice's work and actions and what she has *done* in the past and should *do* in the future.

Reviews and Rankings

There are two goals when providing feedback to employees. First, feedback in the form of things like performance reviews is designed to let people know how they are doing so they can grow as individuals, level up their own skills, and work to fill any gaps in their knowledge or skill set. Second, aside from the value this offers to the individual, the organization also benefits by figuring out which people are performing better and contributing more. The rationale for this is that if there are some people who aren't doing as well as their peers or are consistently failing to improve, the organization would be better off without them.

Frequency of Feedback

According to a 2011 *Wall Street Journal* article (*http://bit.ly/wsj-reviews*), 51 percent of companies do annual performance reviews, while 41 percent do them semiannually. However, more and more companies are beginning to realize that feedback and reviews can have much more of an impact if given more frequently, *if* the feedback itself is helpful to those receiving it. Obviously if feedback provides no new or actionable information, there will be no benefit to getting it more often. However, for feedback that is useful and actionable, greater frequency does lead to greater benefit for both individuals and organizations.

If someone isn't on the right track with something that they're doing, waiting up to a year for their next annual review isn't good for anyone involved. They will likely go through this time thinking they are doing well, leading to a nasty surprise come review time. The psychology of getting feedback shows that people generally react to these sorts of negative surprises emotionally rather than intellectually, a phenomenon known as *amygdala hijacking*.[4] As a result, people are less likely to fully understand and be able to act on the feedback they are being given.

 Smaller, shorter feedback cycles mean that adjustments are smaller and thus easier to make. This is a big driving factor behind teams moving away from the waterfall model for software development toward more Agile practices and a reason why continuous delivery works so well. Annual performance reviews are similar to waterfall in that the delay in getting feedback slows down problem resolution, so organizations should move toward the more Agile idea of continuous feedback.

Ranking System

Especially in larger organizations, various ranking systems are often used to categorize or classify employee performance. One of the biggest changes in recent years is the move away from *stack ranking*, also referred to as *forced ranking* or *forced distribution*. Popularized by then-CEO of GE Jack Welch in the 1980s, this practice is based on the idea that the *top 20* percent of the workforce is the most productive, and the middle 70 percent work adequately. The remaining 10 percent should be fired. This practice is often referred to as "rank and yank." This ranking incentivizes employees to avoid being in the bottom 10 percent.

When individuals in a system are forced to compete with others' accomplishments, this increases the challenge of effective collaboration. Clear, transparent communica-

---

4 Daniel Goleman, *Emotional Intelligence: Why It Can Matter More Than IQ* (New York: Bantam Books, 1996).

1 is not perceived as valuable to the individual, as having information can impact rewards, career advancement, and even whether an individual has a job. Stack ranking, especially when the process is poorly explained, hurts performance instead of helping it, but luckily there has been a marked decline in organizations using it in recent years.[5]

On the other side of things, many startups, looking to move away from ranking systems, do away with rankings and reviews entirely. In the chaos and change that categorizes these early-stage companies, lack of feedback can be detrimental to individuals. Additionally, without any kind of formal procedures or guidelines, it is easy for favoritism to come into play, intentionally or unintentionally. A formal feedback system combined with useful and frequent feedback can provide clear steps forward for people who want to improve and grow their careers.

Looking at these factors, we can see how feedback and rankings around individual performance, rather than being something that impacts only one individual at a time, can impact collaboration throughout entire teams and organizations. Turning performance reviews into a zero-sum game inhibits communication and collaboration, as everyone is more focused on protecting their own jobs than on creating value for the company as a whole, let alone providing the most benefit for customers.

Frequency and formality of feedback play a role in creating a collaborative environment as well. Some formality in the process is certainly a good thing, but consider how much more easily information flows at weekly catch-ups versus big yearly reviews. With shorter feedback cycles, people get more practice both receiving feedback and giving it in return. This leads to greater information sharing in both directions, not just from the top down, creating a more collaborative environment overall.

The Problems with Rock Stars and Superflocks

With the rise in popularity of concepts like "rock star developer" and "10x engineer," many companies and hiring managers are trying to hire those elusive "superstars," hoping to reap the benefits of their supposed 10x productivity. However, focusing too much on these sorts of workers might do more harm than good.

In her June 2015 TED Talk (*http://bit.ly/heffernan-pecking*), international businesswoman Margaret Heffernan used the term "super-chicken model" to describe the way companies hire for elite individuals. This was based on productivity research that evolutionary biologist William Muir of Purdue University conducted on chickens.

Muir found that a regular flock of regular chickens, left to its own devices for six generations, ended up increasing its productivity. Muir also created a "superflock" from

---

5 Max Nisen, "Why Stack Ranking Is a Terrible Way to Motivate Employees," *Business Insider*, November 15, 2013, *http://bit.ly/stack-ranking*.

the most productive chickens, and with each generation selected only the most productive chickens to breed the next. Instead of being even more productive, this superflock ended up with all but three members dead. The "superchickens" were only more productive individually at the expense of the productivity of others.

This outcome can be observed in the workplace as well. A productivity and creative-problem-solving study at MIT (*http://bit.ly/hbr-building-teams*) found that the most productive and creative teams were not the ones created from "superstar" engineers. Intelligence and raw engineering talent weren't at all good predictors of the best teams. Rather, the researchers found that the best teams had higher social sensitivity, gave each other close to equal time to speak, and had more women in them. It was unclear if having more women helped bring about the higher sensitivity to others' mental states and more equal speaking time (women are often socialized to be empathetic, listen more, and interrupt less), but it was clear that the increased social sensitivity, or the ability to recognize and understand both other people's feelings and general social norms, and communication were deciding factors in team productivity.

The Value of Social Capital to a Team

Social capital, or the value of people's social networks and interactions, works through greater information flow, reciprocity and helpfulness, and interdependency and trust. Compare this to a team that is focused around a superstar employee, where help and information are likely to flow only in one direction, there is no interdependency, and there is likely very little trust.

Social capital takes time to develop, and its benefits become increasingly apparent as time progresses. To get the productive teams and organizations we want, we need to stop focusing on "superstar" employees that erode trust and social capital, and instead focus on growing empathy among our existing teams, and working toward cooperation rather than competition.

Communication and Conflict Resolution Styles

With the industry's call for higher product performance and lower costs, individuals are more likely to find themselves facing competing demands for their time and attention. The conflicts that will arise from these demands will need to be resolved somehow. There are several different approaches, which we'll look at here in terms of conflict resolution or negotiation styles.

When we talk about negotiation, we mean communication specifically aimed at reaching an agreement, which can happen in a variety of ways that we will enumerate in the next section. A large part of fostering collaboration as the primary negotiation style among a team or workplace ultimately comes down to communication. We first saw this idea in action when we introduced the devops compact; without effective communication, none of the shared goals, the strategies taken to reach them, or the contingency plans would have been anywhere near as likely to succeed.

Effective Communication

Effective communication allows people to build shared understanding and find common goals as opposed to working only in competition with one another. Aside from simply answering a question or telling somebody what to work on next, there are many different reasons why we, as people, communicate with one another. Four key reasons are increasing understanding, asserting influence, giving recognition, and building community.

Communication helps build resilience among individuals and teams—letting people know that they are not alone, allowing them to share coping strategies, and transferring knowledge between both people and groups—and its effectiveness can have significant impacts on organizations as a whole.

Increasing understanding

A large part of communication is designed to increase understanding, whether that be a clearer understanding of what someone expects from us, a greater depth of knowledge of a technical topic, or anything in between. This kind of knowledge can be shared explicitly, such as through a mentoring session or formal lecture, or implicitly, where people will pick up ideas, norms, and customs through participation in activities like a team hack day or bug-fix session. A culture of learning and social engagement around knowledge sharing can provide additional context and understanding that isn't present with self-learning.

People often end up with large amounts of contextual knowledge and situational awareness around the systems and processes for which they're responsible. Without active dissemination of this knowledge to others, this creates islands of knowledge that are vulnerable to external events in your organization. Having just a couple of people who understand a given topic also increases pressure on those individuals ("No, George can't go on vacation, he's the only one who can fix the database!"), which can increase stress and the likelihood of burnout. Communicating to share and spread understanding is a great way to grow the skills and increase the robustness of your organization.

Many times, understanding includes an aspect of historical perspective. Given the complex systems that we work with and the organic way they grow and evolve over time, it is not always obvious to someone new to a team or project why things are the way they are. This sort of context is greatly important to being able to fully comprehend and contribute to something. This is especially true for operations teams who are tasked with deciding if something is anomalous or not—was this alert a false alarm, or is there an actual issue that needs to be investigated? Being able to communicate historical contexts allows new or more junior team members to grow and develop their knowledge and understanding much more quickly than they would otherwise.

Asserting influence

There are different methods of influence, some that are more positive or collaborative than others. Certainly one can influence others by interrupting anyone who disagrees with them, by being the one who argues the loudest and the longest, or by using some sort of power or coercion. None of these lend themselves well to a healthy or empathetic team dynamic—while influence may be achieved, everyone else is likely to feel resentful. As we'll discuss in more depth later, the most effective way to influence others is to find enough common ground that they will not only do what you want, but will *want* what you want as well.

Giving recognition

Giving recognition is another common reason that people communicate. Giving recognition can improve morale, as people obviously want to feel that their work and accomplishments are noticed and appreciated; it can enhance cooperation between employees as they see each other more as both generous and contributive; and it can help to reinforce behaviors at work that you would like to see more of. Recognition usually has two parts: the identification or realization of something that should be recognized, and the actual communication of that sentiment.

Identifying opportunities for recognition is a skill that takes time—if you aren't in the right mindset (e.g., if you are in a negative mood, stressed out due to a heavy workload, or in a team environment that is incredibly competitive and "everyone for themselves"), it be harder to pinpoint when praise or recognition would be appropriate. Communicating the recognition is a skill as well. Some people feel less comfortable praising others, especially if there hasn't been much recognition in the workplace previously. Recognizing people publicly might feel more uncomfortable than doing so privately, but on the other hand people might feel more recognized if praised publicly, such as in a team meeting.

Building community

Finally, strengthening individual connections with better communication can help build communities. As the MIT study (*http://bit.ly/hbr-building-teams*) mentioned earlier showed, teams with greater ToM and more equal communication are more creative and productive. Building community goes hand in hand with these things. Teams where people regularly talk about topics outside of strictly work-related matters have higher levels of trust and empathy, and are better able to be productive and handle stressful times as a group. People often interact better on an individual level when they are able to see each other as complete individuals, not just email addresses or entries in the company's staff directory.

Community of Practice and Community of Interest

Communities of practice are groups of people who share the same role or concern and meet regularly to improve how they perform within an organization. Every role within an organization has the opportunity to form a community of practice, so there could be one community for developers, one for QA and testing engineers, and another for scrum masters. Communities of practice could also form around specific tools or languages, but in either case they are not restricted to people from any one project or team. These communities tend to work best when they are not mandated by management, but rather allowed to grow and change organically. Community activity may ebb and flow over time as roles and projects do. It is important to note that communities of practice are restricted to those people who are actively participating in the role that the community is focused on, so that learning and discussion will come from people's real-world knowledge and experience.

A community of interest is similar to a community of practice, but instead of being limited to practitioners only, tends to be made up of people who are interested in the management, governance, and communication of the teams involved in an organization. They might take responsibility for overseeing or creating communities of practice, or discuss other higher-level issues that don't have as much impact on the day-to-day, real-world issues that practitioners are discussing. Some communities use the term in a different way, defining a community of interest to be anyone who is interested in discussing a particular topic, team, or technology even if they don't practice it themselves. Both communities of practice and communities of interest are intended as cross-functional, with emphasis being placed on learning and common goals.

There should not be an expectation that employees will become best friends outside of work, and there is a fine line between getting to know someone as a person and getting too invasive or personal; some people are more willing to share personal parts of their lives than others, and that's fine. The key isn't to force community-building interpersonal communication, but to create opportunities for it, gently encourage it, and then allow it to happen naturally. Building relationships and building community both take time; neither happens overnight and neither can be forced.

 Things like shared coffee breaks, shared lunches long enough to both eat and talk, and opt-in activities for people with common interests can go a long way toward building strong communities.

How We Communicate

The methods for communication you choose will, if you're trying to be most effective with your communication, depend on the content, urgency, and importance of your message. This kind of self-awareness will allow you to get your ideas across more clearly, increase understanding within your team, and make it easier for other teams and individuals to work with you. In addition, you'll want to consider what kind of audience you're trying to reach, and how much context and investment from the intended audience will be needed for the communication to be effective. You might also consider how organized, versus more free-form, the communication needs to be.

Different styles of expression are valued in different cultures. Some cultures value assertiveness, the willingness to confront opposing views and express feelings forthrightly during social encounters. Other cultures value indirectness, which requires individuals to read between the lines with the goal of maintaining group harmony.

Communication media

A variety of media or methods exist by which people typically communicate in the workplace. Not every medium is most effective for every situation, and different organizations and teams have different media that they prefer. Table 7-1 breaks down a (nonexhaustive) list of communication methods by a variety of factors.

Table 7-1. Different communication tools and methods

	Immediacy	Audience reach	Investment	Context required	Organization
Email	Low	High	Medium	High	Medium
Impromptu in-person (or video) meeting	High	Low	Medium	Low	Low
Chat	Medium	Medium	Low	High	Low
Formal meeting	Very low	High	High	Low	High
Twitter or other microblogging	Low	Medium	Low	High	Low
GitHub pull request	Low	Medium	Medium	Medium	Medium
Post-it notes	Very low	Medium	Low	High	Low
PagerDuty pages	High	High	High	Medium	Low
Nagios alerts	Medium	High	High	Medium	Low
Books or blog posts	Very low	Low	Medium	Medium	High
Pictures, graphs, and GIFs	Low	Low	Low	High	Low

Let's look at what the columns in this table indicate in more detail.

- *Immediacy* refers to how quickly communication can be established—for example, walking up to someone has high immediacy because you can tap them on the shoulder and interrupt them, whereas email has low immediacy because you can't control how often other people check their email. Meetings can have very low immediacy because scheduling around the availability of people and meeting places can be very time consuming indeed.

- *Audience reach* is how well a medium allows you to reach all of your intended audience, so while an email to an individual has a pretty good chance of being seen by who you want, chat messages will likely be seen only by people who happen to be online (or in a given channel) at the time, depending on what kind of offline messaging and alerting options your chat solution has.

- *Investment* describes how much time and effort is required for people to participate with a given form of communication. Meetings are one of the highest in terms of investment, as people have to take time out of their other work and either go someplace or dial in remotely to participate. An email, book, or blog post requires a medium amount of investment in terms of finding the time to read it thoroughly, but something like chat or Twitter is low investment.

- *Context* is how much context is required for a given communication medium, or how likely misunderstandings are to occur without it. Twitter, chat, and email require high context, because of how easy it is to misinterpret phrasing or tone—in general, the shorter the text communication is, the more likely misunderstandings are to occur because of context being lost. In-person (or video) forms of communication are much lower context because people can see body language, hear voice and tone, and quickly bring up and resolve misunderstandings.

- *Organization* refers to how organized the thoughts or ideas ought to be in a particular medium. Meetings are high organization because they really should have an agenda so people's time isn't wasted. Email is medium because people can choose to organize their thoughts quite a bit before sending, while chat and Twitter are low due to their often rapid nature and short form.

As we'll touch on more in Part IV, there is no one-size-fits-all solution when it comes to communication methods. Even when factors such as urgency and reach are taken into consideration, there are still individual preferences to account for; as with cognitive styles, people often have different preferred communication styles as well. Some people strongly prefer face-to-face communication so they can gather additional context from body language and facial expressions, while others may find that they prefer written communication, as it is easier for them to retain information that way.

Negotiation or conflict resolution styles

How we communicate also involves our negotiation or conflict resolution style, in addition to the communication tools. When negotiating, you might see these different negotiation styles coming into play:

- *Competition*, where someone focuses solely on pursuing their own needs at the expense of others. This might look like a team member who picks "good" projects for themselves (such as ones likely to get lots of recognition) while leaving less glamorous grunt work for other team members.

- *Accommodation*, where someone acquiesces to someone else's needs at the expense of their own, sometimes with the goal of building a better relationship with that person by helping them. For example, one employee might decide to go along with what someone else wants in the hope that that person will remember it and return the favor down the line.

- *Avoidance*, where both parties try to avoid direct conflict, often with an increase in passive-aggressive behaviors, indirect conflict, and tension. In cases like this, you might see long email threads where people try to shift work or blame without being too direct, or there may be a lot of complaining internal to a team about another team, without ever talking directly with the people being complained about.

- *Compromise*, where all sides try to find a mutually agreeable solution that involves everyone giving up a little bit of their own needs in order to try to reach a "fair" outcome. This might look like people reaching a middle ground when it comes to which features will end up going into a given release or when a deadline will be, or coming to an agreement about how much of someone's time another team is able to have on a particular project.

- *Collaboration*, which is similar to compromise in that it is considered win-win, but involves much more creation of mutual understanding, learning, and making sure that all sides genuinely get their needs met. In collaborative environments, you might see people from different teams pairing on a particular project or feature, on-call responsibilities being shared between different groups of people involved in the deployment and maintenance of a product, or people from multiple groups being involved in project planning.

For a team to best work toward its goals, its members must be able to work together. Teams with more collaboration are more productive as a whole, as well as being viewed more favorably by their members—and because lower turnover is usually better for team morale and productivity, this is a positively reinforcing cycle.

Communication Context and Power Differentials

A lot of how we communicate is also impacted by the context of our communications. This is not just the amount of context that various communication media and methods can provide, as just described, but also the situations and circumstances in which communication can take place.

Context and location

Regular communication as part of everyday work is likely to be very different from the communication that takes place during an emergency, such as a site outage or other operational issue. While shared jokes, internet memes, and funny cat pictures might be a good way to build camaraderie and trust during the course of normal work interactions, they can be an unwelcome distraction during an ongoing issue. Companies that rely heavily on chat would do well to create a separate chat room or channel for these situations, such as a "war room" reserved for straightforward, on-topic communication only. This also helps teams review communication later, such as when performing a postmortem.

Finally, whether or not team members are located together can also have a great deal of impact on their communication. If a company is just getting started with allowing remote workers, or simply hasn't given their remote employees much focus or attention, remote communication and collaboration can take a serious hit. If the majority of work-related decisions happen in person, usually outside of a formal meeting context, remote employees might find themselves missing out on valuable information or discussions.

 One way of dealing with this is the practice of communicating as "remote by default." This means using the remote-friendly methods of communication, most commonly email and group chat, for as much communication as possible and as the first choice of method, not a last resort. If, instead of walking over to a colleague's desk to ask a question, an employee posts the question in the team's chat room, remote employees are given a chance to learn and participate in discussions that they wouldn't have before. This leads to more information and better visibility for the entire team, and this can be a reason to favor group chats over one-on-one or private chats for anything that isn't sensitive or might be of general interest. Finally, having a searchable record of communications for future reference can be very valuable as well.

Power differentials

Context is also often informed by power differentials, which can occur for a variety of reasons within an organization. These can be as simple as the power structures built into the workplace, where managers have more power than their reports or senior engineers have more power than junior ones. However, they can also take more subtle forms, with members of underrepresented groups in the tech industry (such as women, people of color, or LGBTQ people) having less power than members of more represented or dominant groups.

These power differentials can have substantial effects on negotiation styles between people. On the one hand, people with less power might avoid any kind of conflict, hoping to avoid being co-opted or having to make compromises they don't want to make, knowing that they have less power and are likely to be the only ones "compromising," which isn't really a compromise at all. Alternatively, the high-power side might also avoid conflict or negotiation because they see no need to: if they can impose their will or solution on others, who have no choice but to accept it, they don't have much incentive to negotiate. It's important to keep these power differentials in mind when considering communication and conflict resolution.

Devops Anti-Patterns: Communication and Interrupting

While it's not necessarily easy to say, "Doing X means you are doing devops," it is often possible to pin down the defining factors of this movement by observing anti-patterns, or rather, "Doing Y means you are not doing devops." Throughout the book, we will illustrate some of these anti-patterns as appropriate, using examples or miniature case studies to help demonstrate why some behaviors or practices aren't effective.

In some organizations, people interrupting and talking over each other is incredibly common. Pay attention to the meetings you attend and count how often people interrupt each other and who does the interrupting. In extreme cases, you might find that only rarely do people start to speak *without* interrupting each other, which leads to lots of time spent repeating things that were said while someone else was talking, as well as people developing tendencies to speak more and more loudly to simply be heard.

This sort of *interrupt culture* is an example of communication that is competitive, rather than collaborative, and offers much less chance for trust to build up between individuals and teams. Communication happens to influence, but rarely to understand, and there is not much in the way of social capital. Cutting down on interrupting not only increases understanding, but also helps people to feel that they are being heard, increasing trust and empathy.

For example, studies have shown (*http://bit.ly/review-gender-bias*) that when women phrase things the same way as men, they are perceived as more "harsh," "abrasive," or "aggressive," while men are praised for how "straightforward" and "take-charge" they are. On the other side, women are often judged negatively for softening their language by apologizing or using hedging words like "just." If they interrupt as much as their male colleagues they are often deemed "unlikeable," but without interrupting, depending on the office culture, it can be hard to ever get their opinions heard. These sorts of contexts can have an enormous impact on how successful our communications are and should be kept in mind, especially when working to improve a team's diversity and inclusivity.

Empathy and Trust

Effective communication, in addition to being crucial for distributing information, is key to building a foundation of trust and empathy between individuals, and that foundation is what enables devops to really work. This goes back to the root of the devops compact that we introduced earlier in the book. In order to continue working toward the same shared goals, we need to be able to empathize with and trust each other.

Creating this compact involves being able to establish and communicate a shared vision or goals—the commonalities that shape the big picture of what teams are working on even as the details differ. In addition to increased empathy and a common focus, a shared vision should give individuals a much clearer picture of organizational or broader goals, which will help direct, inform, and guide autonomous action. Goals that are too vague or that don't seem relevant are harder to fully grasp and realize, and might not provide individuals with the motivation, context, or ability to choose effective courses of action.

Developing Empathy

Empathy, the ability to understand and share someone else's feelings, is a skill that can and should be learned and developed. Its benefits are becoming increasingly well known, both in and out of the workplace. More empathetic individuals are less egocentric, less socially aggressive, and less likely to use stereotypes when considering others. They are also much more likely to compromise during debates or other disagreements rather than tending toward one of the other negotiation styles discussed earlier.

While a great deal of empathy is developed in childhood, there are many ways that empathy can be learned and increased in adulthood as well. We'll take a look at a few of the most common and effective methods and how they can be applied in the workplace.

Listening

Listening is important for building empathy in general, but it can be even more beneficial during disagreements or other heated discussions. Too often when we are disagreeing with someone, we are merely waiting to talk and planning what we are going to say, rather than really listening and trying to understand where the other person is coming from. Instead, try slowing down and forcing yourself to listen, and rather than interrupting, wait until the other person is finished speaking before considering your own response.

Active listening is another good skill to consider here. This involves reflecting what you think the other person just said back to them, paraphrasing or summarizing to make sure that what you heard and understood was what they meant or intended. This makes sure that both parties are on the same page and are talking about the same thing.

 Paying attention to nonverbal cues, such as tone of voice, rate of speech, body language, and facial expressions, is also a key part of listening. Because these nonverbal cues aren't conveyed via text, making sure you have a good video (or at the bare minimum, audio) setup is key if you have any remote employees.

Asking questions

After listening, asking questions can be a great way to build understanding and clarify meaning, often as part of active listening. In addition to asking questions of others, we can also ask questions of or to ourselves. Cultivating curiosity about others, whether they be strangers or other team members, is a habit that can expand our empathy by helping us understand where other people are coming from.

Questions could take the form of "Could you clarify what you meant when you said X?" or something more hypothetical, such as "Where do I think that person on the train is heading right now? What might they be looking at on their phone?," or self-facing, like "What unconscious biases might I have that are impacting my opinions on this?" Combined with listening to the answers we get, either from ourselves or others, asking questions can be a very powerful tool for building empathy.

Imagining other perspectives

Going beyond asking hypothetical questions about what other people might be thinking, doing, or feeling, we can start trying to imagine ourselves in other people's shoes. It's one thing to say that we should assume good intentions, but we can go further and ask ourselves, how might this person be feeling right now when I disagree with them? What good intentions can I identify that this person holds? What might their positive motivations be, and how do they impact the disagreement or discussion that we are having? What valid arguments might they have against my point of view?

Appreciating individual differences

In addition to imagining what other people's thoughts, opinions, and motivations might be, we can teach ourselves to appreciate those differences as another way of cultivating empathy. Working with, genuinely listening to, and imagining ourselves as the various people that we work with can help us break down biases, both conscious and unconscious.

Consider the different working styles described earlier in this chapter and how they complement each other. Starters and finishers, purists and pragmatists, can all combine their skills to bring projects to fruition. Then take this understanding and appreciation and apply it to the other personal and professional backgrounds you might find. Appreciating the benefits of differing perspectives can go a long way toward building empathy among diverse groups of people.

Developing Trust

Trust and empathy go hand in hand: as one grows, so often does the other, and vice versa. Increased trust can help increase the resiliency of a team. Without trust, individuals can be very protective of their projects or areas of responsibility, often to the detriment of their own health or the team's overall productivity.

Imagine, as an example, a team of system administrators so protective of their servers, and so distrustful of anyone else touching them, that they restrict any privileged server access at all to just their own team. If other teams aren't able to install necessary software or deploy code to these servers, this operations team is likely to become a bottleneck, a barrier that other teams will end up resenting or finding ways to work around. This is a typical example that comes to mind when people think of the drawbacks to heavily siloed environments.

That kind of negative impact can become even more apparent when it is a single person rather than a team being too closed off. If only one person knows about or has access to something, they become a single point of failure for that thing. If that thing breaks and that one person is sick or on vacation, the rest of the team might be dead in the water and unable to be productive until that person can be reached, which will either lead to the rest of the team being blocked or that person never being able (or willing) to take time off. With increased trust, this knowledge and responsibility can be shared not only between people but between teams, increasing the resiliency of the organization as a whole.

There are different strategies that can be used specifically for developing trust, however, and both are needed to foster an environment that can be really and reliably collaborative. One of the differentiating factors between a group and a team is the presence of trust. The strategies that we'll cover here include swift trust, self-disclosure, trust but verify, and a perception of fairness.

Swift trust

Swift trust is a form of trust that occurs in short-term or short-lived groups or organizations, and means that trust is assumed to be present at first and then verified as time goes on. First explored by professor of organizational behavior Dr. Debra Meyerson,[6] it is often used in quick-starting groups or teams that lack the time necessary to develop trust the way that would normally occur in longer-term relationships (here meaning any relationship between individuals, not specifically or at all limited to romantic relationships). Because time is limited, teams members will initially assume trustworthiness and then verify and adjust that trust later based on others' actions.

Self-disclosure

Research has shown (*http://bit.ly/trust-self-disclosure*) for some time that self-disclosure is one of the hallmarks of trusting relationships. Being open enough to share things about ourselves can increase feelings of trust and intimacy between people, as well as increase cooperative and collaborative attitudes. Of course, there is a balance that we must achieve when practicing self-disclosure in the workplace. Not enough disclosure, and suspicions may grow; people may wonder what someone is hiding and if they can be trusted. But too much or the wrong kind of disclosure, including inappropriate admissions or a real or perceived betrayal of someone else's confidence, can damage trust and credibility as well.

Trust but verify

The trust-but-verify model, typically used to describe sources of information that are generally reliable but additional research is merited to verify their accuracy, can also be used when you are dealing with sharing professional responsibilities. Someone who waits until trust has already been "earned" before doing something like sharing access to a project they've been working on might find themselves with a chicken-and-egg problem: how can someone earn trust if they're not given opportunities to earn that trust because they aren't yet trusted? Instead, people should be encouraged to share responsibilities with trust given first and followed up by verification. This is also true for sharing power and decision-making ability in addition to things like project work and responsibilities.

---

6 Debra Meyerson, Karl E. Weick, and Roderick M. Kramer, *Swift Trust and Temporary Groups* (Thousand Oaks, CA: Sage Publications, 1996).

Perception of fairness

Trust plays a role in the human side of growing an organization in addition to the technical one. The perception of fairness is very important to employee satisfaction, meaning employees need to be able to trust that they are being treated fairly. One thing that can help in this regard is developing formalized roles, job levels, and pay scales, as well as providing a reasonable amount of transparency in these areas. This can help people to understand the requirements of their role or the processes for pay increases and promotions, which in turn can notably decrease feelings that can threaten trust, such as feeling unfairly overlooked for a promotion.

Sharing risks in addition to sharing responsibilities and resources is key as well. If two teams are sharing work or resources on a project, but only one of them will be negatively impacted if something goes wrong with it, the team with the risk might be distrustful of the team without. In addition, this can lead to a power differential in favor of the team without (or with less) risk and the problems associated with that.

Humane Staffing and Resources

One final consideration we'll discuss with regards to collaboration is the cost to individuals of building and maintaining software that is often expected to be available 24/7/365. A driving factor of devops was the adverse effects that then-current software development practices had on those operating the software or servers it ran on. Practices such as continuous integration and infrastructure as code have improved this, but there are still other considerations.

Availability and Maintenance

When we run websites that our users expect to always be available, the question of when to perform maintenance that requires any kind of downtime or will impact even a subset of services often comes up. From a strictly user-facing perspective, it would make sense to perform maintenance at a time that would impact the fewest users, so a company in the United States whose highest traffic times are during US daytime hours might want to perform maintenance during the US late night or early morning, but that wouldn't necessarily be the case for a company with a primary user base in Asia.

However, that might not be ideal from the perspective of those performing the maintenance. This is not simply a matter of people being unwilling to stay up late or get up early; it's a matter of how alert, responsive, and effective people can be if they aren't sufficiently rested. From an operator's point of view, they should be doing critical maintenance operations when they are most alert and awake. If that strictly isn't possible based on the needs of the users, such as if a maintenance task would take too long and the financial losses would be too great, there are still ways to mitigate the costs to the maintainers.

Employees should be compensated fairly for the off-hours work they have to do. If it is expected as a regular part of their work, that expectation should be made clear in the job description so people can assess whether the position is the right fit for them. Allow and encourage people to take care of themselves and their health—for example, by having them take off the day after they perform late-night maintenance. Make sure that, if at all possible, maintenance tasks are spread out enough or the team is large enough that people have sufficient time to recover between these off-hours shifts. Depending on your circumstances, covering transportation or meal costs for these events would do well too. If job roles change and someone ends up getting off-hours work added to their responsibilities, their compensation should be adjusted to match.

Work–Life Balance

It's important to keep work-life balance in mind when planning your headcount for the upcoming year. Capacity planning is just as important for people as it is for servers. If people on your teams will be required to *regularly* work evenings and weekends in addition to weekdays in order to meet expectations, that is a recipe for poor work, poor morale, and burnout. Devops is about creating sustainable work practices, and how individuals are expected to approach their work–life balance is a key part of that.

While many jobs in operations-related fields have traditionally required this kind of off-hours work—either maintenance, on-call, or nonstandard shifts to provide 24/7 coverage—it is important to keep in mind that these kinds of requirements can be unintentionally biased against people with any substantial responsibilities outside of work. Young, single people without children (or high-maintenance pets) will find it much easier to devote their off hours to work than people with partners, children, or other family responsibilities. People with longer commutes or health considerations will also be more adversely impacted by these kinds of requirements. Part of growing and maintaining a diverse and inclusive team requires taking these things into account and considering how your job requirements can be adjusted to be more inclusive.

Team Size Considerations

Having people responsible for rapid responses to alerts and incidents, either by participating in an on-call pager rotation or having multiple shifts of people working throughout the day, is another consideration. This is one area where larger companies often have it much easier—a larger company is more likely to have multiple teams in different global offices, making a follow-the-sun rotation relatively straightforward to implement.

In this kind of setup, multiple teams (often three) that are distributed around the world will each work during their normal daytime working hours, being physically far enough apart that the end of one shift will coincide with the beginning of the next shift's hours. This enables the teams to collectively provide around-the-clock coverage but without requiring people to work during their local nights.

Even a mid-sized company is likely to have a full team of operations engineers or system administrators who can participate in an on-call rotation, but at smaller or younger companies, this is unlikely to be the case. While you might not think you have enough operations work for a full operations team, you should avoid having only one person be responsible for on-call. This will likely mean sharing on-call responsibilities among as many people as necessary to give individuals a chance to recover and catch up on sleep.

 Even in the short term, sleep deprivation can lead to difficulty concentrating or performing well, irritability or anxiety, and an increased risk of high blood pressure or heart attack—and these effects compound when sleep deprivation is sustained long-term.

Health in general, and burnout specifically, are very real considerations in understanding the overall health of your organization. Prioritizing the short-term financial or material gains for your company over the long-term health of the people within it will lead to long-term losses.

Effective Collaboration with Sparkle Corp

Quickly reviewing the notes from the MongoDB and MySQL discussions, the General noticed that not everyone had voiced an opinion one way or another on MongoDB. Additionally, she didn't have enough information to endorse a specific strategy. "Alice, I'd like to see you pair with Geordie to learn about the features and benefits of MongoDB or continued use of MySQL. Perhaps you both could demo something simple during our weekly demos this week? We'll revisit this discussion next week before continuing implementation of a specific solution. If anyone has anything else to add, please email the team," said the General.

That afternoon, Josie finished up an email to the team. After taking some time contemplating her availability and current projects, she recognized that she had time to provide some support for the project:

I have had previous experience with MongoDB. For use cases without complex transactions, it is really quick to develop and use. I think the reviews service fits this scenario based on our current understanding of the project. I feel that we should sync up with the PM to make sure we have a comprehensive understanding of expectations. We should also include the operations team so that they can provide us feedback about the costs of managing the software. I have some availability to provide subject matter expertise as needed.

Josie generally felt more comfortable composing her thoughts offline and sharing them in a written format such as email, like many introverts do, but she cc'd the rest of the team so they would know what her plans were as well. Embracing Sparkle Corp's "reply-all" culture, Alice and Geordie both chimed in to this discussion, with Alice adding the ops team to the email thread.

Summary

Ultimately, a large part of what makes a devops initiative successful is getting people to work together more effectively than they were previously. There are several different ways in which people can work, especially when their working styles and priorities differ, but getting to a point where people are collaborating is key to getting the most out of them. Much of what is involved in getting to the shared goals and empathy of a collaborative culture is communication, a very necessary skill for any organization that wants to level up their performance.

The relationships between individual members are a large part of what binds these communities together and makes them so beneficial, and these relationships require trust, empathy, and reciprocity. Effective communities are seen much less frequently where there are strict hierarchies in place between members; while individuals can and will have varying levels of knowledge and experiences, the underlying assumption is that everyone has something they can contribute to the company as a whole.

While this might seem counterintuitive for people who have an impression of devops being very heavily technology focused, recall that the original goal was to get two different teams of people talking to each other—devopsdays began as a way to start this dialog, which continues to evolve today. In Part III, we'll expand these ideas beyond individuals to teams and, eventually, organizations.

CHAPTER 8

Collaboration: Misconceptions and Troubleshooting

Problems arise in collaborating effectively when people have differences in professional and individual backgrounds that create friction if not handled. Being able to help people identify, shape, and actively work toward their different motivations and goals is a big part of being able to lead people, either in an official capacity as a manager or in any individual contributor-level leadership position.

We recommend that anyone in this kind of leadership role, especially new managers who moved into management from engineering (management is a career change, not a promotion) take regular action to improve and maintain their management skills. These are skills just like any other that need education, training, and practice to be maximized. A great leader is one who can bring out the best in the people around them, rather than just focusing on themselves or a few "rock stars," and these skills can make the difference between an effective organization and an ineffective one.

Collaboration Misconceptions

Many misconceptions around collaboration ultimately have to do with concerns about how much people are willing or able to learn and grow within their roles or in the organization in general.

You Can't Teach an Old Sysadmin New Tricks

One common misconception about collaboration skills is that people who have traditionally been very siloed off, such as the BOFH (Bastard Operator From Hell, a caricature of a grouchy system administrator referenced in Chapter 3), won't be able to learn to collaborate in a more open or cross-functional environment. The flip side of this is a fear from practitioners, such as veteran system administrators with more "old-school" UNIX backgrounds, that they have to become a developer in order to hold onto their job. Either way, there are often misgivings about what new skills might be required in a collaborative devops environment.

The reality is that new skills absolutely *can* be learned, whether those be new techniques or technologies or more "soft" skills like how to become a mentor or empathize with other people in your organization. It's important to keep in mind, however, that learning new skills takes time and effort; you cannot expect it to happen for free. If you are a manager looking to grow and develop people on your team, provide them with the necessary time and resources (whether that be a budget for books, the option to go to conferences, or in-house training opportunities) and don't expect it to happen overnight.

 New skills require time and practice for everyone. Don't assume that anyone older than you, different from you, or with a different background from yours is incapable of learning.

If you're on the other side of things wondering if your skill set is soon to become obsolete, keep in mind that even with the advent of new cloud-based technologies and containerization everywhere, employers are still looking for a wide range of skill sets. The key is finding a team or position that is the right fit. An early-stage startup trying to get their product off the ground and hosting everything in Amazon's EC2 until they get to that point probably won't have a place for a dedicated UNIX administrator or network engineer, but a bigger, more established company that has its own data centers absolutely will, and despite the hype, larger companies and data centers are not going to disappear any time soon.

You Need to Hire Rock Stars When You're Trying to Grow Quickly

Many startup cofounders, when trying to grow their fledgling companies, place an incredibly high emphasis on raw coding skills. They are trying to get their product built as quickly as possible, to get the user base or funding they need to keep growing their companies. Pure technical talent, however, is far from the only consideration, because if your company takes off, you will have to grow your team along with it. These organizations think that they have to "settle" in terms of the people they hire because they might not have the budget to compete with bigger, more established companies in terms of luring people to them with high salaries, or they might think that hiring an asshole with major coding chops will be worth it in order to get their product out the door.

The problem with this thinking is that it is too focused on the short term; your early employees will set the tone of the company whether you intend for that to happen or not. If these people are too difficult to work with, either you won't be able to hire the people you need at all, or you will end up only being able to hire and retain more difficult people. While it is true that old habits can be broken and new skills can be learned, too often we've seen teams become more and more homogeneous as egocentric engineers, poor communicators, or rude interrupters flock to places where these behaviors are tolerated or even encouraged in the name of the code or the product. In the long term, such a hostile culture, antithetical to the trust, respect, and reciprocity previously described, will not scale.

A Diverse Team Can't Collaborate as Effectively

A concern that frequently arises around increasing a team's or a company's diversity is that it will lead to increased levels of interpersonal conflict. Some people mention concerns around things like "political correctness," worrying that if they increase diversity, their employees will have to stop making jokes. To the first point, while studies have shown that more diverse teams will often see more conflict *in the short term*, these effects are balanced out not only by the fact that the creativity and problem-solving benefits *in the long term* outweigh these costs, but also by the fact that team members will learn collaborate and work well with a wider variety of people.

On top of that, jokes that can be told only in a very homogeneous environment are probably racist, sexist, or problematic in some other way that would make them unsuited for a workplace in general. Certainly, the entertainment that a few get from off-color humor isn't worth the cost to creativity and innovation that a hostile, disrespectful environment causes.

Collaboration Troubleshooting

Dealing with issues between individuals can certainly be tricky; navigating these kinds of conflicts and difficulties is part of what gave rise to the idea of devops in the first place.

Some People on the Team Aren't Pulling Their Weight

One common issue that comes up when working with people on teams is the perception that some team members aren't pulling their weight, are not following through on their assignments and responsibilities, or even are causing issues that other people must take time to help with. This can come up if other people on the team mention it, if the person in question realizes that they don't feel up to the same level as the people around them, or if their manager notices some other way.

The first step toward resolution is clarifying roles and responsibilities. If someone's role is sufficiently vague, or if their actual responsibilities have changed over time in response to an evolving work environment, there could be a relatively simple disconnect or miscommunication regarding what is expected of them. Once these expectations have been clarified, they should be assessed for how realistic they are: does the individual have the knowledge and resources necessary to complete their goals? If more training or education is needed, it should be provided and the employee should be given time to incorporate their learnings. If someone doesn't have the time or workplace resources required to get everything done, that should be addressed as well. Comparing workloads between different employees at similar levels with similar roles can often reveal if work needs to be rebalanced.

Expectations of a Role

When it comes to work, a role is a function composed of a particular set of repeated tasks. There are specific expectations based on the culture of the team, organization, and industry of what a role entails. For example, manager, architect, lead, and project manager all have connotations within a culture that influence and affect people's perception of competence. If someone is an architect, some organizations might not expect them to concern themselves with code, but not every organization defines an architect role in this way. When joining a new team, it is critical to understand individuals' expectations of the role within the culture. Over time, within the same team and organization, role expectations may vary.

If reports that someone isn't performing well come from people other than the individual concerned, such as teammates or managers, work should be undertaken to figure out how accurate these statements are. This is an area where unconscious biases can sometimes sneak in, coloring our views of people in ways we might not expect. This is where having clearly defined, specific, and measurable expectations can go a long way.

In addition to these more contextual reasons, there are personal reasons why someone might not be producing work of the quality or quantity that is expected, such as:

- individual or family health;
- lack of autonomy;
- lack of rewards;
- mismatch in job and expectations on joining a team;
- rapidly changing goals; or
- changing work.

A good manager should make sure employees have appropriate resources to help accommodate these challenges. Solutions may include:

- working remotely;
- flexible scheduling;
- reevaluation of tasks and division of labor;
- training;
- mentorship;
- public acknowledgment; or
- regular one-on-ones with coaching as needed.

Keep an eye out for burnout—employees' physical and mental health are important. Burnout is not solely an individual problem. It's a symptom of a problem within the working environment.

We Need to Decide If We Should Let Someone Go

An issue similar to that of poor performance is deciding when someone is no longer a good fit for the position they are in. As much as we believe that people can and most often want to improve, there are exceptions as well as situations or circumstances that are misaligned enough to not work out anymore. If the issue seems to be one of skill mismatch and at least one training or improvement plan has been tried, make sure that it has been given enough time to work (anything less than a month is likely insufficient, and depending on the training or improvement necessary closer to six months might be in order). If a training only caters to one learning style, a mismatch there would noticeably slow progress.

When creating a development plan, making sure that there is sufficient mentorship available can improve the odds of success. A good mentor, especially one with experience helping others with their career development, can do a great deal to ensure there aren't any persistent roadblocks getting in the way. If you know that your organization lacks the financial or personnel resources to genuinely help develop and train employees, that should be made very clear to the people affected so that they can make an informed decision about how to proceed.

The decision to part ways with an employee isn't necessarily a negative thing. Alignment of goals, values, and priorities is very important, and it's becoming increasingly so to newer generations of employees who have different personal goals and incentives that motivate their professional patterns of behavior. Additionally, goals and priorities can and often do change over time. Regular check-ins with employees, either in feedback sessions from managers or with peer mentors, can detect these changes and potential misalignments early so that if a change in direction makes sense, it can be started sooner rather than later.

Some misalignments don't make sense to try to overcome, however. If someone knows that they are incredibly unhappy working at a large company, if the company grows to that size it's better for everyone to acknowledge that disconnect and allow the employee to leave soon and on good terms rather than trying to force an issue that is unlikely to be resolved any other way. As another example, if a startup gets acquired by a company that then changes the product direction rather radically, you can expect that at least some employees will disagree with the new direction, and it's perfectly fine to not try to force that as well.

Culture Fit and Bias

One final thing to keep in mind is that while the preceding scenarios are good examples of a genuine misalignment or improper fit, the idea of "culture fit" should be carefully scrutinized for conscious and unconscious bias. Culture fit should not mean homogeneity, nor should it mean being exclusive of any differing points of view.

I'm Overworked, Stressed, and Burnt Out

If you are experiencing symptoms of burnout, including anxiety, exhaustion, and decreased satisfaction not only with your job but with yourself, it is important to address the underlying issues sooner rather than later. This is usually not a scenario that will work itself out on its own; rather, you will have to take action.

Short-term strategies

In the short term, find as many ways as possible to give yourself support and space to recharge:

- Take time off where you aren't checking work email or chat.
- Delegate or say "no" to work.
- Reach out to a professional for help—mental health is just as important as physical health.

Longer-term strategies

It can also help to take an inventory of all the responsibilities you have:

- For each one, try to assess if there is anything you can take action on to decrease the stress from that responsibility.

- When you're getting burnt out, it may manifest itself as a more general stress or malaise, so figure out if there is something in particular that is contributing more to your stress and anxiety than you realize.

Identify the single points of responsibility

One thing of note that often causes additional stress is feeling that there is something that is solely your responsibility. You might be the only person working on a given project, a member of a one-person team, or the only person who is interested in making changes to improve organizational culture. Whatever the situation, this can increase the stress and isolation that are part of feeling burnt out. We can't know every specific situation, but we can say that no project, job, or company is worth sacrificing your health for.

 Feelings of stress and burnout can happen any time, but they often become more common around the inflection points of an organization. Being overworked, especially if multiple people on the same team are feeling the same way, can be a sign that an organization is taking on more than it can handle with its current personnel and needs to start hiring more. Talk with the people around you to see if overwork is a common theme that needs to be addressed more broadly.

Finally, take a look at factors in your work environment that might be contributing to stress. If you find yourself swearing at a particular tool quite frequently, it might be worthwhile to see if you can make some improvements to that tool or the workflow around it, or even if you can replace it with something else. The same thing goes for various processes you find yourself using. Talk to team members to see if they have any workarounds or tricks up their sleeves, and keep in mind that this is an area where looking outside your organization for ideas can go a long way.

Some People on the Team Are Feeling Disrespected

Even if you are doing as much as you can to create a diverse workplace rather than a homogeneous one, you might find that some people on your team aren't feeling respected or even safe. Someone might feel that they are being constantly interrupted or that their ideas are not being listened to—for example, studies have shown that women tend to get interrupted more in the workplace than men do, and that their suggestions are given less weight than the same ones made by male colleagues.

These are very real problems that can arise as you work toward building a diverse team, and resources should be provided in support of that goal. Make sure, again, that training and education around general diversity issues—including sensitivity, ally skills and behaviors, and unconscious biases—are encouraged (if not required) for employees and especially managers. Lead by example, from the top down. Also provide as much support as you can to employees who are members of underrepresented groups; this could take the form of company-funded support or social groups or making sure that employees know who their legal and HR contacts are. Startups should formalize an HR department as soon as possible.

Detailed negotiation techniques for when issues do arise are beyond the scope of this book, but overall, be diligent with your listening skills, even (especially) if what you hear is uncomfortable or unexpected. Nobody wants to hear that their colleagues or friends might be harassing someone or displaying other problematic behavior, but given the well-documented risks that people take when speaking up, the rates of false accusations are tiny compared to rates of unreported harassment or abuse.

Be very aware that the resolution you arrive at for these kinds of issues will have a very real impact on the culture of your organization. If someone who has been harassing others is allowed to continue working without any kind of consequences for their actions, that sends a clear message to members of marginalized groups that they are not safe at your company. If reports of feeling disrespected or harassed are dismissed without being fully heard, people will not feel safe, creating an atmosphere where any future issues likely won't get discovered until it's too late.

 A toxic culture is much easier to prevent than it is to repair once trust has been broken, and as we've discussed throughout this chapter and the previous chapter, trust is key to an empathetic and collaborative environment.

Some People Aren't Communicating Enough

When you are trying to break down or prevent silos, a common complaint is that people aren't communicating enough, either within their own teams or across them. Assuming that clear expectations have been set and explained, the best option in these cases is to try to assess the underlying factors that might be affecting people's willingness to communicate, similar to what was discussed in "How We Communicate" on page 87.

If individual people don't seem very willing to communicate, there might be issues of trust at work. This is commonly seen in a culture that used to be very blameful, taking the old view of failure and looking to fire or otherwise punish people for incidents. Over time, people are likely to grow (understandably) fearful of speaking out and may hesitate to provide any more information than the bare minimum. This sort of cultural shift will take time, and people will have to see that speaking up is rewarded rather than punished. Leading by example by facilitating public, blameless postmortems within your organization can work well.

There might also be issues where some individuals respond in ways that feel disrespectful to others, whether or not they were intended that way. Emails and other text-only communication can often come across as brusque or condescending due to difficulties of conveying tone via text communications. Alternatively, you might have a team member who is actively disrespectful to others, generally being unpleasant or outright hostile to others—but maybe not to all others, or in all situations, so this kind of issue might not be apparent to everyone. Someone who will not communicate respectfully might end up being a cultural mismatch with your organization.

Finally, a variety of cultural and personal differences might come into play. On international teams, different cultural customs might make some people seem more reticent or terse when that is simply the most accepted or polite manner of communication for them. Different working styles or personalities can affect this as well, so some people might be more reserved in general, such as not speaking up about their work or accomplishments for fear of sounding like a braggart, while others might prefer a different communication medium than the rest of their team. Giving people opportunities to explain their preferences and letting teams discuss potential happy mediums when those preferences differ can go a long way here.

An Employee (or Candidate) Is Technically Brilliant, but Also a Jerk

Everyone wants to avoid making a bad hiring decision, which is why we put so much effort into our screening and interviewing processes. But sometimes, people will go to great lengths to justify why a bad hire is supposedly necessary, and one common example is the "brilliant but antisocial" engineer. The reasoning that people give is that someone's technical contributions are so good that they outweigh the negative impacts of their interpersonal behavior. A prime example is Linus Torvalds, whose abrasive tirades are tolerated because he created Linux.

We mentioned previously that you do not need to be best friends with all of your coworkers, but you do need to consider the impact that negative behavior can have. This impact is not always easy to measure, but here are some questions you should ask if you ever find yourself making this sort of decision.

- How many people will quit (or choose not to even apply to work for your organization in the first place) because they cannot stand working with this individual?

- How many other people's productivity is being negatively impacted due to arguments with this person or other negative repercussions of their behavior? Keep in mind that "grow a thicker skin" is not an acceptable reaction to this; nobody should be expected to tolerate working in an abusive environment, and just because you didn't personally witness a problematic interaction does not mean it didn't take place.

- If this person's behavior tends to impact women, people of color, or other members of underrepresented groups, how much harm is being done to inclusivity and diversity within your organization? Back channels for communication exist, and word will get around if this person's problematic behavior goes undeterred by management.

- How many hours will be wasted debugging this person's code that they refused to document, or dealing with the fallout of commits that they pushed without following the organization's testing process?

In many cases, the harm that these sorts of people end up doing to an organization, both technically and culturally, does not end up being "worth it," especially if the organization gains a reputation in the industry for tolerating (or even encouraging) this kind of problematic behavior. In general, if faced with a hiring decision where people are saying, "Well, he's kind of an asshole, but…," just skip the "but" and focus on finding candidates who won't detract from your organization.

I Don't Feel Like My Career Is Progressing Within My Current Team/Organization

When we consider our own individual stories, the progression and trajectory of our careers are often some of the most important things that come to mind. At some point, you may start to feel that you are unable to progress any further where you currently are. In some circumstances, this can be a matter of making sure that people are aware of your accomplishments—perhaps you have met all the criteria necessary for a promotion, but you don't want to seem like you're bragging so you keep your work to yourself, so managers aren't aware of all that you've done.

In other cases, there can be issues of conscious and unconscious bias in play. For example, an organization might use "the other engineers at level X agree this person is ready to be promoted" as a big part of the promotion process, but if the group of engineers at level X is very homogeneous (such as all white people or all men), they might end up unconsciously steering more promotions toward people who look like them. If you can work with HR to determine if there is a difference in the rates of promotion between different groups of people, factoring in experience, you may be able to help address this at an organizational level—though this is, of course, a longer-term gain rather than a shorter-term one.

Keep in mind the difference between *mentoring* and *sponsoring*. Much has been written elsewhere about this topic, and Cate Huston, director of mobile engineering at Ride, put it best (*http://bit.ly/huston-allies*) when she said that sponsorship is about having power, and using it to advocate for people with less power. While mentors provide advice and guidance *to* you, sponsors are people who will go to bat *for* you, and it may be that finding a good sponsor to advocate on your behalf can help get you some much-needed traction.

However, if you've considered these options and find yourself thinking things like "the organization/manager is playing favorites against me" and you're not a member of a marginalized group, you may need to consider that there is some requirement, either explicit or implicit, that you aren't meeting. This is not to say that straight white men can't be treated unfairly, but it is also possible that there is some problem with your own behavior that needs to be identified and addressed. It can be tempting and even comforting to blame other people or the system rather than admit that you are at fault or lacking in some way, but introspection and honest self-evaluation are some of the hallmarks of mature engineers.

Take a step back and consider how your own behavior may be impacting others, intentionally or not, and how that behavior aligns with your organization's values. If your organization has stated that empathy is a core competency, or that they have a "no assholes" rule, if you are known for being unpleasant to work with, that can stand in your way as much as any technical shortcoming, if not more.

In many cases, more senior engineering positions emphasize not just technical merit but also people skills—being helpful; sponsoring; mentoring; and allying with others; handling conflict well—and it is well worth everyone's while to make sure they are focusing on these aspects of their performance as well.

Nobody Listens to Me (Anymore)

In larger organizations, as opposed to smaller startups where you can just march into the CEO's office and talk to her directly if you have a problem, it can be easy to feel like you are just a cog in a giant machine and that your voice isn't being heard. This can also be the case if you've been at a company during a growth phase or event—perhaps your department has grown so large that people don't seem to have the same amount of influence they did before, maybe you have a new manager, or maybe even a merger or acquisition has had some noticeable impacts on the culture.

How you choose to proceed will vary based on how much or how little support you are getting from your direct manager. If you are getting a good amount of support from your manager, ask them if they have any advice on how you might have more impact within your team or organization. Especially if you are a more junior employee or new to this particular team or organization, you might find that changes to your working or communication styles can go a long way, and finding a mentor within the organization can help you develop these skills.

If a particular individual or team isn't listening to you, there may be some interpersonal conflicts that have to be dealt with. While it might just be that there are some people you work with whom you don't get along well with, there might also be reactions to a past conflict or event that need to be resolved. We are all human beings, and sometimes we have feelings that impact how well we work with others. If you were unintentionally rude to someone with a request, or missed a deliverable that you had promised, there might be lingering resentments that need to be aired out and cleared up. It's not always easy to admit that you made a mistake, but keep an eye out for how your own behaviors might be impacting your working relationships.

If your direct manager doesn't seem to listen to or respect you, try speaking with them directly first, as it's possible they might not be aware of this. You may also need to bring in their manager or an HR representative to help deal with this. Newer managers especially might not have experience dealing with an increasing number of reports, so management training or a team reorganization might help with that. But if none of these seem to help and your own manager or team still isn't listening, consider that you might be in a hostile or even unhealthy environment, and might be served best by looking for a new position, either within your current organization or somewhere else.

We Just Had a Reorganization or Staff Reduction

The reduction phase of an organization's lifecycle is a natural phase where leadership may reduce product lines or staff count. Depending on the culture of your environment, this may be intensely stressful and scary especially if you haven't experienced one before.

Ask yourself these questions:

Do you know why the reorganization or staff reduction is happening?
 If leadership clearly communicates the reasons for the change, you don't have to fill in the blanks with missing information. Ask this question of your leadership if you don't know the reason. Note that this doesn't mean that you have to or even will agree with the stated reason for the change. Sometimes leadership makes

mistakes. Failure is a learning opportunity; monitor for continued failure that can indicate a bigger problem.

How was the reorganization or staff reduction communicated? Was it timely?

If leadership has taken the time to communicate to everyone in a timely fashion without months of buildup or leaks into the press, you have time to process before everyone in your life is asking you questions. This indicates that the leadership is showing care and concern for the process.

Has your job fundamentally changed? Do you report to the same manager, or have you experienced a decrease or increase in job responsibility, level of job challenge, or autonomy in decisions?

If your job is effectively the same and you're just moving from one name to another, this is a no-op event. Take time to understand why the reorganization or staff reduction is happening, and who it does impact. These are signals about what the company values. If your job has fundamentally changed, make sure to look at your position from the perspective of an interviewing candidate who needs to evaluate the offer before joining a company. Are you being undervalued? Will this change stifle your learning or experience? Do you get along with the new manager?

Have you experienced more than one reorganization in the last 12 months? Companies regularly have a reduction phase in their lifecycle.

If this is the first in a while, this may just be a natural evolution of leadership changing. It's healthy for new perspectives to take ownership of a part of the organization. It minimizes risks to the organization by reducing fragility. If you have experienced multiple reorgs, dig into the causes a little deeper. Did the original reorganization or staff reduction complete, or is this just a long, lingering execution? Leadership will make mistakes that sometimes require a period of shuffling. Take a look at the impact to your health and the value of the job. Does the opportunity it affords you outweigh the personal costs to you?

Is your team underresourced?

If your team has enough people after the reorganization or staff reduction to do the job without a change in cognitive load, this is again a no-op. Take time to understand who was impacted within the organization and understand what is being signaled. If your team doesn't have enough people, and you are constantly firefighting without respite, your skills are atrophying. Being a great firefighter looks great from the inside, but from the outside it looks like a bunch of excuses for not improving.

Based on the answers to these questions you can determine whether the reorganization or staff reduction aligns with your understanding of the culture. At the end of the day, you need to make a deliberate choice about where you work and why. Don't stay somewhere because of a large payout, known as "golden handcuffs" in the industry. Staying for money comes at the cost of your continued health due to increased stress, and you may decide that ultimately, that's not a trade-off you're willing to make anymore.

Remember, you have the option of quitting your job. Not every team or organization is the right fit for every individual. Not everyone is going to care about devops or share your values in other areas, and sometimes the best thing for everyone involved is to find a place that is the right fit.

PART III

Affinity

CHAPTER 9

Affinity: From Individuals to Teams

From job descriptions to performance reviews, many people focus on success only within a single team. Between teams, organizational units, and even companies, however, there exist relationships that impact the speed and value of work. Mark Granovetter, an American sociologist, described the importance of these relationships, the combination of strong and weak links between individuals and the way that information flows over these various links in his 1973 paper, "The Strength of Weak Ties."[1]

Sparkle Corp Development Demo Day

With Josie's past experience with MongoDB, she was able to help Alice and Geordie quickly bring up a couple of virtual machines they will use for comparing and demoing both MongoDB and MySQL. They created a demo of a simple web-based photo application with a star rating feature.

Hedwig, the project manager, and George, the operations engineer, joined the development team's weekly demo meeting to see the progress the team was making as well as to examine the differences between the two products as they manifest in a more real-world scenario.

"I really liked how quickly it was to develop the application with MongoDB. A lot of the features that we've talked about with the review platform already exist in this JavaScript framework, which works seamlessly with MongoDB. That would give us the development time that we want to spend on working on preventing harassment and detecting bullying behavior in the reviews," enthused Alice.

---

1 Mark Granovetter, "The Strength of Weak Ties." *American Journal of Sociology* (May 6, 1973).

"I realized that there is a lot of effort and tooling in place to architect and plan the desired topology structure as well as upgrade and monitor MySQL. Alice really helped me see what benefits we will have to revisit for MongoDB in coordination with the operations team," commented Geordie.

At this point, the Sparkle Corp development team could decide to stick with MySQL. They could investigate with the operations team to understand more about the cost of introducing the new software. They could also pass over the decision to Hedwig, the project manager, who understands the scope of expectations coming from customers. Let's dig into how building affinity can strengthen our organization and help us make crucial decisions.

People Networks

Granovetter described three different kinds of interpersonal ties: strong, weak, and absent, where the strength of a tie is a combination of time, emotional intensity, intimacy, and reciprocity of each tie. He noted that while a combination of strong and weak ties is what binds society as a whole, the weak ties play a much larger role in sharing resources and information than was previously thought. For example, when he interviewed people who were searching for jobs, well over half the participants who found a job through someone they knew had made use of a weak tie, someone they described as an acquaintance rather than a friend and saw less often than twice a week, rather than a strong tie.

In our work lives, we have strong ties with our immediate teams—the people that we work with day in and day out, the people we share office space and coffee with. People outside of these close circles tend to be either weak or absent ties. As Granovetter and later other researchers and sociologists have shown, we can gain a great deal by cultivating the weak ties that we already have, whether with people on other teams at our own company that we rarely interact with, or people in our own fields working at other companies. This chapter will look at how teams function and interact as well as how we can use these ties to make our work relationships even stronger.

What Makes a Team?

Why are there some individuals that seem to work counter to team or organizational goals? To understand this we must understand not only what constitutes a team but also how individuals relate to and identify with the teams they are on.

A team is a group of people working toward a common goal, interdependent with each other, with some familiarity among members. Teams hold a set of convictions expressed by the majority of the participants. Additionally, they have internal and external forces acting upon them that establish and maintain the group identity.

The Work That Teams Do

Work is often broken down into five categories:[2]

Reactionary
> Work that happens in response to something else (such as responding to emails or incoming tickets) rather than proactively

Planning
> Putting effort into scheduling and prioritizing of other work

Procedural
> Maintenance work such as following up on previously sent emails or filling out expense reports

Insecurity
> Work that we do in response to our own insecurities such as checking our personal or organizational reputations online

Problem solving
> Work that requires creativity and focus

Defining Affinity

There is a sixth category of work, called relationship work. Relationship work is a social catalyst, facilitating work so as to shorten the time to get other work done, reducing communication barriers, and building trust based on regard. Affinity is the measure of the relationship strength between individuals, teams, business units, and even companies. It is incredibly hard to measure accurately.

Regardless of organizational structure, companies will often assign a value to roles, creating a ladder of prestige. Individuals will perceive one role as more valuable than another, creating a hierarchy of importance. This hierarchy can be reinforced by company culture based on who receives bonuses, promotions, or other desired outcomes. This ladder can create a false sense of upward motility based on changing roles, encouraging individuals to pursue jobs that they may not be as well suited for or not enjoy as much.

Companies often have multiple teams that need to work together. As companies start to depend on external services, teams need to work with other companies to accomplish goals. Understanding who has the knowledge or skills required and building strong relationships with these different teams, organizations, and companies is affinity. This chapter will look into the human factors that can make or break positive

---

2 Scott Belsky, "The 5 Types of Work that Fill Your Day," *http://bit.ly/5-types-of-work*.

interteam cooperation, discuss strategies for effective cooperation, and examine how these factors can help maintain the devops compact at an organizational level.

Interpersonal Ties Within Teams

Internal forces include a tension between stability and change. Individuals within a group may favor stability through a quest for immutable truths or "best practices." Our tendencies toward stability can work to make a team or a group more cohesive, and natural conflict avoidance may lead people within a team to agree with each other more than they might otherwise. This, of course, has its upsides as well as downsides. A team with too much conflict might not have enough internal stability to accomplish its goals, but too much conflict avoidance leads to a homogeneity of thought that reduces creativity and problem-solving skills.

The external forces that bring teams together tend to be situational. Conflict with another group, such as competition for shared resources, will bind and strengthen team identity, as individual identities and successes are often aligned with the success and identity of the team. Externally imposed goals or deadlines can have a similar effect, as can something that threatens the team's stability or even existence—though it should be noted that while some external circumstances and conflicts can bring some teams together, groups that lack enough initial cohesion and stability or have a great deal of conflict already are unlikely to survive in their original form.

As discussed earlier, the strength of interpersonal ties can be measured by several factors:

Shared time
Simply spending time working together can help to strengthen workplace relationships.

The intensity of the relationship
Overcoming challenges and resolving the conflicts, especially in intense experiences such as resolving a production outage, can bring people together.

Reciprocity of shared stories
Opening up and sharing both personal wins and adversity is a great way to get to know each other.

Reciprocity of support
Taking on-call over holidays, covering a shift when a teammate is on vacation, or assisting someone with an issue they're working on are all great ways to support each other.

It is the combination of all four of these factors that truly makes a tie a strong one; simply spending a lot of time with someone is not enough to really foster a strong connection. A teammate who is always joking around or making sarcastic remarks, never opening up or saying something genuine, is not likely to be someone that we feel like we know or that we are close to, and someone who doesn't reciprocate support like covering an on-call shift or providing a code review isn't a teammate we feel we can count on when things get difficult.

This doesn't mean that people have to get incredibly personal or that we are expected to be best friends with our teammates both in and out of the workplace. Sharing stories doesn't necessarily mean talking about one's families or relationships, but could instead take the form of sharing something you struggled with earlier in your career, a difficult career choice you had to make, or a project that you've been wanting to work on.

Team Culture

The culture of a team can greatly impact the effectiveness of the team's work and the strength of the ties between team members. Rather than talking about culture in terms of "culture fit" and if your teammates are people you'd want to go grab a beer with, it is much more important to focus on culture as the *values* that a team shares and how those values are expressed in practice.

Shared values, when clearly communicated, can be a strong binding force among team members. Making sure that the team's values are understood can go a long way toward preventing or resolving interpersonal conflicts. For example, a conflict could arise between two members working together on a project with a rapidly approaching deadline. One might feel that they should go ahead and ship what they have despite it not being fully tested or feature-complete, as they value following through on promises and making deadlines, while the other might want to wait, valuing only shipping work that meets a certain standard of quality. Who is "right" in this sort of situation depends largely on which of these values the team overall has decided is more important.

It is important that the team's values not be in conflict with either overall organizational or company-wide values or with the individual values of team members. This is an area where the notion of "cultural fit" often arises. As we will discuss in Part V, this concept is not without its problems: it can too often be used to describe common activities, such as drinking beer or being fans of a certain sports team, rather than common goals and values.

When assessing whether or not someone's values are aligned with the team's, be sure to consider whether "values" and "fit" are being used accurately or instead as a way to keep the team more homogeneous.

Devops Anti-Patterns: Culture Fit

The General was working at a startup that was actively trying to hire more engineers. Because the company had been founded by several friends who had gone to college together some years prior, the office had a generally friendly atmosphere. Employees regularly went out for beers together after work, especially among the group of former classmates, who were known for drinking beer in the office together as well.

When candidates were brought in for interviews, if they did well enough on the technical interviews in the morning, the team would invite them out to lunch to see if they were a culture fit. Because of the growing vibe of "beer buddies" in the office, culture fit turned into a question of "Do I enjoy drinking with this person?" The General saw the team dismiss a couple highly of qualified candidates simply because they didn't order a beer with lunch. People decided that they weren't likely to fit in on the team for this reason.

While the most apparent moral of this story might be that if people can only fit in with your team if they are willing to be drunk at work, you probably have larger issues, there is also an important note here about what culture means. Instead of thinking about culture, you should think about *values*—what values are important to your organization and your team? Think of ways that those values might be demonstrated, regardless of a candidate's choice of beverage.

Values can be communicated in a variety of ways, but when it comes down to it, the primary way that people will learn what your team's values are comes down to the team's overall behavior. It matters more what you do than what you say—if you claim reliability as a value but routinely ship software that is late, bug-ridden, or both, people are going to focus more on those outcomes than what you say your values are. Or if an organization claims they value diversity and inclusivity but hires scantily clad women to dance at their official company events, people might rightly question just how dedicated to their values they really are.

This communication of values applies both within and outside a team. Being able to communicate your values outside of your team is critical in an environment where the work your team does or the services they provide interact in any way with the work of other teams. Make sure that other groups know what your values are, what standards you are setting, and what promises you are making about your work and behavior.

This will become apparent in the ways that people from other teams choose to interact—or not—with your own team members. If people are avoiding talking with team members because they have a reputation for being overly critical and difficult to work with, or working around or against your team's rules or systems because they get in the way of what others need to get done, what values are you demonstrating to the other teams in your organization?

Communicating values within the team helps the team to feel and act more unified, especially when onboarding new team members. A lack of consistency here— whether that be different values demonstrated by different team members, or a mismatch between the team's stated values and behavior—will make it more difficult for new members to get up to speed and learn how they should work and act, whether that be different values shown by different people that they are working with and learning from.

In addition to a lack of consistency, a lack of accountability can seriously damage other people's trust in your team as well as the trust between team members. How can people both within and outside the team communicate when they notice a problem or a breach of values? This is not to advocate a blameful environment at all. Rather, blame involves finding someone to pay the price for problems that occurred, while accountability involves ownership, follow-through, and learning.

A 2004 study showed that teams whose members shared values with each other and with their leader had a much higher degree of internal trust than those that didn't.[3] Trust, both between peer team members and toward the team leader, is strongly indicative of higher team and individual performance. The strong ties that this kind of trust engenders are one of the biggest competitive advantages a team or organization can have. In order to maintain a blameless, learning-focused environment, teams' values and culture must match.

Team Cohesion

Team cohesion is the degree to which individual members want to contribute to the group's ability to continue as a functioning work unit. A team with low cohesion tends to take on an "everyone out for themselves" kind of mentality, with team members acting out of self-interest rather than in the interests of the team as a whole. Needless to say, there is less trust, less knowledge sharing, and less empathy in less cohesive teams.

---

3 Nicole Gillespie and Leon Mann, "Transformational Leadership and Shared Values: The Building Blocks of Trust," *Journal of Managerial Psychology* 19, no. 6 (2004).

Other facets of team dynamics include team integration, or the extent to which a team combines individual expertise and work into a unified whole, as well as team solidarity, or the extent to which a team has common interests that bind them together. Team integration is especially valuable for productivity because it allows more knowledge to be shared among individuals, enabling people to work together more rather than keeping knowledge to themselves, and this synthesis of ideas can enable a team to become stronger and more productive than it is as just the sum of its individual members.

Solidarity can keep a team feeling motivated and feeling like a strong unit, but it is important that those feelings not be taken too far to the extreme. Social scientist William Graham Sumner popularized the term *ethnocentrism*,[4] which he described as "the technical name for [the] view of things in which one's own group is the center of everything." In the workplace, this can lead to hostility when teams perceive themselves as competing for scarce resources such as budget.

Ethnocentric attitudes can be observed in phrases that assign value judgments or stereotypes based on other teams. Examples of this are the external conflict seen in some organizations between "dev" and "ops," where problems are frequently thrown over the metaphorical wall and said to be someone else's responsibility, or where work done by other teams is frequently and loudly criticized. This can be observed between any teams within an organization, especially in organizations that subscribe to some form of role hierarchy.

In-group/out-group theory

The idea that external conflict can increase internal team cohesion has been around for decades. Often called the in-group/out-group theory, it is perhaps best explained by Sumner: "The relation of comradeship and peace in the we-group and that of hostility and war toward other-groups are correlative to each other. The exigencies of war with outsiders are what make peace inside."[5] Sociologist Georg Simmel has perhaps gone into the most depth on the topic, specifically in his 1898 article "The Persistence of Social Groups."[6]

Simmel's rule, as it became known, states that the "internal cohesion of a group is contingent on the strength of external pressure." This cohesion was stronger in smaller groups perhaps, as he noted, due to the tendency of smaller groups to have individuals that are more similar to each other. He believed that intergroup conflict

---

4 Boris Bizumic, "Who Coined the Term Ethnocentrism? A Brief Report," *Journal of Social and Political Psychology* 2, no. 1 (2014).

5 Richard D. Ashmore et al., *Social Identity, Intergroup Conflict, and Conflict Reduction* (Oxford, UK: Oxford University Press, 2001).

6 Georg Simmel, "The Persistence of Social Groups," *American Journal of Sociology* 3, no. 5 (1898).

---

accentuates and maintains group boundaries, drawing people together who might normally have nothing to do with each other—the enemy of my enemy is my friend.

A corollary to this rule is that different kinds of groups tend to emerge based on the perceived sources of these external pressures or conflicts. For example, developers might view operations engineers as the source of their problems when the issue might be unrealistic deadlines and expectations being set by upper management. In these cases, the perceived in-groups and out-groups tend to be very strong, indeed shaping the social environment.

When applied in a workplace environment, the intergroup conflict that arises between different groups or teams within the organization can lead to rival interests, with different groups seen as being in constant competition with each other. We want to help members of our own group, or team, at the expense of other groups, and group memberships can become very strong parts of our workplace identities. People tend to form attitudes that stigmatize the out-group members—one example being the "Bastard Operator from Hell" caricature of a system administrator who refers to any and all nontechnical computer users as "lusers," the implication being that they are also "losers." Naturally, these kinds of biases and intergroup conflicts don't lend themselves to a cohesive organization as a whole.

 One way of working against intergroup conflicts, or at least trying to minimize their effects, is by sharing experiences. Shared experiences across group boundaries reduce the risk of future conflict between groups. As mentioned earlier, sharing experiences is key to building trust, and working closely with someone even temporarily, even in what seems like an unrelated situation, can lessen the bias and other-ing that might normally otherwise occur. Exemplified at places like the devopsdays conferences, sharing stories is a big part of what allows people to develop more empathy with each other and thus work together more effectively.

Giving employees the opportunities and encouragement to participate in many different groups in the workplace can also go a long way toward minimizing out-group bias. Known as *crossed categorization*, having people with memberships in many different groups decreases the importance of any given in-group/out-group distinction; makes people aware that those they work with are multidimensional and multifaceted; and increases the interpersonal interactions, communication, and trust between a wider variety of people. It is important that these kinds of interactions not be forced, but allowing interest-based groups, whether a group of colleagues who go hiking together or fans of a particular programming language, to form naturally can generate organizational affinity.

Examining group memberships

The group memberships and social connections of the people creating software can have far-reaching effects on the much greater numbers of the people using it. For example, many social networks have started enforcing "real-name policies," doing things like suspending accounts of users that were not using their legal name. The problems with these sorts of policies are many, but one of the biggest issues is that they can disadvantage or even endanger people who don't go by the name on their government-issued IDs, such as victims of violence or harassment trying to avoid a stalker or abusive partner online, or transgender individuals who aren't "out" in all areas of their life.

Wielded inconsistently across platforms, these policies—which often make exceptions for celebrities (mononymous artists like Bono or Madonna are prime examples of this)—tend to have the most negative effects on groups of people who are already at risk or marginalized somehow by society. Not only that, but they tend to do very little to fight spam, reduce fake profiles, or prevent abuse, all reasons that are given as justification for implementing them.

It is likely that the key decision-making groups around these sorts of policies did not have any trans people, domestic violence survivors, drag performers, or anyone else who could understand the various legitimate reasons people have for not using their legal names online. While it isn't feasible to have a member of every single underrepresented group of people working on every software project ever, it does go to show that the less diverse the group making decisions, the more likely those decisions will have serious negative impacts on people and users outside that group.

It is important to ask ourselves regularly, what kinds of problems are we trying to solve? Are we solving the right problems? Does our team have the necessary knowledge and experience to acknowledge this and to understand the repercussions that their potential solutions might have? If a team tasked with dealing with harassment and abuse on a social network consists solely of straight white men, who overall do not experience these things with anywhere near the same volume and intensity as members of other groups do, can they really be expected to come up with the best solution given their limited experience with and understanding of the problem?

As we work to break down intergroup barriers and foster more communication and shared experiences between teams, we increase the number of weak ties that exist with people who might normally be in our out-groups, with whom we otherwise might only have absent ties. The knowledge and experience that can be gained from these weak ties enables us to create stronger, more creative solutions and to develop products that don't unintentionally harm subsets of the people who use them.

Expanding group memberships

The original view of devops really only considered developers and operation engineers. As the movement was started and the struggles most clearly felt by people with direct experience in these specific areas, this is perfectly reasonable—and it is certainly true that the friction and silos being addressed were real problems that needed to be solved.

It is oversimplifying things, however, to stop there. Most software isn't written for the sheer joy of writing software, especially not software that has to be deployed and monitored by an operations team. In the majority of cases, this software is being sold somehow, in one form or another, by a company, whether publicly traded or not, whose continued existence depends on this software. But ignoring the rest of the company does everyone involved a disservice.

We'd like to expand our view beyond simply development and operations teams. Silos, blame culture, ineffective communication, and lack of trust are significant cultural problems in an organization, no matter if they occur between dev and ops or anywhere else in the company. If we consider, as part of our group memberships, the company as a whole and the industry as a whole, we can take these ideas of trust, affinity, and sharing, and use them to benefit not just engineering departments but entire businesses.

Diversity

When thinking about our group memberships, we must make sure to consider the wide range of groups to which people can belong. Although there are many resources available that go into much more depth than we have space for here, we'll briefly discuss the benefits and axes of diversity and how teams and organizations can work to create inclusive environments that work well for both the business and the individuals working for it.

Benefits of Diversity

Diversity is critical for innovation: the differing ideas, perspectives, and viewpoints that come from different backgrounds are a crucial part of developing new ideas.[7] Diverse teams will be able to develop products that work for a wider customer base due to their unique experiences. The more closely different groups or individuals work together, the more creatively stimulated people tend to be. The tech industry tends to be very homogeneous, consisting mostly of heterosexual, cisgender, white

---

7 Vivian Hunt, Dennis Layton, and Sara Prince. "Why Diversity Matters," Mckinsey.com, February 12, 2016.

men, in proportions much higher than they are found in the general population,[8] which can cut down on its innovation and creativity.

> Strength lies in differences, not in similarities.
>
> —Stephen Covey

A 2006 study from Dr. Samuel R. Sommers, director of the Diversity & Intergroup Relations Lab at Tufts University, showed that racially diverse groups performed better than all-white groups.[9] Heterogeneous groups exchange a wider range of information and discuss more topics than homogeneous ones. Additionally, white people individually performed better in mixed groups than in all-white ones. Similar studies have shown that gender has the same effect: mixed-gender groups outperform groups of all men on individual and group levels.

These benefits are even more pronounced when groups are working on tasks that require creativity or when they are required to interact with nongroup members, where divergent thinking can be helpful. In practice, this means that teams that interact with customers will benefit from increased diversity, leading to increased customer satisfaction. A study conducted by researcher and management professor Orlando C. Richard in 2000 showed that cultural diversity in the workforce led to increased company performance during periods of company and business growth.[10]

Although diverse groups do lead to increased performance at individual, team, and company levels, the drawback is that they can also cause increases in interpersonal conflict, which can lead to lower morale in the short term. It makes sense that differing viewpoints, expectations, and opinions lead to disagreements. It's important to make sure that disagreements are handled well, not just by whoever screams the loudest. Thinking back to the devops compact, we have to know that we are ultimately working toward the same goal, and act with the understanding that we still share that goal in spite of disagreements.

Axes of Diversity and Intersectionality

Many diversity initiatives in tech start by recognizing a lack of women in the workplace. Rectifying the gender disparity is necessary, but not sufficient.

There are many different axes that diversity can take. These include:

- Gender and gender presentation

---

8 Roger Cheng, "Women in Tech: The Numbers Don't Add Up," CNET, May 6, 2015. Web.

9 Samuel Sommers, "On Racial Diversity and Group Decision Making: Identifying Multiple Effects of Racial Composition on Jury Deliberations," *Journal of Personality and Social Psychology* 90, no. 4 (2006).

10 Orlando Richard, "Racial Diversity, Business Strategy, and Firm Performance: A Resource-Based View," *Academy of Management Journal* 43, no. 2 (2000).

- Race and ethnicity
- National origin
- Sexual orientation
- Age
- Veteran status
- Disability
- Religion
- Familial status

Increasing diversity on any one of these axes is important, but one axis does not mean your company is truly diverse, nor that it is a safe place to work for a wide range of people. Intersectionality is defined as the study of intersections between different forms of oppression or discrimination, and how these different forms of oppression are interconnected. The term was first coined by legal scholar Kimberlé Crenshaw[11] and is an important consideration when you are thinking about diversity at your company.

Diversity, like any other devops practice, is not a simple thing that can be implemented once and then checked off a to-do list. It's an iterative process that must be monitored and measured. Your reasons for considering diversity matter, and how successful your efforts are will depend on them. Both initiatives should be undertaken out of a genuine concern for improving the lives of all people in your company and the community as a whole, creating an environment that is not only productive but also inclusive of all the people who can help drive that productivity.

Unconscious Bias

People often think of sexism, racism, or any other "-ism" as an overt or blatant thing, but unconscious biases can be even more insidious in their subtlety. Unconscious biases are shaped from our environments and the times and cultures we live in, and we often don't notice their presence. These are ingrained thought patterns that cause us to assume that men are more qualified than women with the same résumé, for example, without even realizing that we're doing it. The best way to fight against unconscious biases is to become (and stay) aware of them, which is why companies like Google and others are starting to offer unconscious bias training for their employees.

---

11 Kimberlé Crenshaw, "Demarginalizing the Intersection of Race and Sex: A Black Feminist Critique of Antidiscrimination Doctrine," *Feminist Theory and Antiracist Politics* (Chicago: The University of Chicago Legal Forum, 1989).

Hiring Considerations

There are things to be considered throughout the hiring process when trying to improve the diversity of your workforce. We will touch on additional concerns around growing your teams in Part V but here are a few points to consider to make sure that your hiring practices are as inclusive as the rest of your organization:

- Keep an eye out for language that can be exclusionary, such as overtly masculine or militarized phrasing as well as overtly sexist, racist, or homophobic remarks in both job postings and communications from recruiters. External recruiters especially should be given as much guidance as possible on the tone and culture that your company is trying to convey. More specific examples of this will be given in this chapter's case study.

- Be aware of those unconscious biases—even when we mean well, we often inadvertently assume that a résumé is better when it has a name that sounds like a white man's on it. When possible, have everyone involved in the sourcing and hiring processes take unconscious bias training, and keep personally identifying information out of the sourcing process for as long as possible.

- There are recruiters and consultants who specialize in creating diverse teams. If you are struggling with finding as many diverse candidates as you'd like, it might be worth bringing in a professional who has more experience in the area to help.

- While some teams are fond of having candidates submit "homework" as part of the screening process, keep in mind that this might put members of marginalized groups at a disadvantage, whether that be women with family responsibilities or people who don't have the time or inclination to do free work for a company.

Maintaining an Inclusive Environment

It doesn't matter much if you manage to interview and hire diverse employees if you can't retain them. Along with diversity, companies need to start inclusivity initiatives to ensure that individuals in the minority experience belongingness and encouragement to retain the uniqueness within the work group.

A common narrative is the small startup that has hired the first woman on their engineering team. From the rest of the team's perspective, this is great—they're being more diverse, and they now have an internal resource to help them avoid any potentially sexist mistakes! From the woman's point of view, however, it may not feel like an inclusive environment.

Many teams of men, upon hiring their first woman, will do things like say "Hey, guys," when entering the office or a meeting, then look at the woman, wonder if she might feel excluded by that, and follow up with an awkward "…and girls" or "…and gals." This is well intended, but many women say such additions make them feel more awkward and excluded rather than included. On top of the fact that we shouldn't be addressing adult women as "girls," drawing attention to people's differences from the rest of the group fosters a feeling of exclusion.

There is often a cost to members of minority groups in this kind of environment, as they are often expected to take on a great deal of diversity-related work on top of their regular work responsibilities. They are asked to review job postings to make sure they are free of racist and sexist language, or to represent the company and give it a diverse face at industry or recruiting events. They are often asked to represent all members of whatever group(s) they happen to be a part of—no woman is a spokesperson for all women, just like one gay person cannot give insight into what the entire LGBTQ community is thinking or feeling. This is true for all groups that are traditionally underrepresented in tech.

When considering diversity and inclusivity, think about the social groups and activities currently available to employees. Are employees allowed or encouraged to start groups, such as a women-in-engineering group or an LGBTQ group, as a way of connecting with their coworkers and creating safe and supportive spaces? Do people have access to leaders or mentors who are similar to them? If you have several more people of color in junior roles within engineering, but no senior engineers of color or people of color in engineering leadership, for example, those junior employees may wonder if there is room for them to grow at your company.

In terms of making sure an environment is as inclusive as possible, also think about what office activities, especially social or "extracurricular" ones, are opt-in versus opt-out. An opt-in activity is one that employees are not a part of unless they choose to join, whereas an opt-out activity is one that all employees are expected to participate in by default unless they explicitly opt out of doing so.

While it may seem like opt-in creates a barrier to entry that might discourage people from joining, opt-out has the issue of requiring people to admit that they don't want to do something, or provide specific reasons for doing so. For example, many companies view drinking alcohol as the default after-work activity, and startups especially are prone to peer pressure when it comes to drinking, where not going to a bar after work labels someone as different or "not a team player." A new employee is likely to feel uncomfortable having to explain reasons for opting out of this to new coworkers they don't know very well, which is then likely to make them feel excluded. In this example, an office kitchenette stocked with a variety of alcoholic and nonalcoholic drinks, with no mandatory times when "everyone" is expected to partake, is a much more inclusive setup.

Stereotype Threat

Stereotype threat is what happens when people find themselves in a position where they are at risk of confirming a negative stereotype about themselves and the group they are a part of. It has been shown in over 300 different studies (*http://reducingster eotypethreat.org*) to decrease individuals' performance, especially when they expect discriminations based on their group membership or identity. For example, take the stereotype that women are worse at math than men.

Women who are exposed to this stereotype will perform more poorly on math exams than those who aren't, as well as displaying more stress responses such as elevated heart rate and increased cortisol levels. Long-term exposure to stereotype threat can have the same negative long-term effects on mental and physical health that chronic stress does.

Studies have shown that a sense of belonging within a group can help to mitigate stereotype threat. If people are welcomed into the larger group or environment, if they feel that they are genuinely included, they are less influenced by the negative stereotypes that might lower their performance (and health).

There are many things that you can do to make sure your work environment is as inclusive as possible. When thinking about diversity and inclusion within your organization, keep in mind the following tips:

- Make sure that any recruiters you use are aware of your diversity and inclusion goals.

- Send employees to unconscious bias training or an Ally Skills Workshop (*http:// bit.ly/ally-skills-wkshp*).

- Lead by example, and call out problematic language or behavior; don't leave that as the sole responsibility of minority team members.

- Organize employee resource groups. Establish places to address the needs of diverse individuals, including community building, networking, and support. These groups facilitate resilience for the individuals mitigating some of the costs of being different from the majority.

- Audit your work environment. Determine how accessible key elements of the environment are to differently abled employees beyond the government-mandated requirements.

- If you ask people to do the work of reviewing your job postings to be more inclusive, compensate them for that work.

- Pay attention to whether your language or behavior is racist or sexist (or homophobic or transphobic) all the time, not just when people from those groups might be present—preemptively create an inclusive atmosphere.

Creating genuinely inclusive environments benefits not only the individual people in them but also the teams and organizations as whole groups. When people are not dealing with stereotype threat, hostility, or other stressors, they are able to be much more collaborative, communicative, and creative.

Teams and Organizational Structure

From a team to a larger organization, the relationships between individuals becomes more tenuous. British anthropologist Robin Dunbar theorized a limit to the number of people with whom one person can maintain stable social relationships. Through research with primates and the study of neocortex size and its processing capacity, he proposed that this upper limit, now known as Dunbar's number, is around 150 stable relationships.[12] Beyond this size, groups and organizations must use more restrictive rules, laws, and enforced norms to maintain a similarly cohesive group—one of the reasons that larger companies always seem to have more bureaucracy than smaller ones.

Organizations with more than approximately 150 people will require a different set of cultural practices with more restrictive rules and norms to maintain a stable, cohesive group. Yet the more people there are within the organization, the more effort that needs to be made to build relationships between groups to ensure proper information flow and understanding. If these cultural practices restrict how individuals build relationships within the organization, it can have a drastic impact on the organization as a whole.

Social structure influences culture, and culture influences social structure. A culture that embraces the values of collaboration, cooperation, and affinity will impact the underlying organization structures. As with all change, especially around power differentials, moving to this kind of culture can lead to disruptive behaviors. In Chapter 10, we discuss one way of handling these kinds of disruptions.

An organization that isn't placing enough value on these types of interpersonal and intergroup relationships may start to see this coming out in various behavioral aspects. Duplication of work between teams, or groups that are working in parallel on competing or mutually exclusive projects, indicates not only a lack of communication between teams but also a lack of understanding. Tickets that get repeatedly sent back

---

12 R. I. M. Dunbar, "Neocortex Size As a Constraint on Group Size in Primates," *Journal of Human Evolution* 22, no. 6 (1992).

and forth between different groups or projects, or increasingly blameful incident responses, point toward a decrease in trust.

Finding Common Ground Between Teams

How do we build trust, generate shared experiences, and create more inclusive organizations with more in-groups?

The main types of difficulties that can arise when trying to bridge the gaps between different teams are:

- differences in objectives;
- measurement of success;
- differences in leadership; and
- differences in communication styles.

Different teams often have, at least on the surface, different objectives. Though one could argue that every team's objective is to help the company as a whole succeed, the ways that they are expected to get there frequently come into conflict with one another.

The classic example of this in the devops space is a development team, whose goals generally involve getting new features (or bug fixes) in front of customers as quickly as possible, facing off against an operations team whose main goal tends to be something like uptime, making sure that all servers and services are available and usable. These goals can come into conflict in several ways. Deployment requirements or processes designed to minimize the availability impact of deploy errors that support operational uptime goals don't necessarily fall in line with development goals of shipping rapidly. In this kind of situation, developers might also find themselves at odds with QA engineers, whose goals of finding and fixing defects might also end up slowing down release cycles.

Even if the stated goals of different teams don't directly come into conflict, the ways that teams measure their successes might. Key performance indicators (KPIs) used to evaluate organizational progress and success, instead of helping overall performance can end up hindering it if they don't align with what is best for the business (read: the customers who make the business successful).

If developers are measured solely on the number of deploys they do—or worse, the number of lines of code they write—in their efforts to reach those goals they might end up shipping lower-quality code or spend time on features that customers don't want.

If a QA team is measured on how many bugs they find, they could slow down releases by waiting to find as many bugs as they need to meet their quota at the expense of shipping more quickly. Not only are these goals or metrics conflicting, but they might end up causing impacts that are at odds with the overall goals of the business.

Differing leadership and communication styles among teams and the individuals on them can also contribute to gaps between teams. There is a wide range of diverse communication and working styles that can affect how people interact. If these personalities find themselves clustered on teams, as can happen over time due to people's subconscious tendencies to want to hire and work with people similar to themselves, there can end up being communication or working style conflicts at a team level instead of an individual one.

Leaders with different styles or management values can bring about or enhance these differences. A manager with a more hands-on or even micro-management style will likely be at odds with someone with a more hands-off approach who encourages independent experimentation among their reports. Someone who values the appearance of productivity and output over all else might come into conflict with a leader who cares more about nurturing people and relationships. In organizations where consensus between various managers determines things like who gets certain projects or promotions, these kinds of conflicts can have serious impacts.

Despite all these differences, there are ways of finding commonalities between teams and groups that we will examine in the next sections.

From Competition to Cooperation

When we think about teams with differing goals, we often think about teams that are in direct competition with one another. The team that meets their objectives better will likely be the team that gets a bigger portion of its organizational budget for purchasing, more resources for projects, or more headcount. Given these fixed resources, how can teams move from a position of competition to one of cooperation?

As mentioned in Part II, competition occurs when individuals or organizations are striving for something that may be in direct opposition to one another. Competition is driven in many markets by the need to be faster, cheaper, better, or all three. It is perceived as a necessary condition within a free market.

Compliance to fair competition is a cornerstone of how markets have evolved across the world. Principles of this competition law are prohibition of agreements or practices that restrict free trading, banning abusive behavior by dominant firms or practices that lead to such a position, and supervision of mergers and acquisitions that threaten competitive processes. In some ways, competition can help inspire competitors to work harder, to innovate more effective or creative solutions to problems, and to offer more choices to customers.

Too much competition, however, can have a larger detrimental effect overall than the benefits it gains in smaller amounts. The term "tragedy of the commons" is often used to describe this effect, where individuals acting independently and rationally for their own benefit ultimately end up acting contrary to what is best for the group as a whole by depleting some common resource. This phrase, coined as the title of a 1968 essay written by ecologist Garrett Hardin,[13] originally came about describing the effects of unregulated sheep grazing on common or public land, hence the term "commons."

This is a prime example of *game theory*, or the study of the rational choices that people make in the face of problems involving multiple parties, collective action, and interactive decisions. Florian Diekert, a researcher of human interrelations and economics, in his 2012 paper titled "The Tragedy of the Commons from a Game-Theoretic Perspective" argues that the original discussion of this scenario is not entirely realistic.[14] He points out that while cooperation in this type of situation is difficult, especially as the stakes become higher, the tragedy that comes with unlimited individual freedom is not an inevitability.

Indeed, American political economist and Nobel Laureate Elinor Ostrom identifies several factors that are critical to the success of any cooperative efforts in the commons scenario.[15] She asserts that in order for cooperation to succeed, there must be:

- a means of controlling membership in the overall group;
- social networks;
- observable actions of everyone involved;
- graduated sanctions available against individuals; and
- a resource that is not excessively variable.

Ostrom and other game theory researchers have noted that the ability to sanction behavior has a substantial effect on overall cooperation. When noncooperative behavior is collectively punished, cooperative behavior ends up becoming self-enforcing. For example, if every person on a team points out or doesn't tolerate someone interrupting others, that team starts to collectively learn that interrupting isn't an effective way to get your voice heard, and interruptions will tend to decrease over time. But if some people allow interruptions, this self-enforcing behavior will not be seen.

---

13 Garrett Hardin, "The Tragedy of the Commons," *Science*, December 13, 1968.

14 Florian Diekert, Florian. "The Tragedy of the Commons from a Game-Theoretic Perspective," *Sustainability* 4, no. 8 (2012).

15 Elinor Ostrom, *Governing the Commons: The Evolution of Institutions for Collective Action* (Cambridge, UK: Cambridge University Press, 1990).

Free-riding refers to people who reap the benefits of the community without investing in it. This is harmful when it prevents others from participating or contributing. An example of this is a *support vampire*, someone who asks questions without regard to the tone in which the question is asked or how often it is asked, and gets offensive when their expectations are not met. Similarly, a community where sanctions are either not available or not enforced is one that reduces individual contributions as well; if there are no repercussions for noncooperative behavior, game theory shows that individuals will rationally choose noncooperative behavior more and more in order to protect their own individual interests, because the community as a whole is no longer helping work toward those interests.

It follows, therefore, that in order to create cooperative workplace communities rather than competitive ones, you must ensure the presence of the factors described by Ostrom in some respect. Group membership is controlled by the hiring process; social networks exist in the form of organizational and team hierarchies as well as informal and formal social interactions; most people's and teams' behavior is observable to some extent; and a variety of sanctions exist, such as performance improvement plans, removal from desirable projects, budget reductions, and layoffs or terminations.

The final factor, resources that are not too variable, gets interesting. Especially in small startups that are struggling to get off the ground or in larger companies that are facing downturns and downsizing, individual and team behavior becomes observably more competitive and less cooperative than in more stable work environments. Regardless of organizational size, we recommend that you keep these factors in mind when considering how to develop and maintain a sustainable, cooperative workplace environment.

Building Team Empathy

Empathy allows ops engineers to appreciate the importance of being able push [to] code quickly and frequently, without a fuss. It allows developers to appreciate the problems caused by writing code that's fat, or slow, or insecure. Empathy allows software makers and operators to help each other deliver the best possible functionality and operability on behalf of their customers.[16]

—Jeff Sussna

One of the key tenets of the devops movement is developing empathy, not only for people on the other side of the metaphorical wall or in other parts of the company but

---

16 Jeff Sussna, "Empathy: The Essence of Devops," *Ingineering.IT*, January 11, 2014.

also for the customers. Empathy and understanding go hand in hand, and without a deep understanding of what your customers want and what problems you are trying to solve for them (and if those are even the right problems to solve), your business is much less likely to be successful.

Designated ops

For years, operations engineers and system administrators have often been seen as walled off from the rest of the company, as grumpy unpleasant people who look down on the people around them and love saying "no" to things. There are certainly plenty of examples of this in the wild, and it is important for organizations to break down both these toxic behaviors and the perceptions of them in order to be successful. This is especially true for modern businesses where IT and operations are so crucial to the success of the product; gone are the days of one system administrator alone in a server closet somewhere with a network that services only email and printers.

In heavily siloed environments, other teams have historically struggled with getting the services and support they need from their operations teams. Some IT departments had unnecessary processes in place for other people to get help, either for historical reasons or to cut down on requests that were seen as wastes of time (one user who seems to need his password reset at least once a month is a common example). Some departments were spread too thin and lacked the resources to get their own work done, let alone offer any real assistance to other teams. An unstable infrastructure leads to so much time being spent reactively firefighting that no proactive work can get done.

One thing organizations can do to ameliorate this is the idea of having to designate operations engineers for other teams. Teams that tend to need a lot of operational support have a designated contact on the ops team—for example, a web or API development team that needs to do a lot of monitoring, performance tuning, and capacity planning. The idea is that having one designated person gives the dev team a consistent point of contact, rather than having tickets opened and randomly assigned to different people (who then have to re-explain their problems, context, things they've already tried, and so forth) and provides consistency for the members of the operations team as well. A team's designated ops engineer will usually come to their team meetings or standups to keep an ear out for things that will need additional operational support, like new API endpoints being developed that will add extra load to the API cluster—if that will require new hardware, it benefits both teams for ops to be aware of these developments sooner rather than later.

There are a few key points to keep in mind to make this approach work:

Designated, not dedicated
> One of the most important things to remember is that these operations engineers are *designated* for their teams, but not *dedicated* to them. This means under-

standing that the ops team has its own work that needs to get done and that its members cannot and should not be expected to spend 100 percent of their time helping other teams with their work. This also means that the designated ops engineer for a given team is not necessarily responsible for single-handedly doing all ops-related work for that team, rather that they will be the primary point of contact for that team and will generally manage or oversee the associated work. Time and project management skills are very important for making this work for the operations staff, so make sure that they have the support and education necessary for this.

Operations team size

Unless your company is so small that you only have a single small- to medium-sized team in engineering at all, this is not something that can work without a good-sized operations team. Work outside of their normal projects and responsibilities will add further strain, so it is crucial that the team be well staffed enough to accommodate this. At Etsy, which practices this approach, there are approximately 15 operations engineers to a few hundred other engineers; this is not something that can realistically be pulled off with an operations team of just 2 or 3 people.

 Also keep in mind that not all designated ops assignments are created equal. Different teams will create very different workloads for their designated engineers, with some requiring close to no effort aside from keeping a watchful eye out for ops-related happenings (this is common on teams that are removed enough from operations that they don't even know what they don't know, as opposed to other teams that know when they need to ask for operational help), while some will require considerably more effort. You might consider having designations based on projects rather than teams to help spread workload evenly.

Including the good and the bad

Operations has traditionally been a rather thankless profession. If everything is going well, it is nearly completely invisible, but is very highly visible when something goes wrong. It's all too easy for these teams and their members to be overlooked when they perform well but very publicly chastised during issues or outages, especially in blameful environments. Including designated ops engineers in the good or fun parts of a team, and not just speaking to them when you need help, can help foster mutually empathetic relationships. This can be as simple as inviting them to team lunches or dinners or including them on team outings—a little inclusion goes a long way.

A two-way learning street

One of the benefits of building these kinds of relationships between teams is the learning that goes on between people who would otherwise have much less in the way of shared knowledge and experiences. When a team has a designated operations engineer sitting in on their meetings and raising concerns such as how something is going to be monitored, what does it mean for it to be "in production," how to plan for failure and disaster recovery, and so forth, over time they will begin not only to understand the value of these kinds of considerations but ideally to proactively consider them themselves. To get the most value out of this kind of program, however, this kind of learning needs to flow in both directions: operations staff will gain a deeper understanding and appreciation for what other teams are working on. They start to appreciate the motivations and struggles that people on these teams have and stop seeing them as faceless names or email addresses who only come around when they need something. They can bring this understanding and empathy back to the rest of the team, starting to break down boundaries and expand the number of people considered to be a part of, or at least close to, their own in-group.

 In addition to operations, this kind of designation program benefits other teams as well. For example, designated design or user experience teams can help make sure the products people create are easy and intuitive to use, which could be very useful for an internal tools team making something that will be used throughout the organization. If that team, as they often are, were made up of people with mostly backend or system administration experience, if left to their own devices they might come up with a command-line tool that made sense to them but not to anyone who was less comfortable with the command line. Having a designated designer or UX engineer could help them make a tool that was usable for a wider variety of people. Security is another area where having designated engineers working with other teams can make substantial positive impacts, because like operations, security tends to have a reputation for not being the most approachable but should be considered throughout products' entire lifecycles, not just tacked on at the last minute.

Bootcamps and rotations

While programs like designated ops allow people to interact more with other teams, other programs, such as bootcamps and rotations, allow people to briefly join these other teams as a way of expanding their knowledge and skills as well as their empathy.

A *bootcamp* is a term used to describe this approach when it is done at the beginning of an employee's tenure in a given team, where they spend one week or up to several weeks working on teams other than their own. Primarily, people bootcamp on teams that their team regularly works closely with, so a developer might spend one week bootcamping with operations and another with security before jumping into their regular work. The benefit of doing this at the beginning is that when people are first starting, they aren't in the middle of projects for which other people are depending on them, so there are fewer constraints on their time. Additionally, they have fewer pre-conceived notions about other teams or "the way things are," so their fresh pairs of eyes can often bring new insights for how the teams can work together that they might not get otherwise.

When this is done after the beginning of someone's tenure in a particular role, it is often called a *rotation*. Some organizations or teams offer companies the ability to do senior rotations once a year, planned enough in advance that their absence for a few weeks will not be overly disruptive. Senior rotations might also be a bit more flexible when it comes to which teams people might choose to work with. Because they are now well established in their own team and the teams they regularly work with, they might take this opportunity to work on a rather different team—such as an operations engineer working on a mobile development or frontend engineering team—in order to explore different areas and technologies that they might otherwise gain exposure to.

Working as a member of another team has the same overall benefits of a designation program, but tends to build an even deeper foundation of empathy and understanding as well as bringing about much more overlap between different group memberships. In organizations where it is harder to get buy-in for a program of this size, there are other ways to achieve similar results at a smaller scale. Fostering opportunities for people from different teams to pair with each other to work on projects can start building these same bonds in a few hours rather than a few weeks. For example, you could set up an opt-in system where engineers get paired up to work through a backlog of bugs or small ticket items, whether this be for internal products or open source projects that the company either uses or maintains.

Rotations outside engineering

As we have mentioned previously, the principles described in this book can be applied beyond just developers and operations engineers to create and maintain an even stronger company and industry culture. Many tech companies, especially start-ups, tend to value their engineers very highly, but too often this comes at the expense of nonengineering teams. While engineers get branded engineering hoodies and all-expenses-paid trips to conferences, other departments might reasonably start to feel that they are undervalued and underappreciated.

One of the driving factors behind the devops movement was getting more understanding, appreciation, and empathy for operations engineers, system administrators, and IT in general, helping the rest of the company understand the value that these areas provide and how behaviors like throwing deploys over the wall ("worked fine in dev, ops' problem now") affect them. Operations was for too long an area that was either ignored or treated poorly. Now that this is changing in many places, it is crucial that we not unknowingly do the same to other teams that might be in the same boat.

At many companies, customer support falls into this category. They lack the prestige that engineering positions have, but customer support folks are the face of your company to the people using it. They tend to bear the brunt of people's unhappiness the same way that system administrators did when the network was down or a printer wouldn't print. If you, as a product user, call or write into customer support, it is almost certainly because you are unhappy with something, and we have the unfortunate but human tendency to take our frustration out on the people we end up speaking to, even though we know they did not cause our problems themselves. Support teams tend to have much higher turnover rates than other teams, and often feel unappreciated or looked down upon in companies despite the vital role they play.

A *support rotation* can help to alleviate this by having people from other teams spend a few hours every so often answering support emails or triaging incoming customer complaints. In most cases, there will be a lot of the same sort of questions coming in, and with good documentation or pre-created answer templates to use, people can come in and help work through these parts of support queues with a minimum of onboarding effort. This is not to minimize the skill and patience required for the more difficult and less common support cases, of course, but it is a way to allow other groups, often engineers, to both help out with the support workload and, more importantly, gain an appreciation for what kinds of issues customers have (which can be very different from the issues that developers might imagine they have), for the value that support brings to the company, and for how demanding that work can be.

In addition to allowing and encouraging people to switch and rotate between different roles within their own company, some organizations are starting to apply the same principles but between different companies. Often referred to as an *engineering exchange*, two engineers with roughly equivalent roles at different companies will switch places for 2–3 weeks, allowing for the same exchanges of knowledge, shared experiences, and empathy building but at a larger scale. Companies are starting to move away from the competitive, "protect the secret sauce at all costs" mentality from earlier decades, allowing their employees to share information by way of conference talks and open sourcing software, knowing that doing so will not weaken the company but will instead strengthen the industry as a whole.

Of course, the success of these kinds of programs relies on mutual sharing and learning. If one company lets their exchange engineer participate as a full team member, working on actual work, while their counterpart is stuck doing nothing but reading documentation, that is a very one-sided relationship. Returning to the earlier discussion of the tragedy of the commons and factors that can sustain cooperative behavior, the sanctions for such uncooperative behavior might be companies refusing to do future exchange programs with the offending organizations, cutting down on the amount of information those bad actors will get in the future.

For organizations looking to improve their overall and interteam empathy, it is important to examine not only how different teams and groups interact but also the value, real or perceived, of these various groups. Traditionally, functions like IT and support are often seen as cost centers, which do not directly add profit but instead add to the monetary costs of running a company. While the devops movement has started to improve how operations teams are perceived in the workplace as a whole, there is still a long way to go in this regard. Cost center employees often have the most thankless jobs, higher rates of turnover, lower pay, and a higher risk of being downsized during lean times, yet despite being perceived as lower rungs on the company ladder, they can—with the right people, training, and resources—bring incredible gains in areas like customer loyalty or infrastructure stability.

When expanding our view of devops to consider these other teams and how they impact the overall business as well, we believe it is helpful to stop thinking in terms of a ladder of a company hierarchy. The ladder is an overly simplistic model that not only causes misconceptions about career progression (as we have mentioned in other chapters, moving from engineering to management is a career change, not a promotion) but also makes it harder for people to empathize with other groups by positioning them "lower" than others. It also ignores the ways that groups are interconnected and interdependent.

Imagine, instead of a ladder, a rope pyramid—the kind sometimes seen on playgrounds, with taut multicolored ropes all providing enough tension for children to climb and play on (see Figure 9-1). While there is still a hierarchy, in this model it is easier to imagine roles such as IT and support as being the foundation for the other parts of the pyramid, and to realize that without a strong foundation, the overall stability and success of the structure are threatened. A ladder can lose a lower rung and still function, which is why these areas are often viewed as cost centers and are then among the first to be let go, but the value that they bring, even though not monetary, must be considered. If you cut one of the bottom ropes of this pyramid, the whole thing will lose stability.

Improving Team Communication

In addition to having empathy for each other, teams need to be able to communicate effectively in order to truly work well together. Following up on the discussion of communication styles, media, and negotiation types in Part II, this section will look at how these same ideas can be applied at an interteam level. This is a big part of what will take a devops culture from being one that benefits only a few teams or just the engineering department to being something that benefits an entire organization or business.

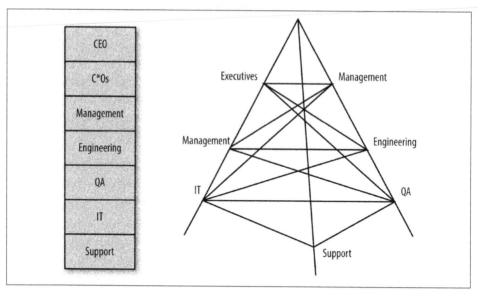

Figure 9-1. Ladder versus pyramid hierarchy

At the simplest level, group communication tends to take on and amplify the individual communications of group members, for better or for worse. In the face of differing communication styles among a group, the most dominant tend to win out. Oftentimes this ends up meaning that the people who speak the loudest, go on the longest, or interrupt the most tend to both dominate group discussions as well as "win" arguments, not necessarily by virtue of their ideas but simply because less argumentative or interruptive individuals will opt out of these discussions sooner. One domineering frequent interrupter in a team can change the entire group's communication dynamic, as other people start interrupting more and more just to get a word in edgewise.

Groups will also look to their leaders for examples of how they should be communicating, whether that be a manager or someone who is authoritative or respected in the group. Leaders who don't communicate well, don't communicate enough, or whose communication styles are detrimental to a cooperative work environment can have similar effects on the communication styles of those around them, so be mindful of the standards that leaders within your organization are setting.

In many organizations, there are often discussions around how much to communicate, and via which media. As we saw earlier, different media are each better suited to different types of communication in terms of reach, urgency, context, and other factors. With these different factors combined with individual preferences, it is often difficult to set guidelines that make everyone happy, but in general it is better to overcommunicate than to undercommunicate.

This is especially true for media where it is relatively easy for people to set up individual filters to suit their preferences, such as email clients that allow automatic filtering of different emails to different folders, or chat programs that allow customizable alert words. While this is not a one-size-fits-all solution, it allows for a fair amount of individual customization and avoids the impression that information is being deliberately withheld, which can foster silos and in-group/out-group attitudes.

Also keep in mind the distribution of individuals and teams within an organization. As teams begin to move across locations and time zones, it becomes increasingly difficult to include everyone with in-person communication. Getting in the habit of communicating in remote-friendly ways, such as email and text chat, by default, not only gives searchable records of what was communicated for future reference but also keeps remote individuals and teams from feeling isolated.

Communication during crises

One of the situations where communication is most likely to falter is during crisis situations such as site outages. While communication during these specific situations is a relatively new field of study, effective communication during crisis situations that involve multiple people and teams in a more general sense is not. The medical field in particular has been researching this for years, and there are several proven strategies from that discipline that can be applied to ours as well:

Cross-functional communication
> People often get used to communicating only with members of their own team or function, which can cause problems during issues that involve troubleshooting or triaging with multiple teams or disciplines. Practicing cross-functional communication outside of these high-stress areas helps these good habits to form. Medical teams do rounds with doctors, nurses, and pharmacy staff; a designated operations or similar program as described previously can have similar benefits in an engineering organization. As individual teams might have divergent communication styles that develop over time, working to set and maintain common standards of communication (such as shared checklists or templates that are used in various situations) can also reduce friction in cross-functional communication.

Assertive communication
> A crisis leaves little time for issues of miscommunication or guesswork, so it is vital that people are comfortable communicating assertively. Being direct does not necessarily mean being rude, however. This is an area where ensuring that people have access to training that can help them communicate directly and effectively can be quite helpful. Cultural differences can sometimes create barri-

ers to assertive or direct communication, as can ways in which different groups of people (such as broken down by gender or race) are socialized to communicate differently. Blameful cultures also often prevent people from communicating directly, so it is important that people are well versed in blameless and nonverbal communication styles.

Specific critical language techniques

Several techniques for making it easier for people to express concern or critique in high-pressure situations have been developed and studied over the years. The *two-challenge rule* recommends that people challenge something they have doubts about up to twice. In crisis situations, it is certainly possible for something to get missed if only said once, especially when there is a lot going on, but challenging more than twice can cause disagreements or debates to go on too long, preventing crucial actions from being taken in a timely manner.

Making sure that people are comfortable speaking up when they have concerns is crucial during crises when the stakes are higher than usual. One technique for this is a strategy called *CUS*,[17] which encourages people to state if they are:

- Concerned about something
- Unsure about something
- Safety is an issue

Another technique, called *SBAR*, offers guidelines for making sure concerns or critiques are expressed in a productive manner. People should make sure to communicate:

- Situational information to describe what is happening
- Background information or context
- An assessment of what they believe the problem is
- Recommendations for how to proceed

These various techniques can be practiced regularly to keep teams in the habit of including each other and communicating as directly and effectively as possible, whether during crises or regular day-to-day work.

Now that we've spent some time examining how to improve affinity, let's take a look at the benefits it can bring to organizations in the real world.

---

17 "Pathways for Patient Safety: Working as a Team," Health Research and Educational Trust, 2008, *http://bit.ly/ pathways-for-safety*.

Case Study: United States Patent and Trademark Office

To get a feel for what a devops transformation looks like within a government organization, we were able to speak with Tina Donbeck, director of the System Configuration and Delivery Automation Division within the Office of the Chief Information Officer at the United States Patent and Trademark Office (USPTO).[18] This office (the OCIO) ensures that customers can perform their day-to-day jobs of reviewing, approving, and adjudicating patent and trademark filings from the American public, by ensuring the technology and tools they use for this work are operational.

Background and Directions

In addition to the director position that she fills, Donbeck is also a Marine Corps veteran and a devops evangelist within her organization. With degrees in psychology and organizational development, after her time in the Marines she spend several years supporting the Department of Navy in their IT workforce development, filling roles such as information systems security officer and program/project manager. Throughout the course of her career so far, she has noted that a common theme has been continuous improvement: "I really enjoy figuring out broken processes and figuring out what makes people tick, what motivates them."

The team that she currently directs is the one that has developed, implemented, and operates the current continuous delivery platform upon which the USPTO's next-generation systems are being developed. This platform touches nearly every aspect of the organization's software development lifecycle and thus her team works fairly closely with several other teams also involved in this cycle, most commonly the Platform Services Devision, the team working with RedHat CloudForms, and the software development teams themselves.

Although they do use CloudForms, RedHat's cloud management and release automation platform, quite extensively, the organization mostly chooses tools that are open source, to avoid large licensing agreements or being locked into a single vendor. These tools include Subversion for source control, Jenkins for a continuous integration server, Sonar for project and quality management, Nexus for repository management, and both Puppet and Ansible for configuration management. Various teams have found that the user communities of these products are a big part of the value they provide, both in terms of being able to answer questions and provide support but also in the new features and widgets that are continually being developed.

To Donbeck, devops means performing continuous delivery efficiently and effectively on the technical side, and being able to coordinate across teams with both trust and a

---

18 All the views expressed in this case study are Donbeck's own and do not necessarily represent those of the US government.

spirit of collaboration in order to produce quality products on the cultural side. Developing and maintaining quality software products, and breaking down barriers that would prevent this work from getting done, is a big part of her motivation and her role as a devops evangelist.

Encouraging Collaboration and Affinity

Working toward an environment of trust and collaboration between teams is an ongoing process and one that is influenced by multiple factors throughout the organization. Donbeck's vision for successful collaboration and cooperation is that people will have "the ability to work together toward a common goal without the need to mark your territory (this is mine, this is yours); collaboration should be open and without fear; there should be no fear that another team or individual is out to throw you under the bus and there should be no fear to fail or make mistakes."

Both individuals and teams are encouraged to work together and seek out feedback on their work and its effectiveness. "We do solicit feedback from our user population with a feature request function on our Division's website where we will capture and analyze a request and put in out our backlog if appropriate. We also hold brown bags and info sessions where we actively solicit feedback from our user community." Code reviews are a required part of every release cycle, to encourage collaboration and frequent feedback between individuals, and new employees on the team are assigned a buddy to show them the ropes.

While some processes, such as required code reviews, are more rigid, Donbeck notes that experimentation with different tools and solutions is not only allowed but actively encouraged. "Our team likes to tinker and we have a sandbox where we try out different tools, widgets, and so on. If it's something we want to push to the larger user population we go through our Enterprise Architecture review process to ensure that the tool/product meets all the governance and security requirements we have to adhere to." This allows for flexibility and innovation while still following all the requirements that come with being a government agency.

Donbeck has had a great deal of success with building community, both strengthening internal community ties and collaborating and sharing with outside organizations as well. Her team took a conference room and turned it into a team "DevOps Workspace" where "it's not uncommon to find 25+ people…working together on an effort—developers, testers, platform support. It's really cool to watch the energy in the room." This setup allows people to actively work together and also encourages drop-ins from other teams that work closely together, rather than relying on meetings. She encourages these teams to work toward a commonly understood end state (in this case, faster, higher-quality deployments) and to have mutual trust and respect for one another. A community space where it feels safe to have discussions and disagreements without fear has been a big contributing factor to that kind of environment.

The USPTO is the first federal agency to host a devops meetup, with their first event having over 100 attendees. Their organization also held an industry day where various vendors in the devops space were invited to come share their products, ideas, and best practices. That event was also well attended, hosting over 100 companies sharing their ideas. They also hosted and sponsored the devopsdays DC 2015 conference, attended by both government and industry participants. These events, in addition to other training offerings for both technical and soft skills, are recommended to employees throughout the organization as a way of encouraging collaborative growth and development.

Balancing Multiple Viewpoints

As with any large organization, there have been some struggles to integrate multiple perspectives and working styles into a cohesive organizational strategy. Devops is sometimes interpreted to mean different things by different people, so there are multiple ideas of what a mature or successful devops organization might look like. As Donbeck noted, "Success likely looks a lot different to developers who are under pressure to produce quality products under tight schedules and operations folks who are often plagued with balancing day-to-day operations of keeping the trains running and innovating their service offerings. There is an acknowledgment that we need a unified understanding with some defined success criteria and it's OK for each functional area to define success differently as long as there is agreement on the main goal."

It can certainly be frustrating to feel like different people or teams in an organization are moving in different directions or even working in opposition to one another, but in fact being able to recognize and discuss these differences is key to being able to work through them. Especially in a larger organization, differing expectations and viewpoints are to be expected, and a team of executive leaders that are able to have conversations about what success looks like and steer their different teams and areas toward a common culture, like the leadership at the USPTO, is a necessary step toward successful cultural change.

While some people might be more resistant to change at an individual level, and some people and teams might not see eye to eye as a result of a previously less open and more blameful culture, efforts can be made at all levels to move past blamefulness, to clear up confusion that arises from evolving roles and responsibilities, and to create a more open and collaborative culture going forward. For example, the CIO went out and purchased small trinkets called "DevOps Doer Mementos" and has handed them out to people in the organization that are taking steps toward creating that kind of devops culture.

Some parts of the organization seem to be changing faster than others, but overall there is a feeling of steady progress, even if it can be slow at times. Support and buy-in from management and leadership in the organization, combined with more grassroots efforts from the teams involved in their day-to-day work, is a combination that is working well for Donbeck and her organization as a whole, and one that other large organizations could learn from.

Regardless of organizational size, speed, or complexity, it is critical to realize that you need to have a common vision, goal, and success criteria in order to successfully execute any kind of substantial cultural or technological change. This ties back to the idea of the devops compact that we introduced in the first chapter. Without a shared understanding and agreement, it is unlikely that any change will be effective or longlasting. Though a completely shared understanding will take time, even an agreement that an understanding needs to be reached and will be actively worked toward is a crucial first step.

Benefits of Improved Affinity

There are a multitude of benefits to improving affinity between teams at individual, team, and organizational levels. Increased empathy and communication helps people feel that their voices are heard and their concerns appreciated, which creates a cycle of improved morale and productivity. Better interteam dynamics create more robust and productive organizations that are able to offer more creative solutions, work more effectively across business units, and iterate more quickly. Improved affinity is good not only for the people working for your business, but for the business as well. In this section, we'll examine how and why this is the case.

Shortened Cycle Time

Cycle time and *lead time* are both measures of work and productivity that have roots in the Kanban system, a scheduling system for Lean production developed at Toyota in the 1950s.[19] Lead time is the time from when a request is made to when the final result is delivered, or the customer's point of view on how long something takes to complete. Cycle time also ends with delivery but begins instead when work begins on a request, not when a request is received. Cycle time measures more the completion rate or the work capability of a system overall, and a shorter cycle time means that less time is being wasted when a request has been made but no progress or work is getting done.

Although cycle time is a term that is often used among Kanban practitioners, it is not unanimously accepted as the best term for what it is often used to describe. Depending on the context, the term can have two different meanings. First is the one just

---

19 Taiichi Ohno, *Toyota Production System—Beyond Large-Scale production* (Portland, OR: Productivity Press, 1988).

described, while the second comes from Lean manufacturing and refers to the average time between two successive units leaving the work or manufacturing process. For this reason, various Kanban professionals have started referring to the first definition as *flow time* to avoid confusion.

> The best moments usually occur when a person's body or mind is stretched to its limits in a voluntary effort to accomplish something difficult and worthwhile. Optimal experience is thus something that we make happen.
>
> —Mihaly Csíkszentmihályi

Flow is a concept that often comes up in discussions about the measurement of work and productivity. Social theorist Mihaly Csíkszentmihályi introduced the concept of flow to describe the mental state of an individual who, in the process of working on an activity, is fully engaged, energized, and content. During his years of research, Csíkszentmihályi has identified six factors that differentiate flow from other mental states.[20] These factors are:

- Intense and focused concentration in the present
- Merging of action and awareness
- Lack of self-consciousness
- Personal control or agency over a situation
- Subjective experience of time is altered
- Intrinsic reward

Flow at an individual level is the state of consciousness in which one feels completely absorbed in an activity that requires preparation and practice, especially an activity involving creative abilities. During a flow state, individuals feel strong, alert, and at the peak of their abilities.

Flow also occurs within a team. Flow within a team is different than flow for an individual. A good example of observing flow is an orchestra, which, while composed of individuals and different instruments, comes together to create something more than the individual sounds. Flow at a team level is more powerful than at the individual level. When people perform as a unit, anticipating each other's actions, it leads to creativity, productivity, and performance. Group flow depends on everyone within the team participating equally. Dominant or arrogant types can ruin group flow.

Csíkszentmihályi also summarized characteristics that facilitate team flow, which include a shared group focus, visualization of work, parallel organized working, spatial arrangements in the workplace, and, perhaps most importantly, treating differ-

---

20 Mihaly Csíkszentmihályi, *Flow: The Psychology of Optimal Experience* (New York: Harper Perennial, 2008).

ences among team members as opportunities rather than obstacles. We will discuss work visualization in more depth in Part IV, as well as how it can be used to bring about more organized working environments. Overall, these characteristics of team or group flow tie directly into groups that have shortened cycle or flow times, less waste, and more productivity.

Reduction of Communication Barriers

Lack of communication, misunderstandings, and other forms of miscommunication are some of the biggest hidden costs in the workplace. Being unable to clearly communicate expectations, whether they be for what a customer wants, what is needed for an internal-facing solution, or for the human side of things such as how people are expected to work together, often leads to those expectations being unmet. Repetition of work, due to either unclear expectations the first time or multiple people unknowingly duplicating each other's efforts, is costly as well. Problems with communication waste time, work, and money.

Improving affinity and trust between different groups of people encourages them to be more direct and honest with their communications. When people aren't comfortable communicating their problems or concerns directly, one common reaction is to become passive-aggressive. If two teams have shared responsibility for some piece of infrastructure and disagree over who should be availabile and perform basic maintenance tasks on that infrastructure but don't discuss it directly, they might see tickets being created and assigned to the other team with no additional communication. Each team is wondering why the other doesn't want to just do their jobs, hoping that assigning them tickets will be enough of a hint, and mistrust and resentment quickly grow on both sides.

Without sufficient trust and empathy, a human communication problem like this might be mistaken for a technical problem. Someone who doesn't understand the value of open and direct communication is liable to suggest technical solutions to this problem, such as a new monitoring solution or a different way of filing tickets, when in reality the problem is the passive-aggressive behavior and the avoidance of any direct confrontation. People sometimes avoid confrontation because it feels too emotional, but letting anger and resentment fester and drawing out issues is much worse than having a brief confrontation or direct discussion that quickly airs and resolves a disagreement.

The better we know each other, the better able we are to accurately interpret and understand other people's communication. This is why it can be very valuable for remote employees to spend their first few weeks on a new team in the office or coworking with other team members as much as possible, to pick up on context, body language, and tone and get to know their colleagues before remote communication takes away most of those nonverbal clues. Having video or at least voice chat readily accessible for remote or distributed teams is also invaluable for this. As beneficial as distributed teams can be, we still need to take into account the effects that distance and technology can have on those communications and connections.

 Technology alone does not create or strengthen connections. Services like Twitter, Facebook, IRC, or Slack allow people to connect with one another, but individuals have to nurture these weak ties in order to strengthen the connections they are building. Features of these services are limited to the perspectives of the teams that build them, so products that are created by more diverse teams will have a wider range of understanding and be able to reach across a wider variety of communication barriers. However, while any of these communication tools can help to strengthen connections, the context depends entirely on the people using them and how they do so.

Trust

The benefits of high-trust organizations versus low-trust ones are numerous. Colleagues who trust each other are able to collaborate more and duplicate less effort. Employees that trust in their organization to support them can take the time they need to invest in themselves and their skills, strengthening the connections in their work and reducing risk of burnout. Creating and maintaining a high-trust environment is key to fostering the relationships and understanding that embody devops.

High-trust organizations are positively correlated with a higher quality of work as well. To someone coming from a low-trust organization, this might seem counterintuitive, as you might think that double-checking or even redoing someone else's work is a way of making sure that they didn't miss anything. However, this sort of behavior, either duplication of work or micromanaging tasks, has a detrimental effect. Over time, people will stop putting in as much effort if they know that someone else will end up redoing or rechecking their work anyway. If they don't feel that they are trusted enough to advance their careers, they also have less motivation to put in genuine effort.

In addition to trust of others, a high-trust organization can have positive impacts on people's trust themselves as well. One of the hallmarks of a more senior individual is the ability to trust their own judgment, to know when they need to ask for help, when to get a second pair of eyes on something, and when they have all the needed capabilities themselves. Someone who is continually being second-guessed by others is not going to be able to develop the skill of trusting their own instincts. Someone who has been taught by a low-trust organization to doubt their own work is not going to challenge themselves to develop new skills and will instead stick to projects that feel safe, which limits the extent to which they can grow and advance.

Trust issues are often seen in organizations that have blameful cultures or overly competitive environments. If everyone has to be out only for themselves, such as if they are facing stack ranking or being fired for making a mistake, people are not going to trust each other and collaborate, inhibiting communication and innovation. Ultimately, if people are not trusted to do the jobs they were hired to do, the most ambitious (or those privileged enough to have more options) will leave for organizations where they are trusted.

Innovation

Building networks that allow individuals to connect both within and beyond the organization encourages bridging that fills gaps in knowledge or innovation within your organization. To be innovative, an organization needs to have a culture of trust and blamelessness, one that will not only reward success but also handle failure well. Innovation requires taking risks, and a blameful culture that punishes risk taking as well as the failures that result will not lend itself to the risk-taking creative behavior that produces innovative solutions.

Organizational trust is strongly correlated with organizational collaboration, as more and more individuals are trusted, connected with, and seen as members of our own groups and circles. Trust in the team, the organization, and the processes they use makes companies more tolerant of risk, as people believe and trust that their colleagues will be able to not only handle but also learn from failures. Being too risk-averse and not knowing how to deal with failure means being less prepared for when failures do happen, and being less prepared and slower to react means that failures will have more of an impact.

In addition to trust and collaboration, innovation is often the result of creative "leaps" that don't necessarily follow a strictly regimented process. While it is difficult to describe exactly what sparks these creative processes, they often come when least expected, when the mind is distracted thinking about something else in the foreground while still ruminating on a problem to be solved in the background. This is why so many people claim that great ideas came to them while they were doing something unrelated to the problem at hand, such as taking a shower or going for a run. Similarly, interactions with other people, especially from outside the organization, can provide new insights from unexpected directions.

Requirements for Affinity

Organizational affinity does not happen overnight, without effort, or without the right circumstances to allow it. In this section, we will discuss what circumstances and characteristics are required for affinity to take place. This is not to say that each of these areas has to be perfect—even in the best organizations these are ongoing works with a focus on constant improvement—but an organization that has serious issues with slack, explicit goals and values, space, or cooperation will find it significantly more difficult to realize all the benefits that affinity can bring.

Slack

Slack in a work system describes a state of not actively working. Often this idleness is perceived as not productive or efficient, but in reality, planning intentional slack is necessary to avoid overassigning work. Focusing on metrics of effectiveness and efficiency around team and individual subscription rates prioritizes measurable tasks over the inherently hard-to-measure relationship work.

Slack is also critical to being able to handle variable work—that is, any work that is unplanned or takes longer to finish than anticipated. To figure out how much slack you need, first you need to understand how variable the work is and then add some buffer on top of that. If you experience exactly 20 hours of unplanned work every week, plan for 20 hours plus the amount of time needed to care for the social network and individual growth. If you experience 20–30 hours of unplanned work every week, you need to allocate more slack.

George and the General are working with their manager to figure out how much work is possible within their group of two people. After a month of using Kanban processes and assigning categories of tasks to unplanned work, they examine the metrics of the workflow and recognize they have 20 hours of unplanned work coming up each week. Taking into account networking time, personal education, and unplanned work, they decide to allocate 40 hours a week of slack, leaving 40 hours as potential scheduled work time.

 In general, the more interrupt-driven a given role is, the more slack will need to be allocated. Thus, operations teams will tend to need more slack than, for example, development teams, in order to effectively deal with the unplanned work that comes from situations like unexpected outages, emergency patches that have to be applied across the infrastructure, and requests from other teams. The more unpredictable a team's workload tends to be, the more slack will be needed as well. Slack is also critical for work–life balance and individual health, both necessities for effective and creative thinking.

Explicit Values and Goals

Many teams find that if they don't explicitly plan for something, it won't get done. As fast-paced and pressure-filled as many engineering environments tend to be today, it is difficult enough to meet even all of their stated goals, let alone anything that goes unsaid. All too often, developing professional relationships is not deemed important enough to plan for, and without planning for it, it is very unlikely that it will happen, leading teams to miss out on the many benefits of affinity described previously.

Both individual contributors and their managers need to understand that relationship work is a valued and important part of their job. If they are oversubscribed with work, relating to others and "wasting" time might not be perceived as valuable. It is crucial to realize that work comes in many forms, and just because someone isn't sitting at their desk actively working on a ticket in a queue does not mean that they aren't making valuable contributions to a team.

Attitudes like this can often be found among groups like old-school system administrators or people who have spent a great deal of time in large corporate environments, as that is what they have learned work looks like over the years. But, as we have shown, building and maintaining relationships provides many benefits for both individuals and teams. It is necessary to make this work explicitly valued, so that expectations are clear. Managers and team leads should express the expected outcomes, and then make sure to celebrate individuals accomplishing these outcomes.

 A skills matrix, used to define what skills and abilities are expected at different levels within an organization or role, can be very useful for explicitly setting goals for this kind of behavior. While there might be several rows in the matrix focusing on technical or "hard" skills and the projects that are completed, there should also be some dedicated to interpersonal and collaboration skills. Valuing humility and active listening as critical to the team and organization encourages strengthened relationships by giving peers the time and space to share their opinions, and recognizing that no single individual is the most important or has all of the solutions.

Adhering to a system like this can help ensure that people are being evaluated fairly with respect to all the different kinds of work they are contributing. Explicitly valuing relationship building can also help you avoid ending up with that one engineer with great technical chops but poor interpersonal skills, if it is well known throughout your organization that such behavior will not be tolerated or rewarded. The things that you measure and reward for are usually the things that you get, and this is just as true of "soft" skills as it is of "hard" ones.

Space

Within a company, create a shared break space that allows for collaboration across teams with the right infrastructure for ad hoc creativity and problem solving. These shared spaces should not come at the cost of individual working spaces, as that encroaches on territory and identity. In-house coffee bars are a good option, providing a mental break from the current tasks, as well as a physical break area. Keep in mind, though, that not everyone drinks coffee, so providing a variety of caffeinated and noncaffeinated refreshments is key to making sure that everyone feels they can participate in these relationship-building spaces.

Some may worry about time away from desks, and *real work*. As mentioned earlier, relationship work is undervalued especially in regard to its crucial role as a catalyst for "real" work. Creating these small spaces to gather and work encourages individuals and teams to work more autonomously to collect the information they need. Also consider, however, that spaces should not favor any one team over another, if possible (e.g., don't place all the bookable conference rooms in one team's area of the office); following this guideline will encourage interteam as well as intrateam relationships.

 Having collaborative spaces in a variety of sizes and configurations is key, though some organizations may be limited by the office space they have available, and not everyone has the ability or resources to remodel their spaces at will. Still, having rooms that range from 1-person phone booths (so phone calls with colleagues or vendors don't disturb the people nearby) to 20-person conference rooms, and from 2-person rooms where people can pair to open spaces where people can come and go as they please, allows people to pick and choose what collaborative styles work for them based on what they're working on at any given time. Further, giving people the time and space to strengthen bonds leads to better retention. We often stay at jobs longer than intended because people make the difference.

One of the problems with open-office floor plans is that they make it harder for anything to happen without being a distraction to the people trying to work nearby, and this includes collaborative or pairing work. Just because this work is valuable doesn't mean it isn't also loud and distracting to someone who is trying to get head down into a tough problem. If you have an open-office plan without any secluded spaces where people can avoid disturbing each other, relationships or productivity (or both) will suffer, so make sure you keep this in mind when evaluating any office space leases or changes.

Collaboration and Cooperation

In addition to providing space and encouragement for employees to cooperate and collaborate with one another, an organization needs to have a culture that really promotes and rewards relationship-building work and behaviors if it wants to realize all the associated benefits. This means rewarding behaviors that involve or encourage cooperation while making sure to avoid either intentionally or unintentionally fostering a competitive environment.

As we mentioned in Part II, using a system such as stack ranking for rating employee performance can be a big detractor from a cooperative environment, because in order for one person to "win" at the stack ranking game, they must ensure that the people around them "lose." By pitting people against each other for promotions, raises, and even just keeping their job, organizations almost guarantee that they will not see any true collaboration.

Similarly, look out for people or systems that reward behavior such as gossiping or tattling to a third party rather than directly addressing issues with the people involved. Passive-aggressive or other indirect behavior undermines trust, which is crucial for cooperation. However, it's important to note that this does not apply to cases when someone feels harassed or otherwise unsafe in the workplace: in many situations, people do not feel safe addressing that behavior directly and should feel comfortable raising their concerns with their manager or HR.

All of these factors combined can work together to create a very effective environment of collaboration and affinity.

Measuring Affinity

It is hard to measure affinity. You can measure the outcomes of affinity, but not affinity itself. This does not preclude taking an active stance toward encouraging the development of community. Rather, you can keep an eye out for signs that members of your organization are growing and developing relationships both among and between teams, as well as fostering connections outside your organization.

Employee Skills and Evaluations

Setting explicit goals and clearly defining values around affinity and collaboration is a solid and necessary step toward achieving those goals, and defining those goals within employee feedback mechanisms is part of that. A good skills matrix or review tool will place an emphasis on areas such as how well an individual communicates.

Clearly, this is an area where the quality of communication matters much more than the quantity, and where peer feedback can be quite useful. For example, consider when employees need information or assistance from one another. Do people know who to direct their questions to? Are they willing to ask the right people, even if those people are outside their team? Are they unwilling to ask for assistance even if their refusal means slowing down their own progress or even blocking someone else? Are they known for derailing meetings, code reviews, or email threads with arguments that most people view as unnecessary or counterproductive?

On the other side of things, pay attention to people who are seen as good sources of information, the people that others turn to when they need help. The best communicators are seen as such good resources often because of how they respond: they do not condescend, they do not see questions as being beneath them, and they help others around them get their answers, even if they don't know the answers themselves or are busy with other things. Good collaborators genuinely want to help other people around them improve and succeed.

By building skills matrices, promotion processes, and rating systems around the qualities that you care about, you will be able to start to see where people's collaborative strengths and weaknesses are. Getting this feedback directly from employees' peers, whether that be their direct teammates or people they work with on other teams, can provide insights into their day-to-day work habits that managers might not get a chance to see otherwise.

Interteam Interaction

If your organization is doing any kind of work or project tracking, that can provide a good place to start when it comes to measuring how work happens when it involves more than one team. If people are diligent about updating tickets when they move between different people who are working on them, this can be a very valuable source of information on the way that work gets done and which people are involved. If you think you can't do this because people don't update their tickets, this is another factor that can be measured and tracked.

Depending on what your organization uses to track larger projects as opposed to work small enough for individual tickets, this can be a good way to indirectly measure interteam affinity as well. It should be noted that, while this isn't strictly required, it will be a lot easier if every team is using common software to track and organize their work rather than every team having their own individual system. Potential points of interest here are:

- How many teams are involved in a given project?
- What was the breakdown of work between teams? How evenly was it divided? Did those divisions make sense, or did one team or team member seem overworked compared to others?
- How much time was spent in various stages of the project's lifecycle? In particular, how much time went into planning and what was the team breakdown during that stage?
- How frequently did misunderstandings occur between teams or project members? Were these misunderstanding specific to a particular group or method of communication?

Both during specific interteam projects as well as during the regular course of their work, it can be interesting to note how frequently or infrequently people seek out members of other teams. How willing are people to ask other teams' members for advice? How often do people ask for clarification versus assuming they know what someone else was trying to communicate? How often do people seek out others for pairing work? These are all good things to look at within individual teams as well, but if you notice these behaviors happening frequently within a team and yet not at all across teams, that might be a sign that something is amiss.

It can also be beneficial to look at how many projects span more than one team versus how many are constrained to only a single team's members. If work does involve multiple teams, does that involvement occur simultaneously, or does one team finish their part and then "hand off" what they've done to another team? While those sorts of hand-offs are not necessarily bad, they might be a sign that more collaboration could be happening throughout the process, and the work should be investigated further to see if any improvements can be made. Similarly, a project that is confined to only one team might not be a problem, but if the results of that work will be used by or will affect other teams, check to see if there are ways to involve those teams throughout the process.

Giving Back to the Community

A large part of what makes the devops movement so strong is its community, the willingness of practitioners to come together and talk about how and what they are working on. Unlike decades prior, there is not an aura of secrecy surrounding industry technologies and practices. In fact, some of the most well-known companies in this space have been speaking openly for years about not only their successes but their struggles and failures as well.

Etsy, well known for their engineering blog *Code as Craft* and the numerous tools they have open sourced, including StatsD, refers to this idea as "generosity of spirit." This generosity includes writing public blog posts about work, speaking at industry conferences, or making open source contributions, and employees are encouraged to participate in at least one, if not more, of these yearly to make sure that they are continuing to enrich and give back to the community. Any organization that gets use and value from conference talks, blog posts, meetups, or open source projects should make a concerted effort to return those favors in kind.

It is people being willing to share their work and ideas freely and openly that makes the community not only strong but also valuable. When people communicate their ideas via media such as Twitter, LinkedIn, or various meetups and conferences, we can make connections and ties that we wouldn't have otherwise, discover solutions and new insights that we hadn't thought of ourselves, and avoid wasting our time working on problems that have already been solved (thanks to the ever-growing body of open source software), allowing us to make better use of our collective time and efforts.

As we discussed earlier in this chapter, part of what makes a cooperative community successful is the idea that bad actors, acting out of self-interest at the expense of the group, can be sanctioned. Only taking from the community and never giving anything in return is not cooperative behavior, and while the generosity of spirit of other organizations will likely lead them to continue to share their knowledge and insights with the community, it would be a loss for the industry as a whole if that were no longer the case.

Sparkle Corp Dev and Ops Affinity

"I like what I see with the possibility of reducing development time on use cases like this review feature, in order to allow us to improve the end user's experience of our service. Based on our current schedule, I think we could spend a sprint on assessing and developing a prototype if you think it's worthwhile," said Hedwig at the conclusion of the demos.

"I have minimal experience with MongoDB. I'd need to sync back with the rest of the team, and find out how much experience they have and how difficult adopting a new project would be," cautioned George. "As a relatively new operations engineer here at Sparkle Corp, I don't want to commit the ops team to something unsustainable."

"Let's keep this assessment open, and keep communicating updates. George, please join Geordie, Josie, and Alice on this project. I will coordinate with the operations team lead to ensure that both teams can have a voice in making the decision once we have more information," said the General.

Summary

Developing and maintaining open, trusting, and communicative relationships is as important between groups working together as it is between individuals. Which groups we consider ourselves members of has a fair amount of impact on our self-described identities, which in turn affects how we interact and work with people based on our perceptions of their own group memberships.

Key to a collaborative organization and industry is finding ways to break down intergroup barriers and expand our group memberships and definitions, so that work, information, and ideas can grow and flow more freely between individuals, teams, and even companies. Sharing stories and ideas between different teams within an organization and even between organizations allows for more trust, and more innovation, and helps maintain the shared mutual understanding that is crucial to a devops environment.

CHAPTER 10

Affinity: Misconceptions and Troubleshooting

The misconceptions and issues that come up around affinity are often similar to those around individual collaboration and communication, but at a higher or more organizational level.

Affinity Misconceptions

People often have differing ideas about the responsibilities and contributions of various teams within an organization, as well as how much affinity and sharing makes sense in a devops environment.

Ops Engineers Aren't as Valuable to the Organization as Developers Are

While it doesn't always refer specifically to operations and development teams, the idea that some teams are inherently more valuable to the company than others is a common one that can be very hard to shake. Part of this stems from tangible versus intangible work. Development work on products that ends up in front of customers is much more tangible to someone who doesn't necessarily understand the details of a team's day-to-day work, as are the mockups that a design team can put together and show. For work that tends to be visible only when it is missing or done poorly (think of a site outage or a rude customer support agent), this is especially true—negative events stick out in our minds much more clearly than positive ones.

The power of organizational affinity and relationships between teams is that teams can support and help each other, rather than getting in each other's way. An operations or internal tools team can stand in the way of developers deploying code, or they could make it very easy for developers to spin up test environments to work on. If the developers are helping the customers, then anyone who can help the developers is making sure that the customers are getting that much more—developers can spend even more time working on their customer-facing products and fixes, rather than waiting for a slow and buggy deploy process or trying to test their changes without a dedicated testing or development environment.

Having programs like designated ops or simply encouraging people—individuals and managers alike—to attend each other's meetings allows for a lot more visibility into what different parts of the organization are working on. This can go a long way toward eliminating the misconception that some teams aren't doing as much or as valuable work. Of course, it could be the case that one team isn't doing as much as it could, but this is more often than not a question of organizational fit versus the inherent worth of the team or its members.

Especially as organizations grow and change, different teams or products might not make as much sense as they once did. Keep an eye out for how different teams and their work fit together in the context of the organization as a whole, but again be careful not to take too narrow a view of what constitutes work.

Sharing Too Much Outside the Company Might Weaken Our Competitive Position

Today's workplaces are indeed competitive ones, and it makes sense that a company wouldn't want to do anything that would put it at a competitive disadvantage in the industry. This viewpoint often leads to companies forbidding employees from doing things like speaking at conferences or open sourcing software. There is the concern that open sourcing software is giving away something for free rather than making a profit by selling it, and that conference talks might give competitors ideas that could help them succeed (as well as conferences taking time away from "real work," which we have already addressed).

Ultimately, however, the tools and techniques that most people are thinking of presenting at conferences or open sourcing in the devops community are not the same ones that their companies are making a profit on. For example, Target is a retailer— they make money by selling physical products to consumers. Giving a conference talk on how they develop the software that powers their consumer-facing website does not take away from the products they are selling, nor impact them at all. When their employees have given talks at devopsdays events and other industry conferences, they are talking about how they *support* and *create* what makes them competitive in their space, not the competitive secret sauce itself.

This is a movement that began with community, with people talking to each other about the problems they were facing and trying to find solutions to them. Developers and system administrators wanted to talk about the cultural and technical challenges ahead of them, but rarely were these challenges domain-specific ones. And with so much talk these days about how good technical talent is hard to find, limiting your employees' participation in their professional communities will limit how attractive your job openings are, and that will be the real competitive disadvantage.

Affinity Troubleshooting

Troubleshooting affinity is often an indirect effort as well. In this section, we will offer some tips for identifying and addressing several common issues that might arise in the course of building and maintaining an open, cooperative culture throughout your organization.

One or More Individuals Are Interrupting Group Flow Dynamics

As mentioned in the previous chapter, group flow is different in nature from individual flow. Some individuals, whether through dominant or arrogant behaviors that can be physical or verbal in nature, may disrupt group flow. Sometimes these individuals are perceived as key performers within an organization. When organizations do not address these behaviors directly, they are silently supporting and reinforcing them.

Beyond impacting group flow, disruptive behaviors can cause stress and frustration leading to other team members leaving the organization. Examples of disruptive behaviors include bullying, abusive language (verbal and email), humiliation, rolling the eyes, individual avoidance, refusing to mentor, refusing to help others, throwing items, and intimidation. Understanding how to respond starts with understanding why the individual is acting out with disruptive behaviors. Causes include power dynamics, displaced frustration, and conflict.

Effective organizations recognize the value of teamwork and collaboration. The first step is setting a commitment to eliminate the behaviors by being clear about the consequences. Ensure that the entire organization cooperates through education and creating a safe space for individuals to communicate violations. There should be a compact within the organization to assuage any fear of retaliation. Develop a code of conduct that defines acceptable and unacceptable behaviors and the process to manage such behaviors. The Geek Feminism website (*http://bit.ly/gf-conduct*) has guidance on creating an effective code of conduct.

If there is a infraction of the code, emphasis should be placed on the behavior, not the person. People don't always understand the impact of their words or actions. Individuals need to understand the direct link between their behavior and its impact on others. If the behavior does not change and there is a recurrence of the infraction, additional steps should be taken. Depending on the locality of your company, there may be different options available to you. For example, anger management classes or mentoring training may be appropriate. If the problem is due to chronic stress within the work environment, identify the stressors, making sure that the individual is getting enough vacation. If the problem is due to conflict, steps need to be taken to address the conflict with mediation if needed.

If remediations don't help, reorganizing the individual into another team, finding opportunities that don't require teamwork, or letting the individual go are options. Parting ways with an employee isn't necessarily a negative thing. It should be noted that making too many exceptions for people who can't seem to work well with others sets a bad precedent and may lead to more individuals who think that bad behavior is acceptable.

One Team Keeps Blocking Other Teams

If you find that one team or group seems to be getting in the way of other teams getting their own work done, the first thing to do is to investigate factors that might be contributing to the blockage. An issue of work not getting done quickly enough might indicate that the team responsible for that work is understaffed for the amount of work they have on their collective plate. Consider the example of designated operations engineers introduced earlier in this chapter: depending on the size of the operations team relative to how many other teams they have to support and those teams' workloads, there might simply be an issue of not having enough people, time, or the right combination of skills to complete everything that is being requested of them.

Teams not fully understanding each others' issues, projects, and requirements is another common cause of blockages. Especially when different groups have very different goals, priorities, and KPIs they have to meet, what is in the critical path for one team might seem inconsequential to another, causing that work to get deprioritized. This might be caused by a lack of communication. If work gets handed back and forth by simply reassigning tickets or something similar, those receiving the work might not be getting enough context to understand its importance, so it can help to ensure that the people involved are having these conversations when work changes hands.

Even if communication is happening, there can still be misunderstandings. Both teams involved should make sure that they reach as clear an understanding as possible as to what needs to get done, what the deadlines and other requirements are, and why this work is important and what its priority is at the beginning of a work handoff. The sooner any misunderstandings get cleared up, the less blockage and delay there will be.

It could be the case that there are company policies, compliance issues, technical limitations, or other reasons why requested work cannot get done, and depending on the organization environment, these reasons might not always be readily apparent. Some people and cultures find it difficult or rude to deliver a direct "no" as an answer, so paying attention to cultural differences as well as nonverbal communication can help.

Other factors in the organizational environment might be fostering a competitive atmosphere rather than a collaborative or cooperative one. If two teams are directly competing for resources such as budget or headcount, and especially if those teams have different goals and metrics they have to achieve, there is unfortunately little motivation for them to help each other out. If this turns out to be the case, that is something that will likely have to be addressed at an organizational rather than an individual or team level.

Direct communication can go a long way toward addressing many of these reasons for blockages, but it is important to go into these discussions with the right attitude. When it feels like someone is deliberately working against you, it is easy to assume that they are acting out of malice or incompetence, and your words and actions will be colored by these underlying assumptions. On the other side of things, people who feel like they are being asked too much or not appreciated for the work they do can get defensive. Both of these are breeding grounds for cycles of dysfunctional and passive-aggressive behavior. To get on the same page, both parties must remember the compact—that everyone is working for the same company and the same overall goals—and agree to try communicating openly and directly to reassess the situation and everyone's expectations.

Some Teams Are Feeling Undervalued

As mentioned previously in this chapter, there is a tendency in tech companies to perhaps overvalue their developers at the expense of other, less "glamorous" or sought-after teams and roles. Understandably, this can cause feelings of resentment from these other teams who perceive that they are undervalued, either relative to their worth in the industry or compared to other parts of their own company. As valuable as developers are, there is much more to having a successful and sustainable *business* than simply writing the software for it.

There are certainly uncontrollable economic forces that drive things like salaries, but what companies often do have control over is how other perks, benefits, and recognition are accorded throughout their organization. Developers and people in other engineering roles often get a budget allocated for conferences, conference travel, and similar events that can be very good for developing both their professional skills and their career network. Make sure that engineering is not the only department being given these opportunities.

If your company is doing things like hosting meetups and giving away high-quality branded swag for engineers as one avenue of recruitment, this is another area where other departments might start to feel overlooked. Nonengineers want to be able to show off their company spirit as well, and while a couple of T-shirts or hoodies might not seem like that big a deal, they can certainly add up to a big decrease in morale over time. And it should go without saying that your company T-shirts and hoodies should be offered in both straight and fitted cuts from the beginning—a woman whose company won't even spring for a shirt that fits her properly is not a woman who will be singing that company's praises.

We discussed previously the importance of space to developing a culture of affinity, and that is another area where imbalances are frequently seen. Anyone who sits at a desk in an office all day is prone to the physical risks that entails, regardless of whether they are writing code or answering support emails. Do not reserve the nicer chairs, better-lit office spaces, or fancy ergonomic standing desks only for engineers. Also pay attention to the availability of conference rooms and other collaborative workspaces and make sure that they are not more accessible to some employees than to others.

Finally, pay attention to which teams and employees are most frequently recognized, whether that be getting profiles on the company's blog or staff page, getting a celebration thrown in a common break area for one of their projects being completed, or getting called out in a quarterly all-hands meeting. Being recognized for effort and accomplishments is a large part of job satisfaction for many people, and hard work and long hours are much more palatable when they are recognized and rewarded, even in smaller ways.

We argue against referring to your developers as "rock stars" in job postings, and it's equally important to not treat them as rock stars in the office while treating other teams and organizations as simply stagehands. That is a breeding ground for resentment and hard feelings, not collaboration.

People Don't Seem to Trust Each Other

Encouraging, developing, and maintaining trust are no easy tasks, especially in an environment where they have been missing previously. Trust, whether that be trust in our peers or in our managers and leaders, is something that has to be earned, not something that can be demanded and then abused. If trust seems to be missing in your environment, that is almost certainly a sign that there are cultural issues that need to be addressed.

A blameful culture is not one that engenders trust, as people are expecting to be punished for mistakes beyond simple accountability and learning. We touched on the concepts of blamefulness and blamelessness previously in Parts I–II; if you are dealing with organizational trust and have not yet read those chapters, that would be a good place to start. If your organization is just starting to transition to a blameless culture from a blameful one, understand that cultural transitions will take time. It takes more time to rebuild lost trust than it does to build trust from a clean slate, so if your culture is healing from being a more harmful one, understand that things are not going to change overnight.

Open communication throughout an organization is key to building an organization of trust. It is not enough to ask individual contributors to be open and honest if managers and executives operate only in secrecy, behind either real or metaphorical closed doors. It isn't enough to simply adopt an open-door policy; most times, people will see this as an empty gesture or be unable or unwilling to risk drawing attention to themselves by asking uncomfortable questions one-on-one. Even in the best organizations, there are often questions around areas like compensation that people are not comfortable asking directly for a variety of reasons, both personal and cultural. Having regular sessions where employees can submit, view, and vote on questions anonymously and then have HR, managers, or executives answer the most common questions will provide transparency and build trust from the top down.

It is important that if you are going to do something like this, you do it 100 percent. Especially in today's world where people and companies are always trying to sell us something, people have a pretty good sense for when they are not being told the truth, whether that be outright falsehoods or simply nonanswers that are cloaked in layers of corporate-speak. The majority of people would rather be told "we can't (or won't) answer that" than be given an answer that doesn't say anything of substance.

In short, trust and communication need to be led by example, which might mean making sure that managers at all levels of the company as well as team leads have adequate training, so that they are well versed in building trust, communicating openly, and dealing with conflict.

Once the culture can support and sustain trust, getting people to interact, starting with relatively low pressure and low stakes, is one of the best ways to build connections between people and teams. Try something like a "mixer" program, where people who opt in are randomly paired with individuals on other teams and then encouraged to spend an hour or so chatting and getting to know each other, usually over lunch or coffee. This can be a great way to expand people's connections without the pressure of having to complete actual work together. Once people are used to these kinds of interactions, having pairs or small groups of people randomly assigned to do tasks like working on a backlog of small, low-priority bugs can also go a long way toward building trust and affinity.

People Are Concerned Solely About Technical Aspects of Work, Not Interpersonal Ones

One of the most common rebuttals we hear to the idea of focusing on affinity, collaboration, and cooperation is that it takes too much focus away from getting work done. While it is true that the primary goal of an organization is not to establish friendships or other interpersonal connections, ignoring the effects that interpersonal relationships can have on an organization, good or bad, is short-sighted. People who hold these sorts of opinions tend to have a very strongly held view about what constitutes "real" work, but this ignores the reality that, with *people* being the ones doing the work, anything that impacts *people's* productivity, either at an individual or group level, does have a measurable impact on "work."

No person or team exists or works in a vacuum. Even at the smallest startup, there are relationships between employees and customers, employees and prospective investors, employees and prospective employees. The larger and more complex an organization, the more these relationships can have an impact on what and how work gets done. Just think of a stereotypical enterprise company that has layers of bureaucracy and processes required to get things done. These processes are the result of many growing and changing relationships between different people, teams, and even organizations within the company. Examining the relationships in an organization can help you figure out what pain points exist, and working to develop said relationships can take steps to alleviate them.

When complex organizations have many different teams, each acting with at least some degree of independence, there will be conflicts. Without any way of identifying or addressing these conflicts, the differing goals and priorities will actively work against the overall success of the organization. Spending time and energy building relationships and developing skills encourages teams and individuals to cooperate rather than compete, and helps the organization get its collective work done. And as anyone can attest who has ever been blocked by what seems like an overly bureaucratic process (e.g., George has to put in a request to his manager, who will talk to the General's manager about something George needs the General to work on instead of just talking to her himself), a dysfunctional relationship in the workplace can absolutely hinder the progress of the "real" work getting done.

Team dynamics can also have an impact on team morale, which in turn affects productivity (as we've discussed in both this part and Part II). So while work isn't about just making friends, it is important to expand our views of what constitutes work. It is more than just sitting at a desk filling out paperwork or writing code—it is also about building the relationships that allow the organization as a whole to function cooperatively and effectively.

Different Teams Seem Like They Won't Ever Be Able to Really Work Together

In established organizations with entrenched relationships and habits, getting individuals to change ingrained responses may be difficult. When teams or groups are used to being in competition with one another, nobody wants to be the first one to alter their behavior; that feels too much like they are giving in or "losing" somehow. If people are used to being in this kind of scenario, changing their behavior means weakening their position, thus there is a strong incentive against changing behavior at all.

However, you cannot expect teams that have traditionally been in competition for resources, with radically different goals, or who have been very siloed off from each other to change their behaviors without any change in the organizational culture or the surrounding circumstances. Shifting from postmortems that ended in someone getting fired or demoted to blameless ones where the focus is on learning rather than punishment, refining the processes or tools that teams use to share work or communicate with each other, or even reorganizing the teams themselves are just a few examples of changes that might be necessary before individual and team behaviors will start to change.

Trust, a necessary component for teams to work well together, does not happen overnight and requires a culture that fosters it. Examine the environment for pressures or behaviors within the teams and organization if teams are having trust issues.

Past Interpersonal Conflicts Are Causing Present Interteam Conflicts

One common scenario that can happen within an organization that decides to undergo some kind of "devops transformation" is that there are teams that have historically been in conflict with each other. Most typically, this kind of friction is seen between development and operations teams, as their goals can in many ways be at odds with each other, but conflict can happen between any two teams that have to work together with differing goals and incentives.

You may find that, even if you have found a way at an organizational level to bring goals into better alignment, redistribute resources or adjust processes, or otherwise minimize friction and conflict between teams, the individuals on those teams still find themselves butting heads. We are all people, and as much as engineers might want to imagine themselves as being incredibly logical, emotions do still get in the way at times like these, especially if past conflicts became incredibly heated.

If the conflict between teams seems to be generally distributed, with no clear sources, it can often help to redistribute people between teams or projects, if possible. People may have formed cliques that can serve as breeding grounds for complaining and us-versus-them mentalities, and rearranging people can help encourage those cliques to break up. People can also form habits around their interactions with others; they may hear something about "the dev team" or "the ops team" and this triggers a kneejerk reaction. Rearranging (or even renaming) teams can help to break those old habits.

It's also possible that there are individuals who have unresolved conflicts that are influencing the behavior of the rest of their teams; this can be especially true if more senior people (who in some organizations tend to also be more opinionated people) are the ones with unresolved negative feelings. Regular one-on-ones with managers, mentors, or even peers can help to identify these conflicts, and it can sometimes do a lot of good to get the people to sit down and talk to each other. With enough time, and with positive changes elsewhere in the team or organization, you may find that people are able to talk things out, apologize for past transgressions (real or imagined), and start repairing their relationships.

Team X Seems to Want to Be Their Own Silo

Similar to the cliques that you might find discussed in the previous scenario, you may end up with groups of people who seem to isolate themselves from the rest of their team, department, or even organization. It can seem that while most people are open to the changes that come with a devops transformation, whether that be reorganized teams, new tools, or revised work processes, small pockets of people are significantly more resistant to these changes.

You'll often see this in people who have roles that have been historically unappreciated or underappreciated, such as IT technicians or even operations engineers. This is the kind of mentality that leads to people hoarding information as a means of job security; because they aren't feeling appreciated in a way that is meaningful to them already in the workplace, they will find a way to make themselves appreciated in some other way.

Even with a movement like devops, which places more value on roles like operations that in previous years or decades were less valued or respected, there can be areas where people still don't feel appreciated, respected, or secure in the workplace. Where devops in theory and practice diverges, you may still find groups of people who aren't thanked for their work, who are seen as "less than" by their peers, or who are treated blamefully rather than blamelessly. Alternatively, self-imposed silos may arise from the expectation of these behaviors based on past experiences, rather than the reality of them, again a knee-jerk reaction to past problems.

Resolving issues like this often involves figuring out which needs these employees have that aren't being met. Maslow's hierarchy of needs can come in handy. For basic needs, think fair compensation. For safety and security, employees need to feel assured that their jobs aren't going to disappear on them—that their work is valued by the organization and that the organization will be forthcoming about things that might impact this like potential layoffs. For belonging, people need to feel comfortable in their workplace and appreciated by their managers and peers, so keep an eye out for any who don't seem to be providing respect or valuable feedback. Finally, self-esteem and self-actualization mean employees who are able to feel proud of themselves and the work they do; if certain positions are treated as grunt work, this can certainly decrease how people feel about the work and the organization.

Looking out for the absence of any (or all) of these needs being met can help point toward areas for improving relationships with groups or teams that seem to be siloing themselves off. As with the other relationships discussed in this book, these working relationships are built on trust, which takes time and effort to build, maintain, or repair. Of course, there are also some people who are contrary to the point of refusing to let trust be repaired, and these people might not end up being a good fit for your changing organization.

People Are Blaming Mistakes on Devops

Significant changes are never without their difficulties, and there are always some people who are much more resistant to change than others. One thing that might happen during transitional periods within an organization is that people who are opposed to the ongoing changes, for whatever reason, will blame them for any issues or mistakes. As an organization starts moving toward a culture of effective devops, there may be people who are vocally opposed to these changes as their way of resisting them.

For example, suppose an organization is making progress on moving away from an infrequent and manual deploy process toward a more automated continuous delivery one. The new automated deployment tools are not perfect right from the beginning; as with every piece of software, there are bugs found that have to be worked out. People who are resistant to these changes may blame these new issues on the new tools, on devops itself, or on the people who are supporting these changes. They might say, "Everything was working well enough before" or "We wouldn't be having these kinds of issues if we had just left things the way they were." They see devops itself as the problem, rather than realizing that every new tool or process will have issues along the way and take time to get used to.

It's important that there be top-down support from management for new devops initiatives if they are to succeed. If leaders within the organization are able to be swayed by a few very loud complainers, it will be difficult for there to be any lasting change. Change doesn't happen overnight, and it's normal and expected for there to be mistakes or bugs along the way. Because there is no one-size-fits-all solution, it will take some trial and error to find the tools and processes that work best for your particular organization.

Provide ways for people to submit feedback on how changes are affecting them and how they think things are going, but pay attention to how often negative feedback comes up and its sources. If many people are finding that a given solution isn't working for them, that is certainly worth investigating and making adjustments, but if only a few negative voices are making a disproportionate amount of noise, be sure to not let them overwhelm changes that are benefiting the majority of people. Not everyone is a good fit for every organization, and someone who is that opposed to change in general—or devops, in particular—may not be a good fit for your organization as it grows.

PART IV

Tools

CHAPTER 11

Tools: Ecosystem Overview

Before embarking on a discussion of how tools can be used to improve and maintain various aspects of culture, we will expand on more definitions and terminology, following up on those described in Chapter 4 to build additional context and understanding across teams. This is by no means an exhaustive list of technologies or terms.

People may have different folk models or different understandings of these terms and concepts. Being explicit with shared meaning allows for more nuanced discussions and better understanding of these ideas.

Software Development

Software development tools help with the process of programming, documenting, testing, and fixing bugs in applications and services. Not restricted to specific roles, these tools are important to anyone who works on software in some capacity.

Local Development Environment

A consistent local development environment is critical to quickly get employees started contributing to your product. This is not to say that individuals should be locked into a single standard editor with no flexibility or customization, but rather it means ensuring that they have the tools needed to get their jobs done effectively.

Minimal requirements may vary in your environment depending on individual preferences, ranging from multiple displays for increased collaboration or high-resolution displays for more comfortable long-term viewing sessions, to specific keyboards, mice, and other input devices. Qualifying the current standard of your local development environment includes determining whether there is a consistent framework that teams share internally and across teams. Consistency of experiences can make it quicker and easier to onboard new employees and have them start making meaningful contributions.

There is a balance to strike between ensuring a consistent experience and allowing employees to customize their workstation and work habits to best suit their own individual needs. Too much customization can lead to isolation of knowledge or the additional overhead of time and effort spent fussing with specialized environment setups. But in recent years employees have started to place more importance on being able to work in their own ways, so not letting them find and express what works best for them can be a competitive disadvantage when it comes to hiring and retention.

 Identify a shared area for documenting the local development environment. Documentation can be stored within a version control repository, an internal wiki, or even a Google Doc. Proficiency with tools will develop with time and practice, so the goal isn't to have documentation that elaborates on every single detail, but enough to get individuals started toward being successful in the environment.

Version Control

Having the ability to commit, compare, merge, and restore past revisions of objects to the repository allows for richer cooperation and collaboration within and between teams. It minimizes risks by establishing a way to revert objects in production to previous versions.

Every organization should implement, use, train, and measure adoption of version control. Version control enables teams to deal with conflicts that result from having multiple people working on the same file or project at the same time, and provides a safe way to make changes and roll them back if necessary. Using version control early in your team's or product's lifecycle will facilitate adoption of good habits.

When choosing the appropriate version control system (VCS) for your environment, look for one that encourages the sort of collaboration in your organization that you want to see. Qualities that encourage collaboration include:

- opening and forking repositories;
- contributing back to repositories;
- curating contributions to your own repositories;
- defining processes for contributing; and
- sharing commit rights.

Some tools lack collaborative features but have been used long enough in your environment that there is a very high level of institutional knowledge around them. In these cases, identify the impact of not migrating to a different tool—for example, hiring capability or time spent on merging different branches—and then try to compare that with the impact of losing so much institutional knowledge. With sufficient process, collaboration can still be implemented with less collaborative tools, but it will not be as easy.

 Lines of code is not an accurate measure of value. There are different types of developers, some that refactor hundreds of confusing lines into tens of lines of simple-to-read abstractions that can be built upon by others in the team. Others focus their attention on finding the bugs hidden within code. Use quantitative measurements as informative trends to encourage the behaviors you want to see. For example, unless you have the skill to qualitatively examine code, don't assume that more is better.

Additional terminology related to version control includes:

Commit
A commit is a collection of actions comprising total number of changes made to files under version control.

Conflicts
A conflict results when two changes are too similar in nature, and the version control system can't determine which is the correct one to accept. In most cases, the version control system will provide a way to view and select the desired change to resolve the conflicts.

Pull request
A pull request is a mechanism that allows an individual to signal that a contribution is ready to be reviewed and merged into the main branch.

Cherry picking
Cherry picking is a way to choose specific commits from one branch and apply them to another. This is useful when you want to select specific changes from a pull request.

Artifact Management

An artifact is the output of any step in the software development process. When choosing between a simple repository and more complex feature-full repository, understand the cost of supporting additional services as well as inherent security concerns.

An artifact repository should be:

- secure;
- trusted;
- stable;
- accessible; and
- versioned.

Having an artifact repository allows you to treat your dependencies statically. You can store a versioned common library as an artifact separate from your software version control, allowing all teams to use the exact same shared library. You build binaries once and only once (even though you could build the same binary again), which helps alleviate complexity by ensuring that the same binary is used throughout test cycles and promotion between builds.

Artifact repositories allow you to store artifacts the way you use them. Some repository systems only store a single version of a package at a time. This can lead to problems describing the history of packages, so you will likely want to increase the duplication factor of package storage to maintain a separate artifact repository per environment in your workflow.

In the early stages of an organization's evolution, it may not yet need to pass certain security compliance requirements. As you grow and pivot along product lines, however, this may change. Having a dedicated local artifact repository allows for a much smoother transition to these requirements.

Ideally, your local development environment has the same access to your internal artifact repository as the other build and deploy mechanisms in your environment. This helps minimize the "it works on my laptop" syndrome because the same packages and dependencies used in production are now used in the local development environment. If the access is limited or blocked, this friction can lead to new ways of doing things that circumvent security and other policies.

Define Policies Early

Establish governance processes early to promote collaboration within the context of your environment and constraints. For example, identify who can push what artifacts, and establish how artifacts are vetted, licensed, and secured. This will alleviate growing pains for out-of-date artifacts.

If you don't have access to the internet within your environment, you need to host your own universe. This includes general software repositories, language-specific package servers, dependency management, and more. A lot of available shared services must be replicated. However, doing this can have several benefits, including shielding your organization from undocumented breaking changes upstream and from having external outages cause internal problems. Relying on the internet for your dependencies means that somebody else ultimately owns the availability and consistency of your builds, something that many organizations hope to avoid.

Additional terminology related to artifact management includes:

Dependency management
Dependency management is the manner and degree of interdependence a software project has on another software project. Different mechanisms exist to expose this dependency. From an artifact level, storing the dependent artifacts for your software is helpful.

Pinning
Pinning is the method of locking down an explicit version of an artifact for an environment. In dependency management, this can be helpful to define the explicit version of a dependent software artifact that works with your project.

Promotion
Promotion is the method of selecting a specific version of software to move toward delivery, generally keyed off the successful passing of tests.

Automation

Automation tools reduce labor, energy, and/or materials used with a goal of improving quality, precision, and accuracy of outcomes.

Server Installation

Server installation is the automation of configuring and setting up individual servers. Hardware manufacturers like HP and Dell provide a tool that works for their brand of hardware.

Some Linux distributions provide operating system–specific tooling as well. As an example, Cobbler and Kickstart can be used to automate the server installation of Red Hat Enterprise Linux or CentOS. Operations staff can write *Kickstart files* that can specify hard disk partitioning, network configuration, which software packages to install, and more.

Hardware Lifecycle Management

Every company has to deal with hardware or lifecycle management in one way or another, though the advent of the cloud and infrastructure or platform services has cut down on the amount of attention this requires to some extent. The hardware lifecycle begins with planning and purchasing (or leasing); continues with installation, maintenance, and repair; and ends with trading in, returning, or recycling.

Infrastructure Automation

Fundamentally, infrastructure automation is provisioning elements of infrastructure through code—treating this code just like the rest of your software, with the ability to recover business through data backups, code repository, and compute resources.

Additional terminology related to infrastructure management includes:

Configuration drift
    Configuration drift is the phenomenon where servers will change or drift away from their desired configuration over time.

MTBF
    MTBF is mean time between failure: the uptime between two failure states.

MTTR
    MTTR is mean time to repair: the length of time that it takes to restore operation to a system.

Availability
    Availability is a commonly used measurement of how often a system or service is available compared to total time it should be usable. Availability = MTBF / (MTBF + MTTR).

Capacity management
    Capacity management is a process used to ensure that infrastructure and other resources are correctly sized to meet current and future business needs in a cost-effective manner.

Snowflake server
    A snowflake server is a server that has gotten to its current, desired configuration by way of many manual changes, often a combination of command-line sorcery, configuration files, hand-applied patches, and even GUI configurations and installations.

When people refer to configuration management in operations roles, often the intended meaning is infrastructure automation. Depending on the system, different parts of it might be automated, including aspects such as which software packages are installed on a server, what versions of those various packages should be used, the presence or absence of various files on the system, or which services are supposed to be running.

"Treat infrastructure code like the rest of your software" means the code is developed using a common local development environment, versioned in version control, versioned in artifacts in an artifact repository, tested, and verified before being put into production.

Infrastructure automation should minimally provide:

Management of configuration drift
Configuration drift can be due to manual changes, software updates or errors, or entropy. A good solution will have a way of preventing this, often by having an individual node regularly check the desired configuration against its actual configuration and self-correcting any inconsistencies.

Elimination of snowflake servers
Infrastructure automation solutions can avoid creation of snowflake servers by ensuring changes are clearly and deterministically defined. You can eliminate snowflake servers by adding management to one piece of the system at a time until the same configuration management recipe can be used to re-create the server from scratch in its desired configuration.

Versioned artifacts of infrastructure code
A good infrastructure automation solution uses version control and an artifact repository. This ensures the code that defines the server configuration can be versioned with all the benefits that come from versioning, such as being able to easily roll back changes to a known good version, or have post-commit hooks that run tests against the infrastructure-defining code. It's also a familiar process such that all team members feel comfortable contributing toward improving the infrastructure code.

Minimizing complexity
By specifying configuration versions per platform type or version, infrastructure automation solutions allow individuals (regardless of role) to manage a heterogeneous environment with a minimum of overhead.

Even in a startup with a small number of systems, it's absolutely critical to not build additional technical debt. Investing in individuals with operational skills that understand the difference between snowflake shell scripts and infrastructure automation will make the difference in whether you are spending time and money on specializing outside of the area in which you are competing.

If the various infrastructure automation tools available do not cater to your exact needs, it's still more cost-effective to help expand the fundamental features or reliability of software that exists in the space rather than rolling your own.

Infrastructure automation leads to repeatable, consistent, documented, auditable, and resilient processes. This frees up time, improves efficiency of staff, allows for more flexibility, and facilitates risk measurement. Infrastructure automation also increases the degree of confidence that the machine setup and deployment are identical, reducing the amount of time spent debugging problems based on system differences.

Contrast infrastructure automation with manual configuration on every single one of a group of servers. Humans performing repetitive tasks leads to mistakes. Systems might be configured inconsistently due to a change in process not configured on older systems or a missed step from the checklist.

Don't institute more processes and checklists. Instead, ensure that sufficient time is allocated to translate these manual checklists into computer-executable scripts. Computers are much better at repetitive tasks than humans are.

With there being so many tangible benefits to using infrastructure as code, it is often one of the first tools that companies investigate in implementing a cultural transformation. Tools can only be understood in the context of the specific environment in use; that is, the specific culture and beliefs of the environment can impact the efficacy of the tool. Which infrastructure automation works best for you will depend on your unique needs.

System Provisioning

While companies once had to plan, buy, and provision hardware in data centers, now they have the option to invest in cloud infrastructure. With on-demand computing, companies can purchase only what they need and scale up and down as necessary. This infrastructure can be purchased and provisioned much faster than physical hardware, and is often more cost-effective for organizations.

System provisioning extends infrastructure automation, allowing companies to define their infrastructure in terms of the clusters of dependent systems rather than just individual nodes. It allows individuals to specify how they want a group of servers to be provisioned once, and then to automatically use that specification as many times as they want later.

Test and Build Automation

In the days of the first computers and compilers, programs were rarely contained in more than one source file. As programs began to grow in size and complexity, developers started to split them out into multiple source files. Standard libraries of code made available to users of a given programming language added to the complexity. With so many different source files needing to be compiled together correctly to get the final program executables, it became necessary to automate the build processes.

Build automation tools today usually specify both how the software is to be built (what steps need to be done and in what order) and what dependencies are required (what other software needs to be present in order for the build to succeed). Some tools are best suited to projects in specific programming languages, such as Apache's Maven and Ant, which, while they can technically be used with other languages, are most often used with Java projects. Others, such as Hudson or Jenkins, can be used more broadly with a wider range of projects.

These tools usually fall into one of three use cases:

On-demand automation
: This tool is run by the user, often on the command line, at the user's discretion. For example, a developer might run a Make script by hand during local development to make sure she can build the software locally before checking it into version control.

Scheduled automation
: This process runs on a predefined schedule, such as a nightly build. Nightly builds are created every night, usually at times when nobody is working so that no new changes are taking place while the software is building (though this is becoming less doable as teams become more globally distributed).

Triggered automation
: This tool runs as specified events happen, such as a continuous integration server that kicks off a new build every time a commit is checked into the code.

Yvonne Lam on Tests, Monitors, and Diagnostics

Often the terms *tests*, *monitors*, and *diagnostics* are conflated, causing more churn within and between teams. In order to work together, teams need to establish a common vocabulary to encode information. This encourages shared knowledge without limiting any individual team member or requiring everyone to know every single detail.

During Sysadvent 2014 (*http://bit.ly/lam-monitors*), Yvonne Lam identified a set of questions a team should ask to build this shared context around tests, monitors, and diagnostics:

- Where is it going to run?
- When is it going to run?
- How often will it run?
- Who is going to consume the result?
- What is that entity going to do with the result?

Lam further enumerated a set of definitions that could be applied to clarify the differences. *Tests* run against nonproduction systems and qualify the system or software readiness. A test generally runs when something changes. *Monitors* run against preproduction and production systems on a schedule. A monitor generally runs frequently or is triggered by an event. *Diagnostics* run against production systems on demand due to an event.

All three of these are needed to most effectively track how various systems are behaving, but being able to clarify that different groups or individuals will have slightly different areas of responsibility here can help maintain a shared understanding and responsibility.

Additional terminology related to testing includes:

Smoke testing
Smoke tests originated with hardware testing to determine whether powering on a device would cause it to start smoking, an indication of a major problem. In software, a smoke test is a very basic, quick test to determine whether the output is possible and reasonable.

Regression testing
Regression tests verify that changes to software do not introduce new bugs or failures.

Usability testing

Usability tests involve testing a product on users to measure its capacity to meet its intended purpose by testing it on users.

A/B testing

A/B tests are an experimental approach in which two different versions of a web page or an application are compared to determine which one performs better.

Blue-green deployment

Blue-green deployment is a release process of maintaining two identical production environments. One environment is considered live and serves all traffic. The final stage of testing a new release is done in the second environment. When tests pass, traffic is routed to the second environment. This deployment process can reduce risk; if something happens with the new release, you can immediately roll back to the previous production environment.

Canary process

In the past, coal miners used canaries as an early warning system to detect toxic gases. When the canaries started to suffer symptoms of exposure, miners knew that the conditions of the mine were unsafe. In software, the canary process involves running new code on a small subset of production systems to see how performance of the new code compares to the old code.

Monitoring

Monitoring is a large topic that can be split into multiple facets—most commonly events and analytics. The methods of information collection include metrics and logs. Monitoring includes gathering basic system-level metrics such as if a server is up or down, how much memory and CPU are being used, and how full each disk is, as well as higher-level application monitoring, which can range from how many user requests a web server is handling, how many items are queued in a queuing system, how long a given web page takes to load, and what are the longest-running queries going into a database. While once solely the domain of system and network administrators, as software grows more complex and teams collaborate more, people are beginning to realize that monitoring is a core reflection of product health.

In general, monitoring is the process of tracking the current state of your systems and environment, usually with the goal of checking whether or not they meet some predefined conditions of what constitutes the desired state. Often monitoring, alerting, and testing are conflated. This leads to confusion about what we are trying to accomplish or build. As mentioned, monitoring usually runs on a predefined schedule while tests are run in response to changes. Alerts are automated communications sent to humans about the results of a test or a monitor.

Metrics

Metrics are the collection of qualitative and quantitative measurements. Generally they are compared against some benchmark or established standard, tracked for analytics, or tracked for historical purposes. Often metrics are siloed within functional organizations, which can impact choosing the right direction for product development.

Metrics are one of the key parts of monitoring; data can be gathered and stored for nearly any part of even the most complex web software, and different teams can have different metrics that they keep track of and use in their work. StatsD and Graphite are very commonly used and a powerful combination for tracking, storing, and viewing metrics.

 There is a community-driven effort to define the set of system and application metrics that should be grouped by protocol, service, and application on GitHub in the metrics-catalog repository maintained by Jason Dixon, organizer of the *Monitorama* monitoring conference. It is a repository of good practices intended to serve as a reference for people looking to build out or expand their metric collection.

Logging

Logging is the generation, filtering, recording, and analysis of events that occur on a system due to operating system or software messages. When tracking down the source of a software issue, one of the first things that engineers often do is to check the logs for any relevant error messages. Logs can be treasure troves of useful information, and with storage getting cheaper and cheaper, just about any log you might want can be saved and stored for later use. Logs can come from the applications you develop, from third-party tools you use, and even from the operating system itself. As there is no logging standard across software, it can be difficult to categorize and qualify events within logs to identify patterns of concern.

A single system can generate hundreds or even thousands of lines of logs a day. In modern environments that have dozens of applications running on hundreds or thousands of servers, the sheer volume of log data can be overwhelming; it is no longer a simple matter of searching through one logfile. Much work has gone into developing applications that handle the storage and searching of logs. The complexities of logging solutions are beyond the scope of this chapter, but their value should not be underestimated.

Alerting

Monitoring and alerting are important not only from a performance perspective, but also from a preventative one, in that they help you find out about potential issues before they become actual issues for your customers. For example, when the US HealthCare.gov site was first launched in October 2013, they originally had no monitoring or alerting to let them know whether or not the website, which had been two years in the making, was up or not.

As United States Digital Service administrator Mikey Dickerson shared in several industry talks, his team was reduced to watching news sources such as CNN report on whether the site was having issues as their original form of monitoring during its first few months of automation. While it is not a panacea, a well-considered alerting strategy could have cut down on some of the embarrassment that came from having those issues be so public.

When reasoning about alerting, you need to consider several factors:

Impact

Not all systems have the same impact. Something that is widespread, affecting multiple systems or a large group of customers, has a much higher impact than something that affects only a small subset of systems or people. Some incidents aren't customer facing at all, or might affect systems that have enough redundancy so as to not have much impact that way. To avoid alert fatigue, as we will discuss in more detail later, alerting should be restricted to incidents that have the most impact.

Urgency

Similar to impact, not all issues are equally urgent. An urgent issue is one that requires a fast (or sometimes immediate) response. For example, your site being completely down such that you are currently losing money or customers is much more urgent than a purely informational blog site being unreachable. Different stakeholders will likely have different opinions about what is urgent, so it's important to consider all the stakeholders when configuring your monitoring and alerting.

Interested party

Primarily, the parties interested in an incident are those affected by it; this could be your customers (or a subset of them) or groups of employees in the case of internal service incidents. Interested parties could also be taken to mean those responsible for responding to an incident. For example, if only DBAs can deal with a particular kind of database issue, it would make sense to alert them, rather than alerting an operations team whose only action would be to call the DBAs.

Resources

What resources are required to respond to a given incident or alert, and what is their availability? Is there enough human coverage to make sure that multiple incidents can be responded to, or do you have only one on-call person that is a single point of failure without backup? Does your organization have the resources to function without a given service, piece of hardware, or individual? These are all things to consider when setting up your alerting.

Cost

There are costs associated with monitoring and alerting. These include the cost of a monitoring service and solution, the cost of storage space for historical monitoring or alert data, and the cost of sending out alerts to humans, not to mention the costs associated with responding to incidents from the responders' point of view and the cost to your company if a given service is unavailable.

In general, alerting is the process of creating *events* from the data gathered through monitoring, with the goal usually being to direct human attention to something that might need human intervention.

Events

Event management is the element of monitoring that acts on existing knowledge around impacts to systems and services. For 24/7 services, this generally reflects the need for real-time information about the status of all of the different components of infrastructure. A system is configured to monitor a specific metric or log based on a defined event and to signal or alert if a threshold is crossed or an alert condition has been met.

With much software development now being done on web software that is expected to be available 24/7, more consideration is being given to handling alerts that occur when engineers are at home instead of in the office. One way of dealing with this is to set up as much automated event handling as possible.

Many alerting and monitoring systems have built-in ways to automatically respond to a given event. The Nagios monitoring system, for example, has "event handlers" that can be configured for different alert conditions. These handers can do a variety of things, from automatically restarting a service that had crashed to creating a ticket for a technician to replace a failed hard disk. Automated event handlers can cut down on the amount of work that operations staff have to do (and likely the number of times they get woken up off-hours as well), but they are not without their risks. It's important to ensure that your failure conditions are clearly defined, that the event handler process is understood well enough to be automated, and that there are necessary safeguards in place to keep the automation from causing more problems than it solves.

No alerting system is 100 percent accurate 100 percent of the time. A *false positive* is when an event is generated when there isn't an issue. If your events generate alerts such as pages that are designed to wake people up off-hours to deal with them, a false positive will disturb someone's sleep unnecessarily. On the flip side, a *false negative* is when an incident occurs without generating an alert for it, which could lead to a longer time before the issue is detected and resolved. There are costs to both false positives and false negatives, and which one is better or worse to risk will depend on your specific issues and environment.

Over time, you will want to tune and adjust your monitoring and alerting as you learn more about the true impact of your issues and events. We recommend monitoring the trends of your alerting, including information such as whether or not any action was taken for each event, how many of your alerts were actionable overall, and how many of them occurred off-hours.

Alert design, or how to create alerts that convey information in the most efficient way for humans to interpret, is a big topic in alerting these days. Etsy developed their OpsWeekly tool (*https://github.com/etsy/opsweekly*) to allow for this kind of tracking as well as categorization of alerts by type of alert and component. Keeping track of alert trends and performing analytics on the alert data can make a big difference in improving the effectiveness of alerts, as well as improving the health and happiness of the humans whose job it is to respond to them.

Just as with other first responders, on-the-job experience leads to implicit knowledge of what alerts are noise. It may be hard to generalize an automated mechanism that handles all cases clearly, but it is important to keep working to improve the efficiency of the alerting system. Alert fatigue, or desensitization to alerts (usually false positives), can lead to slower response to actual issues as well as contributing to burnout.

Environments change: something that was a problem before may not be a problem now due to a change in software function, or perhaps complexity grows and the old way of solving the problem doesn't work anymore. Humans can change to deal with the issue quickly, but algorithms do not have the same adaptive behaviors. Dealing with this constant change is an important part of alert and incident management.

Evolution of the Ecosystem

Over time, from server installation automation to infrastructure configuration and automation, there is a trend to simplify and remove the repetitive tasks that can be subject to human error. With the introduction of containers, the pipeline from the laptop to production has simplified more.

As automation is added to the different parts of the environment, new patterns are discovered. With infrastructure automation, adhering to one version of an operating system is less important, as quickly spinning up a new instance with updated packages on a new system may be more useful from a security standpoint.

Continuous delivery and continuous deployment have freed humans up to focus on what matters. Automated shortened feedback cycles through build automation with tests give us additional confidence and insight into our systems.

The ecosystem will continue to evolve as application development adopts increased operability. Enumerating the 12-factor application (*http://12factor.net*) by hand will go the same way as hand-crafted configurations on servers. When the operable requirements are standardized and automated, employees have the freedom of choice of language and framework.

These trends bring into focus the tools that stress the "we" over "me," building understanding across teams and encouraging time spent on valuable outcomes.

Summary

In this chapter, we have given you an overview of the current ecosystem of tools. While these tools are an important part of a devops environment, it is important to emphasize that they enhance, but can never replace, the interpersonal and cultural aspects of that environment. How tools are used, and the ease with which they can be used, impacts the acceptance and proliferation of specific aspects of culture. When we talk about devops tools, we mean both the tools themselves and the manner of their use, not their fundamental characteristics.

The devops culture is one of collaboration across teams, organizations, and industries. When developing solutions, it is important to think about their impact on teams and organizations, not just individuals. This sometimes means adjusting expectations for the good of the organization, working to find solutions that work for those beyond an organization's "rock stars" or those who have the loudest voices and can have a positive impact on the organization as a whole.

Devops tools stress "we" over "me"; they allow teams and organizations to build mutual understanding to get work done. Your choice of tools is a choice in a common language. Is this language one that benefits your organization as a whole or merely a subset of specific teams? At times, due to the lack of availability of an equally balanced tool, a choice must be made that has a higher cognitive cost to one team over another. Be aware of the cost and empathetic to the teams impacted.

CHAPTER 12

Tools: Accelerators of Culture

Tools are accelerators, increasing our velocity by driving change based on an organization's current culture and direction. When we don't understand our current position or direction, applying acceleration leads to unexpected outcomes with potentially negative impact.

The world changes rapidly; a reflexive response is to follow others in the hopes of mirroring their success. We need to take time to understand our current position, our relationships to other teams, organizations, competitors, and the world at large. This helps frame what we should currently work on, what we should delay, and what to eliminate from our environment.

In this chapter, we move beyond our examination of the current tool ecosystem and present real-world examples of how tools and culture influence and impact each other. We present these studies not to serve as specific how-tos but rather to demonstrate the different ways in which organizations evaluate, choose, and make use of tools within their environments. These studies guide and demonstrate how to reason about tooling choices, rather than recommending any particular tools as a one-size-fits-all solution to all your devops needs.

The Value of Tools to People

We have a long history of using tools to get jobs done more effectively. Moving from typewriters to word processors reduced the cost of making changes and correcting mistakes. Going from punchcards and assembly languages to higher-level languages increases understanding of code.

These tools were not invented as ends in and of themselves—they were all created to make specific jobs easier for the people using them, and that's important to keep in mind when choosing tools. These tools all allow us to collaborate more as software has moved from being written and supported by one person to being written by multiple people, and multiple teams, and having to be understood and maintained by different teams, sometimes years later.

What Are Tools?

Often when tools are discussed, software is the focus—which programming languages, IDEs, text editor, shell, configuration management solution, or chat program to use. Tools are more than software, though: they're essentially anything that helps us achieve a goal without being consumed in the process:

- A server lift cart will reduce injuries and speed up the rack and stack processes within a data center.

- A smaller, lighter laptop creates less physical strain when you're traveling to conferences or bringing a computer through a data center.

- Choosing a hardware RAID solution over a software RAID solution costs more money but offers feature like battery backups and easier maintenance.

The Best Tool

Tools do not have equal value and costs. If they did, we wouldn't need to write this chapter; you could just pick whichever tool meets your requirements. Even among tools that nearly everyone agrees are key, like configuration management or source control, some are better suited for a particular environment.

Tools change based on experience, knowledge, and processes. This means teams can use the same tool and have vastly different outcomes. Tools have to fit within the context of the environment. There is no best tool without context, and context is continually changing.

The Right Tools for Real Problems

For a tool to be widely adopted and implement successful change, it needs to solve real problems. People need to be involved throughout the decision-making processes for a given tool, so their issues, frustrations, and concerns will be discovered, understood, and addressed.

In general, understanding the real underlying issues that tools help us solve will enable us to choose the right solutions and fully understand the complexities of our work. By understanding these complexities, we can work to minimize them and any associated risks, which in turn can help to reduce expenses and ensure that people are focusing on the right areas.

In some organizations, procurement processes are removed from the people who use the tools. This can make a process or cultural issue look like a tool or technical problem.

Growing a new product or organization has different concerns than maintaining an existing one. Decisions should not be made unilaterally by one person based solely on what they find interesting and exciting. Often a tool is chosen because someone just wanted to try it out, and that's not a sufficient reason.

While tooling can be interesting, and the right automation can free up people's time and energy to work on more complex problems, for tools to be effective they need to be chosen for reasons other than being interesting or new.

Embracing Open Source

Open source communities provide a way for individuals to practice collaboration with other individuals. Employees learn the value of managing contributions from other individuals, and how to create contributions that are useful to others. For example, multiple small, discreet commits that focus on one intended change at a time are easier to manage and accept than one large commit that touches many different pieces of code.

Should companies worry that open sourcing their tooling will take away their competitive advantage? If your company's success depends on your tooling, that should be part of your business model, so that you're making money from either the software itself or, as in many companies these days, the support or services for that software.

Contributing to open source is an excellent reflection of company intentions. Open sourcing software within companies encourages teams to contribute to each other's projects rather than reinventing the wheel, and it exposes both individual contributors and managers to the benefits of open source collaboration. Contributing to open source and using open source often go hand in hand as well. Teams that are used to the open source community are more likely to look for open source solutions that already exist rather than writing their own.

Many companies look toward the well-known players in the devops space and their open source contributions, such as Netflix and Etsy, and feel compelled to start writing and open sourcing many of their own tools as well. Despite the benefits of open-source contribution, balance is key here: too far in the other direction, and you end up with Not Invented Here syndrome. This is a term used to describe companies who, on principle, refuse to use third-party tools because they originated outside the company.

There can be various reasons for this behavior, with the most common probably being competition, where companies don't want to acknowledge solutions created by competitors, let alone use them, or fear of software that is external and unknown. Maybe they don't trust that other people could write code as well as they could themselves, or maybe they'd rather write something than figure out how to read and use someone else's code. Some people just like the challenge of creating software that they haven't before, or trying a project written in a new language.

There can be valid concerns about using a third-party solution. If it is something that will be integrated into an existing software project, that project's license might have to be updated or changed to match the license of the new external component. There is also the possibility that the software's maintainer will abandon it, no longer providing bug fixes, security updates, or support, or that future development will introduce breaking changes.

Companies might also not want to be tied to a particular vendor for a variety of reasons. Still, there are serious drawbacks to a case of Not Invented Here. Unless you have a team of security experts, any cryptographic software you write is likely to contain bugs and thus security vulnerabilities. A company not in the business of networking is unlikely to get any benefits from writing their own DNS server; any effort they can produce is unlikely to be better than BIND, and certainly won't be worth the time spent in development, maintenance, and troubleshooting a piece of software that nobody else has any experience with.

 Tools can and will reinforce behavior, which will affect your culture. It is critical to also examine tools when examining behaviors and cultures, and this is where the true importance of your tooling choices lies. Using open source can not only open up new solutions in terms of the tools and technologies available, but it can have a noticeable impact on a culture of collaboration, sharing, and openness as well.

With the large variety of open source projects and communities, when individuals are encouraged to contribute they will build up a wide range of experiences and learn the different patterns that make sense based on their environment.

Standardization of Tools

Working effectively comes down to developing mutual understandings and negotiating to mitigate around the inevitable miscommunication that occurs when teams are trying to navigate multiple goals at once.

Tools can be used to:

- Improve communication
- Set boundaries
- Repair understanding within the scope of the devops compact

Organizations need to standardize tools to balance the challenges and costs of supporting tools that perform the same function. How do we then balance strengthening the organization through standardization, allowing flexibility at the team level, and empowering the individual to be agile and responsive by choosing her own tools?

Consistent Processes for Tool Analysis

Standardization of tools bridges old to new as the technologies being used at a company change. With consistent processes for evaluating, choosing, and retiring tools, organizations will:

- decide upon a tool that meets most people's needs;
- ensure necessary features that were present in an old tool are also features of the new one; and
- ensure that employees are properly trained to be able to effectively use a new piece of hardware or software

Without consistent processes to build the necessary bridges, employees will be resistant to new tools or technologies. Consistent selection processes can minimize risk by making sure that both current and new needs will be met, as well as simply providing reassurance for people who are more resistant to changes in their environments.

Consistency can also help you avoid the sorts of logistical nightmares that can crop up without enough process or standardization. For example, if each team uses a different issue tracker or ticketing system, you will have less visibility throughout the organization, more duplication of effort, and a great deal of time spent trying to navigate and interoperate these various systems.

Exceptions to Standardization

There are exceptions to standardization. If a team needs some isolation or unique requirements, there isn't a reason to force them to use the same tooling as everyone else.

One example is PCI compliance, which requires very strict separation of duties. A team responsible for PCI work is likely to have separate computers running on a separate network from the rest of the organization. In a case like this, a segregated environment allows for different tooling without having a detrimental effect on the organization as a whole. Decisions need to be made on a case-by-case basis.

Even though there are many commonalities, each team and each company has some unique needs and experiences. In the case studies in this chapter, we examine how two companies approach their tooling selection and implementation decisions. While common practices emerge, the tool selection is different based on the stacks within the environments.

Irrelevance of Tools

There are differing opinions on whether or not tools matter, and how much so if they do. The "tools don't matter" viewpoint developed in response to some vendors calling everything "devops" while trying to sell their products regardless of whether or not that label was accurate.

What "tools don't matter" means is two-fold:

- Tooling is not a sufficient condition for a devops culture to exist.
- Tools do not fix broken cultures; tools expose and exacerbate existing conditions in environments.

Ultimately, any "devops solution" that involves only tools while ignoring the *who*, *how*, and *why* of tool usage within an organization is missing the big picture of what devops is about and why it can be so successful. Do not try to solve interpersonal and cultural problems solely with tools and technology.

Failures of Process, Not Tools

A company might fail if it can't figure out how to implement and use configuration management instead of crafting beautiful and unique snowflake servers. Inability to respond quickly to environmental problems causes downtime and thus lost revenue. If you're using configuration management properly, the choice to use Puppet, Chef, Ansible, Salt, CFEngine, or some new CM system that hasn't even been written yet doesn't matter if it does what you need it to do.

 While there are technical differences between tools, what matters is whether the tools have the features that a particular organization needs to solve their problems while facilitating the desired culture.

Conway's Law for Tool Selection

Conway's law, named after computer scientist and programmer Melvin Conway, is the idea that software tends to be developed in ways that mirror the structures and organization of the teams that developed it. This means that in order for two software components to work together if they are each being designed and implemented by a separate team, those two teams must be able to communicate as well.

Conversely, teams that do not communicate well, such as in a heavily siloed environment, will tend to create products that don't work together well either. A corollary to this is that teams choose and use tools in ways that mimic their original structure and communication patterns. Two teams that don't communicate with each other aren't going to start doing so just because the company started using Slack as their new chat system.

The Impacts of Tools on Culture

As tools do heavily influence behavior, give serious consideration to what sort of behaviors different tools encourage or discourage when evaluating your environment, assessing the cultural and technical landscape, and collaboratively defining the goals and visions of the team or organization. Keep in mind that this is an ongoing process that requires continual re-evaluation.

Tools Impacting Communication

Tools shape behavior, so having tools that reduce the friction involved in communicating with other teams makes it more likely that communication will start to take place. If a company doesn't even have any chat software, or if what they use has technical limitations that prevent interteam communication, it will be much harder for communication to happen.

 We stress the importance of communication when it comes to tools because communication can make or break cooperation, collaboration, and affinity within an environment. This is true whether you are discussing tools designed specifically for communication (such as chat solutions) or tools where communication is part of their workflow and usage.

Many times, how a tool is used is more important than the specific tool chosen. Take a ticketing or bug-tracking system, for example. If every team decides that tools don't matter and picks a specific ticketing system that complements their working style, changes are high that down the line, different features and practices will make it incredibly difficult for members of different teams to work effectively together.

Individuals will either have more accounts to manage, or lack visibility into another teams' work.

 This lack of visibility is one of the problems that often plagues siloed organizations. Siloization can lead to duplicated effort, a lack of clarity or detail as to what is being worked on (or whether or not work is getting done at all), and distrust between teams.

Because workplace communities are built on effective communication, the ways that tools either enhance or prevent communication are important to keep in mind. Communication is a key part of being able to work together, and the tools and processes that your company uses for interpersonal communication can have noticeable effects on culture. In addition, every tool that you use has implicit communication inherent to its use.

As mentioned in Part II, there are many factors to take into account with communication. These factors preclude finding a single communication tool that will meet all of the needs inherent to a healthy organization. It is also likely that your communication needs will change as your company grows. While communicating with everyone via chat might make sense at a small startup when everyone can easily participate in one conversation, over time you might find teams leaning more toward email or team wikis.

 ### Measuring Participation

It is critical to understand and measure participation within the larger scope of the organization as your company grows.

Finding the right tools at the right time is an iterative process. Ensuring that all voices are heard in the critical conversations makes for a healthier company. Silence should not be assumed to mean consent to the majority. As evidenced through research on smart teams, teams where everyone has a voice are more effective and productive.[1]

When working with remote employees, invest in high-quality video conference solutions. Ensure that your team members have quality headsets, as the onboard laptop microphones and speakers will lead to subpar experiences that discourage individuals from using the medium. This can lead to remote employees feeling isolated, being left

---

1 Anita Williams Woolley, et al., "Evidence for a Collective Intelligence Factor in the Performance of Human Groups," *Science*, October 29, 2010.

out of important communications or decisions, and in general being less impactful with their work.

It's a matter of choosing the tools, platforms, or methods based on the content, immediacy, context, and other factors of the communication itself. Once these needs are identified based on the types of communication you and your team participate in, you can choose the particular tool of that type based on other needs (such as paying for a chat program or using a free one).

Hollie Kay on Being a Deaf Developer[2]

I've been deaf since infancy. It is not profound; my hearing loss is described as moderate to severe and is mostly problematic at higher-frequency ranges, the range at which most human speech happens. I rely on lip-reading and identifying vowel patterns to understand spoken language. Particular struggles include recognizing the following:

- Consonants, especially sibilants and unvoiced consonants (all consonants are high-frequency sounds, and the unvoiced and sibilant consonants don't activate the vocal chords);
- the beginning (and end) of sentences.

The stereotype of a programmer as a solitary eccentric who's allergic to human company is unfair and inaccurate. As a group, we're a very social bunch. We write blogs, we speak at conferences, we produce tutorials, we mentor. This isn't new, either—it's an atmosphere that dates from before the earliest days of the internet at Bell Labs, or MIT, and scores of other R&D orgs. I love this social world of code, as being able to surround yourself with competent, enthusiastic individuals is a big part of becoming a better developer yourself. But one thing that I've always felt shut out of is pair programming.

Pair programming, in principle, is great—it's like Rubber Duck debugging on steroids. You work together with another person who knows more than you and can guide you, or who perhaps knows less and will appreciate your guidance, or who perhaps knows precisely the same amount as you and can work with you to hash out a solution. Plus, y'know, it's fun. You get to know your colleagues. You get to remind yourself that everyone makes mistakes sometimes. You have somebody to catch you before you deploy that bit of code you are definitely not supposed to be deploying.

But when you're deaf, that dynamic changes and the fun gets sucked out of it. For me, pairing sessions are worse than useless. As a driver, trying to think about the code, type, simultaneously look at the screen in front of me and lip-read the pairing partner beside me, and understand their (often contextless) higher-frequency, spoken English

---

2 *http://cruft.io/posts/deep-accessibility/*

and technical jargon with a ~30 percent success rate is a recipe for misery. Eventually I start staring glumly at an increasingly frustrated navigator before eventually relinquishing control and letting them drive instead, as it's the only way we'll be able to progress. Navigating is even worse—drivers look at their screen pretty much constantly because it's hard to think about how2code and your pairing partner's communication needs at the same time. I know! I know. So I become a passive navigator, and the driver does all the work, and it's just no good for anyone and eurgh. Eurgh!

So it was great to get the opportunity to pair with Rowan Manning on the Pally (*https://github.com/nature/pally*) project, the automated accessibility testing tool built for Nature. Using Screenhero to set up a remote pairing session meant that we could both look at the screen and use text to communicate, losing no information and generating no confusion. This was the first time I've done a pairing session that worked as it should. It's difficult to express what a difference this makes, as I think most hearing people find it hard to appreciate how much information loss occurs in general conversation with a deaf person. Imagine that in your city all the books you've ever read have had ~60 percent of the words in them randomly blanked out with a Sharpie. Then imagine going on holiday to a neighboring city where (mercifully) nobody does that and you can suddenly read an entire book without needing to guess at anything. It's a bit like that.

Tools Impacting Broader Behaviors

This same principle can be applied not only to ticketing systems but also to infrastructure automation, chat systems, deployment tools, and any tool that is used by multiple teams within an organization. While it is important to figure out everyone's requirements and try to meet as many of them as possible, it is unlikely that 100 percent of your people will be 100 percent happy with any tool at all—compromise is pretty much guaranteed. At some point, continuing to argue and debate over which tool to use doesn't gain anything, and may end up causing hostility as arguments continue to occur in addition to all the time lost. It's tempting to say, let's just pick one tool and stick with it.

With those caveats in mind, arguments about which particular tool to use among choices that all fulfill your requirements don't make sense. This chapter isn't going to tell you that X is the One True Y Tool for Devops, because there is no such thing. That would be the same thing as declaring *ed*[3] the true victor in the editor wars. There will never be universal consensus on the "best" tool; the best solution depends entirely on what the specific problem being solved is.

---

3 ed is a line editor for Unix. At one point, it was the default editor for systems and its terseness made it very difficult to use in automation, despite how powerful it was.

Selection of Tools

Selecting a new tool to add to your environment can be a big decision, and one where many people involved are likely to have strong opinions. Here are a few important factors that should be considered during the selection process:

- Product development
- Community health
- In-house customization

This is not an exhaustive list, as availability of features, budget, and interoperability with the current tool set or environment are also important considerations.

We focus on these three factors as these are common needs across organizations, but also ones that have not been covered in great detail anywhere else. Organizations will have varying needs which will dictate necessary features, different budgets, and a variety of existing tool sets within their environment.

All of these factors can have a significant impact on the efficacy of the selection process, so make sure you understand what other driving factors are important to your tool selection.

Product Development

An actively developed product will be quicker to get new features, support newer operating systems and platform versions, and deal with any security vulnerabilities. Using a tool without active development leads to more time spent dealing with bugs or waiting for new features.

How quickly are new features implemented and released? Are these feature requests tracked and regularly evaluated for the product's roadmap? If critical bugs or security vulnerabilities are found, how quickly will they get fixed?

Look at recent releases for the tools you are considering. Pay attention to major and minor release dates, how useful the release notes are (references to specific bugs or ticket numbers are much more helpful when you're deciding if you should upgrade than just the line "bug fixes"), and what the update process is like.

Also consider how much contact you are able to have with the product developers themselves. Will you have any direct developer or support contacts within the tool vendor's organization? Having people assigned directly to work with your account can mean better support, as you are able to have an ongoing dialogue, and it can help ensure your issues get dealt with, rather than disappearing into some unknown ticketing system or email inbox somewhere.

Community Health

Community health is a measurement of the overall health of a group of individuals who are connected through shared norms, values, and behaviors. Communities can evolve for a specific tool, set of tools and practices, or role.

Keep an eye out for community activity as one of the signs of health including:

- rate of response to pull requests;
- mean time to resolution for issues;
- frequency of release;
- content creation (blog posts, articles, news); and
- rate of forum communication.

In addition to being active, the community and its events should also help foster a safe, respectful, collaborative, and inclusive environment. Pay attention to how members of the community treat each other. Consider the following questions:

- Do projects and community events have codes of conduct?
- What is the tenor of discussions on issues and pull requests?

A community where personal insults are thrown around or where sexist, homophobic, or transphobic behaviors are tolerated is not a healthy one. This applies to all communities, not just open source projects. People who use these various tools in their day-to-day work will likely find themselves interacting with other users, maybe attending local meetups or larger conferences focusing on the tools or how to use them.

 As discussed earlier in this chapter, one of the benefits of open source software is that you don't have to reinvent the wheel by working on problems that other people have already solved. An open source solution with a strong community contributing to it can make its implementation even more effective.

In-House Customization

A tool that can be easily customized and contributed to will make for a robust solution that is well suited to both the technological and human aspects of an environment. This is especially important in organizations with a large number of people working with the tool. A tool that deals well with that kind of scale will be able to grow along with your organization, as well as making engineering work easier.

Open source tools are generally the most customizable, as you have the code available and can much more easily both read through it and modify it as needed. This can aid greatly in doing things like fixing bugs, where instead of having to file a support ticket and wait, you can do much more work to identify the bug and even submit a pull request with a fix yourself. Even with closed source tools, pay attention to whether they have something like an API that can be used to develop additional tooling that works with or alongside the tools themselves.

Being able to customize a tool, fix your own bugs, and even add new features and extensions can go a long way toward making a tool easy to work with over time. If you have a feature that is too small or niche to be widely used but would be incredibly helpful for one of your own teams, being able to add that functionality yourself can be orders of magnitude better than having to wait to see if a product's developers ever implement it for you. This can be the difference between a tool that is merely tolerated and one that engineers genuinely enjoy using.

Example: Comparison of Version Control

Version control systems record changes to a set of files over time. CollabNet founded the Subversion project in 2000 as an open source software versioning and revision control system that was architected to be compatible with the widely used Concurrent Versions System (CVS). Subversion 1.0 (svn) was released in February 2004. Technology and habits at the time dictated svn's use and features. Core to svn's architecture is the concept of a centralized repository. This central repository allowed users to control who was and was not allowed to commit changes.

A year later, in 2005, Git was released. It's also an open source software version control system with a focus on decentralized revision control, speed, data integrity, and support for distributed nonlinear workflows. This gives every developer full local control. While you can adopt a centralized workflow and establish a "central" repository, the processes can be flexible, allowing you to use technology as you wish rather than having it defined for you. While the ramp-up time may be a little longer, the functionality allows for quicker organizational changes.

Example: Manual Infrastructure Configuration over Automation

Most of the established infrastructure automation solutions are similar in terms of overall functionality even though their implementations differ. As with all of the tool categories, each tool may reduce or encourage different aspects of collaboration.

In many organizations, system configuration is a manual process. Individuals document the process and upgrade with a checklist. A missed step can lead to systems in an unknown state requiring considerable effort to recover.

When Adam Jacob was developing Chef software (*http://bit.ly/chef-history*), he was trying to create a solution that could work across different organizations. Chef was built to provide abstractions for configuration and management, creating a language that allows individuals to define its infrastructure and policies with code.

Trying to create a language that allows for the nuanced views of developers, system administrators, security operations, and quality assurance engineers is difficult. With Chef, rather than reusing terminology that prioritizes one role over another, Jacob created new terminology, including resources and recipes.

The most important thing to keep in mind is that communication tools are like traveling companions in the rock climbing example we introduced in Chapter 2. They can either be good companions that help us keep the compact we have made, or they can be poor companions that distract us or get in our way. This, of course, will depend on how each of our tools is used; trying to use a low-immediacy medium such as email for things that require immediate replies will cause problems, as will trying to describe something only with words when drawing a picture on a whiteboard would be quicker and more effective.

Finally, when choosing tools it is necessary to balance cohesiveness with flexibility. If there are too many communication methods used, people will have to do lots of searching for the information they need (*was that in an email or a Google Doc or a Confluence wiki page?*) or struggling with how to most effectively reach people (*should I send an instant message or a text message or go to their desk for something like this?*). Too few methods, on the other hand, and you'll cause frustration—we've all heard the stories of companies who hold meetings for everything when too often a quick email would have done the trick.

Our compact, with its focus on shared understanding, will be aided if there are traditions or customs that people can draw upon to help decide on the most effective medium, but only if there is still enough flexibility to choose the right tool for the right job.

Auditing Your Tool Ecosystem

In addition to selecting new tools you may want to introduce to your environment, you must examine the state of your ecosystem. The first litmus test for many tools is whether the functionality exists in your environment. When auditing your environment to identify your tool ecosystem, include information about who has access and overall usage of the tool. Also include information about multiple tools within the same category or overlapping tools in your environment. This will inform areas of improvement that may require additional training or tool replacement.

Alignment with process and individuals' desire to use a specific tool is critical for effective tool usage. Too much process leads to a high cost to individuals, as they are

---

trying to maintain the intricate context around the processes. This effort can detract from project work. Too little process leads to a lack of team cohesion with the proliferation of tools and methods of using them. This can also impact individuals. Time may be spent repairing understanding, and merging work or examining duplicated work. Finding this baseline is key to all aspects of identifying and selecting tools. It is even more important as we try to scale up and down organizations.

Overall, the reason that we use tools at all is to help create environments where people can focus on *solving real issues*. Creating these kinds of environments is a big part of being able to manage a successful team, and this requires ongoing effort. This sort of audit is not something that should be done once and then forgotten about. Rather, people at both individual contributor and manager levels should take a proactive approach to making sure that an effective environment is being built and sustained.

Elimination of Tools

Regular reviews of current processes and tools should be done to make sure that their usage is still effective. Automation and technical debt tracking can help identify processes and tools that should be eliminated. This can help prevent situations where a tool has been causing additional work for those using it, and help identify and eliminate tools that serve the same purpose, reducing both cost and confusion.

These reviews should also involve regular check-ins with employees to discover the underlying stories that are informing and influencing them and their work. Ask questions like:

- What delights/frustrates you?
- What refuels/drains your energy and motivation?
- What value do you perceive from what you currently do?
- What impact do you perceive you have?
- What should we stop doing?
- What should we start doing?

Make sure to ask these questions of the people who spend the most time using these tools in their day-to-day work. Decisions around both selecting and eliminating tools should be done on the ground, so to speak, as the people who use the tools are much more invested as stakeholders than people who don't. These decisions should not be made as top-down mandates from people who haven't had any direct, recent experience with the tools in question.

Improvements: Planning and Measuring Change

Lasting change takes time. Whether software or people, these are complex problems with no quick-fix, one-size-fits-all solutions. The principle behind "SMART" goals[4] states that goals should be specific, measurable, achievable, realistic, and time-bound. SMART change is critical to the workplace organization and culture as well.

Identify the specific problem that you are solving. Before tackling a change, look around and examine what needs to be done. Determine who is interested in the project, who has time, and what the overall value of the project is. Visualize the various options and identify possible projects. Prioritize the projects, and make sure that you are working on solving the correct problems.

Break down the specific project into smaller pieces that can be accomplished and tracked. These smaller pieces are usually much easier to plan for, and therefore easier to reason about and make sure that they are achievable, realistic, and solving the right problems. In order to plan these projects well, you need to identify who you are solving the problem for. What are their needs and motivations? How often are they going to use the solution? Describe the solution: focus on the end goal. Talk to the stakeholders and ensure buy-in. This generally takes time and effort.

Once you know what problem you are trying to solve and who for, you can start to identify possible tooling. Probe the strengths and weaknesses of the various proposed solutions before buying into any single one, and be sure to involve the stakeholders in this part of the process so they can help evaluate potential solutions. Sometimes you may find that there is no existing solution that works well enough, and will have to invent and develop the tooling yourself. While in-house development may seem cheaper in terms of budget line items, make sure you include the time and resources to support long-term.

Finally, keep iterating on these processes, making sure to measure the impact of changes along the way to determine if your solutions are working. The specifics of what you measure will vary quite a bit based on what problem you are trying to solve, but without measuring it is impossible to judge the impact and effectiveness of your changes.

Case Studies

The first case study in this chapter is DramaFever, a streaming video platform that also runs the SundanceNow Doc Club documentary site and the Shudder horror site. Founded in 2009, DramaFever had approximately 120 employees as of mid-2015

---

4 G. T. Doran, "There's a S.M.A.R.T. Way to Write Management's Goals and Objectives" (*Management Review*, 1981).

when this case study was conducted, and its platforms provide content that is international, with 15,000 episodes from 70 content providers, in 15 countries, and an audience of 20 million viewers.[5] To get a deep-dive into how they assess and utilize tools and technologies, we spoke with Tim Gross and Bridget Kromhout, who were working as operations engineers at DramaFever when these interviews were conducted.

Continuing their story from Chapter 2, our second case study is Etsy. Founded in 2005 by Rob Kalin, Jared Tarbell, Chris Maguire, and Haim Schoppik, Etsy is a global marketplace for handmade and vintage goods. Etsy had approximately 785 employees as of the second quarter of 2015. In addition to Ryn Daniels, coauthor of this book, who shared their personal experiences at Etsy, we spoke with Etsy staff operations engineer Jon Cowie to get a feel for how Etsy assessed and utilized tools and technologies.

Information for both case studies was also gathered through published blog posts, presentations, and company filings. Within both of them are examples of how to identify implicit values, adopt desired practices, and evaluate and select tools into an environment, but again we would remind readers that they should refrain from blindly adopting any of these tools or techniques, or using them without a deep understanding and consideration of why and how they can be used.

Examining DramaFever

Tim Gross, who started out architecting buildings instead of software, later pivoted into IT and tool development and ended up becoming the first "DevOps Engineer" working for DramaFever. While his role was predominantly operations-focused, the small engineering team meant that often he was working on development work. In March 2013, the second ops person was hired.

There was no formal or intentional division of roles and responsibilities for the team, just a gradual process that led to the creation of the *ops team*. While the company labeled them as *DevOps Engineers*, the role was essentially operations as reflected in their job description to "manage and automate all aspects of […] infrastructure including site deployments, CDN, and cloud service management" with specific duties to maintain high-availability production AWS systems and on-call. There was no specific devops project.

---

5 Peter Shannon, "Scaling Next-Generation Internet TV on AWS with Docker, Packer, and Chef," October 20, 2015, *http://bit.ly/shannon-scaling*.

DramaFever job descriptions included this statement:

> We believe in helping our engineers to tackle the problems they're passionate about, and our engineers are encouraged to make any piece of our architecture better, if they think they can.

This expresses the pragmatic approach to embrace and encourage diverse viewpoints to identify and solve problems.

In July 2014, Bridget Kromhout joined the DevOps team at DramaFever. Describing the DramaFever technology stack, Kromhout noted that it was entirely in Amazon Web Services (AWS), with a Django/Python web application and growing number of Go microservices. Akamai, a major content delivery network (CDN), provides them with content delivery and edge caching.

Request path code, application code that declares a path that an end user's request will take through the codebase, and all associated services have critical availability and latency requirements above and beyond the requirements of other applications. This request path uses immutable infrastructure that is built using Chef and Packer, and the application code itself has run in Docker containers since late 2013.

According to Kromhout:

> Our application code exists on stateless instances that we autoscale 10x–20x in instance numbers over the course of the week. Our persistence layers are in Elasticache (Memcached, Redis), RDS (MySQL), DynamoDB, and Redshift. We ship logs to ELK and write to Graphite with CollectD and StatsD.

Services that are not in the request path include asynchronous Celery workers, cron jobs, logging aggregation and metrics servers (like Graphite or Logstash), or internal applications like their QA tracker. Kromhout continued:

> Although all of these services are important to our business, they have far less immediate impact on our users. If a cron job doesn't fire and it takes an operations engineer an hour to figure out why, we can spare that time and our users won't notice. If the Django application somehow dies in all availability zones, our users will be unable to enjoy their Kdramas!

Impact of Existing Technology

AWS availability transformed the industry when it launched in 2006. Companies no longer needed to hire for data center management skills. They needed individuals skilled in managing a shared utility service. DramaFever started out in AWS and continues to primarily use the service to provide compute resources. Gross explained:

> We've used Google App Engine (GAE) for some small one-off projects, but any time that these have started to become more heavily used we've found that we wanted to *bring them in* to our AWS environment where we have much more control.

An example of this was our image processing microservice called ImageBoss. It resizes and crops images on demand so that our creative team doesn't have to create so many variants of each art asset. Originally this was deployed on GAE but with only one core available on each node for Go (at the time), the cost of operating it was very high. Moving this into our AWS environment let us tune the application's host environment as we saw fit.

While AWS is perceived as more expensive than other cloud providers, the feature set that DramaFever depends on is unmatched. When asked about the cost analysis of using AWS, Gross explained:

> If we were to switch from AWS to another provider we would need to find replacements for managed services like SQS or DynamoDB, which would almost certainly counterbalance any benefit of moving off. Additionally, our workload is ideally suited for the AWS hourly pricing model--we scale nodes up and down on a regular pattern over the course of a day so we can both reasonably predict our requirements and cheaply scale up to handle bursts.
>
> On top of this, our total AWS bill is totally dwarfed by CDN costs (which are an order of magnitude larger because we stream petabytes of video a month) and engineer salaries. An incremental improvement in hosting costs by moving to another provider would cost us so much in engineering time that it would probably not be worth it.

 When considering existing technology in your own tool selection processes, ask yourself:

- What features are absolutely necessary to have versus which are nice to have?

- What solutions are available right now and which might be available soon?

- How do the features you need balance with the costs of available solutions?

Continuous Impact of Emerging Technologies

As technology evolves and tools emerge in the ecosystem, it can be a challenge to understand whether to adopt a particular tool. For a small company with wide-ranging unplanned work and continuous technical debt accrual, it's important to tackle the most valuable projects first.

Gross described a few problems that his team of two faced in October 2013:

- The main Django application had a slow, nonatomic deployment with complex failures. The Django application was a crucial *request path* application that had strong availability and latency requirements. Using `git clone` was slowing deployment, as well as occasionally failing partway through the deployment.

- Increasing deployment complexity. New Go applications couldn't be deployed with the existing processes. Binaries and interpreted source code had different shipping requirements.

- Separate QA testing and production deployment processes with no audit capabilities.

- Different development and continuous integration environments.

Gross also described additional goals that his team were pursuing:

- Move from a monolithic application to smaller microservices.

- Isolate different versions of the application on the same host within the development and QA environments.

As Gross explained:

> The operations team (which was just two of us at the time) evaluated several options based on merits such as problem-solution fit, our experience with the implementation language, known modes of failure, etc., and landed on Docker. It promised a generic *deployment interface* for us that could solve all the problems.
>
> The big risk was that Docker was still very much a green project (this was October 2013, so version 0.6) and we were not in the habit of deploying non-production-ready projects to production. We knew that we could always fall back to the more mature underlying LXC if things went poorly. We presented this to the senior members of the development team to get their buy-in.
>
> After running trials in the Dev/QA environment, we deployed Docker to production for our main Django application. Only once we had all the kinks worked out did we then move on to containerizing the rest of our fleet of applications.

As with any introduction of technology, additional problems arose that had to be resolved. A continuous integration (CI) environment is one in which work is integrated frequently through automation. Each integration is verified through an automated process that builds and tests the committed code with the goal of detecting errors quickly. Generally this is obtained through spinning up an environment, testing the code, and then destroying the environment.

Within their CI environment, they experienced disk-related problems due to frequent container churn, and to resolve this, they had to change the Docker storage driver used (which was nontrivial to migrate). They also ran into scalability issues with the Docker registry. To resolve the technology issues with the registry they ended up deploying a host-local registry, backed by AWS S3 rather than using a central server.

A third problem area arose when Docker was brought to the local development environment. Gross said,

> Ops had proceeded entirely within AWS without too much trouble. But I failed to make sure we had a good solution for running Docker locally. And because the devel-

opment team had their hands full with new feature work, they hadn't been able to invest the time in educating themselves on the new technology. This meant that when we rolled out `boot2docker` as a local development option, we ended up with a serious training gap that persisted for longer than we'd have liked and caused internal friction. This has been a lesson well learned for us and new infrastructure changes are being designed with more direct involvement from the development team.

 For both existing and new technologies, a careful selection and evaluation process is important. However, for new technologies (either new in general or new to your organization), ask yourself:

- What are the known risks of a new technology?
- What unknown unknowns might you run into?
- What problems are you trying to solve that cannot be solved by existing technology?

Affinity Empowering Adoption of Practices

blameless post-mortems (*http://bit.ly/blameless-post*) with the goal of creating a culture of continuous improvement

—@0x74696d at @dramafever

Makes me glad when @0x74696d references @codeascraft in discussing how @dramafever should treat failure. Thanks for helping us learn, Etsy!

—Bridget Kromhout (@bridgetkromhout)

These tweets, written in February of 2015, illustrate a growing trend of cross-company affinity through knowledge sharing. Kromhout stated that DramaFever has adopted blameless postmortems across the technical teams.

DramaFever also encourages a learning organization through code review. In addition to code review, Kromhout described the cultural challenges of rapid growth and the need to repair understanding between teams through "improved coordination by making explicit our expectations of how services will interoperate. This allows small groups of developers to pursue their own ideas while still maintaining the standards the organization at large expects."

DramaFever encourages transparency. Kromhout said, "Right now developers have full AWS access to the development environment and we've just enabled read-only production IAM access as well." This transparency allows for individuals to learn and observe directly from development environments that replicate production and answer questions about real-world production usage as they occur.

As DramaFever uses AWS technology exclusively, there is no data center presence required and therefore no requirement for employees to be explicitly located near a specific environment. With an international audience, while DramaFever's approximately 120-person team is primarily located in Philadelphia and New York, a number of employees work in alternate locations. In describing the environment, Kromhout said, "We've had employees as nearby as Maryland and as far away as Seoul, with no disruption to their ability to do the same job."

To further facilitate remote employees, DramaFever conference rooms have Chrome-boxes, a business video conference system running Chrome OS, a high-definition camera, and external microphones and speakers. Meetings by default allow for a virtual presence through Google Hangouts, which eliminates the requirement for a physical presence in the office.

 Pay attention to how tools and work practices interact within your organization and teams:

- What values does your team or organization have?
- Do your tools help realize these values in practice or hinder them?
- How transparently are values and processes communicated?

Tool Selection at DramaFever

Due to the budget constraints of working for a smaller company and the inherent cost to large amounts of bureaucratic process, DramaFever is careful about tool selections forgoing for the most part enterprise tools and generally working with open source software.

Kromhout described the process of tool selection as starting "with the intended function or result, and then evaluat[ing] potential tools based on how well they'll meet those needs. The preferences of the person who'll do the implementation matter, but we also have a set of service standards that any choices should meet."

The conversation that takes place when introducing new technology includes determining whether existing solutions will work, why the new technology may be a better fit, and calculating the additional work burden to current staff.

Kromhout explained:

> When deciding whether to roll our own or use SaaS[6] we evaluate costs and benefits, including the costs associated with building something in-house (as staff time is neither infinite nor free).

---

6 SaaS is software as a service, where applications are hosted by an external service provider and made available to customers via the internet.

For example, when we were considering what to do with our logs, we calculated our current log volumes and retention desires, and compared the price of running that on EC2] with ELK versus the price of shipping that quantity of logs to several third parties. We listed what we intended to be able to do with the logs. After getting quotes, and considering how much of our time maintaining ELK took, it made sense to keep using ELK.

DramaFever strives to eliminate downtime even for regular maintenance. Success is measured by the incremental process of completing work associated with eliminating downtime.

Kromhout discussed:

> Creating working infrastructure defined by code is the most important thing, as we aim for hot-swappable everything instead of ever taking the site down for maintenance. The code in question might be bash to work with the JSON that defines our AWS configuration or Chef cookbooks or Python using boto via fabric. We submit pull requests for all such work and have it reviewed and tested by our peers before merging and deploying it. Success is when we create something that works and we can close the GitHub issue and move on to the next one in our Kanban-style workflow.

 It's important to keep in mind what "success" looks like for your organization. Make sure you know what it means for a tool to be considered successful. When considering successful tool selection, pay attention to:

- Who is responsible for making decisions around tool selection?
- What criteria are used to select and evaluate tools and their usage?
- What are you prioritizing, both in terms of engineering happiness and customer happiness?

Many people shy away from using a technology as new as Docker was at the time in their production infrastructure, just as there might also be people for whom Docker does not make sense. The point of this case study is not to talk about Docker specifically, but rather to highlight *why* these engineers ended up choosing it, *what* considerations and tradeoffs they made, and *how* they finalized their decisions around the tools they used.

Examining Etsy

The Etsy technology stack is a PHP application, with a large number of internal services (with a fair amount of interdependence and complexity, not necessarily the more independent microservices that are increasingly common these days) with which they handle things like buying, selling, searching for, and listing items as well as dealing with the payment side of purchasing. There are a few large, well-known payments providers available, which are used by a great number of companies worldwide, but Etsy felt the need for more control over the process, which prompted them to bring their payment processing in-house. This led to the need for PCI compliance and all the considerations that come with that. The predominately on-premise infrastructure is spread across a number of geographically distinct data centers.

Explicit Versus Implicit Culture

Central to establishing a desired specific culture within an environment is defining the set of cultural beliefs and values explicitly. Etsy has been a community-based company from the beginning and clearly states their company values as follows:

- We are a mindful, transparent, and humane business.
- We plan and build for the long term.
- We value craftsmanship in all we make.
- We believe fun should be part of everything we do.
- We keep it real, always.[7]

These values inspire and connect employees as reflected in the 86 percent Connectedness and 91 percent Values alignment scores from the Etsy Progress Report of 2013 (*http://bit.ly/etsy-progress-13*). While Etsy has no devops team, no devops manager, and no devops engineers, these explicit and clear values are reflected in key practices and guide observed behaviors and contributions in the devops community. Etsy's intentional practices include being compassionate, experimentating and iterating, and encouraging a learning organization.

A Culture of Compassion

To be humane, one shows compassion. This compassion is reflected in your efforts to make life better for someone else, even it doesn't make your own life better. Etsy has invested heavily in creating humane working environments for employees through blameless, remote-friendly environments. Etsy also encourages a Thank You culture, where others' achievements of contributions are regularly and publicly acknowledged. IT has a reputation for being a thankless job: invisible when it is working well but called out immediately when there are issues or outages. This is not a humane environment for people to work in, so in addition to being blameless in response to incidents, Etsy actively encourages saying "thank you" when things go well.

---

7 *https://www.etsy.com/mission*

The Importance of Gratitude

"Thank you" or gratitude culture is a critical part of building and improving relationships. Recognizing that others are contributing of their own free will helps people to connect to something larger than themselves as individuals.

Studies have shown that gratitude has significant benefits, including:[8]

Improved health
    Stronger immune systems and lower blood pressure;

Improved resilience
    More ability to handle adversity;

Increased positive emotions
    Higher levels of happiness, joy, and contentment;

Decreased negative emotions
    Lower levels of loneliness and isolation;

Increased collaborative and cooperative behaviors
    Higher levels of generosity and compassion.

 Tools and culture can and do influence each other throughout the lifecycle of an organization. Paying attention to these interactions can help both improve your culture and make your tool usage more effective. Consider:

- What behaviors do you want to encourage among your employees?
- How do people work around or against existing tools or workflows?
- How can tools be used to encourage specific behaviors or values?

Because public communication is encouraged throughout not only the engineering organization but the whole company as well, team-wide emails or instant messages are sent frequently when people want to acknowledge their coworkers for something. People and teams get thanked for fixing bugs, adding features, contributing some-

---

8 Robert Emmons and Robin Stern, "Gratitude as a Psychotherapeutic Intervention," *Journal of Clinical Psychology* 69, no. 8 (2013).

thing to open source, helping unblock someone who was stuck, or even updating documentation. As Jon Cowie, Staff Operations Engineer, revealed:

> One really nice example of 'Thank You' culture is that in our staff directory there's a button where you can nominate somebody for an "Etsy Value Award" for exemplifying one of our stated values. It goes to the recipient and their manager, and gives the sender a nice way to recognize somebody whose work they've appreciated, or who's helped them a lot.

This culture helps foster empathy and closeness, which enables people to work more effectively together, makes them less likely to blame each other later, and creates a more humane environment for all employees.

A Culture of Blamelessness

As mentioned in Chapter 4, blameless environments are defined by individuals being encouraged to share stories and to take on the responsibility of improving safety. John Allspaw, Etsy's current CTO, wrote of Blameless PostMortems and a Just Culture (*http://bit.ly/blameless-post*) in May 2012, describing the transformation of handling errors and mistakes through this blameless approach.

Failure happens. Accepting this as a normal part of business is a first step toward defusing emotional situations. Rather than taking the traditional approach of ascribing this failure to human error with corrective actions of firing, creating more barriers to prevent an individual from doing an action, or assigning more training to the individual, Etsy takes a more systemic approach. Etsy attempts to balance safety and accountability by encouraging the telling of the story through blameless postmortems.

Within a postmortem created with Etsy's Morgue tool (*https://github.com/etsy/morgue*), individuals are encouraged to give a detailed account of:

- timeline of actions and events;
- effects observed;
- expectations;
- assumptions; and
- outcomes and decisions.

Etsy encourages this behavior by committing to not punish individuals for sharing their stories and giving them authority to improve safety by recounting how the events happened. With fear not inhibiting knowledge sharing, individuals become more accountable for their actions, helping to create a safer environment so that others don't repeat the same mistakes.

Being Remote-Friendly

Etsy has an international audience. This means that their applications need to be available 24/7. To create a more humane environment for the individuals supporting the application, this is split across multiple time zones, allowing a greater number of people to be working during their local business hours. This has the additional benefit of creating a greater pool of potential employees to hire from, rather than only considering people living in a couple of locations.

Several tools are used to enable this kind of culture, including IRC for instant messaging or chat, email for longer-form text communication, and Vidyo for video conferencing and collaboration. Etsy practices the idea of communicating as "remote by default," where even people who are local to the same office will use one of these tools whenever possible, rather than simply speaking face to face.

Because the tools are integrated into so much of the environment and workflows, there is relatively little overhead in communicating with these remote-friendly tools. This has the enormous benefit of keeping remote employees in the loop, informed of the decisions being made and able to participate in the conversations taking place.

This enables people to work from wherever they are most comfortable, with the exception of a few positions such as data center technicians, who must be relatively close to the data centers. Comfortable employees are happier with the company, and being allowed to work in a manner that is most effective for them improves both their health and productivity.

 In addition to remote-friendliness, organizations can use tools in a variety of ways to improve the lives and workflows of the people using them. Things to keep in mind include:

- How do tools increase or decrease employee comfort?

- How flexible are your tools? How much can they be customized?

- How do tools impact how people communicate on a daily basis?

Tools Enforcing Practice

Tools play an enormous part in enforcing and encouraging the practices at Etsy. Etsy's remote-friendly culture means that establishing the devops compact and repairing any misunderstandings that occur as part of multiple people working together requires more explicit practice. The cost of additional work toward communication allows for a humane environment to support a 24/7 on-call rotation across multiple time zones. In order to embrace the learning organization and treat people equally, they have adopted strategic processes around communication.

Ad hoc coding sessions and informal in-person conversations are not available as information transfer when supporting remote employees. This means a lot of communication is done in a written recorded format. People email when decisions are made; changes, outages, or issues happen; and to share innovations. Employees rely on creating filters to limit the amount of email, and find it useful to have a searchable archive of all communication.

Internet Relay Chat (IRC) is also critical to the remote-friendly culture fostered by Etsy. Chat bots update channels with information about deploys, alerts, and configuration changes. The chat bots also promote systems interaction—for example, to silence Nagios alerts for upcoming planned maintenance or for code review. Chat bots are also used to promote "thank you culture" by giving each other "pluses" and endorsements.

Most discussion happens in public channels. Channels are transparent and open, allowing for people to pop in to other teams' channels. Work and less-work-related channels are available, as it is recognized that people have more than just work interests. Real-time chat is understood to be potentially interrupting and intrusive, so it's not a problem if people sign out or turn off notifications to get some work done.

Each Etsy employee has a Vidyo client, and remotes have a webcam and headset. Space has been set aside with big-screen TVs and Vidyo hardware to minimize the friction of video conferencing. This "ops cave" was a channel set up by the mostly remote operations team. This permanent Vidyo call setup in the ops team area allows remotes to dial in to whenever they want to hear and see what's going on in the office, or show off their cats. Being able to overhear the ambient noise and chatter helps them drop in to conversations of interest and feel much more included in the team and culture.

Documentation is embraced as a way of doing things at Etsy. For the most part, wiki pages using Atlassian's Confluence software are accurate and up to date—obviously not all pages, but keeping documentation updated is strongly encouraged (especially things like on-call runbooks). Many people take the time to do this. While some companies hesitate to write documentation, saying that it gets out of date too quickly to be useful, Etsy has found that "best-effort wiki updating" has done well enough for them in practice.

Buy or Build

Etsy shies away from the practice of using the latest and shiniest new technologies simply because they are new and interesting. Most of the tools they use are what they already have that is known to work. More information on this philosophy can be found in former Etsy engineer Dan McKinley's blog post called Choose Boring Technology (*http://bit.ly/boring-tech*). The idea is that focusing on implementing new and untested technologies takes time and energy away from innovation on the actual product features, which is where the company's focus ultimately is.

Etsy greatly values what they call "generosity of spirit," which means giving back to the community in as many ways as possible. This can take the form of blog posts, speaking at conferences, mentoring other employees, or contributing to open source projects, either their own or someone else's. This is seen in their tendency to open-source most of the tools that they ended up developing as in-house solutions.

 The general approach for tool selection includes answering the following questions:

- Can we do this using a tool we already know and have expertise in? Is there a compelling reason not to?
- Is there an existing tool that meets our needs? If yes, use that tool.
- Is there a tool that mostly meets our needs and can be extended or customized? Is the tool open source?
- Is there a need or ability, time, and desire to write something ourselves?
- Is the scope of the problem necessary and also external?

Etsy uses and has contributed back to the community for a number of tools, including Nagios, Chef, Elasticsearch, and Kibana. Tools do get replaced if they stop working to the capacity that is required. Etsy wanted to monitor their networking equipment, and has minimal time to monitor when a new device was brought up. At the time Etsy was using Cacti (*http://www.cacti.net/*), but the complexity and manual configuration led to developing and releasing FITB (*https://github.com/lozzd/FITB*).

Border gateway protocol (BGP) monitoring, site monitoring, and synthetic testing are all areas where Etsy selected external services or software due to the nature of the problem space. Looking at BGP monitoring as an example, this made sense to Etsy because BGP monitoring involves monitoring all of the external traffic flows to understand the impact and troubleshooting of routing across networks. There were better uses of their network engineers' time than re-creating such a complex monitoring service that already existed elsewhere, so this was a case when it made clear sense to use an existing tool.

Considering Automation

Over the years, Etsy has done a lot of work to automate various workflows and processes in areas where manual processes were causing problems. One key example of this was seen in the Introduction, where a manual, error-prone deployment process that took multiple hours and was incredibly difficult to roll back was replaced with a more streamlined automated deployment tool, Deployinator. This was not a one-shot change, but rather an iterative process, which has been the case for most of Etsy's automation.

As another example, consider the process of building new servers. Because Etsy runs in their own data centers, not in the cloud, server builds used to be a very manual process, taking hours or even days from when a server was racked to when it was ready to be put into production. The first automation was a collection of a few simple Ruby scripts that dealt with some of the biggest pain points, such as configuring switches and VLANs. Over the next few years, more features were added, bugs were fixed, and more pain points were automated so that now the tool includes a web interface where any engineer, not just members of the ops team, can specify the hardware profile and Chef role and get a new server into production within minutes.

However, Etsy engineers do not try to blindly automate all the things for the sake of automation. They are aware of the *leftover principle*,[9] which states that because only the nonautomated tasks are left for human operators to do, these leftover tasks are either too complex or uncommon to automate or too simple or uneconomic to automate. This can lead to what is known as *deskilling*, where so many tasks are automated away that people will forget how to do them such that over time their skills in those areas will decrease.

Automation can be a great benefit in many situations, allowing for less time to be spent on manual, repetitive tasks and cutting down on errors. It is not a panacea, however. When thinking about automation, ask yourself:

- What are your biggest pain points?
- What can and cannot be automated?
- *Should* certain aspects of workflows be automated at all?
- How will you handle it if the automation you create breaks?

---

9 Tom Limoncelli, "Automation Should Be Like Iron Man, Not Ultron," *ACM Queue*, October 31, 2015.

Measuring Success

In order to deliberately experiment and encourage learning, Etsy has put a high value on transparency and monitoring. The plethora of tools and processes that have been shared expose the strength of this focus. From monitoring system-level performance to business-level metrics, Etsy strives to gather as many data points as possible. This data is made transparent to employees so even individuals without a deep operational understanding can draw insights and conclusions toward iterative improvements. This focus did not develop overnight.

Michael Rembetsy joined Etsy in 2008. He and his team would discover issues through posts on Etsy's customer forums, as there was no real monitoring in the organization at the time. Frequent downtime and reactive discovery led to Rembetsy and other leadership identifying a more sustainable way to run the platform. Rather than trying to plan out a completely exhaustive solution all at once, they began with a minimum viable monitoring solution, starting with the basics of a monitoring solution that would have the greatest impact on customer experience.

There wasn't a clear path on exactly which tools were needed, so they experimented. The goal was about getting insight into what was going on with the site, applications, and all the interlocking components. They selected Nagios, Cacti, and Ganglia to start with due to their familiarity with the platforms, the resulting speed of implementation, and low cost (free).

Over time with frequent iteration and evolution, Etsy has embraced a "measure anything, measure everything" practice. In addition to planning out ahead of time what they wanted to measure, they also made it easy for any individual to get any metric that could be visualized as a graph monitored after the fact. They developed and released StatsD (*https://github.com/etsy/statsd*), a network daemon that runs on the Node.js platform that listens for statistics sent over UDP or TCP and can aggregate to pluggable backend services like Graphite. Data is flushed every 10 seconds, allowing for near-real-time data collection.

There is a shared goal of creating and delivery software. Different teams build monitoring according to their needs. There are no gatekeepers of monitoring; everyone is encouraged to contribute as much as they need or can. With regards to monitoring, they have an explicit understanding:

- If you have questions, ask someone.
- If it causes production problems, the ops team will talk about what you need to resolve the issues.

As an example of the devops compact in action, Daniels described the process of operations working with a very different team, in this case the frontend infrastructure team, to resolve alerts that were paging her. After getting paged in the middle of the night for disk space on a server (every sysadmin's favorite alert to get), she realized that this team had been logging to a disk partition that was much smaller than the standard partition where most logs were stored.

Upon realizing this, she was able to talk with that team about operational best practices for logging, point out some documentation that existed on it, describe the issues that were happening, and suggest a couple of solutions. The frontend infrastructure team then chose and implemented the solution that worked best for them. This combination of blamelessness and information sharing is a key part of creating and maintaining a culture of understanding.

 Monitoring and alerting are key parts of every software environment, as well as areas where effective tool usage can have enormous benefits. Be sure to consider:

- How do your tools differentiate between monitoring and alerting?
- How will your tools and processes handle the different monitoring needs of different teams?
- How flexible and customizable are your monitoring and alerting solutions?

Motivations and Decision-Making Challenges

As is evident in both of these case studies, decisions around the tools that people use day-in and day-out are not ones to be made lightly. Company newsletters, mainstream media, and conference booths will display lists and articles covering the "best" tools for a devops toolchain. How can you tell the difference between a company trying to sell a solution that could be effective in your environment versus a company trying to get in on the devops trend?

Tooling is important to how work gets done but is not in any way the *only* consideration. There is no "devops as a service" that you can buy that is an all-encompassing solution to all your work-related problems. It's important to understand that while tools impact culture, they do not replace it, so be wary of anyone trying to sell you a "bespoke devops solution" that sounds too good to be true—it probably is.

Other motivations outside of our own goals and ambitions come in the form of our interpersonal relationships, such as an organization going with vendor X over any other solution because vendor X took them out to a sporting event and a nice dinner, or the person making the decisions having a friend with a new startup that they want to support.

Tools also might end up getting chosen because they have a good reputation in one way or another; as the saying goes, "Nobody ever got fired for buying IBM." Understanding the motivations behind how decisions get made in your environment can help to inform how these processes might be improved.

Sparkle Corp Effective Tool Usage

"I really found your demo days pretty interesting and educational," said George. "I noticed that you were using a virtual machine on your laptop and managing it separately from the code. Have you tried using Test Kitchen to create a project to manage your virtual machine? The ops team uses it when testing out new implementations of services. That way we can replicate whatever any individual on the team has done."

"No, I hadn't heard of Test Kitchen before. I would love to see what it would involve, especially if it can cut down on spinning up a custom crafted virtual system," said Alice.

"Essentially, we start out with the ChefDK. That's the Chef development kit. It's already baked into all laptops provided to employees at the company," said George. "It sounds like we should coordinate with the IT team and make sure that the documentation is updated about the local development environment for the company. As an operations engineer it was in my new hire documentation. I didn't realize that other teams weren't using it."

George illustrated the ease of setting up a quick Chef cookbook with a precreated Test Kitchen template mirroring the customizations that Alice, Geordie, and Josie had done for MongoDB installation.

"Now, I can commit this back to our centralized Git environment, and any of you can pull down the project to work with it," said George.

Alice tested this out by cloning the project and using the kitchen commands as George had done. After the OS image had synced, she quickly had a test environment up on her local laptop.

"This could be done with MySQL as well, and then we could more quickly evaluate one solution over another with real metrics," said Josie.

"How about we split up into two teams pairing up to get this plugged into our Jenkins cluster? That will let us test pulling the software project down to each platform and evaluate them simultaneously," said George.

In the end, everyone decided that sticking with MySQL made the most sense based on the operational costs. The visualized metrics helped their respective teams see the value of staying with MySQL in the environment. Chef, git, and Jenkins allowed everyone involved to share their work rather than duplicating effort, making it much easier for people from different teams to work together.

The collaborative approach allowed the team to get the reviews application into an initial demo within a week, so the development team could invest more time with the security team in planning their harassment-detection algorithms. The open and ongoing communication helped everyone feel that their voices had been heard and considered, making this a collaborative group decision.

Summary

Ensure you have a clearly defined set of values for your organization. Etsy has a very clear, compelling set of values for the company, and this has helped guide their decisions around the tools and technologies that they use as well as how they're used in people's day-to-day work.

Distill practices based on of the current activities you observe in your team. The practices observed at both Etsy and DramaFever were:

- Blameless environments
- Experimentation and iteration
- Incremental improvement
- Learning organizations

Once you've identified your current activities and practices, you'll be able to determine whether your practices match your values. If you say that you value open source, for example, but end up more often than not choosing closed source vendor solutions or not giving people time to make open source contributions at work, this can be a sign of a mismatch between values in theory and those in practice.

Choose tools based on your culture, skill level, and needs. Your tool selection will vary over time. Having different technical or business needs from other organizations or individuals happens even when you share culture and values. Despite how many of the same values and practices we see in the two case studies, DramaFever ended up with a rather different set of tools. Neither company is universally "right" or "better" overall; you have to know what is right for your organization at the time your decisions are made.

Understand that changes in your culture and tool effectiveness do not happen overnight. Etsy has been working on their monitoring initiatives since 2008, and will continue to hone the craft of their code as they continue to iterate. The rich set of tools they have contributed to the community are not drop-in solutions that will solve your particular problems, although they may help. Change will take time and continued practice.

Know that measuring your progress is critical to obtaining success. If you are at a zero-monitoring state, this is one area you need to spend significant time on. Take more advantage of the benefits that monitoring can offer by reading Jason Dixon's in-depth book *Monitoring with Graphite* (O'Reilly). This book and several other great sources of information are listed in Chapter 20.

Finally, keep in mind that tools are not completely separate from the other three pillars of effective devops. Ultimately, tools are used *by people*, to help them work *with other people*, to create solutions *for people*, and we cannot remove this human side from the tooling equation. Tools can impact and be impacted by how we work and interact, and all of these factors and interactions must be considered in order to bring about significant, lasting change.

CHAPTER 13

Tools: Misconceptions and Troubleshooting

In this chapter, we will cover misconceptions and troubleshooting that can arise around various scenarios related to selecting and utilizing tools in a more general sense. This does not include troubleshooting of specific tools or technologies, as that would be far beyond the scope of this book, but rather the decision-making processes and various tooling workflow problems.

Tools Misconceptions

Many misconceptions on devops-related tooling comes down to the importance of particular tools to a devops solution.

We Use Technology *X*, but Everyone Else Is Using Technology *Y*; We Must Change to Technology *Y* as Soon as Possible

As mentioned in Part I, devops is a cultural movement. Culture includes the technology stack, and wholesale changes—especially when driven by mandates from management—have a cost that decelerates the organization as a whole. Prior to retiring a particular technology, recognize the tools in the environment that have been part of the existing culture, understand individuals' experiences with those tools, and observe what is similar and different between others' experiences. This examination and assessment helps clarify what changes need to be made and whether they need to be made right now.

The one exception to this is upgrades. Upgrades to technology are necessary. The longer you hold off on upgrading, the more debt you incur based on the reliability and testing of compatible upgrade paths. Upgrade too soon, and you could be doing quality assurance testing for the product. Upgrade too late, and you might find the corner cases based on sunset technology.

Copying the tools you see in successful organizations will not necessarily lead to the same observed outcomes in your organization. Focus on the process, not on the outcomes. If technology *X* works in your environment, use it.

The presence of a particular tool or technology doesn't mean that you can't have a successful devops initiative. Using IRC instead of Slack or Hipchat, running servers on bare metal instead of in the cloud somewhere, or having a PHP monolith instead of Go microservices do not preclude devops ideas. So much of the movement is about culture and how people work together, and if you can get people to collaborate just as well with a 20-year-old chat program as with a brand new one, that is more important than which chat program you end up going with.

Using Technology *X* Means We're Doing Devops

There are certainly groups or types of tools and technology that can greatly help with devops initiatives. We've used version control and infrastructure automation as key examples, but it's important to understand *why* they can be so valuable and how that value relates to the human side of software development work.

Infrastructure automation, for example, allows employees to make changes in a more streamlined, reliable way, reducing the risk and friction around making changes.

But without allowing for these impacts on the human side of things, the technological impacts will be greatly reduced. If you start using infrastructure automation but maintain old legacy change control processes that were pain points for developers, you won't see the true benefits that infrastructure automation has to offer. No tool on its own can fix a broken culture. In order to use tools effectively, you need to look at *how* people use tools and *why*, what they are trying to get done, and how tools can help or hinder those efforts.

Simply adding Chef or Docker or Slack or any other tool frequently discussed in relation to devops does not mean that you are "doing devops," because tooling is just one part of how we work together. It's not the presence or absence of a tool that will make or break a devops initiative, but how those tools help or hinder your culture.

We Have to Make Sure We Don't Choose the Wrong Tool

Some people worry that choosing the "wrong" tool will have dire consequences, causing a project or even an organization to fail. This fear can be exacerbated by vendors claiming that you "must" use their products or solutions in order to be doing devops. It is only natural to want to make sure your decisions won't be ones that have significant negative impact.

This much emphasis on the particulars of tools is misguided; rather, you should be giving more attention to how you use tools throughout your organization and what can be learned from the positive and negative aspects of that usage. You won't fail because you chose the wrong tool; you will fail if you choose the wrong way to think about the tool to choose.

To use infrastructure automation as an example, it is unlikely that choosing Chef over Puppet (or vice versa) will have a significant impact on the overall success or failure of your infrastructure automation project. There are certainly small implementation details or particular use cases that may benefit more from one versus the other, but in terms of the big picture, *how* you use an infrastructure automation tool is going to have a much more significant impact than *which* tool you chose.

If you understand the principles of how to use tools appropriately, when automation can be beneficial versus when it isn't, how to choose new tools and implement their usage within your organization, you will be able to continue making tooling decisions to the best of your abilities and, more importantly, learning from your experiences.

This will ensure that you are able to adapt based on the ever-changing landscape of new tools and technologies, so that even if you do choose a tool that turns out not to be an optimal choice, you will not have wasted too many resources or end up stuck with that tool forever. Being able to reason, learn, and adapt your tool usage is far more critical than simply trying to choose the "best" tool in the first place.

You Can Buy Devops-in-a-Box or Devops-as-a-Service

The growing influence and popularity of devops have led to a rapid increase in the number of vendors adding devops-related buzzwords to their marketing copy as a way of trying to get in on the trend. It can be hard sometimes to separate marketing hype from reality, especially if you are brand new to many of these ideas and overwhelmed by the sheer number of products trying to sell devops to you.

To maintain a more balanced view, consider the four pillars; in addition to tooling, consider collaboration, affinity, and scaling. It might make sense to have various tools be "in a box" or "as a service," but as we've shown throughout this chapter, simply having the latest cool devops tools is not enough; you have to use them effectively to be successful.

Devops is about so much more than just tools. How do you sell collaboration as a service? Not a tool that can aid with particular collaboration or communication problems, but the actual act of people working together? What about getting different teams to sit down and discuss their differing goals, priorities, and pain points? You simply cannot buy these things in a box or as a service. Ultimately, so much of the changes that you will need to make come down to getting the people in your organization aligned, creating and maintaining that shared understanding that we've described as the devops compact, and those sorts of changes have to be made internally to your organization.

There are lots of great tools and services. Many companies provide solutions that solve real problems. Keep the four pillars and their interactions and intersections in mind when evaluating and ask yourself if they may be promising something that it doesn't even make sense for them to be able to deliver. (If you replace all instances of "devops" in their marketing copy with "people working well together" and it sounds ridiculous, it's probably not something you should be buying.)

Ultimately, you will have to do the hard work yourselves, with your own people and teams, figuring out what works and doesn't work for your own organization. Lasting overall cultural change cannot be bought, it has to be created from within.

Tools Troubleshooting

Keep in mind when troubleshooting your usage of technology that these are tools, not toys; ultimately you should be trying to choose tools that help you solve problems, not because you just want to try them or because everyone else is using them.

We're Trying to Find the Best Practices for Technology X

It may seem comfortable to seek out the best practice for a particular problem set, but this mindset sets the stage for future problems. When we choose the "best" solution, when it doesn't work out as expected we turn to ways to deal with the cognitive dissonance, which often turns into blame. Here are a few key strategies to apply before diving into solving a problem:

- Identify what the state of the problem is now.
- Identify the musts and nice to haves.
- Identify the individuals and teams that have critical information, and work with them to further qualify the problem. The goal here is to not figure out all the possibilities, it's to figure out what parts of the problem need to have flex, and what parts are critical foundations for what you are trying to do. Having a diverse team with analytical, lateral, and critical thinkers will ensure that you have just enough "what ifs" in your process to discover potential problems without stagnating.

In this identification process, you will discover a particular pattern to the problem. Once you have that pattern, compare it to your available options. Are the options nonviable? What are the consequences of choosing one of those options? What are the consequences of creating something completely new?

Make a decision, documenting the decision process so that it's clear that there was a conscious decision; what flex factors you considered as potential future improvements; and what foundational concerns informed these decisions. It's also important to keep in mind that planning is an integral part of using any tool or technology, especially when that technology involves automation. As much benefit as automation can have, without proper planning you can end up automating a faulty process and make things worse than they were before.

Parallel with the decision and resulting work, ensure that individuals are spending enough time walking through and documenting the "what if?" conditions. In this way, your team can discover a solution that works now, has buy-in, and will be prepared for change as technology evolves and grows as well as prepared for failures in the system as unforeseen problems arise.

We Can't Get People to Agree on One Particular Tool

Within smaller organizations, it can be tempting to try to get agreement from every single person on which tools to use and which to get rid of, and at small enough startups, that might even be possible. As team and organization sizes grow, however, this will get more and more difficult, and at a certain level of organizational size and complexity, it won't even be practical to solicit feedback from every single individual who will be using a particular tool in a timely manner, let alone get everyone to agree.

Once you've accepted that unanimous agreement simply isn't possible at any kind of scale, you can move on to finding which solutions make sense for the most use cases. You'll want to figure out which people will be using tools on a day-to-day basis and optimize for their needs and use cases, rather than focusing on people who will only use a tool occasionally. It will probably make sense to put together a test group, comprising a few people who likely represent the majority of the common use cases for this tool. You might also consider allowing people to be beta testers to help evaluate potential solutions.

Many technologists can be resistant to change, and you might find that people are vocally opposed to having a new tool introduced or an existing one being replaced simply because it isn't what they are used to, rather than any specific problem with it. Consider having a structured way in which people can give feedback about tools they work with that tries to identify how frequently they encounter issues and what those specific issues are, and remember that those who complain the loudest aren't necessarily the majority opinion.

While flexibility is certainly important, in some areas it might make sense to have certain tools that are non-negotiable within a team or organization. For example, if there are certain tools that enable you to maintain SOX, PCI, or some other kind of compliance, it is reasonable to insist that everyone who works within that scope use those tools. You'll probably want to keep these mandatory tools to a minimum, but there are certainly areas where it makes sense to have them.

We've Decided to Adopt (or Retire) Technology X, but People Are Resisting Using It (or Giving It Up)

How open people are to using a new tool in their work may depend a great deal on the process by which that particular tool was selected. If you have a situation where a top-down decision was made, perhaps by a manager who has much less experience with a given tool or workflow than their individual contributor reports, there might be very valid reasons why people don't want to use the new tool. Research into what problems you're trying to solve and working with people who will be using this tool most frequently as described earlier can go a long way toward avoiding this kind of situation.

Pay attention to how you communicate changes and how they are rolled out. If employee computers are centrally managed to the point where software changes can be pushed remotely by IT staff, and if people come in one morning to find that a new piece of software has been installed for them without any kind of explanation for what it is and, more importantly, *why* the change was made, they are likely to resist that change even if the tool does end up being a good solution for them.

Let people know in advance when tooling changes are going to be made that impact them, and give them opportunities to be part of the process as much as possible. You might find that people you hadn't even thought of or known were using a tool have very strong opinions on it. Once decisions have been made, communicate them well in advance of changes going into effect, and give people as much time to transition to the new tool as possible, or to get used to not having it if you are retiring an existing tool. Explain what factors went into the change, how the choice was made, and let people know where they can give feedback or report issues.

This applies to both adding new tools and retiring existing tools, and as with so much else in this book, communication and empathy go a long way in making these changes sustainable and beneficial.

PART V

Scaling

CHAPTER 14

Scaling: Inflection Points

This chapter is aimed at examining and overcoming the obstacles within our organizations at various important points throughout their lifecycles. It might be tempting to simplify this idea to "devops in the enterprise," as many people tend to do when thinking about devops outside of smaller, startup environments. However, this is an oversimplification—while there are certainly enterprise-specific concerns, many of which we will address in this chapter, it is more complete and more valuable to describe how companies change over time, whether that be a startup growing in size or an enterprise organization splitting in two. Scaling is about the evolution, growth, and advancement of the organization as a whole throughout its entire lifecycle.

Understanding Scaling

In a team, department, or organization, it's not always easy to know when a change is needed or in which direction. Although receiving advice on these transitions in advance can be helpful, the change can still feel incredibly counterintuitive.

When we view our progress as part of the evolving landscape that can help or hinder our future endeavors, it can help us to plan, execute, and adjust position with deliberate intention based on our current state—whether the moves are slow and controlled, or dynamic leaps. Through experience we learn when and how to change directions, and to approach different environments with different strategies.

In this chapter, we will take a look at different considerations for the challenges that come with scaling organizations. We will go into depth on how the previous three pillars of effective devops interact with different types of scaling problems, and follow up with some misconceptions and common areas for troubleshooting as we have in the previous chapters.

Considering Enterprise Devops

There is no separate "enterprise devops" with different tools and practices that applies only to companies with a large number of employees. There is not a single definition of success, with a single outcome that every company and organization should strive for. Organizations need to be comfortable building strength with the required agility and balance to navigate change.

The devops compact is just as central to developing strength, balance, and agility within a large company as it is in smaller organizations. A culture of collaboration and affinity strengthens "weak ties," allowing for more information flow throughout the organization. It is the application or implementation of the principles that differs in larger organizations, not the principles themselves.

Some have expressed concern that devops principles can be applied only to greenfield projects at small startups, making it unsuitable for enterprise organizations or legacy systems with accumulated technical and cultural debt, but the research conducted for the Puppet Labs 2015 State of DevOps Report (*http://bit.ly/devops-2015*) showed that this was not the case:

> High performance is achievable if you architect with testability & deployability in mind.

Researchers for the report found that the cultural principles of devops could be applied to organizations of any size, and that technical principles such as continuous delivery and improving deployment processes could be applied to any well-designed and architected software project, even legacy code running on mainframes. A brand new microservice-based project isn't going to be successful because it's new and has microservices—it has to be well-designed, testable, and easily deployable as well. These principles apply to all software projects, old and new.

Growing or Shrinking the Organization Strategically with Devops

Successful organizations must know how to scale—that is, to grow or shrink as needed. Scale can mean different things to different people depending on context. In this way, scale is another example of a folk model, and in order to effectively discuss it within your organization or with others you will need to clarify what kind of scaling you are talking about. For example, scaling might mean:

- Expanding the customer base
- Growing revenue
- Expanding a project or team to meet demand

- Maintaining or improving a ratio of people to systems or money spent
- Growing faster than competitors

To add confusion to the mix, modifiers give weight to what is being done—for example, "large-scale" systems. What is "large" when managed services allow a single engineer to quickly deploy and destroy hundreds of systems in minutes rather than months? Viewed through this lens of the rapidly evolving availability of systems, are there a set of principles, practices, and technologies that apply only to some subset of organizations?

In a word, no. To expand upon one of the case studies we introduced in Part IV, we note that in 2015, Etsy had approximately 800 employees, 1.5 million active sellers, and 22.6 million active sellers with $1.93 billion annual gross merchandise sales. As another example, Target in 2015 had approximately 347,000 employees, and $72 billion in annual revenue. Despite their differences in size, both companies have adopted principles and practices based on their current cultures to select the routes that make the most sense to them today.

Considerations of Deliberate Scaling

Further, trying to identify a single mechanism that solves for all things, especially in eliminating humans from the system, is fundamentally wrong. In the physical world, when architects design buildings they are basing their design on years of education and experience, intuition, and mechanical process. Requirements of building, surrounding areas, history, and environmental studies all influence the design.

Sketching and 3D models lead to the eventual building of a physical structure that can be seen and experienced. Prevailing culture influences the way that architects envision and design buildings and the spaces within.[1] There is no one design for a building that can address all possible requirements in all cases, and this is true for our own software projects and organizations as well.

It's dangerous to assume knowledge about systems based on the individual parts of the system and our own experiences. Building, managing, and using the systems produces a rich, complex set of responses from the systems themselves. Complex systems do not have simplistic, linear failure cases where a singular root cause can be identified. There are many factors, and especially the interactions between them, that we need to take into account when designing and scaling systems.

As an example, a single database server with 50 reads to the same data will respond differently than 50 reads to different data, depending on the software used and how it

---

1 Jun'ichirō Tanizaki, *In Praise Of Shadows* (New Haven, CT: Leete's Island Books, 1977).

is configured. When the database is now distributed, no longer on a single server, the characteristics and behaviors will change again. Don't assume that past behavior will predict future behavior.

The experience of managing this database server will likely give individuals knowledge and experience that they can use to help onboard other people more effectively, helping grow teams and reduce single points of knowledge. Additionally, simplifying how individuals should manage the system in a consistent, repeatable way is critical to reducing complexity. The process of simplification is not itself simple. What works in one environment may be completely wrong in another environment.

Planning for Scaling

Recognizing how your system should behave, and what matters in the grand scheme of things right now, allows you to construct a set of prioritized systems for your current environment. Understanding your goals is vital. Is this a learning exercise? Are you responding to an outage? Are you recovering from a security breach and trying to reestablish trust?

With software, the craftsmanship of design is discussed, and even the progression of the field often leads to an architect title. The stories around software architecture frame our choices, often preventing us from looking at software in entirely new ways. It's not that monolithic software structures are bad, or worse than microservices. Examining technology, process, and conflict strategies ensures we make conscious decisions about the flexibility and inflexibility within our environments. Making intentional decisions about flexible hinges within our organization allows us to approach future change more deliberately, with static or dynamic responses, knowing we have a strong foundation with appropriate flexibility.

Organizational Structure

Restructuring the way teams are organized may facilitate scaling. Small cross-functional teams, whose members comprise multiple skill sets (e.g., frontend and backend development, design, UX, and operations) for a single project or product, have everything needed to get their product off the ground, allowing for high bandwidth between people working on the same product.

There are also benefits to single-function teams, however, such as greater knowledge sharing and specialization within a given team or department. If you find that single-function teams are still communicating and working well with the rest of the organization, don't reorganize just for the sake of reorganization. No matter the overall team structure, it's still critical to have cross-team communication in order to have an effective organization overall.

Hierarchical organizations may stifle innovation and make people feel powerless. The power dynamics and status differences can also facilitate and enhance effectiveness, however. Organizations that attempt massive reorganization to eliminate hierarchies may run into problems when the organization is too flat. Complexity within an organization should strike the balance between being good for the organization and inflicting the least harm to employee morale.

Locality

Having organizations or teams distributed across multiple locations will bring into sharp focus how effective your company's communication skills are as a whole.

Once you have multiple locations, it will become rapidly apparent how much, if at all, your communication and decision-making processes depend on being able to have in-person conversations. If scaling locations is in your short-term to mid-term future, you'll be doing yourself a great service by ensuring everyone's written communication skills.

At a more logistical level, having multiple locations will bring a new set of IT- and infrastructure-related considerations. If only one office or site has access to something vital across the board—whether that be modern printers, a dedicated help desk team, a faster internet connection, or anything else—people working in other locations may start to feel like second-class citizens, a situation likely to hurt both morale and overall productivity. Making sure that the infrastructure between sites can handle normal workloads and work patterns is key, too.

Understanding cultural nuances, and expectations of customers at a global level, also informs how to staff local support offices. With rapid technological change and global competition, determining where your company expends effort to differentiate itself may require more diverse distribution of people.

 In order to grow a company past a certain point, you will have to figure out how to make distributed teams work. Failing to do so will slow down your ability to respond and react to changes affecting your organization, lead to duplication of effort, and decrease individual and team satisfaction as people struggle to bridge these distances effectively.

Team Flexibility

A lot of research has been done on effective team size. Teams that are too small generally lack the resources to get everything done, usually in terms of person-hours or knowledge. Larger teams, especially over 9–10 people, with so many different interpersonal interactions and relationships, can find it much more difficult to make timely and effective decisions. Large teams can also fall prone to *groupthink*, suppressing individual dissenting opinions in the interest of overall group harmony, which can diminish their creativity and problem-solving abilities.

Maintaining a team size of 5–7 people rather than growing the team implies that hiring people means creating additional teams. More teams means more managers and leadership. Management is not a promotion, it's a career change. Promoting from within is critical to maintaining culture; promote those who are capable and interested in a career focused on people.

Too Much Bureaucracy?

One common complaint about larger companies is that there is too much bureaucracy to get anything done. Bureaucracies, defined as the administrative systems that govern any large institution, have often been criticized for being too complex, inefficient, or inflexible. These factors, especially inflexibility, are a large part of why some believe that devops initiatives cannot work at larger organizations. Much research has been done over the years in the field of managerial theory about how to eliminate unnecessary bureaucracy.

Some organizations have taken this to its extreme (*http://bit.ly/nyt-zappos*)—most notably Zappos's move toward *Holacracy* (*http://bit.ly/fc-holacracy*), where all decisions are made through self-organizing teams rather than through a traditional management hierarchy. When Holacracy was introduced, individuals were encouraged to accept the change or take a generous severance package and leave.

Two years after the Zappos announcement about making this transition, 18 percent of its employees have left. There are few organizations with a typical bureaucracy that have invited their employees to leave, so it's unclear whether the severance package allowed those who left to pursue different passions or goals.

Many Zappos employees have noted that under Holacracy career development is less clear, and power vacuums end up getting unofficially filled by people with no management training or experience. Lack of explicit power structures does not mean that power differentials won't exist; they still will, but implicitly and with no formal process for addressing them.

There might be better ways to react to what feels like unnecessary red tape than implementing Holacracy. As described by Max Weber, bureaucracy developed as a reaction to earlier administrative systems like monarchies and dictatorships, where one person's whims had near-complete control over everyone else's with little to nothing in the way of checks and balances. Weber saw bureaucracy as the most efficient and rational way to organize and control human activity, to a point. Recent work around *values-based leadership* seeks to get the benefits of bureaucracy without too many unnecessary layers of management slowing things down.

Organizational Lifecycle

We can examine an organization's lifecycle through two primary lenses:

- Internal and external pressure
- Growth and decline of organizations

There is a fair amount of variety within organizational lifecycles, as new business models and funding methods offer ways for companies to change, grow, and pursue success.

Internal pressure in a growth phase takes the form of an organization growing naturally, hiring employees in order to offer more products, develop more features, work faster, and serve more customers. There may be preemptive hiring in anticipation of future growth, or reactive hiring as people start to realize that current personnel are stretched too thin.

In a decline phase, internal pressure may arise when a company realizes it is not doing as well as it wants and voluntarily starts to downsize or consolidate. How effectively it approaches this kind of change can have a great impact on its future prospects.

External pressure in the decline phase may arise due to national or global economics, changes in competitive advantage, or a company being acquired for reasons such as its product or patent portfolios or being split up and sold in pieces to other organizations. Again, how effectively and quickly an organization can react to such events can impact how well it will do in the future and if it is able to recover from such a decline.

Elimination of Vampire and Zombie Projects

Throughout an organization's lifecycle, it is important to consider whether or not current projects are still adding value to the organization. In growth or decline, identifying vampire and zombie projects can help the organization wade through change successfully. Vampire and zombie projects either hold back growth or speed the organization's decline. Either way, a time of change in the organization is a great time to clean house.

Zombie projects are projects that take up time and resources. Everyone knows that they are "walking dead" projects and yet nobody feels empowered to shut them down, in some cases due to concerns about job security or how the shutdown will impact people.

Vampire projects are projects that feed off the resources and energy of other projects. They're generally hard to recognize as vampires and difficult to kill because of people's beliefs. Sometimes vampire projects arise because of long-standing technical debt, while other times the project's creation was based on poor information.

 The first thing to do when dealing with vampire or zombie projects is to talk to all the individuals impacted and get a better understanding of the situation. A lot of times this can help defuse initial emotional responses that cause the project to linger. Generally people want to work on meaningful projects. Working on a dead project is not meaningful.

Vampire and zombie projects can both be very difficult, because there are core individuals whose lifeblood is essentially feeding the project. They might not even realize how much of a drain the project is overall for the company. When approached with the reality of the project, they may feel that they are being attacked personally. Convincing an individual to abandon "the precious" project to which they have given so much time and effort will be challenging, but it can have immense returns. The people who are passionate about projects, already have passion. You don't have to instill it in them; you just have to redirect that passion to something that has value for your company.

The Impact of Release Cycles

Organizations looking to speed up their release cycle often move from a more waterfall-esque process, where changes take weeks or months, to smaller, more frequent releases. The faster changes can be made, the faster teams can respond to external and internal pressures, such as more rapidly fixing bugs and issues that are discovered.

Failing forward fast makes much less sense in certain areas, however. Two main considerations:

- How easy is it to release software in general?
- How critical are releases?

As pervasive as the internet is these days, not every piece of software developed is designed to be immediately available 24/7/365 or to have constantly updating content. Understand and weigh the importance and complexity of projects and their releases in order to figure out what release cycle makes the most sense for each one. Different projects throughout the organization might work better with different release cadences.

Mobile applications are in most cases restricted by the release processes of their respective mobile platforms, whether that be Google Play, Apple's App Store, or another. Each application store and platform will have its own rules and restrictions and timelines, so it may not be possible to update more frequently than once a week. (Additionally, consider how often a user will be willing to update a mobile app before they decide that the frequency of updates is more of a hassle than it is worth—especially if each update logs them out of the app.)

Embedded software is even more complicated or time-consuming to push out. Software in cars, for example, often cannot be updated easily, so critical issues in it might require a massive, expensive, and inconvenient manufacturer's recall. Software in devices like televisions or microwave ovens may be less concerning in terms of safety, but also is not easy to change once it has been released. With more devices having built-in network connectivity, it's more possible to push out updates to embedded software, but devices that are upgradeable over the air have numerous security concerns that must be considered and addressed.

You must also consider the potential impact of software on the lives of the people who use it. Paying attention to this can help you plan not only release cycles but other aspects of work, such as maintenance windows or on-call rotations for projects, based on their importance.

A social networking site being down, either due to an unplanned outage or to scheduled maintenance, is probably a lot less urgent than a bank's website being down, though that hasn't stopped people from calling emergency services when they couldn't get to Facebook!

A bug that incorrectly tells someone that they have zero followers on Twitter is much lower impact than a bug on an investment website that erroneously tells a customer that the balances in their investment and retirement accounts are zero.

While breaches of personal information are never anything to be taken lightly, they are much more severe when social security numbers, credit card data, or health records are compromised.

How fast you are able to make changes, how fast you *need* to make changes, and the potential repercussions of mistakes in those changes all impact the choices that you will make.

It might seem easier to work on non-web software that isn't expected to be updated as quickly, but that might also mean that it's more difficult to fix bugs that occur. The more you scale in terms of your customers or product offerings, the larger the magnitude of potential outages or breaches.

A publicly traded company now has to consider the impact that their choices have on shareholder value in a much more substantial way than a privately held one. Public companies may have to comply with additional regulations and restrictions, such as Sarbanes-Oxley (SOX) in the United States. SOX compliance requires additional controls around anything that touches financially material data, which impacts how code that interacts with this data can be developed and deployed.

Complexity and Change

There are many ways in which the size, complexity, or inflection points of an organization's growth can affect how they approach devops. The bigger or more complex the organization, the more existing constraints they will likely have to work around (or with); this is true both for large enterprise environments but also in the public sector. In these cases, long-standing bureaucracies limit the amount of collaboration and affinity between teams as well as organizations within governments.

Governments also have more rigid laws that they must consider when adopting disruptive technology and practices. Breaking the rules within an organization may have negative consequences based on bad outcomes; breaking the law has tremendous consequences regardless of outcomes.

Additionally, depending on the organization within the government, contracts and incentives may be driving the siloization of development, operations, and other important teams. If teams have no vested interest in each other's success, the essential groundwork to collaborate and cooperate can be additionally challenging.

Still, there is significant value in helping governmental organizations find a way to limit the focus on risk as with enterprises focusing on outcomes. In the following stories, we will share how to reduce the time to deliver change and decrease costs to taxpayers, while recognizing the concerns around legal consequences from bad production releases and the challenges of collaboration and cooperation between teams.

Scaling for Teams

With a shared sense of work, purpose, interdependence, and responsibility for success, the team collaborates effectively. In this section, we'll look at the different factors that go into helping teams be their best throughout the lifecycle of an organization.

 Organizational structures that lock people into roles or that are fear driven can lead to a focus on optimizing work for the *me,* not the *we.* Choosing processes and tools that favor an individual can lead to short-term gains that are not sustainable for the team or organization over the long term.

The leaders who work most effectively, it seems to me, never say "I." And that's not because they have trained themselves not to say "I." They don't think "I." They think "we"; they think "team." They understand their job to be to make the team function. They accept responsibility and don't sidestep it, but "we" gets the credit. This is what creates trust, what enables you to get the task done.

—Peter F. Drucker

In large organizations, these factors are sometimes separated into specific roles even though as individuals we may have overlapping skills and interests. This can lead to dissonance, as time to build the necessary knowledge is lost. Worse, prestige ladders can evolve where one role is perceived as more important or better than another, hindering the actual transmission of information.

How, then, do we diffuse information across large organizations to track decisions and thus encourage people to feel ownership of or satisfaction in their own work?

Growing Your Teams: Hiring as Scaling

One key element of scaling for teams involves growing those teams. Organizations will have to consider hiring throughout their lifecycle, but especially in growth phases. In this section, we will discuss various considerations around growing teams effectively within a devops environment.

It is important to note that while this section will discuss aspects of hiring and retaining teams that are specific to devops environments, it is not a guide for hiring some mythical "10x devops engineer." Recall from Chapter 13 that devops is not necessarily a job title.

More than hiring people who simply know about infrastructure automation or the cloud or containers, organizations and teams need to focus instead on assessing their specific needs and addressing the interpersonal and cultural aspects of hiring that are key to creating and maintaining a devops culture.

One concern that frequently arises when growing teams is the cost of training employees, both in terms of getting junior hires or recent college graduates up to a level where they can contribute independently as well as providing continuing support and growth opportunities for established employees. Without spending time and money on training and development opportunities, junior members may get stuck doing grunt work—tasks that nobody else on the team has the time or motivation to do—rather than being allowed to level up.

Organizations that view areas like IT simply as cost centers rather than contributors of value may not create the appropriate budget for hiring, viewing it as unnecessary. "We should be automating this work rather than hiring people to do it," they might say, and while there is certainly value in automation, it will never be a complete replacement for humans. Not all work can or should be automated, and often, the more complex automation becomes, the more human intervention is required to maintain and troubleshoot it when it goes wrong. As discussed in Part IV, no automation technique or technology can replace the human components of development, and automation should not be viewed as just another cost-cutting measure.

People often shy away from hiring more junior candidates because they worry that it will take too much time for them to get "real" work done, or that more senior team members will have to spend too much of their time training and mentoring the new people. However, not being willing to invest in training and growing more junior candidates will likely lead to a more homogeneous team, as well as creating an environment less supportive of growth and development in general. Also, keep in mind *Brooks's law*: "Adding manpower to a late software project makes it later." Coined by software engineer Fred Brooks in his 1975 book *The Mythical Man-Month*, this idea, which Brooks himself acknowledges is an oversimplification,[2] neatly sums up how there are costs and overheads to adding more people to a team that need to be considered.

New team members have a ramp-up time before they are productive, and even the most experienced or senior engineer will take some time to get used to a new project and a new code base. There is also the time that existing team members must spend helping the new people get up to speed, which is time that is taken away from other work they might be doing. Communication overheads increase rapidly with team size, and not every task is easily divided into work that multiple people can share. When you are looking to add more people to an existing project, it is important to keep these constraints in mind and consider whether or not additional staffing will be necessary and beneficial.

Subcontracted work

Especially in larger organizations, subcontracted work (often referred to as *outsourcing*) is another option that has to be considered. Historically, areas such as IT or operations that were viewed as cost centers were seen as prime targets for outsourcing by organizations looking to cut costs.

One of the most important things to keep in mind is that while you might be saving in terms of dollars on a budget sheet, there are likely to be increased costs in terms of decreased collaboration and affinity between individuals and teams. Having some

---

2 Fred Brooks, *The Mythical Man-Month* (Boston: Addison-Wesley, 1975).

teams or departments be outsourced while others remain in-house can be a big source of conflict within an organization, either directly or indirectly. Here are some ways that this can manifest, and some solutions for dealing with that conflict:

Outsourcing creating functional silos

One of the biggest problems with silos is the lack of communication and collaboration between them, where people tend to hoard knowledge and information while pushing responsibility onto other groups. When one group is outsourced, they can often feel like nobody is willing to share information with them or keep them in the loop due to their "outsider" status, so make sure that there are clear avenues of communication both ways between in-house and outsourced teams. Using shared communication media (such as a group chat or email list that spans both teams) or encouraging regular status updates can help ensure that information is being shared.

Outsourced teams having "lower" status

In the workplace social hierarchy, either formal or informal, outsourced teams can often feel like they have lower status than in-house teams. At an organizational level, it can help to try to include outsourced teams in team celebrations and the like, because people who feel appreciated and like they are part of a group are often much more motivated at work. On individual and team levels, keep an eye out for any individuals who treat outsourced employees disrespectfully, and do not tolerate such behavior.

Conflicts of responsibility between in-house and outsourced teams

Whether an in-house team is trying to hoard responsibility for themselves, perhaps leaving only menial or tedious work for outsourced teams, or trying to push responsibility (and oftentimes blame) onto the outsourced group, responsibilities between teams can be a point of contention here as well. Regularly and clearly defined responsibilities can help eliminate confusion or tension in this area (along with regular communication), and finding ways for responsibilities or projects to be shared between in-house and outsourced individuals if possible can help foster a more collaborative environment.

While individuals and teams will not be able to fix an organizational attitude that might view outsourcing as simply another cost-cutting measure, focusing on these areas can enable them to make sure that their working relationships with outsourced teams are as effective and collaborative as possible.

 Individuals have strengths and weaknesses. These strengths and weaknesses may become better or worse in association with other people. When evaluating an individual, it's important to view them through the context of the team. Sometimes an individual isn't right for a team, but they are great for your organization.

There is an interesting dynamic that needs to be balanced: ensuring that teams continue to grow and evolve while also maintaining the equilibrium and comfort in knowing the people you work with every day. As an organization grows and declines, change will be necessary. Within a small startup, everyone knows everyone and can have that close personal relationship. As the organization grows from 50 to 100 to more, the binds that tie us to every other individual in the organization weaken.

Retention

In the competitive tech industry, keeping employees is of increasing importance to employers. Employee retention affects not only team productivity, but morale as well. Frequently losing coworkers can cause additional stress to the remaining employees as well as hinting at larger problems with the team or the company. If many employees are leaving for reasons like increased salaries at a new position or because they're worried about the direction the company is heading, that often doesn't bode well for those who stay.

While some reasons employees leave—such as family circumstances causing them to move away from a position that doesn't support remote work—aren't controllable, there are many factors of retention that are. This section will examine those factors, and organizations who want to keep the employees they've put so much effort into sourcing and hiring would do well to consider them.

Compensation

Money isn't everything, and more and more frequently people are choosing healthy work environments and companies they feel connected to over a larger paycheck. Even so, people want to feel like they're being paid competitively. A recent study found that employees who stay at companies longer than 2 years end up making significantly less money—50 percent less over only 10 years[3]—over the course of their careers. Conventional wisdom, especially among individual contributors, says that the best way to get a substantial raise is to change jobs and negotiate a higher starting salary from a new company. On average, employees staying at a company can expect around a 3 percent raise, which is effectively more like 1 percent when taking into account the 2 percent rate of inflation. Changing jobs, however, they can expect an increase of between 10 and 30 percent. Even at a company you love, over time that kind of disparity is hard to ignore.

To help combat this, start by making sure that you are paying competitively from the beginning. Employers are often tempted to offer the lowest starting salary they can get away with to help their bottom line. This often disproportionately affects mem-

---

3 Cameron Keng, "Employees Who Stay in Companies Longer Than Two Years Get Paid 50% Less," *Forbes*, June 22, 2014.

bers of minority groups who tend to make notably less on the dollar than white men. Offering salaries and benefits that are in line with industry averages can help attract these candidates, many of whom have been significantly underpaid at previous positions. Transparency about the salary negotiation process, pay bands (if your company uses them), and other issues related to compensation can help with retention. People want to feel like they are being compensated competitively, but also that they are being treated fairly.

One thing that can help, especially in retaining employees who tend to be penalized for negotiating salary rather than rewarded for it, is transparency around the process for raises. Having a clearly defined and publicly (within the company) documented process is key. A process that relies on people asking or that happens only when managers think of it is far more prone to unconscious biases than one that happens on a regular schedule with clearly defined parameters. Having pay bands rather than simply relying on managers' judgments can reduce these kinds of biases as well. Make sure that everyone, managers and individual contributors alike, is aware of the process around raises (and yearly bonuses, if your company has them) as well as who to talk to if they have a concern with the process.

Nonmonetary benefits

Being paid competitively and fairly is important, but once employees are compensated well enough that they are able to enjoy a good standard of living and save money for the future without having to worry about their rent check bouncing (especially in rental markets like New York and San Francisco), nonmonetary compensation can often be more valuable to them than additional salary increases. For smaller or less mature companies that might not be able to offer the same salaries that more heavily funded or more profitable ones can, these kinds of perks can be a good way to attract and retain talent, especially diverse talent that hasn't been afforded the opportunities to be able to pay rent in such expensive areas.

It is important to note that when we talk about perks, we are not talking about things like beer fridges and ping-pong tables in the office. Those kinds of "perks" tend to create an atmosphere more resembling a frat house than a professional office space, and can be a deterrent for people who feel uncomfortable in such an environment, whether that be women, nondrinkers, or people who simply don't want to play table sports at work. Meals, especially healthy ones that include options for a variety of dietary restrictions, can be a plus, but be wary of offering breakfasts and especially dinners as perks, as those meals tend to indicate a culture where people are expected to arrive early and work late on a regular basis.

Benefits you might consider include:

Remote opportunities
> Whether to attract a wider range of candidates or retain employees who need to move from one of your company's offices (e.g., moving away to have children, to be near parents, or to have a cheaper cost of living), offering the ability to work remotely can be a big benefit.

Educational opportunities
> These might take the form of bringing instructors onsite, sending employees to conferences or training seminars so they can learn new skills or improve existing ones, or providing tuition or textbook reimbursements for people who are seeking continuing education in fields relevant to their profession. Personal and professional development are important to people, so providing them opportunities (as well as time) to pursue these opportunities can be a great benefit.

Flexible work hours
> Unless there is a legitimate reason for requiring people to work specific hours, a little flexibility can go a long way. This, like remote work, shows trust in the employees and teams and respects their lives and responsibilities outside of work. Flexible hours can allow people to pursue hobbies, avoid rush-hour commutes, or take care of family and household responsibilities while getting their work done at times that are convenient for them and the rest of their team.

Work–life balance
> Continually working 50–80 hour weeks has a negative impact on overall productivity, not a positive one. Make sure that employees are allowed and encouraged to come into and leave the office at reasonable times, and to not spend their time at home working or checking email constantly as well. One of the best ways to do this is to provide good examples from management—employees who see their supervisor emailing them at 10 pm or 5 am may feel pressure to respond that late or early, whether that pressure is intentional or not. If employees are on-call, providing extra time off for each on-call shift can be a great benefit also.

Paid leave
> Make sure that your company provides vacation time and that people are using it. Outside of whatever holidays are required by the laws in your country, try to avoid mandating when vacation days should be used. For example, providing 10 days of vacation but requiring that 8 of them be taken during the weeks around Christmas and New Year's leaves only 2 vacation days for the other 50 weeks of the year—which is far from ideal (especially considering not everyone celebrates Christmas). For companies considering unlimited vacation policies, an article (*http://bit.ly/meyer-vacation*) by Mathias Meyer, CEO of the TravisCI continuous integration company, explains how those can also be problematic.

Retirement plans

At the bare minimum, organizations should offer employees the opportunity to contribute to a retirement plan such as an IRA or 401(k). In addition, consider matching employee contributions up to a certain percentage; with fewer and fewer employers doing so these days, this can be a very valuable and competitive benefit if you can afford it. If you cannot, consider doing something like bringing a financial advisor onsite a few times a year to provide complimentary advising sessions to employees.

Health insurance

While some form of health insurance is standard for most full-time employees, health insurance plans can vary widely in their coverage, especially in the United States. More competitive benefits will include a wide range of plans for employees to choose from, dependent coverage, domestic partner benefits, and trans-inclusive healthcare. It can also be a bonus to have the organization pay all monthly costs rather than having those come out of employees' paychecks, or offering access to an online health concierge service to answer employees' medical and insurance-related questions.

Casual dress code

Employers who relax the office dress code reduce long-term and upfront expenses for employees without incurring costs. While business dress may come across as more professional, any tasks that expose individuals to weather or that are physically demanding will affect professional clothing more than casual. For some individuals, having the freedom to choose clothing is one measure of autonomy. In an environment with rigid hierarchies, this is one way to effect change within the organization. When employees at different levels dress more casually, they are more likely to interact with one another, strengthening relationships across the organization.

Transportation benefits

Transportation benefits can include prepaid transit passes, company bus, bike lockers, and even valet parking. By providing mechanisms to ease traffic or parking congestion at the office, employers can reduce the tension that creates competition between employees while lowering the employee's commuting costs. Additionally, within the United States, there are some provisions to transportation benefits up to a certain limit tax-free. These benefits include items such as transit passes, vanpooling, and parking. Check the laws for your area.

Gender-neutral facilities

Providing gender-neutral restrooms creates a more inclusive environment for individuals who may not match stereotypical expectations of binary gender, while also improving accessibility for individuals needing assistance. Local laws will vary with regards to what restrooms and signage are legally required, so this may not be possible to do in every location or for every restroom. Wherever possible, however, gender-neutral restrooms (and locker rooms or showers, if those are provided for employee use) will allow a wider range of employees to use facilities where they feel comfortable and safe.

On-site daycare

Providing on-site daycare can improve overall job satisfaction and attract employees with young children. With reduced absenteeism due to child-care issues, no longer do child-free employees bear the cost of covering for parents both during the day and during on-call shifts.

Overall, employees should not feel like their company is trying to shortchange them when it comes to monetary or nonmonetary benefits. People who feel that they are treated fairly, taken care of, and have a process for addressing any questions or complaints they might have are generally happy employees.

Growth opportunities

Beyond money and work–life balance, one of the biggest reasons that people leave jobs is a lack of opportunities for advancement.[4] Nobody goes into a job expecting or hoping that it will be a dead-end one. People want opportunities to grow their skills and to demonstrate that growth, whether that means more independence, more choice in the projects that they take on, being trusted with bigger projects, or leadership opportunities.

Keep in mind that leadership doesn't just mean management. In some companies, the management track is the only one with clearly defined job levels and the only way that employees can advance in their career, but many technical ICs have no desire to go into management. Leadership for these people can mean leading projects and expanding the impact of their contributions in an organization. Make sure that you have a way for nonmanagers to advance as well. Ideally, this would mean creating a technical track with clearly defined levels of individual contributor growth, as well as a management track.

Having a clearly defined process for growth and promotion is critical for management and individual contributor tracks alike. Make sure that there are definitions of job levels available to employees, with enough detail that people can see clearly what they need to do to move from one level to the next. The process for promotion should be clearly and publicly defined as well. A "process" that consists only of people getting metaphorically tapped on the shoulder by management can be incredibly frustrating for employees who don't get chosen, as well as being rife with opportuni-

---

4 Katie Taylor, "Why Do People Actually Quit Their Jobs?" *Entrepreneur*, July 16, 2014.

ties for unconscious bias to appear. All employees deserve the opportunity to grow, not just those who happen to be friends with their boss or the CTO.

Going along with this, make sure that employees have chances to explore different areas of interest at the company. If a software developer, after several years, wants to explore an interest in operations or security, for example, they will likely go to another company to explore that if their current one doesn't afford them any way to do so. While managers generally shouldn't try to poach employees from other teams, they should be open to the possibilities that people's interests and career goals will change and try to work with that whenever possible. Some companies do what they call "senior rotations," where employees get to take a few weeks to work on teams other than their own once they've been with the company long enough. Whether in their current job area or another one, growth throughout the entire course of their career is very important to people, so providing opportunities for that is necessary if you want them to stick around.

Workload

In general, people are looking for workloads that are challenging but doable. Continuing our discussion of growth opportunities, challenging work that allows people to test themselves and grow their skills is important to their senses of satisfaction about their jobs. In Part II, we addressed several different working or collaborative styles, including starters versus finishers and purists versus pragmatists. If the work that people are regularly being given doesn't align well with the type of work they most prefer to do, that can make their workload feel higher than it is, and disengagement with the work itself is likely to decrease a person's happiness and productivity.

Too much challenge can lead to problems. People might feel that their company or their manager expects too much of them and isn't willing to give them the time, support, or resources they need to get it done, or it might seem like their manager is out of touch with reality and doesn't understand how much work they can accomplish. It might indicate a team that has taken on too much or has an uneven distribution of work, where some employees are relatively relaxed while others are overworked. Whatever the reasons, long-term overworking of people (as opposed to a one-off period of crunch time) can have very negative impacts.

Overworked employees might just end up leaving the company for a different job that doesn't require so much of them. Perhaps even less desirable is the possibility that they will stay, but be suffering from burnout. It is important for managers to regularly check in with the team as a whole and with individual employees to make sure that they don't have an unrealistic amount of work they are trying to take on. Make sure that employees are taking vacations as needed as well. If a team or individual has just finished a period of extra work, such as near the end of a project, encourage them to take some time off, and make sure that everyone is taking at least one good-sized vacation (or even "staycation") per year to avoid burnout.

Burnout

Burnout is a term that refers to long-term exhaustion and lack of interest in work and often in activities outside of work as well. Symptoms of burnout are very similar to those of clinical depression, and burnout has even been called a form of depression in some recent studies. People suffering from burnout may start isolating themselves from others, pay less attention to their own personal needs, have problems sleeping, and have feelings of indifference, helplessness, and hopelessness. It often arises from prolonged periods of stress and overwork, which are far too common in the tech industry, especially in Silicon Valley startups that idealize the "heroic" hacker or "rock star" developer. Mental health is as important as physical health, if not more so, and taking care to avoid burnout should be a priority for every team and every company.

Many tech companies have some kind of on-call position—people whose responsibilities include carrying a phone or pager and responding to incidents outside of standard working hours. It is very important to make sure that on-call is not placing undue stress on people. If at all possible, make sure that the on-call responsibilities are shared between at least two people—this is really the bare minimum. Having only one person on-call 24/7/365 is pretty much asking for that person to get burnt out. No one person should be forced to give up *all* their nights and weekends in perpetuity. Ideally, on-call rotations would be shared between several people, possibly with several rotations as your company grows, to give every individual adequate time to catch up on sleep and relax between their shifts.

If people are part of an on-call rotation, make sure they are compensated for it. Some companies increase the salary of employees who have ongoing on-call responsibilities, some pay extra for each hour that someone carries a pager or for each off-hours incident they have to respond to, and some provide extra vacation hours or days for each on-call shift. If on-call responsibilities are part of a job from the beginning, make sure that the extent of these responsibilities is clarified up front, so employees know what they are signing up for and can negotiate their compensation accordingly. If these responsibilities are added after someone has started, make sure there is an opportunity for them to discuss the details and compensation with their manager.

Culture and "culture fit"

Culture and *culture fit* are terms that are so vague that they can be problematic, often used by people making hiring decisions who seek, either consciously or not, to keep a certain amount of homogeneity within their team, perhaps hiring people who went to the same school, like the same sports, or participated in the same fraternity as them.

This is a misuse of the idea of cultural fit, as it takes very superficial ideas of culture and uses them to create an atmosphere of exclusivity.

Because so much of devops involves culture and how people work together and relate with each other, it is important to define these terms in a way that is productive, rather than exclusive. Culture is better defined as the ideas, customs, and social behavior of a people or society, and when we look deeper into those areas we can see how this definition can make or break someone's desire to stay with a company.

Ideas can mean a lot of different things in the context of a company or a team. Most broadly, an idea for the company is its value proposition, what it is selling, how it has chosen to make money. Some companies' value is essentially in advertising, or selling user data to advertisers. If someone feels that their company's values conflict too much with their own personal ones, or they simply don't have any interest in what the company is doing, there is a force driving the individual away from the company regardless of the company's success.

Ideas might also be interpreted to mean what is considered valuable in a given organization or team. As a typical example, in many organizations, especially before the idea of devops rose to popularity, operations or IT work was often very undervalued. IT was seen as nothing but a cost center. Investment in IT was seen as something to be minimized at all costs, as IT was thought to provide very little to no value to the company.

Similarly, one might feel devalued by their team or manager. If a few team members are very buddy-buddy with their supervisor, and if that friendliness leads the supervisor to listen to them more, the other team members can easily feel that their contributions aren't valuable to the team.

Anyone whose ideas are different from the majority might quickly feel this way as well. We've touched previously on considerations for helping to increase the diversity of a team or organization, but it's very important to consider the impact that this can have on people who aren't "the norm." A lone woman on a team of men, or a person of color in an otherwise all-white team, especially on a team that primarily handles disagreements by way of who yells the loudest, might very well feel that their contributions are neither heard nor valued.

Customs are the traditional or widely accepted ways of behaving, speaking, or doing things. Many aspects of a workplace can be viewed as customs in this light, including:

- How work is assigned, and who is responsible for assigning it
- How members of a team or the same level within the company communicate with each other
- How managers communicate news to their reports
- When people arrive at and leave the office

- Technical processes for doing work
- How promotions, raises, and bonuses are awarded

One of the problems with customs is that they can be hard to recognize as just one way of doing things and not the only way, because once people are used to them they have a tendency to fade into the background. Often it takes a new pair of eyes and a fresh perspective to point out that there might be a better way of doing something.

 It is important to recognize and value these insights; "we've always done it this way" is not a sufficient reason for continuing to do something. Refusal to change or to even consider new ideas is how teams and companies stagnate, often leading to them getting passed over by their competitors. It's human nature to fear change, to reject the unfamiliar, but we should recognize this tendency in ourselves and actively work against it to make sure that we're hearing, considering, and choosing the best ideas, not just the ones we're most comfortable with.

Company customs regarding promotions, raises, and bonuses merit special consideration when you're trying to improve diversity. It bears reiterating that even though we might not want or notice them, unconscious biases can easily creep in here. If these sorts of things are awarded solely at a manager's discretion without people applying, being encouraged to apply, or something like having all employees of a certain role or rank being considered, unconscious biases can (and often do) come into play.

Social behaviors, the last major part of culture, cover a wide range of factors in how people interact. Pay attention to the way people communicate: do more "senior" employees talk down to or talk over those who are lower in the ranks, or are all ideas treated with respect regardless of who they came from? Do people tend to interrupt each other in meetings, or do they wait until others have finished speaking? Is this true among only peers, or with management as well? When people have disagreements, how are they resolved—by calm discussions, by consensus, or by people simply yelling at and over each other until all but one party has given up out of frustration? How do decisions get made?

Social behaviors also include ones that we might more often think of when we hear the word *social*. How do teams get to know each other or bond? There are many benefits to better knowing the people you work with, including greater empathy and more effective communication, but there are more or less effective ways to improve camaraderie. More corporate environments might opt for some awkward ice breakers and trust falls, while startups might tend toward a trip to the nearest bar. The most effective might be something in between, soliciting input from all team members and trying to find something that is agreeable to everyone. Be aware, however, that some people might not feel comfortable giving their opinions publicly. Someone who has struggled with alcohol abuse, for example, would likely be hesitant to explain in front of their coworkers why they don't want to go on a work-sponsored bar crawl. Make sure to give people ample opportunity to give their opinions in a private, safe manner.

Similarly, the ways that people socialize in the office can be very telling as to the overall social behaviors. People will generally notice who frequently goes to lunch or coffee with their team's manager, especially if this is not a privilege afforded equally to everyone on the team. (While it is true, especially at startups that are often founded by people who previously knew each other, that colleagues might become friends at work, it is important to avoid unconscious biases and blatant favoritism in the office.)

Many offices, especially smaller ones, develop activities that often take place after hours or during breaks. Some might have cold-brew coffee or beer on tap, today's equivalent of the water cooler. Some might have ping-pong or foosball tables that employees can use at the end of the day or to blow off some steam. Increasingly common in environments dominated by younger male employees are toys such as remote-controlled helicopters or Nerf guns. These things are not universally bad, but they can be exclusionary of those who don't like them. Someone who doesn't care for kids' toys in a work environment is likely to be pretty upset by getting hit in the head with a poorly aimed Nerf dart in the middle of trying to get work done.

Keep in mind that people might not feel comfortable speaking up against things that happen in the name of "fun"—nobody wants to come across as being antifun. It's hard to be the only one to speak up against something that's been a long-standing part of the culture, and if someone is a minority on the team they might feel even less comfortable coming forward. Making sure that people are comfortable speaking up about their opinions, as well as paying attention to what kinds of activities are common around the office, can go a long way toward promoting a culture that everyone feels a part of.

Overall, a lot of retention comes down to making sure that you are maintaining a compact with your employees, making sure that there is a mutual understanding, shared goals or needs being met, and ongoing development of relationships as per the devops compact we have been discussing. Expectations around culture should be explicitly defined wherever possible throughout the processes of sourcing, interviewing, and retaining employees. With this in mind, we'll now take a look at how these ideas can be applied in the wild.

Case Studies: Growing and Scaling Teams

For this chapter's case studies, we spoke with two people involved in hiring in different capacities: a director of devops at an online marketplace company founded in 2007, and Phaedra Marshall, a technology director at Critical Mass, a global digital marketing and design firm founded in Calgary, Alberta, in 1996. While they are both closely involved with making hiring decisions for technology companies, they approached these decisions in different ways. We'll look at the reasoning behind their different approaches and why each one made sense given their particular sets of circumstances.

Growing and Building Operations Teams

at the director of devops, who originally started his career as a developer and later joined a large ecommerce company that develops software for online stores and retail point-of-sale (POS) systems, and built their operations team from the ground up. He later built from the very beginning the operations team at a digital media and publishing company. At the company, he oversees production operations and corporate IT from the technical side as well as helping to grow both departments.

Looking for an opportunity for a director-level position as well as an environment with plenty of room for learning and growth, the director was drawn to the company due to its diversity and culture. Over half of the company's senior managers were women, including the CTO and CEO, which is much more diverse than most Silicon Valley companies, or even most technology companies in general. It currently has around 125 employees, with about 30 of those in engineering.

In terms of their operations, they run on approximately 50 servers on a combination of physical and cloud infrastructure, with autoscaling (automatically increasing or decreasing the number of servers running in a cloud infrastructure based on some metric such as server CPU load) of up to hundreds of job workers as load necessitates. To them, doing devops effectively means having operations engineers working closely with developers to build "beautifully automated" systems that help the business achieve its goals. This involves teaching developers about operations work and automation in particular and then working closely with them across the lifecycles of the systems they build.

Sourcing and interviewing candidates

In order to make hiring decisions that worked toward this particular vision of devops, the director had to put a fair amount of thought and iteration into the growth strategy for his new team. The devops team at the company, which currently consists of four engineers as well as the director himself, ranges in experience from a junior engineer in his first devops role to a former director making his way back into being an individual contributor. All of these were hires that the director made. Their process involved getting approval from the VP of engineering for the headcount, followed by sharing the job posting on Twitter and the GitHub and StackOverflow job boards. Like many companies, they haven't had a great deal of success with recruiters and have found these industry-specific job boards and networking by current team members to be much more effective at finding the kinds of candidates they need.

The interview process started with two phone screens—one by a current team member, and one by the director himself. Candidates who passed the phone screens earned a full in-person interview, during which they spoke with two engineers, an engineering director, a manager on the business side of the organization, and finally the VP of engineering. Some interviews were more technically focused, while others focused on getting to know the person and assessing how well they would work as a part of the growing team. For the director's team, this meant finding out what they liked and disliked about their previous positions, what they were looking for, and what excited or discouraged them when it came to work environments.

The director notes that he tried to find out if candidates have any strong opinions (on text editors, or SQL versus NoSQL, or their favorite Linux distribution) and whether or not those opinions are so rigidly held as to be completely inflexible. The company has found that people who refuse to change their minds about things tend not to be people who fit in well to their team environment. Interviewing with people outside of their direct team, such as with the business manager, is useful for finding out if candidates work well with other teams, especially nonengineering teams.

Strong Opinions, Weakly Held

Paul Saffo, a technology forecaster in Silicon Valley, wrote in 2008 (*http://bit.ly/saffo-opinions*) that the best perspective he had found for dealing with environments that involve at least a moderate degree of uncertainty, as so much of the tech industry does, is to have "strong opinions, weakly held." The strong opinions part meant making sure he arrived at a conclusion, usually guided by his intuition if necessary, rather than refusing to take a stance or form an opinion at all.

Weakly held means looking to be proven wrong, seeking out things that don't fit with the current conclusion, and being willing and able to change his mind based on new evidence. Many people have found that this is a desired perspective for candidates, as someone who cannot form strong opinions will not be a strong decision maker or leader, but someone whose opinions are too strongly held is likely to back themselves into a corner and be less able to recover from mistakes.

Problems with "Hero Culture"

When it was pointed out that their job posting was glorifying *hero culture*, where "heroic" behaviors—such as working long hours and single-handedly troubleshooting and "firefighting" to keep services up and running—are looked upon as desirable, the director realized that their hiring process needed some improvement.

The problem with this kind of culture is that it is unhealthy, with long hours and working weekends leading to burnout as well as physical and often mental health issues. Additionally, it tends to attract people who are more interested in being "heroes" for their own recognition or gain than they are in working effectively as part of a team. Though the glorification of hero culture in the job posting was inadvertent, it was affecting the types of candidates the director was getting for the positions he was trying to fill.

Examples of these kinds of job descriptions include:

- Asking for candidates to "give 110 percent" or "go above and beyond," phrases that tend to be indicative of teams with little to no work–life balance. In addition to being unhealthy, these kinds of requirements are biased toward singles and away from candidates who have family responsibilities (or simply want to get home at a reasonable hour most nights).

- Describing a team that "works hard and plays harder." You are hiring employees, not friends, and expecting your employees to spend their nonwork hours at work social events, especially when those events tend to be heavily focused on alcohol, is off-putting to many candidates.

- "Awesomeness" or some other vague quality. A term like this is vague enough to be close to meaningless, and attracts the sort of people who think they exude "awesomeness," which often goes hand in hand with egotism and unwillingness to learn or listen, excluding groups like women and people of color who tend to suffer from impostor syndrome.[5] This includes asking for candidates who self-identify as "rock stars," "ninjas," "wizards," and the like as ways of describing their skills.

- Assigning homework or otherwise requiring applicants to prove their knowledge is another tactic that shows a lack of respect for employees' time and that tends to be biased toward people with fewer responsibilities outside of work. Not all screening exercises are bad—ones that involve walking through hypothetical scenarios to get a feeling for a candidate's thought processes and values can be very beneficial, for example—but relying too much on trivia questions can be very off-putting to candidates.

These and similar requirements that emphasize hero culture tend to create workplaces where employees are often losing sleep, which itself leads to degradation of creativity, productivity, and empathy, as well as eventual job dissatisfaction, loss of self-confidence, and burnout.

---

5 Impostor syndrome is a term used to describe high-achieving individuals who are unable to internalize their own successes and thus worry that they will be found out as frauds or impostors.

Job Postings and Recruitment Issues

When examining their job descriptions under this lens, the company looked a great deal at how their recruiting strategy as a whole was portraying them. They maintained their previous decision of not using recruiters, because too often recruiters, especially third-party ones, can also lead to issues, as recruiters who don't share your values won't necessarily represent your company well, and may be incredibly off-putting or even offensive to candidates. The following examples are not from the director or the company, but are an example of the kinds of things to especially watch out for in either job descriptions or messages from recruiters (internal or external).

Lack of effort or attention to detail

If an email begins with "Dear %%FIRSTNAME%%, we are looking for someone to fill a %%JOBTITLE%% position," that's a clear sign of someone who copied and pasted from a template and couldn't even be bothered to glance over their email for these very obvious mistakes before hitting send. Even copying a potential candidate's skills from their LinkedIn profile isn't always a sure bet, especially without proofreading; sending an email to someone asking to discuss their "experience with backend development and drinking beer" is a clear indication that someone either didn't double-check their work or is hiring for a very unhealthy company culture. Copying and pasting the same form letter to every member of a team is a lack of effort that will not go unnoticed by those teammates—word about companies who use these tactics gets around.

In the same vein, asking a potential candidate to recommend some other people if they aren't interested in the position comes across as incredibly lazy. These days, nearly every company is actively hiring. If they knew any qualified candidates they would be talking to them themselves, not doing free recruiting work for someone else's company. People are often willing to give recommendations, but to friends or colleagues they know and trust, not to complete strangers who bother them with repeated unsolicited emails.

Exclusionary or unprofessional language

Look out for language in job postings or recruiting emails that is likely to alienate candidates. Exceptionally masculine language—"crushing code," "rock stars," and "are you a [TECH] weapon" are likely to be off-putting to people who don't fall into a stereotypically masculine mold. Even worse than this is overtly sexist or homophobic language. A job description that lists "making it rain on them hoes" and "partying with rock stars" as job perks and "being totally gay for code" as a requirement is wildly inappropriate in a professional context, pointing to a company that is likely to be hostile to women or LGBTQ people. Saying that you're looking for a "nice dude" who is "under 30" does the same thing, and specifying gender and age is often illegal depending on the country you're hiring in.

Misplaced focus on technology

Many engineers are excited by getting to use new technologies, so it makes sense that companies might use those technologies to get people interested in their jobs. Too much focus on tech, especially without doing due diligence, can backfire, however. If you're asking for experience in a particular technology, do your research. Asking for 10 years of experience in a product that has only existed for 2 years makes it look like you don't know what you're talking about at all—probably not the impression you're trying to give.

Something else to be aware of is that candidates are more and more often interested in what a company is doing, not just the technologies it's using. If your technology is interesting with good reason, feel free to mention it, but sending an email to a potential candidate that talks *only* about the tech without even mentioning what that technology is building and what the company does is a mistake. An engineering team that is always using the latest "hot" new bleeding-edge tools (and again, descriptions like "hot" and "sexy" are very likely to alienate large groups of potential candidates) isn't necessarily going to sell your team very well.

Linting Your Job Descriptions

Linting is a term in computer programming that describes programmatically searching for suspicious, dangerous, or nonportable code constructs that are likely to cause issues. Engineers can "lint" their code to do this kind of analysis on it, checking for common errors or style problems, before they commit it to the main code repository.

A similar tool exists for analyzing job descriptions or postings, or recruiter emails, to check for some of the common issues that we have described here. You can use this tool yourself at joblint.org to catch some issues you might not be aware of, and to remind you of what you should check for in the future.

The company later revised their job postings and got rid of these "heroic" descriptions; they now highlight the team's cultural values, including work–life balance. For example, they note that they give every on-call engineer an extra day off after each weeklong on-call rotation, to help counteract the stress and sleep deprivation that is so often part of being on-call. They also work to optimize away the unpleasant parts of working in operational areas by doing things like rotating who is responsible for responding to walk-up questions and other interruptions from colleagues, and using a ticketing system to track these requests.

Other examples of better job postings include:

- Mentioning general skills rather than specific technologies. Instead of saying you want someone with two years of Puppet experience, try advertising for concepts such as automation of repetitive tasks and configuration management. Also assess whether or not a specific number of years experience is required; in many cases it isn't, and those kinds of hard requirements will leave out candidates who are qualified.

- Call out important cultural values. By culture, we're not talking about having a team who drinks beer and plays foosball together, but rather cultural values such as empathy, effective communication, getting rid of silos, and work–life balance. (Of course, don't mention values that your team doesn't have—lying about your culture to get hires will quickly be discovered and word will spread.)

- Make sure your job descriptions are gender-neutral and free of aggressive terminology. You're looking for somebody who can write code, not "crush" code.

- Specifically call out your company's commitment to diversity if that's something you're working on. Mention perks that will appeal to a wide range of applicants; instead of a beer fridge and ping-pong table, talk about a culture that encourages people to leave work on time, parental leave, and training opportunities.

More Diverse Hiring Resources

Model View Culture, an independent publication writing on issues of culture and diversity in tech, has a list of 25 tips for diverse hiring (*http://bit.ly/mvc-diverse*). It is an excellent collection of resources for anyone looking to improve the diversity of their teams.

The new job posting has been working very well for the director and his team—they've had five successful hires, with only one person who didn't end up being a good fit. They've managed to take their infrastructure from one of entirely unmanaged "snowflake" servers to one that is completely automated, because of the people they've hired. Their team worked to hire engineers who are enthusiastic believers in automation and testing, and then let them do their best work without being micromanaged. This led to a complete overhaul of their automation and testing infrastructure, providing the entire engineering organization with simple, well-documented tools that everyone knows how to use and contribute to.

Developing Individuals and Teams

We move now to Critical Mass, where technology director Phaedra Marshall has a 15-year history working with technology across industries including higher education, finance, media, and advertising. To her, devops means leveraging the coding skills of developers with the operational knowledge of system administrators to provision and operate reliable computing systems at scale, something that is important regardless of the specific industry those systems are supporting. She wants to take existing job descriptions and positions and create an environment where both kinds of technologists can really play to their strengths.

As a team lead, her focus is on growing and improving her team, similar to the director previously described, but at over 700 people, Critical Mass is operating at a much larger scale than the online marketplace company. This necessitates different specific hiring practices, even though their general objectives are the same.

Because their organization is so large, they have staff recruiters who work full-time in-house to find qualified candidates. This has enabled them to work with the recruiters very closely, making sure that they are very closely aligned with the team and company visions, and avoiding some of the potential recruiter missteps mentioned previously. If a team lead or hiring manager isn't satisfied with the candidates they are getting from the recruiters, it is their responsibility to work with the specified recruiter to try to resolve those issues.

The interview process consists of a phone interview, which usually lasts around 30 minutes and covers a candidate's work history, followed by a number of on-site interviews. The exact number depends on the team and the type of position a candidate is interviewing for. For example, an entry-level developer would be requested to come to only one on-site interview, but the higher level the position a candidate is being considered for, the more interviews they are likely to have.

Developing and Growing Team Members

Once the interview process has been completed and a hire has been made, every employee is assigned a *Career Developer*. Career Developers act as mentors to the employees assigned to them, which is usually a number around four; the company has found over time that no Career Developer has been very effective with more than seven mentees, as they all have other work assignments and responsibilities as well. The primary goal of a Career Developer is to help employees succeed at the company, in whatever form that takes, as they would much rather have an employee change positions or teams within the company than be dissatisfied enough to leave entirely. Each Career Developer meets with their mentees individually at least once a month.

The company uses a type of feedback called *360 feedback* for performance reviews. In this method, feedback is gathered from a variety of people in an employee's immediate work circle, often including their immediate peers, their direct reports if they have any, and the person (or people) they report to. In this case study, 360 feedback is provided anonymously, and a Career Developer will receive a copy of all the feedback for their mentees. In this way, they can help their mentees process that feedback, by, for example, coming up with a performance improvement plan if there was significant negative feedback or helping employees make concrete plans toward their short- and long-term career goals. This is a large part of how Career Developers help their mentees, in addition to offering general career direction advice or assisting with perplexing technical issues.

As their focus on career growth and mentorship shows, Critical Mass takes retention very seriously as a key part of their hiring and employment strategy. They have realized that while monetary compensation is important, there are other ways of making employees feel valued aside from simply increasing their salaries.

In their weekly technology staff meetings, all team members are encouraged to talk about what they're working on and describe the contributions they've made to those projects. Once a month, employees are asked to nominate one of their coworkers for a *spot bonus*, which combines the interpersonal satisfaction that comes from peer respect and recognition with a monetary bonus.

Letting employees explore multiple interests and grow their careers in the directions they choose is an important retention strategy as well. The technology lead shared a story of a frontend developer on her team who was very valued on the team, but wanting to do something beyond JavaScript and CSS. He discussed this with his Career Developer, who brought it to the attention of the tech lead, and together the three of them came up with a way for the developer to start spending at least 25 percent of his time each week working on other creative technology projects. This slight modification to his responsibilities allowed him to grow his skill set, gave him the opportunity to work in an area of technology that excites him, and let the company retain a talented (and much happier) developer.

These two case studies taken side by side show how, even though both companies have the same overall objectives (to hire and retain talented engineers), their sizes and specific situations led them to different hiring and retention techniques. At different scales, these two organizations both focused on the sort of culture they wanted to create and maintain, and developed their hiring and retention strategies to fit these goals.

Hiring only for skill or experience with a particular technology is akin to skipping over all the material in this book except for the section on tools—these technology-focused "hard skills" are only a small part of the overall picture of what makes devops so effective. If you hire someone who has worked with your particular stack before but is a poor culture fit or lacks critical thinking, learning, and troubleshooting skills, what will happen if you need to switch technologies in the future, or add a new one to your stack?

On the other hand, if you find a developer who has great people and learning skills, her ability to pick up new things will be a much better benefit in the long run. Keeping this in mind as you grow and develop your teams will make your hiring practices and your organization in general much more effective.

Team Scaling and Growth Strategies

The team in some ways can be viewed as a separate organism. To ensure healthy teams within a scaling organization, solid collaboration and affinity skills are crucial, so you may wish to revisit Parts II and III. Additionally, there are three key strategies to strengthen the team throughout its lifecycle:

- Keeping teams small and flexible
- Fostering collaboration
- Managing conflict

Next, we'll take a look at how these different strategies can impact team health and productivity.

Keeping Teams Small and Flexible

As organizations grow, teams may grow without thoughtful design. Large teams are less likely to share knowledge or learn freely from each other. The lack of familiarity within the team of each member's strengths and weaknesses leads to less workload flexibility. Tasks align to individuals, which often creates bottlenecks, especially as individuals become circular dependencies in complex scenarios.

What is the state of your environment now? Do you have single points of knowledge on particular topics or services? This is often a situation that occurs in small startups where individuals take on a number of roles and responsibilities in order to get the job done. As the team grows, these single points of knowledge need to be monitored. This is hidden fragility in your environment that will lead to out-of-band retention heroics if this person decides to leave your company, or worse, suffers some kind of life-altering event preventing their continued employ.

In the 1960s, psychologist Frederick Herzberg interviewed a number of engineers and accountants, formulating a motivation hygiene theory (see Figure 14-1) about job satisfaction and job dissatisfaction factors that act independently of each other.[6]

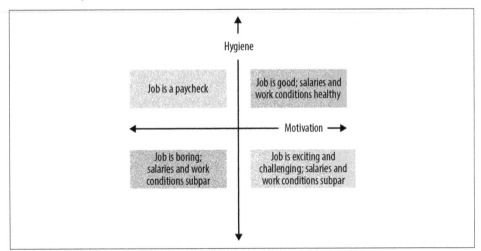

Figure 14-1. Motivation hygiene theory

Motivators improve job satisfaction and include factors like challenging work, appreciation and recognition for achievement, perceived responsibility and autonomy, and the opportunity to do meaningful work. There are five critical elements that empower and motivate individuals:

- Freedom
- Challenge
- Education
- Personal meaningful contribution
- A positive environment

Hygiene factors remove job dissatisfaction and include job security, fair salary, benefits, work conditions, and vacation.

Based on Herzberg's motivation hygiene theory, J. Richard Hackman and Neil Vidmar did research on the optimum group size in the 1970s.[7] They composed groups rang-

---

6 Christina Stello, *Herzberg's Two-Factor Theory of Job Satisfaction: An Integrative Literature Review* (Minneapolis: University of Minnesota, 2011.

7 J. Richard Hackman and Neil Vidmar, "Effects of Size and Task Type on Group Performance and Member Reactions," *Sociometry* 33, no. 1 (March 1970).

ing from two to seven members to assess the impact of size on process and performance in a number of varied tasks. After the tasks were completed, they asked the participants questions about their feelings on the group size and the assigned tasks. Based on this research, they found the optimum group size was 4.6 individuals, so try to limit your team size to around this number. Depending on whether there are a lot of consensus-driven decisions, choose an odd number, like three or five.

Hackman and Vidmar also identified a set of factors that contributed to dysfunctional teams as teams grew into double digits:

- The cost to communication and coordination chores grew exponentially so that less time was spent working.
- More handoffs led to more mistakes and miscommunication.
- Overall team cohesion was weaker.

 Over time, a team will become more effective at its current work, and will either add more responsibility or change direction. If the team is reaching a size that will start to limit effectiveness and requires additional people to get the work done, consider splitting the team, or reducing the responsibilities.

Teams should change as needed to maintain effectiveness within and between them. Small organizations allow for interactive team communications where everyone knows each other on the team, and so communication is high bandwidth. As organizations grow, per-person bandwidth decreases and you reach a point where everyone doesn't know everyone else within the organization. Team sizes should remain small in order to maintain enough communication and shared understanding to enforce the devops compact throughout the organization.

Fostering Collaboration

In Part II, we covered the importance of understanding individual backgrounds, goals, cognitive styles, and mindsets. We also discussed the organizational pressures that impact teams, and the negotiation strategies employed to deal with conflict. Here we focus on the key elements that make or break a team facing scaling challenges.

Support from leadership and management is critical in endorsing effective collaboration. There must not be disincentivizing performance programs like stack ranking. Better yet, desired behaviors should be incentivized.

When researching smart teams, David Engel and cohorts discovered that the most effective and productive teams were made up of members that "communicated a lot, participated equally and possessed good emotion-reading skills."[8] Even when remote teams were studied, the collective intelligence observed in local teams was critical in remote teams. Whether local or not, teams consistently rate higher in effectiveness and performance with these critical skills. We distill these findings into the following characteristics of a high-functioning collaborative team:

- Positive interdependence of team members
- Effective communication
- Individual and group accountability

Positive interdependence of team members

Interdependence within the team is exhibited by a coreliance and responsibility to each other. This trust and respect takes time to build in a new team, and has to be reestablished with every new team member who joins or leaves the group.

Over time, individuals learn about the strengths and weaknesses of the other members of their team, and learn how to delegate activities based on context and availability of team members. Effective brainstorming allows for the team to participate equally in the discovery of ideas, and then work through ideas and determine which ones to work on now.

One skill derived from participating in hackathons is creating *quick teams*, groups that form, work together, and disband in a relatively short period of time compared to traditional teams in a workplace environment. There is an established deadline, and mutual reliance on one another to get the project done. Winning teams quickly identify the strengths and weaknesses of the group, seeking out additional individuals who can balance the team.

Research has shown that individuals act in one of three ways within the work environment—as givers, takers, or matchers:[9]

- *Givers*, people who give more than take, help others without expecting in return.
- *Takers*, people who take more than give, strategically help only when the benefits to themselves outweigh the cost.
- *Matchers* will work along a spectrum trying to maintain an equal balance of giving and receiving.

---

8 David Engel et al., "Reading the Mind in the Eyes or Reading Between the Lines? Theory of Mind Predicts Collective Intelligence Equally Well Online and Face-To-Face, *PLoS ONE* 9, no. 12 (2014)

9 Adam M. Grant, *Give And Take* (New York: Viking, 2013).

Each individual on the team has a set of preferences for reciprocity. This is yet one more way individuals can have conflict within a team.

Learning When and How to Ask for Help

Within a team context, it's absolutely crucial to gauge when context may not be clear and respond in ways to obtain additional information. It may be easiest for the individual to create understanding based on individual context, and get something done. Yet this has longer-term costs. One of the hardest things for individuals starting out at companies that grow from startup to established business is this change in context, and needing to work toward the team and organizational goals rather than just working based on their isolated understanding.

In a group of people who have not formed strong team bonds, asking for more information or help can be misconstrued and viewed negatively. For an experienced employee, it can be even harder to ask for help. There is this misconception that we can and should be self-reliant experts in all things as we progress in our careers.

Another reason people may not ask for help is not wanting to incur an obligation. The act of asking for help may create a sense of obligation or cost to the individual. In a healthy organization, individuals won't be "keeping score" of these sorts of obligations, but will focus instead on what needs to get done for the good of the team or business as a whole.

There are three key types of giving (see Figure 14-2):

- Time
- Knowledge
- Money

Most of our activities will fall somewhere on these spectra. When you are looking at the overall value and cost to individuals, it helps to think along these three axes. For example, activities like mentoring and giving feedback may be more costly than providing introductions.

When considering how to be a better "giver," think about the areas you enjoy and where you benefit from giving, and focus on those aspects. Sometimes the intended recipient doesn't need what is being offered, so don't waste your resources in that area. For example, if someone asks for emotional support for something, that doesn't imply that they need or want feedback or your personal knowledge.

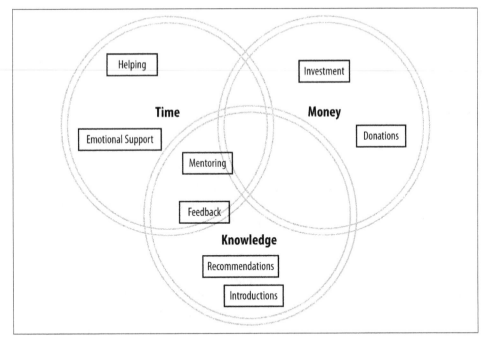

Figure 14-2. Types of giving activities

Challenges and Changes

By not asking questions, we limit the opportunities for maintaining mutual understanding and common ground, set a model of behavior to junior individuals in the industry that can exacerbate lack of understanding, and waste valuable learning and execution time with having to redo work.

The first part of asking for help is restating your assumptions to try to narrow understanding between individuals. In an environment where individuals have formed strong bonds, the terseness of the "belay communication" (to revisit our rock-climbing metaphor from Part I) is sufficient for both individuals to understand the state as they progress through the objective.

New projects or team members and new management require additional communication until sufficient time and energy have been invested. When teams are stretched thin, they can take out their frustration when something isn't working as smoothly as before on whoever and whatever is new. Recognize the pain points of change. Don't blame the new people for not being psychic or treat the new technology as wasted effort.

When a team is tasked with supporting others, they may need additional support in understanding when and how to say "not right now." Give people permission to allocate time to focus on other projects and sufficient *recess* time. When people start to burn out from giving too much of their time or knowledge, they react in dysfunctional ways that harm relationships. For example, they may become intolerant or sarcastic to customers. When these behaviors arise, the problem is not necessarily with the individual but the system.

Effective communication

Interdependence within teams can be either helped or hindered by their communication strategies. We discussed communication in Part II, which we recommended reviewing with a focus on effective communication. In addition, when considering scaling within your environment, there are additional challenges to consider.

Diversity

With any luck (and of course with the requisite attention and effort), your teams will diversify as they grow. As discussed previously in Parts II and III, increased diversity may lead to increases in interpersonal conflict in the short term before those differences resolve into increased empathy, creativity, and problem-solving abilities in the long term. The added stressors that can arise from organizational inflection points can certainly add to this tension.

It's important to make sure that team managers are aware of these sorts of difficulties that can arise and have had training relating to inclusivity and unconscious bias. As organizations grow, it can be a great help to have dedicated HR representatives for teams or departments so that both individual contributors and their managers have designated points of contact if and when issues arise.

Individual and group accountability

Individual accountability is the ability to acknowledge and assume responsibility for outcomes based ion one's own actions and behaviors. When individuals know that coworkers are committed to quality work it increases team cohesion and identification. If asked "Are you committed to quality work?," most people would respond "yes." Generally, people want to do their best when given the freedom to do so. If all the individuals on the team can say, "Yes, my teammates are committed to quality work," that implies trust, shared values, and team cohesion.

Defining Quality

It's important to define quality explicitly within your team and organization. Being transparent with your customers about how you define quality, and encouraging them to share their understanding of quality, allows for a stronger alignment of product outcomes, operability, performance, and learning. Providing clear quality metrics allows for individuals to hold themselves accountable.

Additionally, for each role within an organization, work quality can differ in definition. For example, for the team writing code, a focus on quality code may drive them to spend more time on a release to the detriment of other teams that also need time. Coming to a common understanding about quality, and what matters to different roles, can help reduce unnecessary conflict in approaching problems.

First described by W. Edwards Deming in the 1950s, a *quality circle* refers to a group of people who do the same or similar work, and are most often aligned in terms of what they view as quality work. It's important to get people on the same page in this respect, both to increase cohesion within a team (because team members are most frequently performing the same or similar work) but also because working toward this shared definition of quality work helps minimize misunderstandings, enforcing the devops compact.

Team accountability is the ability to acknowledge and assume responsibility for outcomes based on the team's actions. Key to individuals accepting team accountability is trusting each other and holding each other accountable for behaviors and actions. In high-performing teams, individuals will respectfully confront and hold each other accountable when problems arise. The shorter the lag time between the identification and discussion of a problem, the faster that problem gets resolved. The longer the problem exists, the more mistrust and reluctance to work as a team can grow.

Managing Conflict

In Part II, we talked about negotiation strategies and conflict. Companies will gain a number of ingrained habits and behaviors over the course of their history. For the health of a team, management must help individuals align their internal vision with the company and team's vision, encourage individuals and their team skills, and provide incentives that align the norms and desired behaviors.

In some respects, conflict can be healthy to a team. It exposes the team to new ideas and perspectives. If there is zero conflict on the team, that indicates that there is a homogeneity that needs to be addressed. It is our obligation to bring value to our organization. If we're just redundant, we can't be surprised when we're culled from an organization. Healthy conflict resolution skills are necessary for individuals, teams, and organizations to grow.

 ### Model Desirable Behaviors

Model the behaviors that you want to see within team meetings. When individuals see their management complain about issues with their peers rather than addressing those problems directly, they will copy the same patterns of behaviors. This applies to individual contributors in any kind of mentoring or leadership position; even if you are not a manager, people may be looking to you for guidance and following your lead when it comes to work behaviors.

On the other hand, conflict does not mean tolerating or encouraging bullying behaviors. Bullying behaviors should be eliminated from the environment, and not justified by the perceived value that the bullies may bring. Bullying behaviors can be identified by how the target of said behaviors feels, whether that be oppression, humiliation, demotivation, or belittlement. Even more egregious is when the person exhibiting bullying behaviors is in a position of leadership or management. Some examples of bullying behaviors include:

- blaming individuals for errors;
- criticizing someone's ability;
- threatening job loss;
- using insults or put-downs;
- belittling or denying accomplishments;
- engaging in exclusionary tactics; and
- yelling or screaming.

These sorts of behaviors can be indicative of a sick or unhealthy work environment. It can be tempting, especially in smaller environments during growth phases, to overlook such behaviors in individuals with a great deal of technical skills, with the reasoning that someone's hard or technical skills outweigh their lack of soft or interpersonal skills—or even abusive behavior. However, because of the influence these individuals may have and how that influence can spread in larger organizations, allowing or encouraging these bullying behaviors can lead to an increasingly toxic environment that will become less healthy and productive over time.

Conflict within the team

Within individual teams, there can be many different sources of conflict. We'll discuss a few of the most common ones here, as well as potential solutions that can be applied either at the individual or team level.

Alignment with team goals

As we have discussed before, not every position is going to be a match for every individual. People have different individual preferences, motivations, and working styles, and that's quite all right, as that diversity is part of what makes teams and organizations so resilient. This makes it possible, or even likely in larger organizations, that people might find themselves in a team whose work priorities or working styles don't align with their own.

Whether this is due to a lack of interest in a team's priorities or projects, interpersonal conflict with peers or managers, or a mismatch in working styles, an individual might find themselves at odds with the rest of their team. It is generally in everyone's best interest that this be resolved, as a negative attitude, increased conflict, or decreased quality of work due to this mismatch can end up negatively impacting the rest of the team. Regular and frequent one-on-ones with both peers and managers can help to identify and resolve these sorts of issues sooner rather than later.

 The ideas of *perfection* and *execution* are ones that we have frequently come across in our own experiences, as discussed in Part II with the terms *starters* and *finishers*. This is an area where being moved to different projects or different tasks within a project can go a long way toward minimizing conflict.

One of the benefits to larger organizations is that they often have a wider range of opportunities for people to move between teams or even internal departments. As discussed in Part III, providing people with the opportunity to participate in bootcamps or rotations in between teams can help them to identify not only mismatches but teams where they might be better aligned, and these sorts of changes should be encouraged rather than discouraged.

Alignment with organizational goals

Similar to misalignment with their team, people might find themselves misaligned with their organization as a whole and its goals. This is increasingly likely to happen after an inflection point such as a merger, acquisition, or reduction event, but may also happen at other points within the organizational lifecycle. For example, some people work best in smaller startups and may become increasingly uncomfortable once their organization grows past a certain size.

A major value misalignment between an individual and the organization as a whole is harder to overcome than a team misalignment. It is important to realize that if this sort of problem arises it's not necessarily due to any fault or wrongdoing on either side, and to help the individual move on to a place that is a better fit with a minimum of hard feelings. This can improve the likelihood that they will be a reference or referral for your organization in the future, rather than just a burnt bridge.

Misaligned incentives

In addition to misaligned goals, priorities, or working styles, incentives can also become misaligned as organizations, teams, and individuals grow and change. Again, this may be more likely to happen after some sort of scaling event such as a merger or acquisition.

Regular one-on-ones can again be useful to identify these sorts of conflicts, and an HR representative can provide a great deal of benefit when the incentives in question are monetary. However, you may run into issues such as someone being incentivized by money when the organization they are a part of is in a decline phase, or perhaps being more motivated by quality work than they perceive the rest of their team or department to be. Incentives may be addressed at a team or organizational level, but they should be dealt with in one way or another as quickly as possible, before negative feelings and demotivation spread from an individual to the rest of their team.

Conflict external to the team

While conflict can certainly occur within a team, it tends to become more prevalent beyond the team as a department or organization grows in size. Indeed, conflict between teams was one of the primary factors that motivated the start of the devops movement. Most frequently, this conflict tends to stem from a misalignment of motivations or expectations between teams.

Push back on unrealistic expectations

It is incumbent on the management for a team to push back on unrealistic expectations. It can also fall to management to determine when and if expectations of a given team are in fact unrealistic, especially among teams with a higher percentage of newer or more junior members of the organization.

Over time, teams may find the expectations placed upon them becoming more unrealistic. For example, if you are using a designated ops model such as that described in Parts III and IV, your ops team have more and more expectations placed on them over time as the organization grows and there are more teams to support. If these expectations increase before the headcount for the ops team does, these expectations or requirements may soon become unrealistic, and it falls to that team's manager to deal with that. Individual contributors, depending on their level of influence within the organization, don't have the same kind of pull that their managers do, and that needs to be taken into account.

Assess team alignment and capacity

If a team has reasonably realistic expectations placed upon it but regularly fails to meet them, it can be due to a number of reasons. The most immediate result is that the team may end up losing the trust of dependent teams. Is the team holding itself accountable to commitments? We discussed accountability of teams and individuals earlier in this chapter, but keep in mind that broader organizational changes can lead to misalignments in both individuals and teams that should be sought out, identified, and addressed.

Is the team over capacity in work? Make sure that the work the team is doing is the most important, and valuable to the company. Again, pay attention to how realistic the expectations placed on this team are, especially if the organization has grown recently. As we've said previously, devops is not a way to get twice the amount of work out of the same number of people, so make sure that teams are sufficiently staffed to meet the expectations placed upon them. Time, energy, and personnel are all needs that must be met in order for a team to meet their own demands.

Scaling for Organizations

Larger scaling challenges occur at the organizational level. Decisions need to be taken down to the level where the data is known within the appropriate teams and with individuals. This requires sufficient coordination and data transparency so that enough data flow is happening around these decision points. Solitary teams working in isolation will build tools that may help others incidentally, but primarily serve the needs of the individual team.

Centralized Versus Ad Hoc Teams

Centralizing teams to provide support functions leads to burnout and one team trying to be everything to all other teams. Efficient support teams can make things seem to just work. If its value is not visualized and communicated across the organization, the support team can be perceived as lower value, especially in organizations where the prestige ladder is in effect. This can be disastrous for morale, and over time impact the whole company as the team loses effectiveness.

Ad hoc teams that encourage the collaboration of individuals from cross-functional purposes to design, build out, and communicate decisions will allow for multiple perspectives, and ease change. It also allows individuals to transcend tribal boundaries.

We can't measure the capacity of a human—how much and how integral they are to an organization. Once they are gone, the impact of their leaving becomes clear if we have not sufficiently understood their value. Try to be aware of decisions that create single points of authority and responsibility, which can lead to fragility within the organization.

Build Out Leadership

Build out a collaborative leadership team that can drive daily change, tackle emerging opportunities and challenges, and monitor critical paths. These different tasks need to be spread across the leadership team. Tools that enable collection of task metrics will assist in better quantification and qualification of people needed for this team.

Regardless of what part of the organization is experiencing scaling pains, there are key behaviors that leadership needs to exhibit when handling the challenges that arise. These modeled behaviors include accountability, focus, and follow-through; consistent actions and mutually reinforcing values within leadership help to create a healthy organization.

A culture of accountability

In general, accountability is acknowledgment and assumption of responsibility, and this is true at an organizational level as well as at the team and individual levels. We can consider accountability both from a team or individual perspective, which generally involves being responsible for project and individual results as well as learning and development activities. Finally, we can consider accountability from a leadership perspective, which tends to have additional financial and regulatory responsibilities.

An important question to ask regardless of perspective is, "Who decides that we should be held accountable, and who decides what we do?" Through the process of answering this question, you'll be able to identify who defines accountability and why accountability matters. A culture of accountability includes clear reasonable expectations, positive consequences that follow quality performance, and negative consequences following poor performance.

As mentioned in Part III, a key misconception about accountability is the idea that it is about ascribing blame, or that encouraging accountability leads to a fear culture. Overlooking performance issues and avoiding accountability encourages individuals to copy the avoidance behaviors, and lose trust in each other as well as in management. Organizations can foster fear cultures, impacting individuals' ability to be personally accountable. When people get blamed for something without having the *authority* necessary to fix or improve it, cultures turn from those of accountability into those of fear and blame.

Another misconception about accountability is that individuals will naturally hold themselves accountable. Even in self-managed or self-directed teams, leadership needs to establish and encourage behaviors that are valued. An overemphasis on personal accountability without providing clarity and linkage to the business goals can lead to increased mistakes and miscommunication. With the complexity of organizations, a large number of competing goals and requirements are in place, which can make self-direction and self-imposed accountability more difficult.

This doesn't mean that people can't and won't be self-motivated, but managers who expect their reports to proactively come to them with issues or mistakes may be leaving open potential gaps in accountability. This is especially true when moving from a blameful to a blameless organization: if people are used to getting punished for mistakes or lower quality, they will naturally be wary of coming forward with these sorts of issues. Individuals will need coaching and guidance on how to hold themselves and others accountable without returning to blameful or fear-based behaviors.

Organizational flexibility

Bigger organizations, especially ones that have been around for many years, are considered to be much slower to change and adapt. This is true in many cases; by necessity, it will take more time and effort to roll out changes to thousands or hundreds of thousands of people than it will to make the same changes to fewer than one hundred simply by virtue of how many people are impacted.

One of the benefits of a more agile style of software development is the rate at which changes can be made, with shorter feedback cycles meaning that changes can be made sooner rather than later in response to new information, leading to less wasted time and effort. How flexible an organization can be depends a great deal on another factor: how teams are organized and the processes that affect their interactions.

Typical questions to ask when considering the flexibility of a large organization include:

How do people communicate between teams?
> In an ineffective environment, people will have to go up in the management hierarchy at least one level in order to communicate across to different teams or individuals at their own level. This process gets more inefficient the more levels there are and the more expansive an organizational structure gets, if for no other reason than that a greater number of people are required to be involved.

Does the decision-making process require a formal meeting?
> If making changes requires some form of paperwork, and if that system still has very manual components that haven't been automated, that is another way that scale can inversely affect flexibility and productivity.

How far up the management hierarchy does someone need to go in order to make a change?

If individuals are having to get managerial approval at levels above their own direct manager to make changes that affect only their team's work, they are very likely to feel that their hands are unnecessarily tied.

Case Study: Government Digital Service, GOV.UK

In the following case study, we present the Government Digital Service (GDS), a unit of the UK Government's Cabinet Office primarily based in Holborn, London, that is responsible for transforming government digital services.[10] In 2010, Martha Lane Fox put together a report entitled *Directgov 2010 and Beyond: Revolution Not Evolution* (*http://bit.ly/fox-directgov*). Formed in April 2011, GDS is overseen by the Public Expenditure Executive (Efficiency & Reform).

Explicit Culture

The Government Digital Service has established seven digital principles (*http://bit.ly/7-digital*):

- Digital by default
- Putting users first
- Learning from the journey
- Building a network of trust
- Moving barriers aside
- Creating an environment for technology leaders to flourish
- Don't do everything yourself (you can't)

> Starting with users isn't just how we should be making tech, it's how we should be making government.
>
> —Jennifer Pahlka, *Code for America Summit*

We can see here that there are values and prohibitions explicitly present in these principles. For example, "putting users first" is a value stating that the user is a higher priority than, say, an engineer's desire to experiment and learn a new tool or architecture, and "don't do everything yourself" is a type of prohibition. It's important to note that there are more positively stated values than negatively stated prohibitions; while it might be easier to tell people what *not* to do, describing the behaviors

---

10 All the views expressed in this case study are our interpretations of information provided and do not necessarily represent those of the UK government.

you *do* want is usually much more effective at creating a desired culture or atmosphere.

In conjunction with these digital principles, the GDS has also established 10 design principles (*https://www.gov.uk/design-principles*):

- Start with needs
- Do less
- Design with data
- Do the hard work to make it simple
- Iterate. Then iterate again.
- This is for everyone
- Understand context
- Build digital services, not websites
- Be consistent, not uniform
- Make things open: it makes things better

These design principles reflect further on one of the digital principles listed earlier: putting users first (in this case, by focusing on all aspects of the user experience, not just the backend code). Critical to their culture is the idea that transformation is not just the hardware and software technology; transformation is also changing the experience of users. An example of this was the implementation of the Claim Carer's Allowance digital service (*http://bit.ly/gds-service*).

 Making their culture explicit rather than relying on implicit understanding (which often leads to misunderstanding) has allowed the GDS to clearly focus on the specific types of changes they want to make to their area of the government.

Planning

Planning is an important part of any software development– or digital service–focused organization. By explicitly stating what they want to accomplish and when, in addition to establishing what their priorities are for a given time frame, teams can greatly increase the likelihood that they will meet their goals. This ties in closely with having an explicit culture—it is much less likely that you will reach your goals if you can't define them well enough to plan for them.

The GDS team's process of planning changes involves them spending enough time examining possible solutions, and the value of the solutions offered, to make sure that they are choosing the one that can best meet their needs while staying in line with their digital and design principles. They also speak to other teams throughout the government in order to coordinate efforts and make sure that no existing team is actively doing the work that they themselves are planning to work on. This is a straightforward-sounding but critical step to make sure that everyone is on the same page and working as effectively as possible without wasting time on duplicated effort.

Once data on the project and its requirements has been gathered, they evaluate potential solutions, both open source and commercial. They create a prototype, and share it across teams including the development, operations, and service managers. This enables them to get feedback from as many of the key stakeholders as possible before committing fully to a solution, again to minimize wasted effort if they end up changing directions and also to make sure that everyone's needs are being met by potential solutions as much as possible.

 When planning projects or other efforts within an organization, especially one operating at scale, pay attention to:

- Are any other teams or groups already working in this area?
- How can efforts be coordinated or combined with other teams?
- Who are the stakeholders and decision makers who need to be involved?
- How will you define success for this project?

Challenges

One of the challenges within governmental agencies is the frequent duplication of effort between different groups (see Figure 14-3). Each group has to provide core infrastructure elements for their application in addition to work that is the focus or expertise of their specific group. Because these core services are not centralized, each team or group must spend additional time to hire specialists with these skills.

Creating multitenancy platform services within the government would save service teams time by providing a centrally supported service that meets all the security and privacy constraints required by law. Instead of having each team provide and maintain their own services that meet these requirements, providing the services centrally would allow service teams to focus on the areas, skills, and requirements that are unique to them. Key requirements for such a multitenancy platform within the government were:

- It should be self-service;
- Multiple service providers must be utilized; and

- There should be isolation of code, data, and logs.

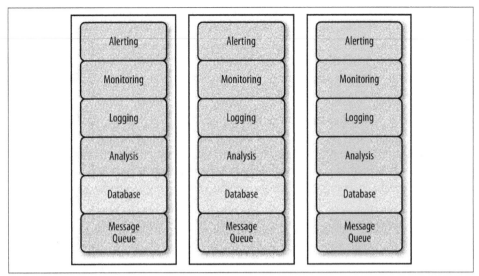

Figure 14-3. Duplicated services across governments

Having a self-service application gave individuals complete control of the aspects of the applications needed, allowing the platform teams to focus on platform improvements, rather than getting the services they require. This encourages specialization for the service and platform teams.

The second requirement of having multiple service providers prevented vendor lock-in, encouraged competitive pricing, and removed single points of failure. During the deliberation over the project's requirements, the importance of using multiple public clouds rather than only one was surfaced. Knowing this requirement in advance ensured that they were able to avoid using vendor-specific features that would have created lock-in and made it harder to change providers or expand to include more of them after the fact. Later, however, the GPS decided to not make this a requirement after all, as going with open source solutions provided them with the same flexibility.

The third requirement and most essential to a multitenant platform was complete isolation of code, data, and logs between agencies. This was necessary in order to make sure that each group or agency was able to meet its own individual security and privacy constraints, without which the platform would not be usable and could not be considered a success even if the other two requirements were met. While the details of this challenge might be unique to a government agency, plenty of organizations also have various legal requirements that must be met (such as PCI, SOX, or HIPAA compliance), all of which must be part of planning processes from the beginning in order to avoid potentially wasting effort.

Building Affinity

One way the GDS builds affinity is participation in Global GovJams (*http://www.govjam.org*). A GovJam is similar to a hackathon in that participants have a limited amount of time—in this case, 48 hours—to complete the projects they are "jamming" on. Inspired by Global Service Jams and Sustainability Jams, GovJams are loosely themed, with individuals voting on ideas and creating teams that focus on the public sector.

Once the teams form, they talk to constituents to discover their needs. Unlike traditional hackathons, a Jam focuses on cooperation between people interested in improving and innovating. The Global GovJam unites and connects people from all over the world through a common theme and shared central platform for the prototypes. Additionally, participants collaborate and share using Twitter with the hashtag #ggovjam.

Then teams build prototypes using what's available and what they are able to make work given their collective experience and expertise within the 48-hour window. They demo regularly and watch how others experience and use the product, improving the product based on their learning. Ideas and help are shared between teams, as the focus is ultimately on benefiting their constituents rather than on winning a prize for themselves. This focus on collaboration has been a great way to bring that same collaborative mindset back to the GDS.

A second way the GDS builds affinity is regularly blogging to share information about the organization, its aim, and the projects it is working on. While still complying with various security and privacy regulations, GDS employees are encouraged to write posts that go on the group's public-facing blog. Their posts have been on topics ranging from new products or services that are available to constituents to ways that they are trying to improve their culture and processes. It not only puts an approachable face on the group but also helps build habits of both learning and sharing.

Finally, the GDS builds affinity by participating in the open source community. GOV.UK (*https://www.gov.uk*) is built on open source software. By using open source software, it helps technologists focus on user needs. They have made their code available at *https://github.com/gds-operations* and *https://github.com/alphagov*.

James Stewart, director of technical architecture at GDS, recounted the general approach for tool selection, shown in Figure 14-4, via a quote from JP Rangaswami:

> For common problems use *Opensource*.
> For rare problems use *Buy*.
> For unique problems use *Build*.

Essentially, this embraces the idea that everyone within a team should be solving the everyday problems with open source, contributing to the community for the problems that affect it as a whole. Contributing to open source is more than just commit-

---

ting code and includes items like documentation, bug reports, and illustrations. For the problems that are rare, buy products to solve them. Finally, for the unique problems that are specific to your organization or team, building your own solutions is effective.

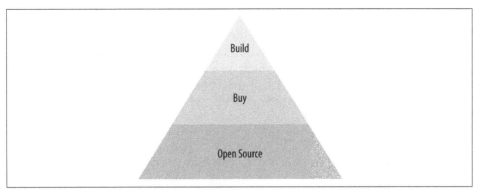

Figure 14-4. Build, buy, open source pyramid

Overall, the Government Digital Service is working on creating and maintaining an explicitly defined culture that values focusing on users and solving user-facing problems; embraces design and overall experience as well as code; and focuses on using Agile practices to reduce waste, iterate more quickly, and help simplify digital and technological services for the rest of the government. Their focus on collaboration and affinity as well as their own values and prohibitions has gone a long way toward creating the kind of culture the government will need to be successful going forward.

Case Study: Target

The last 10 years have seen significant changes in how, where, and when people shop. Target customers need to have readily available access anywhere and anytime; the technology underlying the company is critical in its being able to rapidly adjust strategies to the evolving landscape within the supply chain as well as to customer demands.

As Target is a large organization, adoption of devops culture was not a unilateral top-down decision. Multiple teams started their devops journey separately, and then banded together as results showed the success of their chosen strategies. Information for this case study was gathered through published blog posts, publicly available presentations by Target employees, and company filings.

Examining Target

Target Corporation is a retail company headquartered in Minneapolis, Minnesota. Founded in 1902 by George Dayton as Dayton Dry Goods, Target had approximately

347,000 employees as of mid-2015, as noted earlier. They are the second largest importer in the United States as of 2015. Along with brick-and-mortar Target stores, they have expanded to the banking, pharmacy, and healthcare sectors.

As a modern retailing company, Target has a long record of technical innovation (*http://bit.ly/target-history*). In 1988, Target deployed UPC scanners at all Target stores and distribution centers, changing the in-store experience from shorter lines to better-stocked shelves. This innovation through the years has manifested in outward and inward supporting technology from price-checking stations, cash registers, hand-held devices for checking stock, gift registry stations, applications to ensure that distribution centers stock the right inventory at the right time of year, and more.

Starting with Desired Outcomes

In a large organization with a long history, the journey toward change often can feel like a jumbled maze with lots of twists and turns. The well-traveled path includes best practices that minimize risk. The organization reflected the complexity built up over time. When taking the 10,000-foot view, it would be very hard to define a specific starting point for Target's devops journey.

In reality, there was no single starting point. Multiple teams started from different points. Heather Mickman led the API and Integration Development team and Ross Clanton led the Ops Infrastructure Services team, two teams that were working on implementing devops into the organization. The paths each team took weren't easy, and some began without using the word *devops* at all. Instead, they used language to describe the desired outcomes, such as "leaner, faster, higher quality service delivery," which encompassed the devops philosophy. Heather Mickman explained:

> I had to stop using the term *devops*; it had become a loaded term with a lot of misinformation and misconception. As I would have conversations with peers and other senior leaders within the organization, I literally saw them shut down when I said "devops."

Mickman's decision to stop using the term *devops* because it had become so loaded demonstrates the power of *folk models*, first introduced in Chapter 2. You might encounter similar reactions within your own organizations, with people's preconceived notions distracting and detracting from discussions. As Mickman found herself, you might also have an easier time effecting change within an organization if you focus on the desired outcomes and changes rather than the terminology at first. Change occurred through phases, starting with individual change agents, grassroots efforts, top-down support, and then scaling successful strategies.

Focusing on the desired outcomes and being aware of the sensitivity to language is a critical process to adopting change. Telling the compelling stories that will evoke and inspire change doesn't require the use of the word *devops*. It was important to understand the current landscape within Target—how individuals were affected by existing efforts.

Affinity Within the Enterprise

Target leadership encouraged affinity within the enterprise by promoting the existing culture of organizational learning. Embracing the idea of organizational learning, as well as encouraging everyone to level up, allowed them to scale change through the organization. The four elements they focused on were:

- Experimenting
- Testing
- Failing
- Succeeding

Widespread experiences with different teams gave Ross Clanton insight and empathy around each team's challenges and the misaligned incentives, hand-offs, and accountability within the organization.

Clanton's devops journey at Target began with seeking out guidance to help resolve these challenges. Many recommended the book *The Phoenix Project: A Novel About IT, DevOps, and Helping Your Business win* by Kevin Behr, Gene Kim, and George Spafford. After reading *The Phoenix Project*, Clanton bought additional copies and gave them out to others in his teams, and even held an off-site event to role-play the various scenarios within the book.

He teamed up with other technology leaders within the organization, including director Heather Mickman and engineering leader Jeff Einhorn, to find partners throughout the organization to help drive the common changes needed together. This was critical to help "mind the gap" between the different silos; different organizations had different priorities and challenges that they needed to overcome. Together, they reached out to other experts in the field, including leadership at Netflix, Google, and Facebook, to understand the applicable patterns that they might adopt into their own organization.

It's important to note how they embraced learning and driving change within the organization as well as looking outside of it for inspiration. If you only look within your own organization for ideas and strategies, you run the risk of ending up with the same practices, habits, and patterns you already have—at least some of which must not be working too well if you are trying to make significant organizational changes.

Don't fall victim to the cargo cult mentality, making changes only because others are doing the same thing and you want to replicate their results, but also don't underestimate how valuable outside experience and expertise can be.

At the DevOps Enterprise Summit in 2014, Ross Clanton described his devops journey at Target as connecting people across the organization. After obtaining success within limited teams, they started bringing the message to the wider audience within Target in a variety of ways:

- In February 2014, they held the first internal devops mini-conference with guest speakers Rob Cummings from Nordstrom, and Michael Ducy from Chef.
- They set up regular events, inviting additinal external guest speakers, including Jeff Sussna, Fletcher Nichol, Ian Malpass, Sean O'Neil, and Jez Humble. These internal events helped yield a growing grassroots movement, from 160 attendees at the first event to over 400 in a February 2015 event.
- To encourage people who wanted to learn more about these topics, they started a weekly Automation Open Labs program as an open-ended Q&A session.
- They also started a monthly demo session, which was an opportunity for community members to share their work, get feedback, inspire, and be inspired.

They adopted consistent messaging across "coaches" within the organization by converging the Lean, devops, and Agile movements to grow cross-discipline coaches; fostered deliberate quality practice through highly immersive coaching sessions; and also encouraged employees to share their experiences externally at *http://target.github.io*, all as ways of increasing affinity both within their organization and beyond it.

Tools and Technology Within the Enterprise

Mickman's team was charged with the building out of application program interfaces (APIs) to simplify the growing complexity of systems and organizational silos at Target.

Over time in a waterfall-driven organization, the tendency is toward hierarchies and processes that minimize risk. Roles become rigid, and teams specialize in a single service that becomes tightly coupled with other services within the organization. This leads to longer release cycles to communicate potential change across the organization, which in turn leads to greater risk.

Development of APIs was seen as a way to tackle the growing cultural and technical debt of the organization. As a retail company, Target tackled important APIs like product, store location and hours, promotions, and pricing. The APIs evolved, allowing Target to quickly test and learn how to optimize experiences with customers as well as partners like Pinterest.

The Importance of Security to Devops

In December 2015, the wish list app from Target was reported to have a personal data leak. The key element of an API is to provide the communication interfaces for software to talk to each other. Often when developing software, companies focus on how the software is expected to be used rather than how it could *possibly* be used.

When you create software that allows software to communicate, you create software that allows humans to talk to the software too. Often authorization and authentication barriers are put into place to qualify who can talk to and use software. Authentication ensures that an entity is who it says it is. Authorization defines the access policies around what an entity can do.

In the case of the Target vulnerability, the API appears to not have a rich set of authorization or authentication. The process of adding authentication to a service can be difficult, especially if you enable individuals to find a wish list based on known information without having to create a user profile. While the individual who creates a wish list wants to share their identifying information with an organization, the individual reading the wish list might not. So not having authentication on the wish list might not be a bad decision.

The challenge, then, is creating a safe service that doesn't give out personally identifying information (PII) to individuals who don't already know it, while also providing a way to search PII for matching people's wish lists. The core weakness in the API is a clear set of access policies around entities. An unauthenticated, unauthorized entity should not be able to access PII, even with a user ID. Ideally the user IDs are not something that can be easily guessed. In some ways, in the Target case it seems as if having any kind of information about an individual could be construed as authorization to obtain all information about an individual.

This highlights the importance of every part of the organization being part of the transformation. In organizations that have a lot of accumulated cultural and technical debt, we will continue to see these kind of impacts as the long existing silos are slowly bridged.

For Target leadership, it was important to find the right tools to enable the outcomes that they wanted to see. As discussed in Part IV, there are differing opinions among both individuals and organizations as to whether or not specific tools matter, or if only the ways in which tools are used is ultimately important. Target is of the opinion that tools do matter, as the right tooling allowed them to have more "full-stack" ownership of their platform and API, rather than having those be separate and siloed.

To accomplish this, they have been using a combination of the OpenStack platform for cloud computing, Jenkins for continuous integration and continuous delivery, Chef for infrastructure automation or configuration management, and GitHub for source control. This combination has been particularly powerful for them, as it enabled much more transparency in the development process. Instead of developers having their own separate offline code reviews, they now use GitHub pull requests, which their operations staff loves because they now have visibility into what changes are happening and can more easily be active participants in the development process.

On top of this, they have found that using Hipchat for internal communication has been very beneficial, with *chatops* becoming more and more integral to their development processes. With Hipchat, they have found that not only can teams easily communicate among themselves, but they can also communicate with other teams more easily. Because they've been using chatops to stream in alerts and events into appropriate channels, they have a real-time view of their development ecosystem that has enabled them to respond to incidents much more quickly than before.

Target has measured the success of their new tooling initiatives in part by the growth in the number of APIs they have, which has increased from 30 in October 2014 to 45 in February 2015. The number of APIs was important because it allows teams and services to integrate and work together, again rather than being siloed and separate. Not only has the volume of both internal and external API requests increased, but this has all happened while the site has remained stable, with a consistently low number of incidents per month. Finding the right combination of tools that helped them to collaborate more while eliminating some of their previous pain points has been a large part of their success.

 Be sure to define what success means for tool usage within your organization. Focus on the outcomes you want to achieve, figure out what your pain points are, and then look for tools to solve those problems rather than looking for problems that can be solved by a specific tool or technology.

Sharing Knowledge Within the Enterprise

After obtaining success within limited teams, Mickman and Clanton started bringing the message to the wider audience within Target. One mechanism to drive this change across the organization was to hold quarterly internal devopsdays events where they also brought in speakers from other organizations, including Rob Cummings from Nordstrom and Michael Ducy from Chef, to keynote. As mentioned previously, this helped to bring in new ideas as well as drive interest in their own devops initiatives and progress.

A second strategy they adopted was to ensure a consistency of messaging throughout the organization. They had the idea of *coaches*, where various subject matter experts in areas like Lean, devops, and Agile would help coach or mentor other individuals or teams to help teach and share information. They found that by converging these topics into one and by growing cross-discipline coaches, they were able to build a more consistent folk model internally, so that more people were on the same page when talking about various devops-related concepts.

Holding immersive coaching sessions throughout the organization was another method of scaling up the initiatives that had been working so well for them within a few individual teams. Open labs that people throughout the organization could attend helped scale up how much people could teach and share knowledge, and "automation hackathons" gave even more people a chance to participate in these changes and be empowered in their own work.

These are only a few of the ways that Target has been able to not only find tooling and collaborative solutions that worked for them but also share what worked (and what didn't) throughout their organization. A combination of top-down support and grassroots efforts to drive change at individual and team levels has been working quite well for them.

 Indeed, this approach—letting individual contributors and teams drive changes stemming from their own in-depth experiences—is necessary for any organization to feel confident they are making the right changes, but executive and managerial support is also necessary to make these changes not only happen, but stick.

Summary

We face challenges in our environment based on our past decisions, as well as our current objectives. If we approach these problems from the individual, team, and organizational level, we can successfully assess, plan, and overcome them. Indeed, the key challenges to adopting devops are, in essence, scaling challenges. The barriers that can exist at various levels get magnified with history, impacting how we approach the various inflection points that occur in organizational lifecycles.

Sometimes we need to reevaluate current processes and backtrack. Sometimes we need to be slow and careful in our approach; at other times, we need to be quick and dynamic. Success comes with continual practice, and learning from mistakes.

Scaling successfully is the art and science of realizing when and how to change direction as necessary to navigate the ever-changing environment. Just as with outdoor climbing, there are no marked colorful routes that will guide your way for your particular circumstance. Leveling up the necessary individual, team, and organizational skills will prepare you, and the same basic principles of effective devops will apply regardless of organizational size and complexity.

CHAPTER 15

Scaling: Misconceptions and Troubleshooting

Let's examine some common scaling challenges that individuals may come across, and how to troubleshoot them. This chapter will cover areas relevant to both managers and individual contributors, and while you might find the ones directly applicable to your current role more helpful, it can provide valuable insight to read and understand what challenges people in other roles are facing as well.

Scaling Misconceptions

As we discussed in the previous chapter, there is more to scaling than simply being a very large organization or doing some separate "enterprise devops."

Some of Our Teams Will Never Be Able to Work Together

Often devops origins are described in terms of developers and operations teams at odds with each other. In general, teams can get into a state of high tension and conflict due to compiled misunderstandings. As mentioned in Part II, conflict is not bad. It's an important signal for a healthy organization. It is critical to ensure that teams are not at odds with each other. With personal reconciliation, there is a one-on-one repairing of understanding, while team reconciliation requires a much more complex process. It's important to repair the intrateam bonds, as well as the processes that have led to the failures.

Often the initial stages of repair are very difficult and awkward as teams relearn how to interact with each other. It takes time and the accumulation of positive experiences to rebuild the trust between teams. One bad experience can disrupt progress that has been made.

Behavior patterns to monitor for:

Criticism
> Personal attacks on character traits

Contempt
> Statements or behaviors that come from a relative position of superiority

Defensiveness
> Self-protection statements or behaviors

Stonewalling
> Emotional withdrawal from the interaction

Blanket accusations
> Statements that include "they always" or "they never" (or "we always/never")

If teams are in an "us" versus "them" pattern, this exposes a key problem with identity. Within an organization, it's critical that teams align on vision and the definition of success. If one group feels like their goals are impacted by lack of information and transparency from another group, they may be putting pressure on the second group with emotional overtones. This can escalate tensions between the teams.

The effect will be exacerbated by distributed teams. When different priorities and goals for success collide, conflict increases and takes extra effort to resolve. With distributed teams, it's important to make the resolution process fair to all individuals so they feel part of the resolution.

Research shows that site visits can help coworkers build rapport, strengthening shared compact and helping develop trust and understanding around the way individuals communicate and work.[1] As much as you can, give people agency around when and how these visits take place, and build transparency into the whole process of getting teams to start working together. People hate feeling blindsided by decisions that directly impact them, even if they might otherwise appreciate the results of those decisions.

Having two groups be at odds with each other in such a way that it impacts their work can also happen when two organizations or companies are being merged together, and it's important to ensure that, as much as possible, there are stakeholders from both groups present and involved going forward. This can help reduce the likelihood of "us versus them" patterns becoming entrenched.

---

1 Pamela J. Hinds and Catherine Durnell Cramton, "Situated Coworker Familiarity: How Site Visits Transform Relationships Among Distributed Workers," *Organization Science* 25, no. 3 (2014).

This mentality can also be seen in people who have built up an island of dependency on them and their knowledge as a form of job security. These individuals enjoy being a single point of failure or bottleneck for knowledge transfer, as they believe this makes them too valuable to the team or organization to ever get rid of. This can negatively impact their relationships with their peers, and steps should be taken to spread out their knowledge as well as repair those relationships—including the one of mistrust that usually exists between these individuals and the organization they are a part of.

We Need Total Executive Buy-In to Start Making Changes

As a manager, you have a fair amount of influence on your direct reports and their effectiveness. If there is significant pushback from upper levels of management, act as a metaphorical "shit umbrella"[2]—that is, shield your reports from as much of the bullshit that would get in the way of them doing their work as possible.

If people are making unrealistic demands of your team, you can either protect your team from distractions or simply funnel all those requests and demands to them (the "shit funnel").

Do what you can to empower your own team, giving them as much leeway as possible to experiment with their tools, workflows, and practices within the team. Depending on the culture in your organization, you may find it easier to persuade the powers that be with actual results, such as being able to show the results of an experiment demonstrating that a new tool or workflow is more effective than the existing ones. Make sure you're doing as much as you can to both shield your team from naysayers and let them figure out the best ways of working for them.

We Don't Have the Budget to Do Any Hiring Right Now So We Can't Start Doing Devops

In smaller or rapidly growing organizations, changing the culture to a more devops-focused one can be as simple as making sure that you hire people with these skill sets and mindsets, but not every team or organization is in a position to do a lot of hiring—or any at all. Luckily, it is absolutely possible to do devops without hiring a brand new group of "10x rock star devops engineers."

Create a shared understanding of goals
> In order to get people on board with an idea like devops, you'll first need to make sure that everyone is on the same page with what that means. Make sure that you are able to communicate not only what you want to change in your environment,

---

2 This phrase originates from Todd Jackson, a former group product manager for Gmail at Google, who said that as a manager, "You can either be a shit funnel or a shit umbrella."

but also *why*. Especially in larger environments prone to reorganizations, people might be suspicious of a change that sounds like fluff or just buzzwords, so be sure that you can talk about specific changes you want to make and the specific benefits you expect to see from them.

Provide and encourage learning opportunities
As we discussed in Chapter 8, it is certainly possible to teach an old sysadmin new tricks, so to speak. A devops transformation will likely involve learning both new soft skills and new technical skills, such as how to facilitate blameless postmortems as well as how to use Docker. Make sure that training is available for any skills you want your employees to have, as well as encouraging a learning environment and growth mindset throughout your organization.

Create an environment where devops principles thrive
In order for these sorts of changes to stick, you will need to create an environment where it is in people's best interests to make. If you want people to communicate more or do more mentoring, make these skills explicit parts of your skills matrices or career development plans. If you want to discourage rude behavior, encourage people to call it out when they see it (if they feel comfortable doing so) and make sure there are consequences for disruptive or abusive behavior. It is difficult to have an environment where collaboration and assholes can both thrive, so if you find yourself tolerating jerks, chances are you're actively working against a collaborative devops environment.

When you are trying to change an existing environment and the habits and behavior of the people in it, you'll want to start with small steps. Make sure you provide clear goals, ongoing learning opportunities, and an atmosphere of trust, empathy, and collaboration.

Scaling Troubleshooting

There is no one-size-fits-all solution that can provide all the answers to scaling challenges for every organization. Instead, this section will present some common scenarios that arise as organizations grow and change over the course of their lifecycles.

Management Is Insistent That We Stick With *X*, and Doesn't See the Value of Devops

As we saw when we discussed Target in the previous chapter, at some point there has to be management buy-in to make these sorts of changes in an impactful and lasting manner across an organization. However, as they also saw, this doesn't mean that that approval has to be there from the very beginning. Starting with just one team, giving that team some time to experiment, and then reporting those changes to management once there are positive results to show can be a useful, if not immediately gratifying, way to show others the value of these sorts of changes.

If the problem lies with upper management, see if you can get your manager on board to help with the changes you want to make. They may:

- work around restrictions already in place;
- negotiate with other managers on your behalf;
- decide to let you experiment within your team; and
- shield you from any repercussions.

If your direct manager doesn't see the value of devops, it will naturally be more difficult to effect change, but you can still look for allies within your team in a similar manner. If your manager insists on using tool or methodology X, is there a way that you can use that alongside a new tool or practice Y, and see how the two compare over time? Read up on ideas like "managing your manager" and see if there aren't ways you could be communicating why you want to make changes more effectively, such that your manager can feel the benefits as well.

Teams Are Spread Too Thin

When teams are consistently not meeting their requirements or deadlines and you've determined that there are not overly unrealistic demands being placed on them, the most likely cause is that there aren't enough individuals working on given tasks or projects to meet the demands. Take the time to reassess both project workload and deadlines; you may find that you need to shift people between projects or adjust deadlines to match what can realistically be accomplished by the current team.

You may also find that you need to hire more people, especially during a growth phase, but also keep an eye out for this during decline phases, where you may discover you have reduced headcount without reducing project scope or workload to match. It might be tempting to try to get the same amount of work out of fewer people to cut costs, but beyond a certain point, that simply leads to lower-quality work and burnt-out employees. It's important to keep your expectations for what people can accomplish grounded in reality.

One way to get effectively more work out of the same number of people is essentially enabling them to work smarter, not harder. Rather than looking to longer hours to accomplish more, look to your current tools and processes for ways they can be improved. Talk with the people on your team about their workflows and what tools and technologies they use to accomplish their work, and look for ways that these can be made more efficient, so that less effort or time is wasted. You may need to look outside the organization for ideas, but also solicit suggestions from the people currently on your team. It might take some time and effort if people aren't traditionally used to having their ideas or voices be heard, but you might get some very valuable information from the results.

Decisions Aren't Being Made Well

Realizing that decisions are regularly resulting in undesirable outcomes ("we decided to try X and it ended up making things worse instead of better") or that decision-making processes seem to involve a lot of wasted time and effort, is a common pain point as organizations grow and change. Decisions that were made easily when your entire engineering department could fit in the same room have become long, drawn-out affairs now that your organization has grown to contain multiple departments around the world. Here are some ways to address this:

Examine processes

It's easy for there to be increased confusion around the ownership of various problems as an organization grows. When issues or projects span multiple teams, you may find that they either slip through the cracks and lack enough ownership or become a source of conflict as multiple teams contend for ownership. The latter situation especially can lead to ineffective decision-making processes, as too much arguing makes it difficult for anything to ever get decided. On the other side of things, top-down decisions, while they tend to dramatically reduce the amount of arguing that goes on, tend to leave people unhappy with the process, if not the results.

Recognize clarity issues

If there is a lack of clarity around what decisions need to be made or what their impacts are, or if there are too many unknowns surrounding the outcomes, you may also find increasing analysis paralysis.

Monitor the weight of process

People avoid making decisions if there is so much process that the process itself gets in the way of work getting done or reaching an outcome in a reasonable amount of time.

Weigh productivity versus risk

When people are avoiding making a decision, it impacts productivity. Take a moment to understand the risk of making the wrong decision. If the cost to being wrong has minimal impact, continuing to avoid making a decision is wasted time and may impact the usefulness of the decision.

Make incremental change

Recognizing most decisions are not irreversible helps to change the frame of understanding. When we recognize that we can change our minds after the fact, it eliminates some of the analysis paralysis that arises from too much choice.

Create safe spaces to experiment

Mistakes teach us how to analyze risk appropriately and make good decisions when needed. This is another area where having a blameless culture rather than a blameful one can have a big benefit, as people will be more able to focus on reaching the best outcome rather than simply covering their asses.

 Keep track of the decisions you are making. Continuing to do the same thing and expecting to see a different result is a source of wasted effort, and the definition of insanity. By tracking decisions and outcomes, you can course-correct and gain more confidence in the decisions that you make.

We're Having Problems Attracting the Talent We Want

Make sure to educate human resources about the requirements of the job, attend local meetup groups, rethink requirements of the job, and give back to the community. In environments where the history of your organization is impacting how many or what kinds of candidates apply to your positions, there are a few additional steps that may assist.

Acknowledge the history and the challenges in the environment. Be prepared with answers for questions that will come up about issues that have been reported. The fact that an individual did research on your company, read the reviews on Glassdoor, and still showed up for the interview is good! Encourage your current employees to talk about their work, either through presenting or participating in open spaces at conferences. Ensure that the process for vetting presentations and participation is transparent and clear.

Identify whether the problem is with the hiring process, or with the individuals interviewing. Create an interview training program and pair interview, allowing more people within the organization to become better interviewers. Figure out if any of your interview techniques might be turning away potential candidates. Full-day or multiday interviews, or interviewers who are overly confrontational in their style, are likely to discourage candidates from applying or accepting offers, and tend to discourage diversity within the organization as well.

On a related note, it might be the case that certain individuals within your organization are problematic in some of their actions or workplace behaviors. If issues of this sort have gone unresolved for long enough, it may be difficult to surface information, as people will have seen that problematic behavior is accepted and may have given up trying to report or resolve the issue. Removing such problematic individuals from the organization may be necessary to attract more candidates, especially if the problematic behavior is racist, sexist, or similarly discriminatory.

It will also help to know your target audience for potential new hires, and to address this realistically to get the most from your potential candidate pool. If you are a large enterprise organization with a history of being slow to respond to industry changes, you probably shouldn't be looking to poach current startup employees. Be aware of and up front about your organizational issues and limitations, which will help you align your searches with your audience as well as avoid getting a bad reputation for misleading hiring practices.

Morale Is Suffering After a Reorganization or Staff Reduction

The reduction phase of an organization's lifecycle is a natural phase where leadership may reduce product lines or staff count. Changing cultural norms have led to increased transparency as individuals post reviews on experiences, salary, and interview information. Glassdoor is one site where employees can post this information anonymously, and potential employees can read and rate their interest in a position.

The processes that are followed when a company enters this phase are a reflection of the culture. How and when leadership communicates the impending change can cause cognitive dissonance if the internal perception of culture and the implications of the message are not in sync.

A disconnect in how different individuals are valued can also negatively impact morale. If the company then transmits a message that underperformers are being cut, and a valued member is cut from the team, the remaining team members have to create the missing context in order to resolve the cognitive dissonance.

Change that is not handled well can demoralize the individuals still at the company; decrease cooperation, collaboration, and teamwork between individuals and teams within the organization; and increase outages and absenteeism due to stress and illnesses. Depending on the reasons for the reorganization or reduction, this could result in the opposite outcomes than desired.

When a reduction of workforce is imminent, don't try to hide it. The larger the organization, the more opportunities for leaks, whether due to people caring and trying to reconcile their feelings about the process, or someone making poor decisions about sharing sensitive information. If the news gets into the press before you have informed your company, you'll end up with people stressing out over the possibilities of losing their job, or losing valuable coworkers.

If your company has had an event of this nature and handled it poorly, due to the ever-increasing transparency of shared experiences, it is critical that it addresses any remaining internal issues and embraces the opportunity for transparency.

Review and repair your hiring practices. Ensure your hiring practices are a positive experience. Even if there are bad reviews, great individual experiences with the phone screen and interview process can help to repair your image.

Seek out entry- and junior-level candidates. Mentor and educate them. These individuals will cost more money in the short term, but will help you in the long term. They bring different perspectives and can revitalize your efforts in hiring.

Finally, fire your bullies. Track and measure the impact of individuals on the team. Don't excuse bad behavior because it's someone who is really smart or productive. Their behaviors impact the rest of the team, and may impact your interviewing prospects.

We Don't Know If We Need a Full Team for X

Even if a project or role might not have enough day-to-day work to necessitate hiring more than one person, single-person teams can be a recipe for burnout and single points of failure. The *bus factor* is a number describing how many people a team or project would have to lose in order to lose its institutional knowledge or ability to progress (or, how many people could get hit by a bus before the project/team would be unsalvagable). Lower numbers here are worse, because there is less margin for error or extenuating circumstances.

Single-person teams, by definition, have a bus factor of one: if that one person gets hit by a bus or (less dramatically) gets sick, wants to take a vacation, or leaves the organization, where will you be then? Look for ways that you can share knowledge, even without enough workload to hire a full team. Pairing and keeping documentation up to date are great places to start.

Burnout is another serious issue with single-person teams. If someone is the only person who knows how to do certain things, there will likely be pressure on them—either internally or externally imposed—to avoid taking time off or getting sick. Without any real time to recharge, their stress levels will continually increase—and so will the likelihood that they will end up leaving the organization, either because they proactively look for a job where they aren't a single point of failure or because stress and burnout end up forcing their hand. If you can have several people sharing responsibility and knowledge part-time rather than one person full-time, that ends up being better at both an individual and an organizational level.

PART VI

Bridging Devops Cultures

CHAPTER 16

Building Bridges with the Four Pillars of Effective Devops

One of the key factors that gives devops staying power and enables far-reaching influence is its flexibility. As we have illustrated throughout this book, there is no *one way* of doing devops; it does not require a particular piece of software or process, nor is it limited to web startups.

There are certain stories (Netflix and Etsy) that tend to be repeated as examples of successful devops implementations. These are not all-inclusive when it comes to ways that organizations can use the four pillars of effective devops to improve their productivity. While organizations like Etsy, which is well-known for its cultural and technical practices, certainly have important stories to share, we deliberately shared a wider range of stories than only those traditionally told in devops circles. The diversity of stories we have examined in no way nullifies the importance of devops, but rather is key to understanding its significance in the way we work and the industry as a whole.

When people tell stories about devops, they often talk about silos. A common trope is that of development and operations teams so siloed off from each other that they barely communicate at all, let alone collaborate effectively, and one thing that people look for is how to break down those silos. We prefer to think of devops in terms of a more constructive metaphor, rather than a destructive one.

Rather than silos, we view different teams or organizations as *islands*. In order to maintain a healthy, thriving ecosystem, a group of islands needs to be able to share resources, transfer knowledge, and even have inhabitants moving between them. Thus, we need to build bridges between the islands. The more bridges we have, the more robust our island network will be. The stories we tell with the four pillars of effective devops are how we build these bridges between the islands of different individuals, teams, and organizations.

The Significance of Stories

Throughout this book, we have emphasized the importance and significance of stories, and now that you are familiar with our four pillars, you will hopefully be able to see how they are working together to impact your own stories, past and present.

> The stories that people tell are the container that holds their world together and gives meaning to their lives.
>
> —Andrew Ramer

In some ways, devops is about understanding and potentially changing our core beliefs about our identity. When we internalize beliefs on identity based on roles and reject people because their behaviors don't match our beliefs, it impacts which engineers we admire, who we consider viable candidates for our job openings, how we interview, and who we consider "in." Devops means that instead of saying something like, "I'm ops because I innately do these things," we should instead be saying that, "I'm ops because I do these things now." This takes us back to the growth mindset that we want to encourage, rather than a fixed mindset: it's not that you either "do devops" or you don't, it is about how you examine and approach problems.

To understand why devops has gained such traction within the industry, we can examine its significance across multiple perspectives. Central across teams and organizations, it has a function that impacts the lives and work structures of individuals as well as the industry as a whole. Examining different company cultures gives us the opportunity to understand and interact with a diverse set of individuals. It also gives us the opportunity to understand the relationship of devops with newer philosophies that will arise.

As individuals, when we examine, listen, and share our stories from personal experience we strengthen our sense of belonging within the community, obtain comfort through the shared group values, and gain additional understanding of events that occur. As a group, we are improving communication through common symbolism, reducing conflict through shared meaning, and increasing cohesion through common values and conceptions of reality.

Explicit and Implicit Stories

While people have always had a great fondness for telling stories as a means of communication, this is not the only way that we end up demonstrating our histories and our cultures.

Explicit stories tell stories in a direct narrative form. These are the most common, and repeated as examples. We knowingly and deliberately tell these stories.

Implicit stories share information about our culture, histories, and actions. We aren't directly telling these stories.

We often don't consider the implicit stories when we talk about our devops journeys. For example:

Encouraging a candidate to join our team
> During the interview process, we often unknowingly share information about what is valued at the company. Mentioning long weekend hours signal to individuals that work and life commitments may be unbalanced. It might also signal that people are passionate about the product.

Writing a blog post
> What information is included, and the level at which it's written, communicates to individuals what is valued and expectations of knowledge.

Presenting at an industry conference
> The level and role of the individuals presenting at industry conferences communicates trust and transparency as well as a lack of prestige when individual contributors across the company are encouraged to speak.

Alice Goldfuss, Site Reliability Engineer, New Relic

Devops, to me, was about blending development and operations mindsets to create solid software and reliable platforms. It was about automation and tests and good incident management.

But devops can be much more than that; it can be a whole culture. After all, teams need to understand each other before solving shared problems. In fact, devops culture is such an obvious way of functioning that at first I didn't realize I was a practitioner. Of course you should communicate with other teams. Of course incidents should be blameless. Of course you want diverse talent. Of course.

I'm fortunate to work at a company that has striven to incorporate devops values into everyday engineering processes, without need of buzzwords or kick-offs. We have blameless incident retros, embed SREs on development teams, and provide transparency whenever possible. For example, our engineering organization is governed by a processes repo that any engineer can contribute to, and we send out monthly newsletters with the latest process changes.

I feel I can talk to almost any engineer in my company and find a sympathetic ear and willingness to help me with my current project. Because every production engineering team is in an on-call rotation, we all speak more or less the same language and support each other's ups and downs. In fact, we are growing toward a skill set of blurred lines, where software engineers can troubleshoot Linux and SREs write systems tools and web apps.

Is it perfect? No, of course not. When you're paged at 3 am for someone else's code, you want to throw blame and put up walls. But having official processes in place against this means no one gets hurt due to temporary feelings. Having a culture that supports interest across disciplines means people stay longer. And realizing the value of well-balanced teams creates room for junior talent.

If this is what devops is, then everyone should be doing it.

Devops in Theory and in Practice

It is one thing to discuss how something works in theory, and another to put it into practice. Anyone who has made a change to a piece of software has at some point said to themselves (or to their teammates) that "this should work *in theory*" but remained a bit uncertain about how that change will manifest when put into production.

We all have mental models about how we see the world and how we think things should work. Whether we realize it or not (and we often do not), these models guide our thoughts and behaviors in our day-to-day lives. This is referred to as *theory in use*, or how our theories or mental models play out when they are being used. However, when asked about how we see the world or how we think we would behave in a given situation, we often give different answers—how we think we act or how we wish we acted, called our *espoused theories*, is not always the same as how we do act.

For the most part, people are not trying to be deceitful when their espoused theories differ from their theories in use. It is human nature to believe that we would act in what we believe is a better, more positive, more idealistic manner than what happens when we are confronted with the stresses and realities of situations. So while a manager might say that of course he would let his reports decide the best way to proceed when dealing with an outage, in practice he might fall into micromanaging behaviors—and not even be aware of that difference.

Real-World Case Studies: Stories Showing Practice

We have shared real-world case studies throughout this book to illustrate the realities and varieties of the theories in use of devops practices. It is one thing to say that you have a blameless environment, and another thing to have one.

Keep this in mind when attending conference talks or reading blog posts about how other organizations are doing devops and making comparisons with your own organization. It can be easy to get discouraged when it feels like other companies have cultures that are so far ahead, but they might have differences between their espoused theories and theories in use.

It can also be frustrating to see the same people or organizations speaking about what they are doing, or having others talk them up as being these "industry thought leaders." You might think, "Well, that's great for them, but the reality is that some of those things just won't work in our organization." Change may be more difficult in some organizations based on their specific challenges.

While we would argue that a great deal more cultural change is possible than people might think, it is certainly true that different organizations and industries have different requirements and restrictions, and not every change you might want to make is possible. If you have to maintain PCI compliance, for example, there are certain workflow changes around aspects like your servers that handle credit card processing that you simply cannot make, as well as restrictions that you must follow to be compliant. This doesn't mean, however, that there aren't still significant gains that can be made elsewhere in most organizations.

Learning from Stories

Holism is the theory that parts of a whole are in intimate interconnection and thus regarded as greater than their sum. This applies to the four pillars of effective devops: while they can be considered individually, the strength of the devops movement stems from understanding all four and their interactions.

Through stories, we can learn:

- Why particular tools or technologies were chosen
- How people interact with each other and use different tools to accomplish their goals
- How tools enabled goals (or didn't) in the real world
- How different teams and organizations worked through various problems
- Things that worked and, more importantly, why they didn't work

In the next chapter, we'll discuss various forms of knowledge and learning that exist among teams, groups, or organizations, as well as look at changes that can be made to encourage more of this kind of affinity and learning.

Building Connections with Stories

In addition to considering how different parts of an organization are interconnected, it is also important to think about how we, as practitioners and as human beings, are connected as well. It is not possible to completely divorce any kind of discussion on software or technology from the people who create it and the people who use it. Our software is made by people, for people, and focusing our conversations entirely on the technical while ignoring the interpersonal is ultimately short-sighted.

Stories enable us to build connections with each other. When we shared our own stories in Chapter 1, we did so with the hope that readers would be able to connect with us, both to understand where we are coming from and start drawing parallels with their own stories. Sharing stories helps us see each other as real people, not as an anonymous faceless mob or just a screen name and a cartoon avatar, and to start interacting with and empathizing with each other as such.

By sharing and discussing the breadth of experiences found in these various stories, we hope that readers will be able to:

- recognize that other's different experiences will lead to differences in culture;
- learn how to ask questions to determine whether an organization that professes devops matches their own expectations and fit;
- increase tolerance of others' views;
- observe others' and their own experiences, comparing and contrasting these multiple viewpoints; and
- increase ability to articulate their own beliefs and values.

In the final two chapters of this book, we will examine various stories or narratives that impact us as individuals, the effects these stories have on how we work together, and what it means to create healthy, sustainable organizations where individuals can thrive.

Summary

Some readers might be surprised by how much we have discussed cultural factors in this book, rather than spending more time on technical ones. Culture—as defined by the values, beliefs, goals, and practices shared by the people in an organization—has much more impact on implementation of devops than specific tools or technologies.

As we've discussed before with the notion of the devops compact, devops is about creating understandings and shared goals that allow for long-term, sustainable working relationships between individuals and teams. Similar to how someone with a strong understanding of fundamental engineering concepts can readily pick up new programming languages, organizations with a strong understanding of the cultural aspects of how people work together can more easily adapt to use different tools and technologies.

In order to build the relationships and connections that effective devops requires, we have to be able to both learn from and connect with one another. Stories—whether those told on Usenet, the ones shared at the first devopsdays conference back in 2009, or those written out in this book—provide us with mechanisms and narratives for this learning and connecting.

CHAPTER 17

Bridging Devops Cultures: Learning from Our Stories

Stories are a big part of learning, for both the people telling the stories and the people hearing them. You might think of learning as just being about learning how to use a new tool, picking up a new programming language, or improving some other technical skill, but the context around how and why various tools and technologies are used can have just as much impact, if not more, as their technical details.

Luckily, stories are a great way of sharing the cultural context around the use of tools within a specific environment. For example, Netflix's Chaos Monkey (*http://bit.ly/ netflix-chaos-mnky*) explicitly tests failure in production by having an application randomly crash virtual servers. The stories shared of the Chaos tools in use at Netflix illuminate values of the organization including:

- practice at resolving failures when engineers are at their best during the day versus at 2 am;
- standard of writing software that degrades rather than fails; and
- expectation of failure as a mode of software operation.

In this chapter, we'll cover various aspects of this cultural context that demonstrate the values of a team or organization, either implicitly or explicitly. We'll then cover ways to encourage learning between teams and even organizations, looking at how to foster this sort of learning in your own environment.

What Stories Can Teach Us About Culture

As we stated in Chapter 1, a large part of culture consists of the values, norms, and knowledge shared among groups of people. It is one thing to talk about culture, however, and another thing to see or hear how that culture manifests itself in day-to-day work.

This section examines five key aspects of culture: values, prohibitions, myths, rituals, and ideas. We will examine how these aspects are established in everyday work environments as well as give suggestions for examining them in your own culture. Aspects such as these are how we teach other people about our cultures, whether those are new people who are joining your organization or the audience of a talk you are giving at a conference.

 It's important to keep in mind that you can use these cultural aspects in stories you are telling, but you should also pay attention to them when you are listening to and learning from stories yourself. When you are listening to someone tell a story, either informally or formally, what are they saying about their culture? What parts of their culture are implicit versus explicitly stated? By noticing what elements of cultural context are most valuable to learn from, you will get better at both learning from other people's stories and at teaching others through your own.

Values

Every organization has values, but the described values that exist in theory don't always match the values demonstrated in practice. Values are the principles, standards of behavior, and judgments of what is and isn't important within an organization.

How organizational values are communicated, both within and outside the organization, is important. Most frequently, the espoused values are written down somewhere. These value statements can be found in places like a company's website or other promotional material, job descriptions, employee handbooks, or motivational posters with phrases like "Customer Satisfaction" or "Teamwork." These values might also be repeated verbally in situations like organization-wide meetings or press releases.

Values in theory and in practice

These verbal and written descriptions state principles, but when it comes to everyday life in an organization, where theory most often diverges from practice is in the behaviors being demonstrated.

Many people have heard the phrase, "the standard you walk past is the standard you accept." Lieutenant General David Morrison, currently serving as Australia's Chief of Army, said this in a 2013 statement regarding acceptable behavior in the Australian army during the course of an investigation of sexual harassment by officers. He noted that it is one thing to say that harassment will not be tolerated, but if there are no consequences for harassing behavior, that actual behavior becomes the standard rather than the stated value.

The same holds true for the workplace. Morrison also stated that the responsibility to set and enforce standards of behavior falls especially to those in leadership roles or other positions of power. This is important, as it avoids blaming victims for bad behavior that happens to them (an unfortunately common occurrence) placing the responsibility instead on the people who have the power and obligation to enforce behavior and set consequences.

However, this is not to say that only managers or leaders can speak up when they see bad behavior happening. As noted in Part III, behaviors and consequences enforced by the group as a whole are most effective for maintaining a communally beneficial standard of behavior overall. This means that everyone who has the ability to safely do so should do their part to set and enforce values. It also prevents people on the receiving end of bad behavior, who are often members of underrepresented or marginalized groups and have less power and safety with which to act, from being solely responsible for how other people behave.

Another way in which values can be expressed is in how different teams are treated throughout the organization. As also mentioned in Part III, it is common in startups for engineering teams, especially web and mobile development ones, to be valued more than other, nonengineering teams. While this usually is not explicitly stated, it becomes apparent through behaviors such as allowing more flexible schedules or remote opportunities for engineers; giving them a higher budget for swag, training, and travel; and giving them more recognition for their accomplishments.

Differing team and organizational values

Moving from overall organizational values to a more granular level, individual teams can end up having rather different values from each other, and this can cause conflicts throughout an organization as well. We've discussed previously how different values were at the heart of the issues that sparked the devops movement. Shipping features quickly and site stability are examples of different engineering values. But how work gets done or how it is evaluated are not the only values that teams and organizations need to consider. Some other examples of values are:

- "Move fast and break things"—that is, valuing forward motion over all else
- Valuing teaching and sharing—individual versus collective knowledge
- Valuing building an inclusive and diverse team versus growing a team quickly
- Encouraging people to speak their mind however they want versus creating a place where people feel safe
- Valuing being a team player versus being a "lone wolf"

- Prioritizing quality of work over quantity of hours worked
- Encouraging people to eat three meals a day at the office versus encouraging them to spend time with their families

Differences in these or any other values between teams, especially when the differing teams have to work closely together, can be a source of conflict. The key is not in never having differences or disagreements in the first place, but rather in how teams work to communicate and resolve these kinds of disagreements when they do arise.

Whether or not people are willing and able to communicate their individual and team values to others is a good indicator of how well the organization will be able to effectively work with a diverse group of individuals and their possibly disparate working styles and values. This ties back to the idea of the devops compact we introduced in Part I—communication in the beginning is used to create a *shared understanding* of not only the goals but also the general strategies that will be used together, and an environment of *trust* allows people or teams to work semi-independently toward that goal.

Obviously this cannot happen without the shared understanding of the goal, strategies, or values—how will people know what they are working toward if this is never discussed or communicated? The more siloed and less communicative an organization begins from, the more communication they are likely to need to reach a shared understanding, and the more time it will take to reach a trustful, blameless environment that can maintain that state.

Communicating and teaching values

How do values get communicated between teams, individuals, and organizations? How do we determine how much overlap and sharing already exist with our values and goals, how do we best communicate what is most important to us, and how do we resolve conflicts between differing values?

Ask people to prepare
When these kinds of discussions need to happen, tell people to prepare for them. Get key stakeholders to define what their values are, explain why they are important, and prioritize them. "Because they just are" is not useful to help defuse conflict when resolving disagreements in values. Make sure everyone involved has a chance to share and discuss their values and viewpoints, to ensure that everyone's voice is heard.

Level up communication skills
This might mean management training so that managers throughout the organization are skilled in dealing with conflict effectively, or providing communication training to individual contributors of all levels, but it's important to start develop-

ing good communication habits in people and breaking unproductive ones as early as possible.

Talk face to face, if possible

Whether this means in person or with video conferencing, it's important to remember how much of what we communicate is nonverbal. So much of the context and nuance gets lost in written communication that it is much easier for misunderstandings to occur that way. People who are more comfortable with written communication can take advantage of the preparation step to write out their thoughts while still presenting them face to face later.

Document, review, and iterate

People won't always remember what was discussed in a given meeting or conversation, or schedules might mean somebody wasn't able to attend. In addition, miscommunication is still possible and people can have different interpretations of what was said and agreed upon. Having a written record of what happened allows you to review it and gives you a solid starting point to continue the conversation and keep working to reach a common understanding.

Keep information visible and shared

Finally, it is important that everyone be able to see the conversations that took place and what decisions were reached, especially around values that impact their daily work. In order for values to be truly shared, they cannot be hidden away or decided behind closed doors and then handed down as edicts. Without visibility, there can be no conversations, and conversations are necessary for shared understanding.

 In general, try to use the same classes of tools and the same general strategies you use for technical work to do this sort of community-building, "soft" skills work. Not only will people already be familiar with the general workflows of the tools, but it will reduce the friction that can come from learning to use a new tool. For example, if your teams are already using GitHub's pull requests for collaborating on code, they can use them to collaborate on documents specifying the team's or organization's values as well.

Looking around the industry, it is incredibly gratifying to see that we are starting to talk about sustainable work practices based on not glorifying long work hours, and instead have started sharing coping strategies and encouraging our coworkers to take vacations. Pretending that stress, overwork, burnout, and other such issues don't exist won't make them go away; all that will do is make people afraid to speak up and reach out for help when they are struggling. When you consider your team and organizational values, be sure that you do not forget this human side of things.

Prohibitions

Prohibitions are things that are known or described as being dangerous or forbidden. However, whether this knowledge is implicit or explicit can vary greatly among teams, as it's often found in the form of tribal knowledge not explicitly documented. Some examples of prohibitions in environments include:

- running commands as `root` in production rather than using `sudo`;
- testing changes to production configuration in production (even if it is just a monitoring script);
- committing code to version control prior to testing;
- moving forward with deployment without passing tests;
- running arbitrary code from the internet on company systems; and
- deploying to production on Fridays or right before heading home.

These prohibitions can be technical or nontechnical. It is important to keep in mind that the more explicit they are, the easier it will be to communicate them to new people joining the group. If nothing is written down or explicitly stated, how is someone supposed to know they are committing a faux pas until after the fact?

This is an area where people of different backgrounds might have different social or cultural expectations that come into play, such as *ask* versus *guess* cultures (described in Part II). Clarifying and documenting expectations around both values and prohibitions can go a long way toward keeping the devops compact self-enforcing.

Technical prohibitions might be documented in code comments or, more frequently, wiki pages or other shared documents. A wiki page describing how to deploy code to production might be expected to have some prohibitions in the form of "Be careful to look out for *X*" or "Warning: Make sure *Y* happens at this point before continuing." These sorts of prohibitions can often be traced back to previous mistakes that were made and then documented in the hopes of preventing their recurrence.

Nontechnical prohibitions often take the form of an employee handbook or a code of conduct. While there are other texts that go into much greater depth as to why codes of conduct (*http://bit.ly/conduct-101*) are important, we will simply say here that they are a much-needed way to detail inappropriate behaviors, enforcement policies for violations, the process for reporting violations, and consequences for violations in a given environment. All companies should have an employee handbook and all events should have a code of conduct that lays out types and examples of prohibited behavior, the ramifications of violating the rules, and how to report issues or violations if you see them.

Describing and teaching prohibitions

For both technical and nontechnical prohibitions, it helps to be as specific as possible when describing them. This is especially true for more social or cultural prohibitions; something that states only "don't be an asshole" (as too many do) leaves itself up to interpretation as to what constitutes someone "being an asshole." This then turns reporting a violation into one person's word against another, and people with less power or privilege in a given community or organization often feel less safe reporting violations for this reason. On the other hand, a prohibition such as "no sexually explicit content in talks or on slides" provides a much clearer picture of what is not allowed.

In many cases, it can be helpful to explain why a particular prohibition exists. This not only provides context that can help guide people's decisions, but also makes the rules feel less arbitrary. People are less likely to push back against rules and prohibitions when there is a clear reason behind them. For a technical prohibition, this might take the form of an example of what happens if a prohibited thing is done (or maybe a link to a postmortem from an event that caused the prohibition to become necessary). Some people might think it is not needed to state why more social/nontechnical prohibitions like codes of conduct are necessary, but we feel that you cannot overstate that everyone's health, safety, and security are prioritized.

Finally, it is important to pay attention to how prohibitions and rules get enforced. Is your environment a blameless one, or does it look for someone to make an example of? Are the consequences or repercussions that happen in line with what is stated? For example, if a code of conduct says that someone who violates it will be removed from the event, does that happen? Not following through on these sorts of prohibitions sends the message that they are not *really* important, so make sure that you do not set forth consequences that you do not intend to act on.

 Additionally, keep an eye out for rules being enforced inconsistently. If there are individuals in an organization who seem to be allowed to break the rules, this not only sets a bad example for the rest of the organization, but it also creates an environment where different people are held to different standards at the expense of everyone's safety.

Myths

We have mentioned the importance of stories several times throughout this book, along with the impact that they have on culture. A myth is a traditional story or belief that is shared among a culture or community that explains "why" and influences behavior, but often is not based on factual data.

Harmful impacts of myths

Myths can vary in whether or not they are harmful. More lighthearted ones might take the form of superstitions: among most operation engineers, there are superstitions around being on-call and jokes like "do not anger the on-call gods" by saying something like "this on-call rotation hasn't been too bad so far." Some myths can cause more long-lasting problems with how people think, how they interact with others, and how they deal with the industry around them.

A prime example of a harmful myth is "girls are bad at math." This phenomenon, introduced in Chapter 9, is referred to as *stereotype threat*. It describes how people will very often perform more poorly in situations when they have been told or reminded of negative stereotypes that apply to them (such as girls who are told that "girls are bad at math" performing worse on a math test). This is in large part due to the psychological power that stories can have upon us, negative or positive. When people have to worry about proving or disproving other people's negative perceptions of them (and other members of their group or people like them), the pressure and mental overhead placed upon them is enormous.

Another harmful myth is "I'm not technical." In an industry that increasingly glorifies engineers, people in disciplines outside of engineering can stop believing in the value of their own skills and discount their contributions in the workplace. Engineers should not be put on pedestals at the expense of other employees, as it takes more than just engineering skills to grow and maintain a successful business.

Another problem with this myth is that it indicates a fixed mindset rather than a growth mindset. People tend to say "I'm not an engineer" or "I'm not technical" as if it were some immutable fact that could never change, which discourages them from ever picking up programming or operations skills. The myth that engineers are more important than anyone else in turn discourages engineers from learning anything about the business or customer-facing aspects of the organizations they are a part of. While these technical versus nontechnical silos are broader than "dev" versus "ops," they are still silos that can prevent an organization from reaching its full potential.

Examining myths

When we come across myths like these, we should be asking ourselves as a community not only what harm might they be causing but also how we can work to counter their effects. The various coding bootcamp programs that exist are good for raising the technical skills of people outside the industry looking to get into engineering, but we need to consider how we treat nontechnical people within our industry and organizations. How can we encourage and grow technical and engineering literacy in nonengineers? How can we encourage business literacy among engineering staff? What can we do in our interviewing processes to help combat the negative effects of stereotype threat?

Different organizations and companies will have myths and stories that are unique to them, but it is important to keep an eye out for them, to examine the effects they have throughout the various groups and communities that make up our industry, and to keep questioning and iterating on how we can improve the stories we are telling.

Rituals

Rituals, or formalized modes of behavior that members of a group or community regularly engage in, are useful not only for building community but also for determining where a community's values lie. From a more sociological perspective, the idea of a formalized ritual often has a more religious meaning, but behavior need not be quite that formalized in order to be considered a ritual—the extent to which the knowledge of it is shared among community members as well as the regularity of its practice really help give an activity or behavior ritual status.

Rituals have long been used as a way of bringing a community together by helping to build a shared identity based on participation in the ritual. A fairly obvious example of this is the "rushing" of fraternities or sororities and the hazing that often happens to new or prospective members. Participating in these shared, traditional behaviors helps to instill a feeling of camaraderie and group membership once the rituals are completed.

Rituals within a community

As we've discussed in earlier chapters, building a community and instilling a sense of group membership is key to developing strong collaborative relationships within an organization, and rituals can be an effective way of doing this. However, it is important to be aware of whether or not the rituals that we've created are exclusionary, who they might be leaving out, and how those exclusions can harm both individuals and the community as a whole. Consider a few examples of rituals that might be seen at various tech companies:

Regularly working until 9 or 10 pm
> Not only is a ritual like this a problem for employees that have obligations outside of work (such as a family to care for), but it can also promote a culture that is devoid of any balance or boundaries between work and not-work. When managers are some of the people working late all the time, it can make that behavior seem required, even if they say that it is not.

Celebrating milestones or goals with drinks or at a bar
> Celebrations can be a great way to recognize the work that people have done, but there are many different ways to celebrate. An alcohol-focused culture that only ever has celebrations at bars or encourages excessive consumption can be not only unfriendly for anyone who doesn't drink (or drinks less) but also can be downright unhealthy.

Referencing memes and pop culture in chat

With the growth in popularity of chatops, it can become more and more common for chat bots to share memes, pop culture references, or other inside jokes. Again, while shared jokes can be a way to increase camaraderie and ties between team members and teams, they can also feel exclusionary to anyone who doesn't get the references or jokes in addition to blurring the lines between what is and is not acceptable for work. What seems like an innocent joke or GIF to one person can be offensive to someone else. In their quest to differentiate themselves from the beige cubicles of large corporations, many startups tend to adopt an "anything goes" attitude, but this is not conducive to a genuinely inclusive work environment.

Competing in a 100-pushup challenge in the office

This is another example of an activity that can be a way to facilitate group bonding but isn't necessarily inclusive of people with different levels of physical ability. Especially in startups with a younger median age, team activities can tend to skew toward those enjoyed by a very specific subset of the population. Things like fantasy sports teams; foosball, ping-pong, or pool tables; and fitness challenges can give off a "tech bro" kind of vibe. This isn't to say that they shouldn't be allowed, and it might not be possible to find an activity that every single person will love, but it's important to pay attention to the type and variety of activities and rituals and who they might be unintentionally favoring or excluding.

Providing free meals and snacks at work

While free meals can be a nice perk, providing meals like breakfast and dinner can give the impression of encouraging employees to spend more and more hours in the office, rather than encouraging a work–life balance and having hobbies and interests outside of work.

Designating times to bring dogs or children to visit

Again, keep in mind that while some people might love dogs, not everyone is a dog person (and some people have allergies) and that's OK. This can be another great way to encourage bonding between employees, but consider having designated dog-free areas or a dedicated child-care space—especially in an open-office floor plan where noise can quickly become a huge distraction.

A theme that becomes apparent when discussing these rituals is that of balance and consideration. All the rituals just described can be used in a positive way, to bring people together using shared experiences, which can help with collaboration and affinity, but they all also have aspects that might make people feel uncomfortable or excluded. Usually this exclusion is implicit and probably unintentional, but sometimes it can be made explicit under the guise of "culture fit," which should be avoided. Be sure to encourage a variety of rituals to be as inclusive as possible.

Other sorts of rituals can exist around how organizations work: a CEO might have weekly office hours to answer questions in an open forum, a VP might make appointments to have lunch with everyone in their division once a quarter, or employees might be strongly encouraged to participate in support rotations to get a feel for what kinds of issues customers are writing in about. Rituals of this sort can help to create a company culture just as much as the ones just described, but these sorts tend to be less problematic as they involve more strictly work-related issues rather than social ones.

Changing and creating rituals

One final consideration around organizational or cultural rituals and practices is how often do rituals get changed or created, and how explicitly those changes are communicated throughout the organization. A company that has had the same rituals for five years might find that they have been outgrown, and no longer reflect the current organizational values or the way people want the organization to behave going forward. An organization that is growing, especially in terms of its diversity and inclusivity, should encourage the creation of new rituals that include new people and processes.

It is important to continually examine our rituals to understand the impacts that they can have both on work productivity and how employees interact, and why they are (or are not) important and meaningful. "It's always been done this way" is not a solid reason for doing something technical in a particular way, and as it turns out it isn't a good reason for interpersonal and cultural rituals either.

Ideas and Knowledge

"It's always been done this way" not only is not a good reason for continuing to do something, but it is also indicative of a fixed mindset, rather than a growth one. One area where this can often be seen is that of so-called "best practices." These are ideas or procedures that are commonly accepted or prescribed as being the most correct or most effective, but this sort of thinking can be problematic in fields as fast-paced as web operations or modern software development.

People look to the ideas of best practices for a variety of reasons. They can be a way of trying to minimize risk, something that we see manifested in other ways such as adding monitoring or deploying smaller changesets. If someone is trying to complete work in an area where they have no prior experience (common at startups with much smaller teams), they might look to industry best practices for guidance. It's also human nature to want to believe that there is some objectively best way of doing things.

Searching for the "best" ideas

The problem is that there is often not one "best" way of doing something, nor is there one "best" solution that applies equally well to every situation. With as complex and varied as our products and architectures tend to be today, with as many different moving pieces as there are, and with so many different technologies to choose from, what works best for one organization might be quite ineffective for another, and what worked best at one point in time might not still be the best solution 6 or 12 months down the road.

People want to resolve cognitive dissonance, that mental conflict that arises over incompatible ideas. If we can shift from a culture of "best" to one of "appropriate now" or "design pattern," we can alleviate future dissonance that comes from having to replace one "best" thing with a different thing that is somehow also "best." If we stop using "best" as some sort of immutable, absolute label, we can stop the dissonance that comes from those things not working as well as we expected or having their effectiveness change as our needs and restrictions do.

What makes people accept an idea as a "best practice" or an "appropriate now" solution? People can display preferences for how they accept evidence, just as they have individual preferences around their working and learning styles. For some, an authoritative figure is enough. Others require direct experience doing something themselves in order to accept that it works and how well. These needs can cause conflicts based on how we communicate.

 Though it likely isn't practical for someone who prefers direct experience to be able to try every potential solution themselves, knowledge of their preferences can impact other people's communication styles, such as including more detail about what was tried, providing links to additional or background reading, or adding graphs or other measurable results.

Mindsets and learning new ideas

People also vary in regards to how, when, and why they seek out new knowledge and ideas. It might not be a surprise to hear that having a fixed versus a growth mindset can have a lot of impact in this area. A fixed mindset tends to discourage people from seeking out or accepting new knowledge. If someone with a fixed mindset has built their sense of self around the idea that they are smart, having to learn new things or change their mind about something would challenge this idea; fixed-mindset individuals tend to be the ones more strongly rejecting new ideas, especially those that contradict previously held knowledge.

Alternatively, someone with a growth mindset, who might see their successes as a result of learning and effort rather than some innate intelligence, is often more likely to not only seek out new knowledge but also to accept it as being true. People with a growth mindset are necessary for any healthy organization to continue to grow and improve. Luckily, it is possible to move from a fixed mindset to a growth one; check out the Chapter 20 list for more on this topic.

Interorganizational Interactions

In addition to the stories and experiences that come from within a given organization, there is also great value to be had by sharing stories in between organizations. How organizations approach this idea can be a good indicator of how likely they are to be successful in creating a lasting devops culture.

As it turns out, organizations can have fixed or growth mindsets as well, in much the same manner that individuals can. A fixed-mindset organization might view its success as innate and inevitable, whether that comes from being an enterprise that has been successful for years past or a new startup flush with VC money. This fixed mindset might cause them to ignore signs that they are struggling or discourage any change from how things are currently being done.

A growth mindset in an organization tends to cause that organization to focus a lot on continually learning and improving, viewing its success as something that requires continual effort rather than being guaranteed. These organizations will seek out new ideas, try new solutions, and look for better ways of doing things both technically and culturally, rather than assuming that what they are currently doing is the best.

How do organizations seek out new information? What interactions do they have with other organizations? The most common ways that interactions and informational exchanges take place tend to be through industry conferences, smaller community events, and engineering exchange programs.

Conferences and Travel

Conferences can be a very valuable way of getting outside one's own organization and learning from other practitioners in the industry. Individuals can go to conferences that focus on a particular technology, such as a specific database solution or programming language, or events that cover a somewhat broader topic such as mobile development, web performance, or web operations. Conference talks can range from very technical to highly cultural, and there can also be a great deal of value in the hallway track, the often serendipitous meetings that occur in the halls (or lunch tables or coffee lines) at these conferences.

The costs of traveling

There are costs to traveling to conferences, however, and not just the monetary costs that come from flights, hotels, per diems for food and ground transportation, and admission to the conferences themselves (if your organization does not currently have a training or education budget that includes these kinds of costs for conferences, now is a great time to start creating one). There is also a mental, emotional, and even physical cost to conference travel that should be considered for attendees as well as speakers.

For any conferences that require travel, people will have to make arrangements for childcare, pet care, or house sitting, the costs of which are usually not covered by organizations' travel policies and can put more of a burden on people who tend to shoulder the majority of domestic responsibilities (usually women). Frequent travel can cause anxiety or stress just from the logistics of traveling as well as being away from home. Being separated from friends, families, and coworkers can cause isolation and even strain relationships, especially if frequent travel leaves one person taking care of the home and children much more than they are used to. Jetlag and illness are real concerns as well.

Many organizations have some sort of policies in place regarding travel. Common policies might include having a fixed budget per employee for training and conferences per year, a similar budget per team or per department, a fixed number of events that each employee is allowed to attend, or a rule differentiated by who is covering the travel costs—for example, "you can attend X conferences where the conference pays for travel and lodging, and Y that the company will pay for as a speaker, and Z as an attendee."

When creating or examining travel and training policies, keep in mind that not everyone has the ability to get an event to pay for their flights and hotel stays. Many conferences do not pay these costs at all, will only pay if people negotiate for them up front (which can adversely impact women, who are both socialized to negotiate less as well as often being penalized when they do), or will only pay more popular, established speakers. The latter might mean that your organization is sending the same people over and over, rather than giving less experienced speakers or more junior employees the same chances to participate.

Conference safety considerations

Expecting people to speak at conferences in order to attend them, while it can help reduce costs in an organization if speakers are able to negotiate travel and lodging reimbursement, prevents people who have no desire to speak from gaining valuable learning and networking opportunities. Not everyone wants to be a public speaker, and while public speaking is certainly a skill that can be learned, some people would strongly prefer to give back to the community in other ways, such as writing blog posts, writing technical documentation, or contributing to open source software.

There is also a risk to speaking up and being a kind of public speaker that disproportionately impacts members of underrepresented groups in the industry. Threats and harassment can and do happen, and an organization should not require that someone put themselves forward in a way that makes them feel unsafe just to attend a conference or training.

Unfortunately, even attending conferences as a member of an underrepresented group can be a less-than-positive experience. If your organization has a policy that only one person from the company or team can go to a given event, consider that people might feel and even be safer if they are traveling with someone they know and trust. Ensure that there are resources in place, either in person or remotely, for employees who have safety considerations when traveling and attending industry events, and make sure that they are allowed to do things like expense cabs so they can travel more safely.

Finally, keep in mind that conferences will be a different experience if someone is there to speak versus there to recruit or simply to learn. A speaker might find themselves less able to concentrate on the talks preceding theirs due to nerves, while if you send employees with the sole purpose of recruiting potential new hires (or selling a product), that focus can also take away from their ability to learn, especially if that means staffing a booth rather than attending talks.

 Conferences are a great way to share knowledge throughout the industry, and should be part of your organization's or team's budget and plans. Make sure that you allow for people to attend, in a capacity that is comfortable for them, at least one event per year so they can grow their skills, expand their networks, and enhance the team and organizational knowledge.

Other Community Events

Other, smaller community events such as Meetup groups can also be a great way to share knowledge in between organizations in the industry. Because Meetups have a local focus, there typically should not be travel and lodging costs associated with them. While one could attend a Meetup while they were traveling for other reasons, most of the time people just attend meetings where they live.

These kinds of groups usually have much smaller sizes than a typical conference, but that can significantly reduce costs for both attendees and hosts. In many cases, a local organization will allow a Meetup group to host an event in their office space free of charge, only asking in exchange for a few minutes to speak about job or sales opportunities the company has to offer. Hosting or even just attending these events can be a good way to find new potential candidates.

In most larger cities, groups or events will already exist for a variety of topics, perhaps with more variety and more specificity than with larger conferences, due to the much lower overhead of creating a group or event. Lower costs make it much easier to start new groups as well, so if you live in a place with a smaller tech scene or find a particular technology that doesn't have a group yet, starting one can be a great way of engaging and sharing knowledge with the local community.

Hosting a series of speakers can help you get additional perspectives and share knowledge. It is possible to bring in speakers to meetings that are private and internal to just your organization, but that doesn't involve any sharing with the rest of the community at large—and without a sense of reciprocity or giving back, an organization might over time become a less desirable place to speak. Hosting speakers at events that are open to the public (and having video made available online, either live or after the fact), like Etsy's Code as Craft speaker series, benefits not only your organization but other organizations as well.

With even less overhead than hosting these sorts of smaller events, running a public-facing technical blog allows organizations to share knowledge with the rest of the community—and you might find that you have employees who much prefer writing to public speaking. A tech blog can be useful for increasing familiarity with the organization's name and culture in the industry (always a plus for hiring and recruiting), providing background information for new employees, and encouraging other organizations to start sharing their stories as well.

Engineering Exchanges

As we discussed in Part III, engineering exchanges, or programs where a pair of engineers at different organization swap places and roles with each other for some relatively short period of time, can be a fantastic way of sharing ideas and knowledge in between organizations if executed properly.

It's possible to get a much more nuanced, and perhaps more realistic, view of how an organization operates through an exchange program than through a conference talk or blog post. In the latter two, there can be a tendency to put on a good public face and maybe gloss over any less-than-perfect details, not in the sense of lying but perhaps not sharing the entire picture. There's not anything particularly wrong with this, but in terms of learning from each other, being able to see and reason about the messy things and the not-so good parts can create a much more complete understanding.

Engineering culture and openness

Again, how open an organization is willing to be with an exchange program will determine how successful that program is. An organization that doesn't let outside engineers working with it do or learn anything of substance is less likely to be invited to participate in future exchange programs for not holding up their end of the deal. This exchange is another form of a compact or social contract; there must be a shared understanding, both parties must participate, and there can be internally enforced negative ramifications for not playing fairly.

Whether or not engineering exchanges are allowed or disallowed, or encouraged or discouraged if they are allowed, can say a lot about organizational mindset. Pay attention to how engineers are treated on both sides of an exchange program:

- Are some teams or managers more likely to participate than others within a given organization?
- Are participants going to an exchange still expected to be online, check email, and do their regular work during the exchange, or are they allowed to more fully immerse themselves in it?
- Are participating engineers regarded positively for their participation or treated like traitors to the organization?
- Are new ideas or suggestions stemming from an exchange immediately (or abnormally rapidly) dismissed or given fair consideration?
- How much work are incoming exchange participants allowed to do? Is it meaningful work or busy work?
- Are incoming engineers allowed to speak in meetings or only observe?
- Do these engineers leave with anything (schwag such as stickers, mugs, or T-shirts; notes they may have taken; a significant piece of work they accomplished) or empty-handed?

If your organization or team feels like it is stagnating, or having the same arguments over and over with no agreement in sight, having a fresh set of eyes and insights can often be a breath of much-needed fresh air. While it is hypothetically even possible to bring in an exchange with someone with a specific skill set, it is more recommended to not use an exchange program to solve specific problems but rather to practice having a growth mindset and exploring new possibilities and ideas.

Encouraging Interorganizational Affinity

What do you do if your organization has a fixed mindset rather than a growth one? How can you tell if your organization has a fixed mindset in the first place?

Discouraging Fixed Mindsets

One of the most common symptoms of a fixed mindset is sticking rigidly to the idea of "we've always done it this way." This is not to say that only the latest bleeding-edge technology should be used; indeed, there can be great value in sticking to tried-and-tested technologies over something that hasn't even been used in production for more than a few months. If an organization is willing to assess and evaluate technologies and tools based on how well they solve problems and decides that for many problems, sticking with what they already use and know is better, that's one thing. But rigidly refusing to ever seriously consider changing anything, especially processes, is indicative of a fixed mindset.

Also keep an eye out for sentiments such as:

- "That's fine for Facebook and Netflix and Etsy, but we aren't that kind of organization."
- "We're a high-performing organization; we don't need devops."
- "This is an enterprise; that kind of thing doesn't work for us."

While it is important to know your organization's strengths and weaknesses, what sort of engineering or organizational values you want to maintain, and what hasn't worked for you in the past, it's important to watch out for statements that imply that this is how things always have been and always will be, rather than just how they are right now. Compare this with an individual fixed mindset: "I'm not good at math" versus "I'm working to get better at math right now"—at an operational level, this might look like "Devops wouldn't work for us" versus "We're looking for ways to get people to collaborate more."

Start with Small Changes

One of the most recommended ways to move from a fixed mindset to a growth one is to use *small, repeated actions*, and using smaller, frequent successes to reinforce new habits and thought patterns. At an organizational level, this might involve:

Don't try to change everything overnight
A lot of a fixed organization mindset can come from multiple individuals who have had bad experiences with change before or who are risk-averse for various reasons. It can help to start with smaller changes; rather than overhauling the entire deployment system all at once, start with a part of it, even if that part is as small as fixing incorrect documentation. Look for small things that can be changed and improved, and help build confidence that change not only improves things but also doesn't necessarily mean massive issues or outages.

Focus on the process, not on the end result
If management or leadership at an organization has an idea in their heads that devops is only for startups or not relevant to them, trying to push a goal of a "devops transformation" or a "devops team" or something to that effect is unlikely to be successful. In a case like this, focus on the actions you'd like to change, whether that be implementing configuration management or changing how people approach monitoring or addressing whatever your biggest pain points are, and emphasize the reasons for the changes rather than getting too "big picture."

Start with just one team

There is a cost to change, and the larger the impact or scope of a change, the larger the costs can be, both in terms of implementing the change but also the risk if the change is a mistake somehow. (This is why continuous delivery of smaller code changes is so often a good idea!) Rather than trying to change an entire department or organization at once, it might be easier to get buy-in to change just one team to start to lower the cost and the risk. You might try a team that is more isolated, to minimize impact on the rest of the organization, but there is also benefit to experimenting with a team that interacts with others, so that other people can see and feel the benefits and maybe start to become interested in adopting new tools or practices themselves.

Make a habit of learning

Changing a mindset, whether it be individual or organizational, involves changing our habits, and a key habit to a growth mindset is learning. Encourage people to share interesting things they've learned at daily standups or weekly status meetings—even if it's learning something that *didn't* work. Start a mailing list where people can share interesting articles or blog posts they've read and can discuss them with others. Encourage people to go to local meetups and share their takeaways from those as well. Making a positive habit of learning in small ways can make its benefits more apparent and pave the way for larger-scale organizational learning and cultural changes.

Overall, one of the best ways to break down resistance to interorganizational affinity is to understand the mindset that causes it. While managers can help by doing things like creating budgets for conferences or implementing a speaker series, individual contributors can also help to showcase the benefits of knowledge sharing between different companies and organizations themselves, in ways that can minimize risk and fear while still helping to effect cultural changes.

Summary

As we've illustrated in this chapter, there are a multitude of ways that culture can manifest itself, in terms of its values, prohibitions, rituals, myths, and ideas, and thus, there are just as many ways that a devops culture can be formed within an organization. There are certainly common themes that people and teams should keep in mind, the most important of which is that the combination of individual and organizational mindset can make or break a culture's ability to grow and learn.

A fixed mindset, with people holding fast to thoughts such as "that will never work for us" and "but we've always done it this way" is unlikely to be able to make any significant and sustainable changes, with that fixed view becoming a self-fulfilling prophecy. On the other hand, those with a growth mindset, with a focus on individual and organization learning and the assurance that growth and change can be achieved with individual and collective effort, is much more likely to succeed in the changes that they are trying to make.

Even with a growth mindset, lasting changes toward a culture of collaboration and affinity will not come overnight, and these changes will look different from organization to organization. It's important to keep this in mind and remember that this is OK. Not every organization has to have the same values or the same culture, but finding out what your values are is key to shaping the culture you want. Values will exist in an organization whether they are implicitly or explicitly defined, but the more explicit and clear they are, the easier they are to learn from.

CHAPTER 18

Bridging Devops Cultures: Fostering Human Connections

In addition to helping us learn about successful technologies and effective cultures, stories also allow us to form and maintain strong interpersonal connections with each other. As we discussed in Part III, the strength of the ties between individuals and groups has an overall positive effect on an organization's health and productivity.

Stories are a way for us to foster these sorts of connections at an individual level. Learning what we value in our own individual narratives, the stories that we tell about ourselves, can help us to understand and empathize better with others. In this chapter, we'll discuss some of these narrative elements and how they relate to the overarching cultural context of devops. We'll also see how these individual stories can add up to impact organizational health and how you can work toward creating healthy cultural systems rather than unhealthy ones.

Individual Stories and Narratives around Work

Some people shy away from getting too personal (or interpersonal) in the workplace, saying things like "I only care about the work" or valuing technical skills more highly than anything else. But unless you are a one-person organization creating software only for yourself, you work with other people and you create software for other people; the interpersonal aspects of work cannot be erased from the equation.

In this chapter, we'll examine various ways in which individual stories can play out in the workplace and the impact that they can have on organizational culture, and vice versa. From when people join an organization to how they end up leaving it, these narrative aspects are a key part of an organization's culture and how healthy it is for the people working in it.

Taylorism and the Value of Individual Stories

In the late 19th century, an American mechanical engineer named Frederick Winslow Taylor began putting together his theories on management as it pertained to improving workflows and thus economic efficiency and productivity. His original goal was to improve manufacturing operational efficiency by applying the scientific method to the development of manufacturing processes. While he did have several ideas that are still important in many industries today, such as the reduction of waste and the standardization of best practices, one big part of Taylorism that has with good reason fallen out of favor is his low regard for most individual workers in his systems of work:

> The man who is [...] physically able to handle pig-iron and is sufficiently phlegmatic and stupid to choose this for his occupation is rarely able to comprehend the science of handling pig-iron.

Taylor espoused the idea "that there is a difference between the average and the first class man [...] that the first class man can do in most cases from two to four times as much is known to few." In essence, the Taylorist view holds that the majority of individual workers were incapable of improving their working methods at all, despite the fact that these workers were the most familiar with the details of the methods and processes they used.

He believed that improvements could only be conceived of by specialists who were "above" those workers. It ignores the value that the individuals bring, the emotions and behaviors that impact the systems they manage. Compare this with the theories of Lean and the Toyota Production System, where workers on the manufacturing lines were assumed to have deep knowledge of their systems and encouraged to come up with ways to improve their processes.

Considering individual strengths and opinions, and letting the people most familiar with the work recommend ways to improve it, has long been one of the foundations of most successful devops environments. Indeed, the movement originally started with workers who noticed flaws in their processes—namely, silos causing lack of collaboration and communication between developers and operators—and started thinking of ways to change how they worked to improve these processes.

Hollie Kay on Devops

Devops is one of the most game-changing things to have come out of the shakeups in tech over the last few years, and the best thing about it for me is that it blows right through the partisan, divisive culture that can spring up between isolated dev and sysadmin departments. I'm all over bringing different types of good techs together and narrowing the gaps between them.

The question of whether tools or culture is more important to the concept of devops is one that has been around nearly as long as the term itself. As we have explained throughout this book, we strongly believe that culture—with its effects on how people work, why they work, how they interact when working together, and how they make decisions related to work, *including* which tools and technologies are used and how— is more encompassing of the essence of the movement.

Culture is obviously strongly tied to people; the same tools and policies being used by a different group of people with different goals, working styles, and interpretations can result in a very different culture or work environment. Were it not for the fact that the work we're discussing is done by people, ultimately for other people, these types of conversations would not be happening. Therefore, it is important to consider how people work, how they think, and what motivates them, as we discussed in Part II.

Culture is also very strongly tied with values, both at an individual and an organizational level. Recognizing the importance of individuals, respecting their expertise around their own areas of work, and letting people shape both their own narratives and influence those of their team and organization are key values of a healthy and effective devops culture. In these next sections, we'll look at how values can manifest themselves both implicitly and explicitly.

Celebrating Individuals

Which individuals are the most celebrated can say a lot about a team or company's values. One way that this manifests itself is when new hires are celebrated. Oftentimes, the hires that are celebrated most are the high-profile individuals, well-known "rock stars" in the industry that may have been poached at great expense from another company. This can send a message, albeit usually unintentionally, that these high-profile people are more important than anyone else and that their "poaching" is worth more than retaining existing employees. If it feels like the signing bonus and salary for a new "rock star" are taking away from the budget for raises, bonuses, or anything else that would benefit existing employees, resentment and attrition can quickly grow.

More senior roles are often celebrated more as well, and with biases both conscious and unconscious leading to companies that get more and more homogeneous as you get higher up, this means that a narrower group of individuals is being more visibly celebrated. While nobody wants to be called out or celebrated because of what group memberships they have (anyone who has been called out with, "Hooray, we finally hired *a woman*," as if that's her only characteristic worth mentioning, can attest to this), it is important to celebrate the less visible and more junior hires as well, to show them that they are valued and welcomed in your organization.

When people join an organization, they are joining an established community. How we welcome people to our communities can reveal a great deal about the health of those communities. We spoke with Nicole Johnson, an enterprise field solutions architect for Chef working out of New York, who has spent the past eight years specializing in varying areas of infrastructure virtualization, cloud computing, operations, and automation, about her feelings on devops and its community.

Nicole Johnson, Enterprise Field Solutions Architect

It is important that we recognize the power of devops, not just for established practitioners and community members, but that we continue to be welcoming to new devops community members, regardless of background or industry. We are seeing large enterprises—traditional industries, such as banking and manufacturing—benefit from the power of devops. It's not just about *automating all of the things*, but it's about embracing a way of working throughout an organization that empowers and embraces each member as a valuable and important part of that team. Recognizing that effective collaboration is not necessarily a function of tools, but embracing the culture of devops, breaking down silos within that organization, and eventually leveraging opportunities to collaborate in other places.

Having made the journey from a more traditional area of technology to an organization that embodies devops at Chef, it is very clear to me that wholeheartedly embracing this way of working allows the right environment for a meaningful and sustainable transformation. I have worked with many organizations whose primary roadblocks were not technical, but organizational—primarily founded in their siloed approach. Breaking down those barriers is a crucial step in moving forward with an IT and organizational transformation.

I have had significant focus on automation of systems deployment, application deployment, and testing for a number of years, and in my experience, devops is what has helped many organizations complete that last mile of automation. The reason that they have fallen short is typically not because of a technical roadblock, but because of siloed operations and lack of collaboration.

As a new member of the devops community, that made it immediately apparent to me that devops is one of the primary factors that has enabled organizations to succeed in transforming the way that they do business through a commitment to a collaborative culture, and a combination of utilizing infrastructure as code, automation, and continuous delivery. What I have quickly learned since is that there is so much more to devops, and I am grateful that the community has been so welcoming.

A person's first experience with a community, whether that be an organization full of new colleagues, a conference that they've never attended before, or the community of devops practitioners worldwide, can have a lasting impact on how they view that community and whether or not they end up considering themselves a part of it.

 It is important to keep that in mind when we, as more established members of the groups we are a part of, encounter and interact with new members. It is one thing to say that we value diverse perspectives, and another thing to treat people respectfully when we disagree with their ideas—another example of implicit values in action.

Promotions

Another area where values can be readily seen is that of promotions within an organization. Which promotions get announced, and how widely, can be another way that a culture implicitly shows its values, especially if there are inequities in this process as well. If announcements are left entirely up to managers' discretion, biases can again come into play, conscious or not, which can lead to the situation of men's successes getting more visibility than women's, or one team getting more recognition than the rest of the organization. These sorts of situations breed resentment from individuals or teams who feel that their contributions are less valued.

Feeling appreciated is one of the key factors that predicts job satisfaction, so doing something like setting a standard policy for how promotions are announced can go a long way toward making people feel like they are being treated fairly. This policy could be as simple as guidelines such as, "Promotions to level X get announced at an individual's team's next weekly meeting, while promotions to level Y get announced at the next department-wide meeting."

Creating standards and policies for the way that career growth is handled throughout an organization can help to level a playing field that has historically been rather imbalanced, as well as help foster a culture of fairness and appreciation throughout the organization.

Going Remote

With ever-climbing costs of living in big tech areas like San Francisco and New York, more and more people are looking to live in places that are less crowded and more affordable. Whether they are spouses looking to raise a family in a more suburban area or single people who are simply tired of spending so much of their income on rent, there are many valid reasons why people would want to work remotely, and with high-speed internet connections being nearly ubiquitous and video conferencing software advancing as it has, there are fewer and fewer technical reasons to not allow remote work for positions where it makes sense. (A role that involves something like testing a variety of hardware might not lend itself well to remote work if the hardware is too large to reasonably ship or if there is a lab it has to be tested in, and a data center technician has to be reasonably close to the data center, but most software-centric roles could be done remotely without issue.)

One objection heard fairly frequently from managers who are new to remote work is, "How do I know someone is working if I can't walk by their desk and see them working?" The visibility of the work that people do is an interesting idea, but as it turns out, managers cannot tell the difference between people who work 80 hours a week and people who merely pretend to.

 Pretending to do work is something that can happen in the office just as easily as remotely, so if you are concerned about how much work will get done, consider addressing these concerns in other ways, such as during the interview process, rather than forcing everyone to work from an often-expensive office.

While remote work does have its own unique challenges around how to allow for collaboration, communication, and visibility of work, an organization that refuses to allow employees to work remotely even for positions that could handle it is saying quite a bit about its values. Often this is an implicit value judgment rather than an explicit one. This kind of culture often tends to keep processes around "because that's how it's always been done" even if those processes could be improved. Disallowing remote work reflects a culture that values the appearance of doing work more than the effectiveness of the actual work. Metrics such as number of hours spent in the office or number of lines of code written are not good indicators of work quality.

How an organization reacts to an individual wanting to change teams or locations can indicate a lot about organizational health and flexibility. If a company is measuring the wrong metrics, such as focusing on how many hours each person is in the office rather than the quality of their work or if they are meeting their deadlines, they are likely to see a decrease in actual work output as well as employee satisfaction. As we discussed in Part II, there are numerous benefits to having a variety of working styles collaborating as part of a team or project. Forcing everyone to work the same way in terms of when and where they work stifles these differences in working styles, rather than embracing them and learning from them.

Finally, consider how changes such as moving between teams are communicated throughout the organization. How much transparency is encouraged or even allowed says a lot about a company's transparency in practice, regardless of what it might say it values in theory. Are individuals allowed to communicate openly about the fact that they want to change teams or move locations? Do their immediate colleagues know about these potential changes, or are they kept in the dark until the change happens? Who communicates these changes to the rest of the department or organization—the individual who made the move, their manager, or nobody?

Leaving a Company

An individual leaving a company is another area where how a change is communicated can have a big impact on the surrounding people and teams. One of the first things to note is how much notice people are expected to give, not just to HR or their manager, but also to the people they work most closely with. Depending on the scope of the person's responsibilities, they might have considerable amounts of both work and knowledge that need to be transferred to others. Again, this can say a lot about what is valued within an organization: is it the appearance of "being a team player," or is it transparently sharing knowledge so team members can be more effective?

Some organizations strongly discourage people from sharing the news of their impending departure because they believe that news would be bad for the rest of the team's morale, but we would argue strongly against this practice. People leave companies: this is a simple fact and something that everyone with any work experience at all understands. Not letting people communicate that they are leaving significantly limits how much work and knowledge can be effectively transferred, removes the chance for other people to ask questions about the work being transferred, and can have more of a negative impact on morale because of the secrecy. Keeping the simple fact that someone is leaving a secret does not engender a culture of trust; people will start to wonder what else is going on that is being hidden from them.

Again, the amount of transparency that people are allowed to have about their choices and the reasons behind them tends to fall in line with organizational transparency as a whole. More transparency tends to encourage more trust in the organization and vice versa. There is likely to be some difference in how departures are handled if someone leaves voluntarily versus if they are fired or asked to leave, but the amount and method of communication can demonstrate a culture of trust and honesty, or one of their absence.

Why people leave organizations

Keeping track of why people are leaving can be a valuable source of information about potential problem areas in an organization, assuming that people are able and willing to talk honestly about their reasons. Unfortunately, the situations where an organization would benefit most from understanding the reasons are the ones where reasons are less likely to be freely given. If someone felt unsafe or harassed and wasn't able to get any resolution to that situation, they are unlikely to feel safe explaining that situation during an exit interview. Or, if someone was repeatedly trying to improve broken processes or fix cultural issues but never made any headway, they might feel that re-explaining their issues would have no point and no chance of changing anything.

However, there are a few common reasons why people frequently leave organizations that merit some consideration, as they reflect on the organizational culture as a whole, rather than being solely individual reasons:

Not respecting people's time

Not respecting employees' time in the office is bad enough, but expecting that they dedicate their time outside of the office to work is a sure way to start losing people who have any kind of external interests or responsibilities. People who have outside interests and who are able to take breaks, disconnect, and recharge are often more focused and productive when they are at work, and additionally, a culture that favors people without any nonwork responsibilities tends to quickly become a homogeneous one of young, single, heterosexual men. We would argue that companies should not expect people to be working or even checking email outside working hours (dire circumstances and on-call rotations being the exception) in the first place, but if those are requirements, they should be explicitly stated with reasons given up front, in the job description, so people at least have an honest understanding of the job they are taking. Not doing so is asking for burnout and attrition.

Not respecting people

If people do not feel respected by their peers, their manager, or their organization, they are not likely to stick around for long if they have any other options. It is commonly said that people don't leave jobs, they leave managers, but more often than not, what this means is that people leave when they feel that their manager doesn't respect them or trust them, rather than leaving because of simple disagreements or personality clashes. If someone was hired to do a certain job but is micromanaged to the point of not being able to do it, they are likely to feel that their skills would be better appreciated elsewhere. The same thing goes for feeling that a manager will not go to bat for them or advocate for their career advancement in any way.

Not earning trust in return

Trust in any relationship has to go both ways. Organizations, especially startups, often ask a lot from their employees, whether that be working longer hours than originally agreed on, working on a project that doesn't interest them because it is important to the business, or even taking a pay cut during tough financial times. This often involves personal risk, especially for employees who are members of marginalized groups, and that risk requires trust that, like any trust, has to be earned. If people feel that the company is not going in a direction or under leadership that merits that kind of trust, they will often go somewhere else that does.

Even if people don't come forward explicitly with these reasons, you can look for patterns such as multiple or frequent departures from people working under a certain manager, a culture where many people end up working nights and weekends even if that is not "officially" required of them (remember that implicit expectations can have a noticeable effect, especially on less experienced employees or those who feel the need to prove themselves more), or departures that happen during or after some significant changes in organizational leadership or direction. These can be signs of a community that is not as aligned with its members as it perhaps ought to be.

Cultural Debt

While technical debt refers to the eventual consequences of technical decisions, such as system design, software architecture, software development, or technology choices, *cultural debt* is the term used to describe the eventual consequences of cultural decisions, including hiring and firing decisions, what community standards are created and enforced, organizational hierarchy, and values.

The same ideas around technical debt apply to cultural debt as well, namely that it will need to be repaid at some point and that the longer one goes without addressing the issues surrounding it, the more interest accumulates and the harder it will be to get out of debt in the future.

Examples of cultural debt include:

- Hiring an engineer who is known to be incredibly difficult to work with (or to be a serial harasser or someone who always gets way too drunk at company events) and requiring other people to work around him or quit rather than asking him to leave or change his problematic behaviors

- Too many layers of middle management causing unnecessary processes or slowing down cycle time and being unwilling to restructure or reduce headcount at all

- A conference or community event known for not having or enforcing a code of conduct such that it has become known as an unsafe space for members of underrepresented groups in that community, yet bad actors are continued to allowed to attend (or even still invited to speak) at the expense of other people's safety, perhaps because of how well known they are in the community

- Mailing lists where abusive language is allowed or even encouraged, making it less likely that new members will join and contribute to the list

- An organization where there has developed a vicious cycle of being always working and always available, where people do things like send emails late at night knowing that other people will also be working and likely provide a quick response, and where nobody wants to be the first one to work less and give the appearance of not being a team player

When considering the health of your organization, it is important to consider cultural debt as well as technical debt if you are trying to improve the organization's effectiveness overall.

This sort of situation is not one where there are any reasonable immediate or short-term fixes; you cannot force people to tell you the truth about why they are leaving a position, especially if there are trust or safety issues involved. You can, however, keep an eye out for other indicators of cultural issues, as well as continuing to foster a culture of safety, inclusivity, blamelessness, and trust.

The Health of Systems

When people consider the health of an organization or company, the first thing that comes to mind is often financial health. How much profit and revenue are there? How does year-over-year growth look? How is market share or customer acquisition doing? Sometimes organizations or teams might look at things like hiring rates or attrition rates, but often those are considered to be much less important, especially if things are going well enough financially.

As we've discussed previously in this book, problems like burnout need to be taken seriously, as they impact not only team and organizational morale and productivity but also the health of the very people that create our organizations and our industry. It is important that we analyze not just individual factors that can affect burnout and health, but systemic factors as well. For both managers who are trying to make a positive difference to individual and organizational well-being and individuals looking to take their career in a healthier and more balanced direction, it is necessary to be able to identify health factors within a system or organization.

Unfortunately, this sort of information can be hard to come by, especially for an organization you aren't currently a part of. People don't often discuss issues like stress, burnout, anxiety, and other health concerns as they relate to work for a variety of reasons: they don't want to be seen as weak or not a team player, they don't want to discuss something so personal in a professional context (despite how much overlap there often is in reality), or they don't even know that their issues are shared by others and worth discussing. In an interview or a hiring webpage where a company is trying to sell itself to potential employees, it is unlikely to mention high attrition rates, the number of employees who have burnt out, or any other "negative" aspects of their culture. How are we to find out how healthy an organization really is?

Examining Sick Systems

In 2010, a blogger and student of forensic anthropology and psychology who goes by the screen name Issendai wrote an article describing what they refer to as *sick systems*, dysfunctional or unhealthy relationships—either personal or professional—that keep people in them despite being unhealthy or negative. The four qualities or rules for a sick system are described as follows (here in the context of a workplace environment):

Keep people too busy to think

If people in a workplace are too busy to spend much time thinking about things, they will be less likely to realize how negative or unhealthy their environment is. This can be expanded to include keeping people too busy to talk to each other, discouraging taking breaks at water coolers or coffee stations because that is "wasting time," and discouraging interaction with people outside the organization. This last one might come with reasoning along the lines of "company loyalty," but discouraging people from looking outward at all, whether it be for solutions to technical problems or for social ones, is usually not a good sign.

Keep people tired

Similar to keeping people busy, keeping people tired can also keep them from thinking too hard about the way things are going. This does not just mean physically tired, but mentally and emotionally exhausted as well. If someone is too busy putting out fires all day and is the only one on-call all night, they are very unlikely to have the physical or emotional energy to try to add some automation or fix some subpar processes, let alone try to overhaul the way on-call is handled or look for another job. We have noted throughout this book that significant, lasting change requires effort and will not happen overnight, so it follows that if people do not have the energy required to sustain change and form new habits, things are likely to remain as they are. Being tired in a work context could also mean someone who has given up or is close to burning out, who has decided (correctly or not) that nothing is going to change any time soon and is only working for a paycheck, not out of any intrinsic motivation. More people working in this state adds to organizational inertia and makes the whole organization more tired.

Keep people emotionally involved

The more emotionally involved people are, the more likely they are to stick with something. This is especially true if their sense of self-worth is tied to the success of their team, product, or the organization as a whole. It is quite common to see rather extreme loyalty being intentionally fostered at early-stage startups, where passion for the product or company is supposed to motivate people to forgo work-life balance, a competitive salary, a real vacation policy, and so on. Encouraging conformity within the organization as well as an individual identity that is closely tied to the group can get and keep people emotionally attached. Organizations might accomplish this by providing so much free branded apparel to employees that their wardrobes consist mostly of items with the company's logo; by providing breakfast, dinner, dry-cleaning, or other perks designed to keep employees in the office longer and longer; or by making decisions at "optional" post-work social events so that anyone who decides to skip those events has less say in what goes on in their group. The idea of "golden handcuffs," or deferred benefits such as stock options that vest over a period of years to discourage people from leaving the organization, are another way of keeping people involved and invested.

Reward people intermittently

The allure of intermittent rewards is something that has been studied extensively in psychology, with a well-known example being that rats who receive a food pellet every single time they press a lever will press it only when they are hungry, while rats who get a food pellet only intermittently will press the lever more often, as they don't know when they will be able to eat next. While our minds are undoubtedly much more complex than those of rats, the same principles can be applied to humans as well. Video games and gambling exploit this quite well. In a workplace, this might involve managers who are very inconsistent with what feedback, if any, they give to their reports, or a system of raises, promotions, and bonuses that is not at all transparent.

What does this look like overall? This might be an organization that seems to thrive on crisis, where people are always working reactively rather than proactively, always too busy fighting the next fire to ever get ahead of anything and make any significant progress toward paying down any of their technical debt. All that firefighting might require people to always be checking and replying to emails, chat messages, and pull requests from their phones, even on evenings and weekends, and not just during rare short-term crunch periods. This might look like an organization full of employees that are so busy, so burnt out, or so attached to the company that they have few to no hobbies, interests, or commitments outside of the office.

Some of these examples might sound to some people like they are somewhat extreme or even contrived, but they are unfortunately all too common in various parts of the tech industry these days. If you haven't seen or heard of a single example of cultural debt or an unhealthy system, make sure that you are working as much as possible to create an environment where people feel safe enough to raise concerns they might have.

Creating Healthy Systems

a When we are able to identify these qualities that can keep people in a sick system, working for an organization that doesn't have the best interests of its employees at heart, we can then turn these attributes around to identify what would make an organization a *healthy system*. These qualities can then be described thusly:

Create time to think and reflect

Moving beyond simply allowing people time to think, a healthy system should actively encourage it. This might mean requiring (or strongly encouraging) managers to schedule regular one-on-one meetings with all of their reports, creating spaces in the office designed for people to work and socialize together, or setting up a program for matching people in either a formal mentorship capacity or an informal social one so that thoughts and ideas can be shared. People should feel comfortable thinking about different solutions to problems or different ways that people can work together. Ideally, this sort of work environment will be blameless so that experimentation is allowed but doesn't lead to people being thrown under the bus. Managers can encourage even more reflection and consideration by doing things like having CEO office hours, where anyone in the organization can talk to or ask questions of company executives, having communication go both ways rather than being a top-down, one-way affair.

Encourage people to rest and recharge

As much as possible, encourage people to think about how much work they can do realistically and to not try to take on more. This kind of change will need to be led from the top down, by example, as people will tend to mirror the actions of their managers or leaders even if those leaders' words say something different. Make working nights and hours be the exception, not the rule, and if it starts becoming a regular occurrence, proactively fix your planning processes until you are not regularly planning to do more than you are able to fulfill during normal business hours. Make efforts to pay down both technical and cultural debt, even if that means taking some time away from "regular" work in the short term in order to make tools or processes better in the long term. Don't keep people on a treadmill of always working reactively because there is never time to work proactively. Actively seek out and listen to solutions from people who are in the thick of things, and give them enough authority, time, and resources to work on activities that will benefit them in their day-to-day work as well as supporting the organization's goals.

Encourage involvements outside of work

Similar to encouraging people to be well rested and work proactively rather than reactively, a healthy system will encourage people to foster and develop interests, hobbies, and even commitments outside of work, realizing that this makes them happier and more well-rounded, which will in turn help them be more productive. Prioritize quality of work over quantity of hours in the office. Don't require people to invest all of their time, emotional energy, or especially identity into your organization or product, but rather cultivate a diversity of experiences and interests. Make sure that people are spending time out of the office, perhaps implementing a minimum vacation policy and again leading by example, having managers and executives visibly taking time out of the office (and disconnecting) as well. Make sure resources are available to help employees struggling with stress, anxiety or other mental health issues, and burnout.

Reward people fairly and regularly

While it is true that intrinsic motivators can be a great deal more powerful than extrinsic ones, the reality is that people have rent to pay and often families to support, and people deserve to be fairly compensated for their time and effort. Make sure that all managers throughout your organization are using the same procedures, time frames, and guidelines to review compensation so that people under different managers don't end up being treated wildly differently when it comes to raises and bonuses. Organizations should make sure that they have standardized pay bands that are being used consistently, and regularly evaluate compensation to make sure everyone falls within the appropriate bands. Keep in mind that unconscious bias is a real thing and that women are often socialized to not negotiate and are treated differently when they do. Make sure that your recruiters and hiring managers are not using this to "save money" by offering significantly lower salaries to members of marginalized or underrepresented groups. Whatever your policies around raises and bonuses end up being, you can lower employees' stress by clearly and publicly documenting those policies, rather than keeping people guessing.

People who are evaluating organizations, such as those choosing between different job offers or just deciding whether they want to stay at their current job at all, can look at these four attributes and see where organizations fall on the spectrum between healthy and unhealthy. It is unlikely that any organization will fall entirely to one extreme or the other, but you can certainly figure out which aspects are most important to you and prioritize or evaluate accordingly.

Organizational and Individual Health

Even in systems that are not quite as unhealthy as the sick systems described earlier, there are other ways in which systemic or organizational factors can prove to be unhealthy for individuals. One key example of this is found when we examine diversity and inclusivity in our workplaces. Research has shown that women working in male-dominated environments, such as those found in nearly every engineering organization these days, display physiological signs of stress nearly constantly (in addition to dealing with harassment, microaggressions, or any other forms of gender bias).

This stress can have noticeable and lasting impacts on health. Women who work in environments that are over 85 percent male (again, unfortunately, like most engineering departments) show ongoing disregulated cortisol patterns. Cortisol is a stress hormone that appears at varying levels over time, both short-term and long-term, but for these "lone" or "token" women, their cortisol levels and patterns are much higher than those with regular daily stress patterns. Over time, women's bodies become used to this chronic, stressed-out, "fight or flight" mode of existing, and it can take years after leaving such a workplace for a more diverse one for their cortisol level to re-regulate and return to normal.

Cortisol at high levels can have very negative impacts on physical and emotional health, causing or contributing to problems such as a weakened immune system, decreased thyroid function, and even the breakdown of bone, muscle, and connective tissue in small amounts. While the research done so far has focused only on gender differences, it stands to reason that anyone in a position of feeling like a "token" indi-vidual, being the only one or one of a few people like themselves and dealing with stereotype threat, would face these same health-impacting consequences of that stress. People of color and LGBTQ individuals almost certainly have to deal with these sorts of issues as well.

Other stress- and health-related issues in an organization can be amplified by a lack of work–life balance. Studies have shown that high-pressure, always-on environments tend to amplify the effects of sexism, racism, ageism, and other forms of biases. These sorts of organizations tend to be focused most highly on the number of hours that people are in the office, which tends to negatively impact people—most often women and older employees—who have caregiving responsibilities outside of work.

Environments where people are expected to routinely work long hours also tend to favor people who will not question the status quo, whether that be the amount of time people are expected to work or the inclusivity of the overall environment. Not only are they bad for long-term productivity and health, but these types of high-pressure, long-hours environments can add further stresses for people who don't fit the stereo-type of a hoodie-wearing engineer who looks a lot like Mark Zuckerberg.

One common misconception around hiring "devops engineers" is that you will be able to hire one person with the skills of two differ-ent roles, someone who can be a full-time developer and a full-time operations engineer, but without the cost of hiring two separate people for that. This is neither accurate nor realistic, nor would it be sustainable even if it were true. Trying to get one person to do the work of two people will lead to lower-quality work and burnout in the long term, as well as earning your organization a reputation for treating employees poorly.

One problem with these sorts of issues is that they are often subtle, worsening in impact and intensity over time and being difficult to identify, both externally and internally. In sick systems, gaslighting frequently causes people to doubt their own perceptions and feelings about their experiences, leading them to think that they are overreacting or imagining things when in fact they are doing neither. In such situa-tions, it can be difficult to identify how negative an environment is. Additionally, long-term stress and acclimation to cortisol and other stress hormones make such an environment feel normal when it ought not to be.

Identifying Healthy and Unhealthy Cultures

How can you identify a sick system or unhealthy work environment before you join it? Or, if it is an environment that worsens over time, how can you notice this and determine when it is time to leave? In addition to the qualities of "healthy systems" described earlier, keep an eye out for the following, whether in an environment you are currently in or in questions you might ask during an interview process:

How do decisions get made?

Does the process for making a decision vary based on the estimated impact that choice will have, or do even the smallest choices require a laborious approval process? How much authority do engineers (or any individual contributors) have to make decisions during their normal, day-to-day work? Are more junior team members given the leeway to experiment, to make their own choices and deal with the consequences as part of their learning process? For larger decisions, is a consensus required from all impacted parties? Do some people seem to not be held to the same processes as others? Who has decision-making power in an organization can say quite a lot about its culture and how easy it is to effect change within the organization.

What does a typical release cycle look like?

In addition to more straightforward questions such as whether or not there are automated tests and generally how often a release happens, release cycles can show a great level of detail about cycle time and lead time, as introduced in Part III. As the saying goes, "don't let the perfect become the enemy of the good," meaning that trying to get something to some definition of "perfect" or always wanting to add "just one more thing" can prevent you from releasing something that is good enough in a timely manner. A team or organization too focused on "perfect" is likely to find itself iterating too slowly to gain or maintain customers —though there are plenty of other reasons cycle speed might be too slow as well.

What does a ticket's lifecycle look like?

Who creates tickets when there is ticket-sized work that needs to be done? How do tickets get assigned: does the person creating the ticket choose someone to assign it to, or do people on a given team or project pull tickets out of some sort of receiving queue, or is there one person per project who reviews and assigns tickets, or some combination of the above? How do tickets get prioritized, and how consistent is the prioritization across varying individuals and projects? How often do tickets get due dates assigned to them? Watch out for places where everything has an urgent due date or nothing has one at all, as this can indicate issues with being able to prioritize work well.

How much risk is too much risk?

Similar to looking at how decisions get made, how an organization or team responds to risk can say a lot about it. When risks are taken, what areas do they tend to be in? Are they risks around using a new tool or technology, or around whether or not customers want or need a new feature idea? Are some people given more freedom to take risks than others—is a startup CTO allowed to rewrite large parts of the product as part of a pet project he had because nobody can stand up to or question him, while the rest of his organization has processes and rules that they are required to follow? Any sort of "cowboy developers" that don't have to play by the same rules as everyone else can be problematic for a team or organization.

The relative health or sickness of a system is an important area for consideration when either evaluating job offers or debating whether or not to stay in a given organization. If all else were equal, the healthier environment would easily be the one to choose, but not only are organizations rarely so evenly matched in all factors, but it can be very difficult to tell from the outside (or even an interview) what a culture's health will be like. If you have the ability to talk frankly with people who currently do or recently have worked at an organization, that can provide valuable insight into what you might expect there.

Summary

How we interact as individuals with each other and with our organization is a large part of how organizational culture is created and maintained. The stories and narratives we tell about our own work can help us to recognize those same narratives in other people, growing empathy and strengthening connections.

We've discussed the ideas of both *technical debt* and *cultural debt*, the lasting consequences of past decisions on technology and culture, respectively. Both are relatively easy to come by and relatively hard to shake once they are there. Similarly, bad habits —such as treating everything as a crisis or replying to emails all night, every night— are hard to break. While individuals and their stories can have significant impacts on the organizations they are part of, keep in mind that as an individual, your first responsibility should be taking care of your individual health, not that of your organization.

As you continue along your own devops journey, it is important to keep in mind how valuable sharing stories can be. Pay attention to what your stories say about your culture and its values, both explicit and implicit; how effective you are at connecting with and learning from other individuals, teams, and organizations; and how both technical and cultural debt can impact the health of your organizations and the people in them.

CHAPTER 19

Conclusion

You made it all the way to the end of this book—congratulations, and thank you for reading! We covered a great deal in this book, sharing a variety of stories from a range of individuals and organizations. It is possible that you will not have the time to change every single thing you might want to, or that not every aspect of what we describe as an effective devops culture will be relevant to your current situation. Remember that there is no one-size-fits-all solution. It is important for you, either individually or with others, to identify your most pressing concerns that need to be prioritized now, the changes that can be delayed until some later date, and those that don't currently matter to you at all.

We've shown you that there is no prescription for the One True Way of doing devops, devops in a box, or devops-as-a-service. We've shared ideas and approaches for improving individual collaboration, team and organizational affinity, and tool usage throughout an organization, and how these concepts allow organizations to change, adapt, and pivot as necessary. You have learned how these common themes can be applied in different ways to every organization that wants to improve both the quality of their products and the efficiency and well-being of their employees.

These principles apply regardless of what language you're programming in, what tools you use to manage your infrastructure, or whether or not you're using the latest, shiniest container technology. If you have a strong understanding of how the four pillars of effective devops can work together to maximize shared goals, promote shared understanding, and develop healthy sustainable workplace values and practices, you will be well on your way to creating a culture that will last much longer than any one tool or trend. Developing this understanding of how people work together and how to maintain and repair these working relationships is what has given devops its staying power.

Devops is not something that belongs solely to web companies or small startups, nor is it something that applies only to development and operations teams. More than just a sea change around software development practices, the principles and ideas found in the four pillars touch all parts of an organization, and can be used even by large enterprises or government agencies. There are many ways that these theories can be put into practice, and it's important to not focus so much on other people's stories that you lose sight of your own.

Recall that no matter what the specifics of your organization's culture or journey look like, the end goal is not to have some fixed number of deploys per day, to use a specific open source tool, or to do things simply because other organizations have been successful doing them. The end goal is to create and maintain a successful organization that solves a problem for your customers. Take the time to proactively define these goals and the values and ideas that you want to help you get there, regardless of your industry or size. Don't wait until you find that your implicit values have been defined for you and it feels too late to change them.

Your Next Steps

You most likely started this book hoping to gain some guidance and insight into making effective cultural and technical changes within your own organization. So what should you do next?

Check out the materials listed in the Chapter 20 list. This section contains a variety of books, articles, and videos that we found useful or interesting, reference material that was cited earlier in this book, and links to texts that we imagine will be helpful to anyone interested in devops or other cultural changes.

Start prioritizing what you see as the biggest issues that you would like to make progress on, in your organization, on your team, or in your own work habits. Depending on where you are coming from, it might seem like there are so many changes you want to make that it's hard to see where to start, so ask yourself what you find the most frustrating in your everyday work, where you see yourself or your colleagues spending a lot of unnecessary time or energy, and what you think could help make you immediately more effective in your work.

Share your perspectives with your team and organization. Find common ground and alignment, and work together to effect change within your organization. Whether you're an individual aspiring to be a critical change agent, or executive within your company, you can and will have impact.

Examine which changes can be done individually, which are collaborative within teams, and which need to be addressed at an organizational level. One thing to keep in mind throughout this process is that you need to be adaptable and open to change. It's human nature to be at least somewhat change-averse, but spending too much time in situations where all change only seems to be for the worse can exacerbate this tendency to an unproductive degree.

Keep an eye out for learned habits and thought processes that can inhibit effective growth and change. As you work to prioritize what your most pressing issues are, you should start to understand where any unhappiness or frustration you have at work are coming from. In addition to suboptimal tools or processes, you might find learned helplessness, learned expectations (either self-imposed or based on others' expectations of who you are), or learned role adherence, any of which can prevent forward movement. Remember to avoid the trap of "but we've always done things this way"!

If you are in a leadership role within your organization, you have the added responsibility of helping firmly establish the culture your organization will have going forward. Remember that the devops compact relies on a *shared understanding*—as a leader, it is up to you to help establish this shared understanding within your organization, to define what "doing devops" successfully means to you. Remember that your culture has values regardless of whether they are explicitly or implicitly stated—but explicitly stated ones are much easier to reason about, discuss, and change.

While it does require top-level support, lasting change cannot come only in the form of a top-down mandate. Changes that impact an entire organization need to have buy-in throughout, which means that leaders need to help develop a collective voice, finding effective ways for individual voices to be heard without getting in the way of decisions being made. This also means creating an environment of strong support and low hostility, where people are not afraid to ask questions, to try new things, or to speak up about things that aren't working.

Finally, be sure to reread chapters of this book as you need them, or even reread the whole thing in six months to a year, in order to get fresh perspectives and reevaluate progress as your teams and organizations are changing.

Creating Effective Devops

Devops is not just an item on a checklist. While you can certainly prioritize and accomplish specific changes within your organization, devops is not something you are ever truly *done* with. Instead, it is an ongoing and iterative process. Shared understanding must be continually maintained and renewed, or else it will not remain shared for long.

Devops is also not something that you can accomplish solely by creating or renaming a team, changing some job titles to have "devops" in them, or buying the latest and greatest containerized platform cloud synergies as a service. You cannot buy or install devops, and it doesn't require (nor is it precluded by) any particular tool or technology. It is not something that is relevant only to developers and ops teams, or even only to engineers, and it isn't something you can accomplish by passing responsibility for it onto someone else.

Instead, devops is about understanding, empathy, and interconnectedness, and while you can prioritize and focus on different aspects of it or different chapters of this book at a time, its strength really comes from the interplay of all four pillars together. Combined, these pillars form and strengthen the foundation of an ongoing culture with sustainable workplace practices and cultivated relationships between people.

Devops is about encouraging every member of the organization to contribute to provide value to the whole. As with an orchestra, it takes practice, communication, and coordination and doesn't idolize a couple of "rock stars."

Devops is about invitations to be involved in the ongoing change process, gratitude for wins that occur in every team within the organization, and explicit rejection of bullying behaviors. As with a garden, it takes continued feeding, watering, and weeding to nurture the organization toward sustainable growth and business success. And just as buying a bouquet of precut flowers cannot be considered gardening, simply buying a tool that claims to be a "devops solution" cannot be considered devops. It is the ongoing work to build *and maintain* a culture that makes devops truly effective.

With an ongoing shared understanding of the four pillars of *Effective DevOps*, we can all work to transform our organizations and the industry itself to be more productive, sustaining, and valuing. Please share your stories on our website, *effectivedevops.net*, so that we collectively grow and learn as a community. Sparkle on.

CHAPTER 20

Further Resources

What Is Devops?

- Apache HTTP Server Project. "About The Apache HTTP Server Project—The Apache HTTP Server Project." *https://httpd.apache.org/ABOUT_APACHE.html.*

- ComputerHistory. "Jean Bartik and the ENIAC Women." Posted November 10, 2010. *http://bit.ly/bartik-eniac.*

- Dekker, Sidney. *The Field Guide to Understanding Human Error.* Farnham, UK: Ashgate Publishing, 2006.

- Dekker, Sidney, and Erik Hollnagel. "Human Factors and Folk Models." *Cognition, Technology & Work* 6, no. 2 (2004): 79–86.

- ENIAC Programmers Project. "ENIAC Programmers Project." *http://eniacprogrammers.org.*

- Humble, Jez. "Continuous Delivery vs Continuous Deployment." *http://continuousdelivery.com/2010/08/continuous-delivery-vs-continuous-deployment.*

- Humble, Jez, and Farley, David. *Continuous Delivery.* Upper Saddle River, NJ: Addison-Wesley, 2010.

- Poppendieck, Mary, and Thomas David Poppendieck. *Implementing Lean Software Development.* Upper Saddle River, NJ: Addison-Wesley, 2007.

- Walls, Mandi. *Building a DevOps Culture.* Sebastopol, CA: O'Reilly Media, 2013.

Collaboration: Individuals Working Together

- Friedman, Ron. "Schedule a 15-Minute Break Before You Burn Out." *Harvard Business Review*. August 4, 2014. *https://hbr.org/2014/08/schedule-a-15-minute-break-before-you-burn-out*.

- Greaves, Karen, and Samantha Laing. *Collaboration Games from the Growing Agile Toolbox*. Victoria, BC: Leanpub/Growing Agile, 2014.

- Gulati, Ranjay, Franz Wohlgezogen, and Pavel Zhelyazkov. "The Two Facets of Collaboration: Cooperation and Coordination in Strategic Alliances." *The Academy of Management Annals* 6, no. 1 (2012): 531–583.

- Heffernan, Margaret. "Why It's Time to Forget the Pecking Order at Work." TED-Women 2015, May 2015. *http://bit.ly/heffernan-pecking*.

- Hewlett, Sylvia Ann. "Sponsors Seen as Crucial for Women's Career Advancement." *New York Times*, April 13, 2013. *http://bit.ly/nyt-sponsorship*.

- O'Daniel, Michelle, and Alan H. Rosenstein. "Professional Communication and Team Collaboration." In *Patient Safety and Quality: An Evidence-Based Handbook for Nurses*, edited by Ronda G. Hughes. Rockville, MD: Agency for Healthcare Research and Quality, US Department of Health and Human Services, 2008. *http://bit.ly/comm-collab*.

- Popova, Maria. "Fixed vs. Growth: The Two Basic Mindsets That Shape Our Lives." BrainPickings.com, January 29, 2014. *http://bit.ly/fixed-vs-growth*.

- Preece, Jennifer. "Etiquette, Empathy and Trust in Communities of Practice: Stepping-Stones to Social Capital." *Journal of Computer Science* 10, no. 3 (2004).

- Schawbel, Dan. "Sylvia Ann Hewlett: Find a Sponsor Instead of a Mentor." Forbes.com, September 10, 2013. *http://bit.ly/hewlett-sponsor*.

- Silverman, Rachel Emma. "Yearly Reviews? Try Weekly." *Wall Street Journal*, September 6, 2011. *http://bit.ly/wsj-reviews*.

- Stone, Douglas, and Sheila Heen. *Thanks for the Feedback*. New York: Viking, 2014.

Affinity: From Individuals to Teams

- Fowler, Chad. "Your Most Important Skill: Empathy." ChadFowler.com, January 19, 2014. *http://bit.ly/fowler-empathy*.

- Granovetter, Mark S. "The Strength of Weak Ties." *American Journal of Sociology* 78, no. 6 (May 1973).

- Herting, Stephen R. "Trust Correlated with Innovation Adoption in Hospital Organizations." Paper presented for the American Society for Public Administration, National Conference, Phoenix, Arizona, March 8, 2002.

- Hewstone, Miles, Mark Rubin, and Hazel Willis. "Intergroup Bias." *Annual Review of Psychology* 53 (2002).

- Hunt, Vivian, Dennis Layton, and Sara Prince. "Why Diversity Matters." McKinsey.com, January 2015. *http://bit.ly/mckinsey-diversity*.

- Kohtamäki, Marko, Tauno Kekäle, and Riitta Viitala. "Trust and Innovation: From Spin-Off Idea to Stock Exchange." *Creativity and Innovation Management* 13, no. 2 (June 2004).

- Mind Tools Editorial Team. "The Greiner Curve: Understanding the Crises That Come with Growth." MindTools.com, N.d. *http://bit.ly/greiner-curve*.

- Schwartz, Katrina. "How Do You Teach Empathy? Harvard Pilots Game Simulation." KQED.org, May 9, 2013. *http://bit.ly/teach-empathy*.

- Sussna, Jeff. "Empathy: The Essence of Devops." Ingineering.IT, January 11, 2014. *http://bit.ly/sussna-empathy*.

Tools: Accelerators of Culture

- Allspaw, John. "A Mature Role for Automation: Part 1." KitchenSoap.com, September 21, 2012. *http://bit.ly/allspaw-automation*.

- Caum, Carl. "Continuous Delivery vs. Continuous Deployment: What's the Diff?" Puppet blog, August 30, 2013. *http://bit.ly/cd-vs-cd*.

- Coutinho, Rodrigo. "In Support of DevOps: Kanban vs. Scrum." DevOps.com, July 29, 2014. *http://bit.ly/kanban-v-scrum*.

- Cowie, Jon. *Customizing Chef*. Sebastopol, CA: O'Reilly Media, 2014.

- Dixon, Jason. *Monitoring with Graphite*. Sebastopol, CA.: O'Reilly Media, 2015.

- Forsgren, Nicole, and Jez Humble. "The Role of Continuous Delivery in IT and Organizational Performance." In the Proceedings of the Western Decision Sciences Institute (WDSI), Las Vegas, Nevada, October 27, 2015.

- Friedman, Ron. "Schedule a 15-Minute Break Before You Burn Out." *Harvard Business Review*. August 4, 2014. *http://bit.ly/hbr-breaks*.

- Humble, Jez. "Deployment pipeline anti-patterns." *http://bit.ly/humble-anti-patterns*.

- Kim, Gene. Kanbans and DevOps: Resource Guide for *The Phoenix Project* (Part 2)." IT Revolution Press, N.d. *http://bit.ly/kanbans-devops*.

- Konnikova, Maria. "The Open-Office Trap." *The New Yorker*, January 7, 2014. *http://bit.ly/open-office-trap*.

- Ōno, Taiichi. *Toyota Production System*. Cambridge, MA: Productivity Press, 1988.

- Rembetsy, Michael, and Patrick McDonnell. "Continuously Deploying Culture." Etsy presentation at Velocity London 2012. *http://vimeo.com/51310058*.

Scaling: Inflection Points

- Clark, William. "Explores Motivation Research—A Boss' Tool." *Chicago Tribune*, August 4, 1959.

- Cole, Jonathan R., and Stephen Cole. "The Ortega Hypothesis." *Science* 178, no. 4059 (1972): 368–375.

- Engel David, Anita W. Woolley, Lisa X. Jing, Christopher F. Chabris, and Thomas W. Malone. "Reading the Mind in the Eyes or Reading Between the Lines? Theory of Mind Predicts Collective Intelligence Equally Well Online and Face-to-Face." *PLoS ONE* 9, no. 12 (2014).

- Grant, Adam M. *Give and Take*. New York: Viking, 2013.

- Griswold, Alison. "Here's Why Eliminating Titles and Managers at Zappos Probably Won't Work." *Business Insider*, January 6, 2014. *http://bit.ly/holacracy-unlikely*.

- Hackman J. R. "The Design of Work Teams." In *The Handbook of Organizational Behavior*, edited by Jay W. Lorsch. Englewood Cliffs, NJ: Prentice-Hall, 1987.

- Hackman, J. Richard, and Greg R. Oldham. "Motivation Through the Design of Work: Test of a Theory." *Organizational Behavior and Human Performance* 16, no. 2 (1976): 250–279.

- Kurtz, Cynthia F., and David J. Snowden. "Bramble Bushes in a Thicket: Narrative and the Intangibles of Learning Networks." In *Strategic Networks: Learning to Compete*, edited by Michael Gibbert and Thomas Durand. Malden, MA: Blackwell, 2007.

- Mickman, Heather, and Ross Clanton. "DevOps at Target." Posted on October 29, 2014. *http://bit.ly/devops-target*.

- Puppet. "2015 State of DevOps Report." *http://bit.ly/2015-state-of-devops*.

- Rose, Katie. "Performance Assessment with Impact." devopsdays Silicon Valley 2015. Posted on November 13, 2015. *http://bit.ly/rose-perf-assess*.

- Shannon-Solomon, Rachel. "Devops Is Great for Startups, but for Enterprises It Won't Work—Yet." *Wall Street Journal*, May 13, 2014. *http://bit.ly/wsj-devops-enterprise*.

- Tanizaki, Jun'ichirō. *In Praise Of Shadows*. New Haven, CT: Leete's Island Books, 1977.

Bridging Devops Cultures

- Fox, Martha Lane. "Directgov 2010 and Beyond: Revolution not Evolution." GOV.UK, November 23, 2010. *http://bit.ly/fox-directgov-2010*.

- Gillespie, Nicole A., and Leon Mann. "Transformational Leadership and Shared Values: The Building Blocks of Trust." *Journal of Managerial Psychology* 19, no. 6 (2004).

- Indiana University. "Women in Mostly Male Workplaces Exhibit Psychological Stress Response." EurekAlert, August 24, 2015. *http://bit.ly/women-male-workplace*.

- Reed, J. Paul. *DevOps in Practice*. Sebastopol, CA: O'Reilly Media, 2013.

Recommended Conferences and Meetups

- !!Con (*http://bangbangcon.com*)
- AlterConf (*http://www.alterconf.com*)
- Berlin Buzzwords (*https://berlinbuzzwords.de*)
- CoffeeOps (*http://www.coffeeops.org*)
- CSSconf EU (*http://www.cssconf.eu*)
- devopsdays (*http://www.devopsdays.org*)
- Infracoders (*http://infrastructurecoders.com*)
- JSConf EU (*http://www.jsconf.eu*)
- Open Source and Feelings (*http://osfeels.com*)
- Open Source Bridge (*http://opensourcebridge.org*)
- Monitorama (*http://monitorama.com*)
- SassConf (*http://sassconf.com*)
- Strange Loop (*http://www.thestrangeloop.com*)

- Velocity (*http://conferences.oreilly.com/velocity*)
- XoXo (*http://www.xoxofest.com*)

Recommended Podcasts

- Arrested DevOps (*https://www.arresteddevops.com*)
- DevOps Cafe Podcast with John Willis and Damon Edwards (*http://devops cafe.org*)
- Food Fight Show (*http://foodfightshow.org*)

Index

fostering, 74-79
  learning fundamental skills, 74
  moving from fixed mindset to, 332
  recognizing your strengths/progress, 76
growth opportunities, 254
guessers/guess culture, 69

H

Hackman, J. Richard, 269
Hamilton, Margaret, 20
Hammond, Paul, xv, 27
Hardin, Garrett, 136
hardware lifecycle management, 182
health insurance, 253
health of individuals
  and team size, 98
  organizational factors affecting, 348
health of systems, 344-351
  and sick systems, 344-346
  creating healthy systems, 346-348
  identifying healthy/unhealthy cultures,
    350-351
  organizational factors affecting individual
    health, 348
HealthCare.gov, 189
healthy cultures, 350-351
Hefferman, Margaret, 82
help, asking for, 272, 273
hero culture, 261
  (see also "rock stars")
Herzberg, Frederick, 269
Hewlett, Sylvia Ann, 71
hierarchies
  ladder vs. pyramid, 143
  work roles, 66
hierarchy of needs, 172
high-trust organizations, 153
Hipchat, 292
hiring
  diversity considerations, 130
  growing teams via, 247-250
  job postings/recruitment issues, 263-265
  problems with "hero culture", 261
  sourcing and interviewing candidates, 260
  when teams are spread too thin, 299
history of devops, 19-30
  advent of proprietary software and stand-
    ardization, 21
  advent of software engineering, 20

  age of applications and the Web, 24
  age of the network, 22
  Agile infrastructure, 27
  beginning of devopsdays, 28
  current state, 29
  developer as operator, 19
  growth of software development methodol-
    ogies, 25
  open source software, 26
  proprietary services, 26
Holacracy, 242
holism, 311
hours, flexible, 252
HR (human resources) department
  and diversity, 67
  role in attracting talent, 301
human connections
  and bridging of cultures, 335-351
  using stories to build, 312
human error
  as anti-pattern, 55
  "old view" vs. "new view" of, 14
humane staffing, 96-98, 219

I

IBM (International Business Machines), 21
ideas
  culture and, 257, 325-327
  learning new, 326
  mindsets and, 326
  search for "best", 326
imagination, empathy and, 93
implementation, time needed for, 49
implicit stories, 308
in-group/out-group theory, 124
incentives, misalignment of, 278
inclusive environment, 130-133
individual accountability, 274
individual differences, 94
individual growth (see growth mindsets)
individual stories
  around work, 335-343
  Taylorism and value of, 336
influence, asserting, 85
infrastructure automation, 41, 182-184, 205
infrastructure concepts, 40-42
  artifact management, 41
  cloud computing, 41
  configuration management, 40

About the Authors

Jennifer Davis is a global organizer for devopsdays (*http://www.devopsdays.org/*) and a local organizer for devopsdays Silicon Valley, and the founder of Coffeeops (*http://www.coffeeops.org*). She supports a number of community meetups in the San Francisco area. In her role at Chef, Jennifer develops Chef cookbooks to simplify building and managing infrastructure. She has spoken at a number of industry conferences about devops, tech culture, monitoring, and automation. When she's not working, she enjoys hiking Bay Area trails, learning to make things, and spending quality time with her partner, Brian, and her dog, George.

Ryn Daniels is a senior operations engineer working at Etsy. They have taken their love of automation and operations and turned it into a specialization in monitoring, configuration management, and operational tooling development, and have spoken at numerous industry conferences including Velocity, devopsdays, and Monitorama about subjects such as infrastructure automation, scaling monitoring solutions, and cultural change in engineering. Ryn is one of the co-organizers of devopsdays NYC and helps run Ladies Who Linux in New York. They live in Brooklyn with a perfectly reasonable number of cats, and in their spare time enjoy playing cello, rock climbing, and brewing beer.

Colophon

The animal on the cover of *Effective DevOps* is a wild yak (*Bos mutus*). This formidable yet friendly bovid occupies remote, mountainous areas of the northwestern Tibetan Plateau, the highest dwelling of any mammal.

The wild yak's distinguishing characteristics include high, humped shoulders and shaggy, dark fur that hangs nearly to the ground. It is one of the largest members of the *Bovidae* family, which also includes the American bison, the African buffalo, and domestic cattle. Males can reach between five and seven feet high at the shoulder and weigh up to 2,200 pounds; females are typically a third of that size.

Bos mutus is extremely well adapted to its high-altitude habitat, with a large lung capacity, high red blood cell count, and warm, woolly coat. In spite of their bulk, wild yaks are also very adept climbers, using their split hooves and strong legs to navigate rocky, icy terrain. Their dense horns, which curve out from the sides of their broad heads, allow them to dig through snow for food. Conversely, they are very sensitive to warm temperatures and move seasonally to avoid the heat.

Wild yaks are gregarious and peaceful herbivores, feeding on grass, herbs, and lichens. Female yaks gather with their young in herds of as many as 100; males tend to be more solitary, traveling in groups of around 10. Together they travel long distances to obtain vegetation.

Though the yak population is thought to number over 12 million worldwide, that figure mostly comprises the smaller domesticated yak (*Bos grunniens*). The wild species is considered vulnerable, reportedly declining more than 30 percent in the last 3 decades. Its most serious threat is poaching, although interbreeding with domestic yaks is another factor. The wild yak's average lifespan is about 23 years in the wild.

Many of the animals on O'Reilly covers are endangered; all of them are important to the world. To learn more about how you can help, go to *animals.oreilly.com*.

The cover image is from *Lydekker's Royal Natural History*. The cover fonts are URW Typewriter and Guardian Sans. The text font is Adobe Minion Pro; the heading font is Adobe Myriad Condensed; and the code font is Dalton Maag's Ubuntu Mono.

Learn from experts.
Find the answers you need.

Sign up for a **10-day free trial** to get **unlimited access** to all of the content on Safari, including Learning Paths, interactive tutorials, and curated playlists that draw from thousands of ebooks and training videos on a wide range of topics, including data, design, DevOps, management, business—and much more.

Start your free trial at:

oreilly.com/safari

(No credit card required)

CPSIA information can be obtained
at www.ICGtesting.com
Printed in the USA
BVHW05s0545120718
521391BV00005B/91/P

9 781491 926307